SELECTED MATERIAL FROM

THE ART OF PUBLIC SPEAKING

Ninth Edition

STEPHEN E. LUCAS
University of Wisconsin–Madison

SPEECH 105 FUNDAMENTALS OF PUBLIC SPEAKING
HOWARD COMMUNITY COLLEGE

McGraw Hill Learning Solutions

Boston Burr Ridge, IL Dubuque, IA New York San Francisco St. Louis
Bangkok Bogotá Caracas Lisbon London Madrid
Mexico City Milan New Delhi Seoul Singapore Sydney Taipei Toronto

The McGraw·Hill Companies

Selected Material from
The Art of Public Speaking, Ninth Edition
SPEECH 105 Fundamentals of Public Speaking
Howard Community College

This book is a McGraw-Hill Learning Solutions textbook and contains select material from *The Art of Public Speaking*, Ninth Edition by Stephen E. Lucas. Copyright © 2007, 2004, 2001, 1998, 1995, 1992, 1989, 1986, 1983 by Stephen E. Lucas. Reprinted with permission of the publisher. Many custom published texts are modified versions or adaptations of our best-selling textbooks. Some adaptations are printed in black and white to keep prices at a minimum, while others are in color.

4 5 6 7 8 9 0 QWD QWD 14 13 12 11 10

ISBN-13: 978-0-07-729579-0
ISBN-10: 0-07-729579-X
Part of
ISBN-13: 978-0-07-729678-0
ISBN-10: 0-07-729678-8

Learning Solutions Manager: Heidi Freund Degheri
Learning Solutions Specialist: Nicole Schmitt
Production Editor: Nicole Baumgartner
Printer/Binder: Quebecor World

Stephen E. Lucas is Professor of Communication Arts and Evjue-Bascom Professor in the Humanities at the University of Wisconsin–Madison, where he has taught since 1972. He received his bachelor's degree from the University of California, Santa Barbara, and his master's and doctorate degrees from Penn State University.

Professor Lucas has been recognized for his work as both a scholar and a teacher. His first book, *Portents of Rebellion: Rhetoric and Revolution in Philadelphia, 1765–1776,* received the Golden Anniversary Award of the National Communication Association in 1977 and was nominated for a Pulitzer Prize. His major articles include "The Schism in Rhetorical Scholarship" (1981), "The Renaissance of American Public Address: Text and Context in Rhetorical Criticism" (1988), "The Stylistic Artistry of the Declaration of Independence" (1990), and "The Rhetorical Ancestry of the Declaration of Independence" (1998), for which he received the Golden Anniversary Monograph Award of the National Communication Association. He is currently working on *Words of a Century: The Top 100 American Speeches, 1900–1999.*

Professor Lucas has received a number of teaching awards, including the Chancellor's Award for Excellence in Teaching at the University of Wisconsin and the National Communication Association's Donald Ecroyd Award for Outstanding Teaching in Higher Education. His lecture course on "The Rhetoric of Campaigns and Revolutions" is among the most popular on campus and has twice been selected for statewide broadcast in its entirety by Wisconsin Public Radio. Professor Lucas is featured in the Educational Video Group's program on the history of American public address, and he has appeared on the History Channel's documentary on the Declaration of Independence.

Professor Lucas has directed the introductory public speaking course at the University of Wisconsin–Madison since 1973. Over the years he has been responsible for numerous teaching innovations and has supervised the training of hundreds of graduate assistants. In addition to participating in public speaking workshops and colloquia at schools throughout the United States, he has served as a judge for the major national English-language public speaking competitions in China, has lectured at numerous Chinese universities, and has conducted workshops for Chinese instructors on teaching public speaking.

Stephen Lucas and his wife, Patty, live in Madison, Wisconsin, and have two sons, Jeff and Ryan. His interests include travel, sports, art, and photography.

Contents in Brief

Contents

CHAPTER 1

Speaking in Public

CHAPTER 4 84

Selecting a Topic and a Purpose

CHAPTER 7 174

Supporting Your Ideas

CHAPTER 8
Organizing the Body of the Speech
204

CHAPTER 9
Beginning and Ending the Speech
226

CHAPTER 10

Outlining the Speech

252

CHAPTER 11

Using Language

270

CHAPTER 12

Delivery

CHAPTER 13

Using Visual Aids

CHAPTER 15

Speaking to Persuade

CHAPTER 17

Speaking on Special Occasions

CHAPTER 18

Speaking in Small Groups

484

APPENDIX

Speeches for Analysis and Discussion

A–1

Preface

If it is true, as Walter Pater said, that "a book, like a person, has its fortunes," then fortune has indeed smiled upon *The Art of Public Speaking*. As the book enters its ninth edition, I am deeply appreciative of the students and teachers who have made it the leading work on its subject at colleges and universities across the United States.

In preparing this edition, I have retained what readers have identified as the main strengths of previous editions. The book continues to be informed by classical and contemporary theories of rhetoric but does not present theory for its own sake. Keeping a steady eye on the practical skills of public speaking, it offers full coverage of all major aspects of speech preparation and presentation.

Throughout *The Art of Public Speaking* I have followed David Hume's advice that one "who would teach eloquence must do it chiefly by examples." Whenever possible, I have tried to *show* the principles of public speaking in action in addition to describing them. Thus you will find in the book a large number of narratives and extracts from speeches—set off from the text in a contrasting typeface. There are also many speech outlines and sample speeches. All these are provided so students can *see* how to formulate specific purpose statements, how to analyze and adapt to audiences, how to organize ideas and construct outlines, how to assess evidence and reasoning, how to use language effectively, and so forth.

Because the immediate task facing students is to present speeches in the classroom, I have relied heavily on examples that relate directly to students' classroom needs and experiences. The speech classroom, however, is a training ground where students develop skills that will serve them throughout life. Therefore, I have also included a large number of illustrations drawn from the kinds of speaking experiences students will face after they graduate—in their careers and in their communities.

Also as in previous editions, I have been guided by the belief that a book intended for students who want to speak more effectively should never lose sight of the fact that the most important part of speaking is thinking. The ability to think critically is vital to a world in which personality and image too often substitute for thought and substance. While helping students become capable, responsible speakers, *The Art of Public Speaking* also aims at helping them become capable, responsible thinkers.

Features of the Ninth Edition

Given the enthusiastic response of teachers and students to the changes made in the eighth edition, I have kept the basic philosophy and approach of the book intact. At the same time, I have made a number of improvements in response to advances in technology and to the evolving needs of students and instructors. These improvements cover a broad range of subjects and are discussed below.

Sample Speeches

From the very first edition of *The Art of Public Speaking,* one of its distinctive features has been the use of sample speeches with commentary that illustrate the principles of effective communication and that students can study as they prepare their own speeches. This edition contains six new complete sample speeches with commentary. Two are introductory speeches and appear in "Giving Your First Speech" (pages 81–83). Two are informative speeches and appear in Chapters 10 and 14. Two are persuasive speeches and appear in Chapters 15 and 16. There is also a new sample introduction and conclusion with commentary in Chapter 9.

In addition, the appendix of speeches for analysis and discussion following Chapter 18 contains three new student speeches—one informative, one persuasive, and one commemorative. As in previous editions, all the sample speeches throughout the book have been carefully chosen to illustrate a variety of speech types and organizational methods, including Monroe's motivated sequence. All the new full speeches, with the exception of the sample outline with commentary in Chapter 10, are included on the CD-ROM and video supplements to this edition, so students can view the speeches in addition to reading the written texts.

Speech Videos

A strong video program is crucial to any public speaking textbook. Because speeches are performative acts, students need to be able to view speakers in action as well as read their words on the printed page. This edition of *The Art of Public Speaking* includes a new volume of *Speeches for Analysis and Discussion.* Available in both DVD and VHS, this video program includes a total of nineteen full student speeches, ten of which are new to this edition. All together, there are five introductory speeches, seven informative speeches, four persuasive speeches, and three commemorative speeches.

These speeches reflect the diversity of today's society and college classroom. They are presented by speakers of many backgrounds, deal with a wide range of topics, and employ several kinds of visual aids. Special attention has been given to providing examples of extemporaneous delivery, as well as to showing speakers in a variety of situations. Some talk from behind a lectern, but just as many do not. Some speak from note cards, while others use regular sheets of paper. Depending on the kind of speech and the personality of the speaker, some are more informal in presentation style, while others are more formal. Whatever their manner of delivery, however, all the speeches are meant to illustrate the principles of organization, audience analysis, supporting materials, creativity, and language that are discussed throughout the book and that are central to effective public speaking in any context.

In response to requests from instructors, the new DVD and VHS of student speeches also includes a paired set of "Needs Improvement" and "Final Version" speeches. Both are informative presentations on "The Hidden World of Chili Peppers." The needs improvement version contains many of the flaws that typically appear in student presentations early in the term—inadequate preparation, underdevelopment of ideas, sloppy organization, and ineffective use of visual aids. The aim is to show students—rather than just tell them—some of the things to avoid if they want to craft a successful presentation. Once students have seen the needs improvement version, instructors can show the final version, in which the flaws have been corrected.

The contrast between the two versions of the speech is sufficiently stark that it should be readily apparent to students why the final version is stronger—in content and delivery—than the needs to improve version. There are enough differences between the two versions that showing both back-to-back should spark a lively and fruitful class discussion. Here, as elsewhere, my aim is to provide materials that allow students to *see* the principles of effective public speaking in addition to reading about them.

Finally, it is worth noting that all the entries on the DVD of sample speeches for the 9th edition include an option for closed captioning, which can be activated as needed.

Speech Preparation Checklists

To help students keep on track as they prepare their speeches, I have added 14 speech checklists to the book. Included are checklists on ethical speaking, framing the specific purpose and central idea, phrasing and organizing main points, creating a preparation outline, composing introductions and conclusions, using supporting materials, and preparing and presenting visual aids. These checklists are also available on the Student CD-ROM and can be printed out in case instructors want students to submit them with their speeches.

Commemorative Speaking

Many instructors have asked for more coverage of commemorative speaking, which is treated in Chapter 17. Examples of commemorative speeches include eulogies, testimonial addresses, and dedications. The aim of a commemorative speech is to pay tribute to a person, a group of people, an institution, or an idea. Almost everyone will deliver this kind of speech at some point in his or her life.

Because a commemorative speech depends so much on the creative use of language, it provides an excellent opportunity for students to gain experience with an aspect of public speaking that is less likely to be emphasized in the informative and persuasive speech assignments. Including a commemorative speech assignment is also valuable because it takes account of the diversity of student aptitudes and backgrounds. Some students who have difficulty with the more didactic informative and persuasive speeches shine on the commemorative speech, which rewards a somewhat different set of skills and sensibilities.

Given the fact that it is only 3–4 minutes in length, the commemorative speech can usually be worked into the syllabus with relative ease. For years I have used the assignment with great success as the final speech of the term, and students often say it is their favorite presentation of the entire course.

In response to the growing interest in commemorative speaking, I have expanded the coverage of it in Chapter 17. I have also added a second sample commemorative speech. In addition to the speech printed in Chapter 17, there is now one in the appendix of sample speeches at the end of the book. Both speeches are printed in their entirety, both are available on the DVD and VHS of student speeches that accompanies this edition, and both are included among the full speeches on the Student CD-ROM.

PowerPoint

As the use of PowerPoint has become ubiquitous in almost every venue for public speaking, the need for students to understand how to use it has grown apace. Many schools now provide students the opportunity to employ PowerPoint in the classroom, and employers increasingly assume that students who have taken a public speaking class will have had some exposure to PowerPoint.

Accordingly, in the eighth edition I added a new appendix following Chapter 13 explaining how PowerPoint can be used to enhance a speech without either dominating it or enfeebling its content. This appendix explores the pluses and minuses of PowerPoint, how to plan where to employ PowerPoint in a speech, how to use the resources of PowerPoint most effectively, and how to work PowerPoint into the delivery of a speech smoothly and expertly.

The response to this appendix has been extremely favorable, and I have updated it in this edition to keep pace with changes in PowerPoint. Because PowerPoint is a visual medium, the appendix also includes a five-minute informative speech on the Great Wall of China that illustrates the use of PowerPoint. This speech is reprinted in full—with commentary—at the end of the PowerPoint appendix and is available on the DVD and VHS videos that accompany the book, as well as on the Student CD-ROM.

In addition to the material in the PowerPoint appendix, the Student CD-ROM for Chapter 13 contains five new video clips that include the use of PowerPoint. Instructors who emphasize the use of PowerPoint can also turn to "The Hidden World of Chili Peppers," a new informative speech that is reprinted in the appendix of sample speeches at the end of the book. This speech provides an excellent model of how to employ PowerPoint and is included on the Student CD-ROM and the DVD and VHS supplements to this edition

Finally, for students who need more guidance on the technical details of PowerPoint than can be covered in the book, the Online Learning Center Web site for *The Art of Public Speaking* includes step-by-step tutorials for both PowerPoint 2002 and PowerPoint 2003. The tutorials can be accessed at www.mhhe.com/lucaspowerpoint.

Taken together, the PowerPoint appendix, the Student CD-ROM, the DVD and VHS videos, and the online tutorials provide the most comprehensive set of teaching materials for PowerPoint available with any speech textbook. They give the kind of guidance students need to use PowerPoint effectively and responsibly—in the classroom and beyond.

Internet Research

Students and instructors alike have commented positively on the section in Chapter 6 titled "Searching the Internet" ever since I added it in the 6th edition. Readers of this edition will continue to find coverage of search engines and virtual libraries, as well as a compendium of specialized research sources. They will no longer find a discussion of metasearch engines, whose benefits have been eclipsed by a combination of their own internal defects and the rapid expansion in the capabilities of individual search engines such as Google, Yahoo, and All the Web.

This edition retains the 8th edition's expanded section on "Evaluating Internet Documents" and its new section on "Citing Internet Documents." Too often, students either forget to cite Internet materials in their speeches or cite them in passing by saying something like, "As I found on the Web," or "As the Internet states." In addition to explaining the need for precise, accurate citation of Web sources, I provide two examples of such citation from classroom speeches. These excerpts are included on the Student CD-ROM, so readers can see how Internet citations can be woven into the delivery of a speech.

Diversity

As society has changed since the first edition of *The Art of Public Speaking* in 1983, so has the book. In each edition, I have sought to relate the principles of effective speechmaking to students of diverse backgrounds, values, and aspirations. This new edition continues my efforts to make sure the book is respectful of and applicable to all of its readers.

Rather than treating diversity as a subject to be highlighted in boxes for marketing purposes or to be tossed into a chapter or two for its own sake, I have woven the subject into the fabric of the book from beginning to end. This is evident from the section on public speaking in a multicultural world in Chapter 1 to the treatment of audience analysis in Chapter 5 to the material on inclusive language in Chapter 11 to the speech by Nelson Mandela accepting the Congressional Gold Medal in Chapter 17.

In addition, there are scores of stories, speech excerpts, outlines, examples, photographs, and other materials that reflect the diversity of contemporary life and its implications for speechmaking. This new edition also reflects the increasingly global context in which much public speaking takes place—including excerpts from student speeches delivered in China's 2001 and 2002 collegiate English-language speech competitions. In a variety of ways, large and small, I have sought to instill respect for people of diverse cultures, backgrounds, and orientations and to encourage an inclusive approach to the art of public speaking.

Student CD-ROM

Bridging the gap between the printed page and the spoken word has always been the greatest challenge facing a public speaking textbook. The innovative Student CD-ROM that accompanied the 8th edition brought the art of public speaking to life, and it has been fully updated for this new edition.

Specially marked icons in the margins of the book direct readers to the appropriate resources on the CD. Those resources have been carefully designed to help students master the skills, concepts, and principles discussed in the text. Let me say a word about each.

Speech Videos

Continuing one of the most popular features of the 8th-edition CD, the new version contains 70 video clips that demonstrate the principles of public speaking in action—including 36 brand new clips. Fully integrated with the text, each clip has been chosen to illustrate a specific aspect of speechmaking. Running in length from 20 seconds to a minute and a half, the clips are distributed evenly throughout the book. Most are from student presentations. The remainder are from public figures and include such models of rhetorical excellence as Barack Obama, Winston Churchill, Martin Luther King, Ronald Reagan, Mary Fisher, and Elizabeth Dole. All video clips offer the option of closed captioning.

A second CD presents 18 full student speeches for analysis and discussion. Included are introductory speeches, informative speeches, persuasive speeches, and commemorative speeches. All full speech videos offer the option of closed captioning. Eight of the full speeches are also accompanied by an outline of the speech, which scrolls alongside the video as it plays. Together, the excerpts and full speeches provide students with more than two hours of video.

Interactive Study Questions

To reinforce key principles and ideas, the CD contains a comprehensive set of study questions for each chapter. These questions are fully interactive, use a variety of formats, and systematically cover all the major concepts discussed in the book. Entirely different from items in the *Test Bank,* the questions have been written both to quiz students and to help them learn. After students enter their answer for each question, they receive not just an indication of whether the answer is right or wrong, but *feedback* that explains the correct answer.

Speech Outliner

In addition to video clips and study questions, the CD includes a speech outliner that guides students systematically through the process of organizing and outlining their speeches. As students use the outliner, they move step by step through each element of the speech from title through bibliography. Tutorial screens explain the organizational methods involved in composing each part of the speech, and the outliner automatically formats the speech in accordance with proper outlining principles. It also allows students to save, revise, and print their work, as well as export it to their own word processors.

Outline Exercises

Six interactive outlining exercises give students additional help in developing their skills of speech organization. These exercises present scrambled outlines that students can rearrange in the correct order by using standard drag-and-drop procedures. As in other parts of the CD, the aim of these exercises is to put the resources provided by computer technology to the best possible pedagogical use.

Bibliography Formats

The CD also presents a comprehensive set of sample citations for both Modern Language Association (MLA) and American Psychological Association (APA) formats. Covering 30 types of source material—from books, essays, and newspaper articles to government publications, personal interviews, television programs, and Internet documents—these sample citations have been fully updated for the 9th edition and are especially valuable to students as they prepare their speech bibliographies.

Speech Preparation Checklists

Fourteen checklists help students keep on track as they prepare their speeches. Included are checklists for ethical public speaking, for framing the specific purpose and central idea, for phrasing and organizing main points, for creating the preparation outline, for composing introductions and conclusions, for using supporting materials, and for preparing and presenting visual aids. The checklists have been revised for this edition and now appear in the book as well as on the CD.

Glossary of Key Terms

Throughout the book, key terms are defined in the margin as they appear in the text. Those key terms are reproduced on the CD, where they can be accessed either by chapter or via a master glossary arranged in alphabetical order. Whether students are reviewing for exams or working with the study questions on the CD, they can instantly check the meaning of any key term at the click of a mouse.

Key-Term Flashcards

A set of electronic flashcards for each chapter provides another resource for studying key terms. In addition to being fully interactive, the flashcards include an audio option for students who are aural learners. Developed especially for *The Art of Public Speaking*, the flashcards provide another example of how students can profit from advancements in instructional technology.

Notepad

This edition again includes a Notepad feature that allows students to take notes as they are using the CD and to save those notes as a .txt file on their computer's hard drive.

Online Learning Center with PowerWeb

Accessible at www.mhhe.com/lucas9, the Online Learning Center (OLC) provides a wealth of resources that supplement *The Art of Public Speaking*. Among those resources is the Top 100 American Speeches of the 20th Century. The OLC includes at least one link to a Web site with a transcript of each speech. Many of the links also furnish historical background about the speech and/or links to additional sites with information about the speaker, speech, or occasion. Whenever possible, a link has been provided to a site that contains a full or partial audio presentation of the original speech.

My aim in developing the Top 100 Web site was to provide a readily accessible way for students to learn more about the rich history of public speaking. One way to incorporate the site into class is to have each student give an informative presentation about one of the Top 100 speeches. Students often find this a fascinating assignment that broadens their horizons beyond the boundaries of their classroom.

The Online Learning Center also includes overviews, outlines, and learning objectives for each chapter of the book, practice quizzes, worksheets, speech evaluation forms, and key-term crossword puzzles. In addition, it is integrated with McGraw-Hill's Public Speaking PowerWeb, which keeps students up to date and helps them find topics for their presentations by reprinting recent speeches of public interest, as well as news and journal articles related to current issues and to public speaking in general. PowerWeb also provides weekly updates, links to *New York Times* articles, and a robust search capability.

Two recent additions to the Online Learning Center are the Bibliomaker and the Questionnaire Maker. The former is a software program that automatically formats bibliography entries in either APA or MLA formats. The latter allows students to create electronic audience-analysis questionnaires, to distribute them to classmates via e-mail, and to automatically tabulate the results.

As with the CD, icons in the margins of the book guide readers to specific elements of the Online Learning Center.

Integrated Teaching and Learning System

The Art of Public Speaking has an exceptional set of print, video, and electronic resources for students and teachers alike. Some of these resources are found in the book itself; others are supplemental to it. Taken together, they provide a fully integrated teaching and learning system. In addition to the Online Learning Center and the Student CD, both of which were described earlier, the integrated teaching and learning system includes the following elements.

Sample Speeches

Chapters 7, 14, 15, and 16 contain full sample speeches with commentary, as do the appendixes on "Giving Your First Speech" and "Using PowerPoint." Chapter 10 has complete preparation and speaking outlines, both with commentary, and Chapter 17 has four full sample speeches. The end-of-book appendix consists of seven additional speeches for discussion and analysis, all of which are also available on video.

Critical Thinking Exercises

A set of Exercises for Critical Thinking accompanies each chapter, and the *Instructor's Manual* provides dozens of additional exercises that can be used as homework assignments or as the basis for classroom activities and discussion. In keeping with the experiential nature of speechmaking, these exercises require that students *work with* (rather than simply memorize) the principles presented in the book.

Student Workbook

Containing exercises, checklists, worksheets, evaluation forms, and other materials, the workbook gives students additional assistance with all the major elements of effective speechmaking. Instructors teaching online classes have found it highly valuable, but it has become a staple in many traditional classes as well.

Annotated Instructor's Edition

The *Annotated Instructor's Edition* provides a wealth of teaching aids for each chapter in the book. These aids include instructional strategies, class activities, discussion questions, speech assignments, and related readings. The *Annotated Instructor's Edition* is also cross-referenced with the *Instructor's Manual* and the other supplements that accompany *The Art of Public Speaking.*

Instructor's Manual

Running to more than 500 pages, the *Instructor's Manual* provides a comprehensive guide to teaching from *The Art of Public Speaking*. The manual contains outlines for each chapter of the book; discusses the end-of chapter exercises; furnishes supplementary exercises, speeches, and classroom activities; offers suggested course outlines and speaking assignments; and provides 32 additional speeches for discussion and analysis.

Test Bank

The *Test Bank* furnishes more than 2,000 examination questions based on *The Art of Public Speaking*. As a special feature, it also offers preconstructed quizzes for each chapter in the book, as well as three complete final examinations.

The *Test Bank* is also available electronically in McGraw-Hill's EZ Test program. In addition to reproducing questions from the *Test Bank,* this program allows instructors to add their own questions, to create multiple versions of a single exam, and to export exams for use with course management systems such as WebCT, BlackBoard, or PageOut. There is also an EZ Test Online service that helps instructors administer online exams and quizzes that have been created with EZ Test.

Selections from the Communication Teacher

This edition marks the sixth volume of *Selections from the Communication Teacher* that I have compiled to accompany *The Art of Public Speaking*. Like its predecessors, the new collection covers a host of topics related to the teaching of public speaking, including audience analysis, critical thinking, diversity and multiculturalism, informative speaking, persuasion, and general instructional methods. All six volumes are available with this edition of the book. Taken together, they reprint more than 380 brief articles that offer a wealth of practical ideas for classroom use.

Videos

There are several videos of student presentations that accompany *The Art of Public Speaking,* including a new collection that offers 19 speeches, 10 of which are new to this edition. Instructors who adopt *The Art of Public Speaking* can also select from several "Great Speeches" videos that accompany the book. Among the selections on these are Martin Luther King's "I Have a Dream" and Barbara Bush's 1990 commencement speech at Wellesley College, both of which are reprinted in the book.

Two other videos—*Be Prepared to Speak* and *Speaking Effectively to 1 or 1,000*—introduce students to the public speaking process and provide helpful advice on dealing with stage fright. Both videos are entertaining as well as informative, and either can be shown early in the course to help prepare students for their initial speeches.

Overhead Transparencies

The 9th edition of *The Art of Public Speaking* comes with a binder of 157 full-color overhead transparencies. Created to be of maximum value for lecture presentations and classroom discussions, they include a wide range of graphics, illustrations, and exercises from the textbook, as well as additional exercises and classroom activities from the *Instructor's Manual.*

PowerPoint Slides with Video Clips

There is also a collection of more than 400 slides for instructors who use PowerPoint in their lectures and discussions. Instructors can use these slides just as they are, or they can modify the slides to fit the needs of individual classes. As a special feature, 50 of the slides include video speech clips as well as text. The PowerPoint slides can be found on the Instructor's Resource CD-ROM described below.

Instructor's Resource CD-ROM

For the convenience of instructors, the *Instructor's Manual, Test Bank, Selections From the Communication Teacher, Teaching Public Speaking Online, Teaching Public Speaking, Handbook for Teachers of Non-Native Speakers of English,* PowerPoint slides with speech video clips, Overhead Transparencies, and Classroom Performance System questions are all available on a single CD. Like the other computerized resources that accompany *The Art of Public Speaking,* this CD is available in both Mac and Windows versions.

Teaching Public Speaking Online

This supplement was new to the 8th edition and has been fully revised and updated for the 9th edition. Written by Professor Jennifer Cochrane of Indiana University and Purdue University at Indianapolis, it provides a wealth of practical guidance for instructors who are adapting *The Art of*

Public Speaking for use in an online environment. It draws upon Professor Cochrane's pioneering experience with online instruction to explore how one can teach an intellectually rich, practically rewarding public speaking course via the Web.

From Oratory to Public Speaking

Reprinted from my essay on "Public Speaking" in the *Encyclopedia of Rhetoric* (Oxford University Press), this pamphlet presents a synoptic view of major developments in the practice and teaching of public speaking during the 20th century, and it illuminates the role of public speaking as a powerful historical force.

Teaching Public Speaking

Written primarily for beginning instructors, *Teaching Public Speaking* reprints my essay of the same title from *Teaching Communication: Theory, Research, and Methods* (Lawrence Erlbaum Associates). This essay presents an overview of the pedagogical philosophy behind *The Art of Public Speaking,* discusses a number of practical classroom issues, and is available on the Instructor's Resource CD.

Handbook for Teachers of Non-Native Speakers of English

Developed for instructors who have ESL students in their public speaking classes, this 60-page handbook focuses on the central issues that should be considered when working with students from different linguistic and cultural backgrounds.

Online Learning Center

Instructors and students alike can take advantage of several outstanding online resources in conjunction with this edition, including the Online Learning Center with PowerWeb, which we discussed on page 00. In addition, instructors using *The Art of Public Speaking* have full access to McGraw-Hill's PageOut, which allows teachers to create personal course Web sites by using a template provided by McGraw-Hill.

Special features of PageOut include an interactive course syllabus, an online grade book, online testing, and capability for posting personal files and discussions. All online content for *The Art of Public Speaking* is supported by Web CT, Blackboard, and eCollege.com. For more details, check with a McGraw-Hill representative or visit www.mhhe.com/pageout.

Audio Abridgement CD Set

This six-CD set presents an abridged, spoken version of *The Art of Public Speaking.* Designed with today's multi-tasking students in mind, this "book on tape" allows listeners to review while commuting, working out, or just sitting down to study. All chapters in the book are included with the exception of Chapters 10 and 13 (Outlining and Visual Aids), whose contents are intrinsically visual rather than auditory. Each chapter on the CD runs approximately 15 minutes, focuses on key concepts, and, when possible, incorporates audio footage from speeches used as examples in the book.

Acknowledgments

"'Tis the good reader," said Ralph Waldo Emerson, "that makes the good book." I have been fortunate to have very good readers indeed, and I would like to thank the reviewers and focus-group participants whose names appear on page xxx for their many helpful comments and suggestions.

In addition, I would like to express my gratitude to the students at the University of Wisconsin whose speeches provided the material for so many of the examples in the text; to Mary Rossa and Sarah Meinen, who assisted with the research for this edition; to Jim Ferris, who once again provided a valuable sounding board on numerous issues; and to members of the Communication Arts 100 teaching staff at the University of Wisconsin, who helped me by collecting sample speeches and by identifying rough spots in the 8th edition.

Special thanks go to Amy Slagell for doing a marvelous job generating new questions for the *Test Bank*; to Jennifer Cochrane for her splendid supplement on using *The Art of Public Speaking* in an online course; to Susan Zaeske for help on a variety of fronts; and to Sue Vander Hook for her expert formatting of the *Instructor's Manual*, *Test Bank*, and *Student Workbook*. Above all, I am indebted to Paul Stob, whose work on all the supplements and contributions to the book itself have improved this edition immeasurably.

I am also grateful to Carl Burgchardt, who provided permission for me to incorporate parts of his pamphlet *How to Give Your First Speech*, originally written to accompany the 5th edition of *The Art of Public Speaking*, into the appendix on "Giving Your First Speech"; to Randy Fitzgerald, Director of Public Relations at the University of Richmond, and Paul Porterfield, Director of the Media Resource Center at the same school, for their time and effort in helping me secure the videotape of Sajjid Zahir Chinoy's "Questions of Culture"; and to Nie Lisheng, Editor-in-Chief of *21st Century*, for permission to include on the Student CD video excerpts from speeches presented at China's national English-language public speaking competition sponsored by *21st Century*.

I also owe thanks to many people at McGraw-Hill. Nanette Giles provided overall editorial direction and a keen sense of vision that will be sorely missed now that she has moved to a different position. Rhona Robbin was an invaluable source of editorial wisdom who kept the entire project moving inexorably forward. Nancy Garcia oversaw the book's technology program, while Leslie Oberhuber directed an outstanding marketing campaign.

It is easy to forget that preparing a manuscript is only the first of many steps in producing a book. As in the previous two editions, Susan Trentacosti was a masterful project manager whose dedication and expertise are evident on every page. I was also fortunate to again have Laurie Entringer as the book's designer. A textbook is more than just words on a page. Laurie made sure the content and design of the book worked hand in hand.

This is the third edition to benefit from Barbara Salz's expertise as a photo researcher. As always, she produced a superior photo program—not an easy task when one is limited primarily to pictures of people giving or listening to speeches. I would be remiss if I did not also thank Phil Butcher, Emily Barrosse, Steve Debow, and Ed Stanford—all of whom made sure the book had sufficient resources to maintain its commitment to excellence.

Finally, I am indebted to my wife, Patty, whose love, support, and counsel remain a mainstay of the book and of my life.

Stephen E. Lucas
Madison, Wisconsin

Reviewers and Focus Group Participants

Richard Armstrong
Wichita State University

Kim Berry
Ozarks Technical Community College

Mila Brisbon
Borough of Manhattan Community College

Deborah Craig-Claar
Penn Valley Community College

Terry Cunconan
Central Missouri State University

Jean Fish-Davis
Pueblo Community College

Linda Dickeroff
George Mason University

Shelton Hill
Palomar College

Rebecca Franko
California Polytechnic State University

Terry Helmick
Johnson County Community College

Frank Irizarry
University of Florida

Jerilyn Kamm
University of Nebraska

Susan Kilgard
Anne Arundel Community College

Kathryn Kiser
Longview Community College

Brian Kline
Gainesville College

Linda Kurz
University of Missouri

Angela Latham
Triton College

Rona Leber
Bossier Parish Community College

Mark Lewis
Riverside Community College

Marcia Litrenta
Harper College

Jody Littleton
Parkland College

Krista Longtin
Indiana University–Purdue University

Sujanet Mason
Luzerne County Community College

Martin McDermott
Brookdale Community College

Steve Netti
Vincennes University

Jim Schroeder
Holmes Community College

Richard Soller
College of Lake County

Ruth Stokes
Trident Technical College

Elliott Street
Meridian Community College

Katherine Taylor
University of Louisville

Sharon Terrill
Riverside Community College

Kay Weeks
Abraham Baldwin Agricultural College

THE ART OF PUBLIC SPEAKING

CHAPTER ONE

Speaking in Public

Wilma Subra had no intention of becoming a public speaker. After graduating from college with degrees in chemistry and microbiology, she went to work at Gulf South Research Institute in New Iberia, Louisiana. As part of her job, she conducted field research on environmental toxins—often in minority communities located near large industrial polluters. She found that many families were being exposed to high, sometimes deadly, levels of chemicals and other toxins, but she was not allowed to make her information public.

Frustrated by these restrictions, Subra left her job, created her own company, and has devoted the past two decades to helping people fight back against giant industrial polluters. She works with families and community groups to conduct environmental tests, interpret test results, and organize for change. Because of her efforts, dozens of toxic sites across the country have been cleaned up, and one chemical industry spokesperson calls her "a top gun for the environmental movement."

How has Wilma Subra achieved all this? Partly through her scientific training, partly through her commitment to environmental justice. But just as important is her ability to communicate with people through public speaking. "Public speaking," she says, "is the primary vehicle I use for reaching people. When you have an important message, it's the best way to engage people and get them involved."

If you had asked Subra early in her career, "Do you see yourself as a major public speaker?" she would have laughed at the idea. Yet today she gives more than 100 presentations a year, not including radio, television, and newspaper interviews. Along the way she has lectured at Harvard, testified before Congress, and addressed audiences in 40 states, as well as in Mexico, Canada, and Japan. "When I was in college," she says, "I never dreamed I'd need public speaking, but now I use it almost every day."

The Power of Public Speaking

Throughout history people have used public speaking as a vital means of communication. What the Greek leader Pericles said more than 2,500 years ago is still true today: "One who forms a judgment on any point but cannot explain" it clearly "might as well never have thought at all on the subject."[1] Public speaking, as its name implies, is a way of making your ideas public—of sharing them with other people and of influencing other people.

CD 1: VIDEO 1.1

View John F. Kennedy, Martin Luther King, Barbara Jordan, Ronald Reagan, and other speakers in action.

During modern times many women and men around the globe have spread their ideas and influence through public speaking. In the United States, the list includes Franklin Roosevelt, Billy Graham, Cesar Chavez, Barbara Jordan, Ronald Reagan, Martin Luther King, Jesse Jackson, and Elizabeth Dole. In other countries, we see the power of public speaking employed by such people as former British Prime Minister Margaret Thatcher, South African leader Nelson Mandela, Burmese democracy champion Aung San Suu Kyi, and Kenyan environmentalist and Nobel Prize winner Wangari Maathai.

As you read these names, you may think to yourself, "That's fine. Good for them. But what does that have to do with me? I don't plan to be a president or a preacher or a crusader for any cause." Nevertheless, the need for public speaking will almost certainly touch you sometime in your life—maybe tomorrow, maybe not for five years. Can you imagine yourself in any of these situations?

You are a management trainee in a large corporation. Altogether, there are seven trainees in the program. One of you will get the lower-management job that has just opened. There is to be a large staff meeting at which each of the trainees will discuss the project he or she has been developing. One by one your colleagues make their presentations. They have no experience in public speaking and are intimidated by the higher-ranking managers present. Their speeches are stumbling and awkward. You, however, call upon all the skills you learned in your public speaking course. You deliver an informative talk that is clear, well reasoned, and articulate. You get the job.

You are married and have three children. One of your children has a learning disability. You hear that your local school board has decided, for budget reasons, to eliminate the special teacher who has been helping your child. At an open meeting of the school board, you stand up and deliver a thoughtful, compelling speech on the necessity for keeping the special teacher. The school board changes its mind.

ONLINE LEARNING CENTER

To read the words of famous speakers, log on to the Top 100 American Speeches of the 20th Century at www.mhhe.com/lucastop100.

You are the assistant manager in a branch office of a national company. Your immediate superior, the branch manager, is about to retire, and there will be a retirement dinner. All the executives from the home office will attend. As his close working associate, you are asked to give a farewell toast at the party. You prepare and deliver a speech that is both witty and touching—a perfect tribute to your boss. After the speech, everyone applauds enthusiastically, and a few people have tears in their eyes. The following week you are named branch manager.

Fantasies? Not really. Any of these situations could occur. In a survey of 480 companies and public organizations, communication skills—including public speaking—were ranked first among the personal qualities of college graduates sought by employers. In another survey, college graduates in the work force were asked to rank the things they found most essential to their career development. What was at the top of their list? Skill in oral communication.[2]

The importance of such skill is true across the board—for accountants and architects, teachers and technicians, scientists and stockbrokers. Even in highly specialized fields such as civil and mechanical engineering, employers consistently rank the ability to communicate above technical knowledge when deciding whom to hire and whom to promote.

Nor has the growth of the Internet and other new technologies reduced the need for public speaking. As one communication consultant states, "There are more avenues to reach people than ever before, but there's no substitute for face-to-face communication." To be successful, says business leader Midge Costanza, you must have "the ability to stand on your feet, either on a one-to-one basis or before a group, and make a presentation that is convincing and believable."[3]

The same is true in community life. Public speaking is a vital means of civic engagement. It is a way to express your ideas and to have an impact on issues that matter in a democratic society. Look back for a moment at the second of our three hypothetical situations, the one in which you persuade the school board to keep the special teacher who has been helping your child. Why did the school board change its mind? Not simply because the facts were on your side (though they may have been) or because you knew more about education than the school board (which you probably do not). The school board changed its mind because of your *speech*—in which you presented a compelling case for keeping the special teacher.

The point is that public speaking is a form of empowerment. It can—and often does—make a difference in things people care about very much. The key phrase here is "make a difference." This is what most of us want to do in life—to make a difference, to change the world in some small way. Public speaking offers you an opportunity to make a difference in something you care about very much.

The Tradition of Public Speaking

Given the importance of public speaking, it's not surprising that it has been taught and studied around the globe for thousands of years. Almost all cultures have an equivalent of the English word "orator" to designate someone with special skills in public speaking. The oldest known handbook on effective speech was written on papyrus in Egypt some 4,500 years ago. Eloquence was highly prized in ancient India, Africa, and China, as well as among the Aztecs and other pre-European cultures of North and South America.[4]

In classical Greece and Rome, public speaking played a central role in education and civic life. It was also studied extensively. Aristotle's *Rhetoric,* composed during the third century B.C.E., is still considered the most important work on its subject, and many of its principles are followed by speakers (and writers) today. The great Roman leader Cicero used his speeches to defend liberty and wrote several works about oratory in general.

Over the centuries, many other notable thinkers have dealt with issues of rhetoric, speech, and language—including the Roman educator Quintilian, the Christian preacher St. Augustine, the medieval writer Christine de Pizan, the British philosopher Francis Bacon, and the American critic Kenneth Burke.[5] In recent years, communication researchers have provided an increasingly scientific basis for understanding the methods and strategies of effective speech.[6]

Your immediate objective is to apply those methods and strategies in your classroom speeches. What you learn in your class, however, will be applicable long after you leave college. As you read this book, keep in mind that the principles of public speaking are derived from a long tradition and have been confirmed by a substantial body of research.[7] The more you know about those principles, the more effective you will be in your own speeches—and the more effective you will be in listening to the speeches of other people.

Similarities Between Public Speaking and Conversation

How much time do you spend each day talking to other people? The average adult spends about 30 percent of her or his waking hours in conversation. As you will see, there are many similarities between daily conversation and public speaking.

Children learn the art of conversation by trial and error. A toddler says "Cookie!" to persuade her father to give her a snack. A five-year-old tells a little story to entertain Grandma and gain admiration. If neither of these things works—the cookie isn't forthcoming, Grandma is not amused—well, back to the drawing board. Next time the child will try it a slightly different way.

By the time you read this book, you will have spent much of your life perfecting the art of conversation. You may not realize it, but you already employ a wide range of skills when talking to people. These skills include the following:

1. *Organizing your thoughts logically.* Suppose you were giving someone directions to get to your house. You wouldn't do it this way:

> When you turn off the highway, you'll see a big diner on the left. But before that, stay on the highway to Exit 67. Usually a couple of the neighbors' dogs are in the street, so go slow after you turn at the blinking light. Coming from your house you get on the highway through Maple Street. If you pass the taco stand, you've gone too far. The house is blue.

Instead, you would take your listener systematically, step by step, from his or her house to your house. You would organize your message.

2. *Tailoring your message to your audience.* You are a geology major. Two people ask you how pearls are formed. One is your roommate; the other is your nine-year-old niece. You answer as follows:

> *To your roommate:* "When any irritant, say a grain of sand, gets inside the oyster's shell, the oyster automatically secretes a substance called nacre, which is principally calcium carbonate and is the same material that lines the oyster's shell. The nacre accumulates in layers around the irritant core to form the pearl."
>
> *To your niece:* "Imagine you're an oyster on the ocean floor. A grain of sand gets inside your shell and makes you uncomfortable. So you decide to cover it up. You cover it with a material called mother-of-pearl. The covering builds up around the grain of sand to make a pearl."

Many skills used in conversation also apply in public speaking. As you learn to speak more effectively, you may also learn to communicate more effectively in other situations.

3. *Telling a story for maximum impact.* Suppose you are telling a friend about a funny incident at last week's football game. You don't begin with the punch line ("Keisha fell out of the stands right onto the field. Here's how it started. . . . "). Instead, you carefully build up your story, adjusting your words and tone of voice to get the best effect.

4. *Adapting to listener feedback.* Whenever you talk with someone, you are aware of that person's verbal, facial, and physical reactions. For example:

> You are explaining an interesting point that came up in biology class. Your listener begins to look confused, puts up a hand as though to stop you, and says "Huh?" You go back and explain more clearly.
>
> A friend has asked you to listen while she practices a speech. At the end you tell her, "There's just one part I really don't like—that quotation from the attorney general." Your friend looks very hurt and says, "That was my favorite part!" So you say, "But if you just worked the quotation in a little differently, it would be wonderful."

Each day, in casual conversation, you do all these things many times without thinking about them. You already possess these communication skills. And these are among the most important skills you will need for public speaking.

To illustrate, let's return briefly to one of the hypothetical situations at the beginning of this chapter. When addressing the school board about the need for a special teacher:

- You *organize* your ideas to present them in the most persuasive manner. You steadily build up a compelling case about how the teacher benefits the school.
- You *tailor your message* to your audience. This is no time to launch an impassioned defense of special education in the United States. You must show how the issue is important to the people in that very room—to their children and to the school.
- You tell your story for *maximum impact.* Perhaps you relate an anecdote to demonstrate how much your child has improved. You also have statistics to show how many other children have been helped.
- You *adapt to listener feedback.* When you mention the cost of the special teacher, you notice sour looks on the faces of the school board members. So you patiently explain how small that cost is in relation to the overall school budget.

In many ways, then, public speaking requires the same skills used in ordinary conversation. Most people who communicate well in daily talk can learn to communicate just as well in public speaking. By the same token, training in public speaking can make you a more adept communicator in a variety of situations, such as conversations, classroom discussions, business meetings, and interviews.

Differences Between Public Speaking and Conversation

Despite their similarities, public speaking and everyday conversation are not identical. Imagine that you are telling a story to a friend. Then imagine yourself telling the story to a group of seven or eight friends. Now imagine telling the same story to 20 or 30 people. As the size of your audience grows, the manner in which you present the story will change. You will find yourself adapting to three major differences between conversation and public speaking:

1. *Public speaking is more highly structured.* It usually imposes strict time limitations on the speaker. In most cases, the situation does not allow listeners to interrupt with questions or commentary. The speaker must accomplish her or his purpose in the speech itself. In preparing the speech, the speaker must anticipate questions that might arise in the minds of listeners and answer them. Consequently, public speaking demands much more detailed planning and preparation than ordinary conversation.

2. *Public speaking requires more formal language.* Slang, jargon, and bad grammar have little place in public speeches. As angry as she is about industrial pollution, when Wilma Subra speaks to a congressional committee, she doesn't say, "We've damn well got to stop the greedy creeps who pollute whole communities just to make a few more bucks." Despite the growing informality of all aspects of American life, listeners usually react negatively to speakers who do not elevate and polish their language when addressing an audience. A speech should be "special."

3. *Public speaking requires a different method of delivery.* When conversing informally, most people talk quietly, interject stock phrases such as "like" and "you know," adopt a casual posture, and use what are called vocalized pauses ("uh," "er," "um"). Effective public speakers, however, adjust their voices to be heard clearly throughout the audience. They assume a more erect posture. They avoid distracting mannerisms and verbal habits.

With study and practice, you will be able to master these differences and expand your conversational skills into speechmaking. Your speech class will provide the opportunity for this study and practice.

Developing Confidence: Your Speech Class

One of the major concerns of students in any speech class is stage fright. We may as well face the issue squarely. Many people who converse easily in all kinds of everyday situations become frightened at the idea of standing up before a group to make a speech.

If you are worried about stage fright, you may feel better knowing that you are not alone. A survey conducted in 1973 asked more than 2,500 Americans to list their greatest fears. To the surprise of the researchers, the largest number of people—41 percent—listed speaking before a group among

stage fright
Anxiety over the prospect of giving a speech in front of an audience.

their greatest fears.[8] Amazing as it may seem, many Americans appear to consider public speaking a fate worse than death.

In a more recent study, researchers concentrated on social situations and, again, asked their subjects to list their greatest fears. Here is how they responded:[9]

Greatest Fear	Percent Naming
A party with strangers	74
Giving a speech	70
Asked personal questions in public	65
Meeting a date's parents	59
First day on a new job	59
Victim of a practical joke	56
Talking with someone in authority	53
Job interview	46
Formal dinner party	44
Blind date	42

Again, speechmaking ranks near the top in provoking anxiety.

Nervousness Is Normal

Actually, most people tend to be anxious before doing something important in public. Actors are nervous before a play, politicians are nervous before a campaign speech, athletes are nervous before a big game. The ones who succeed have learned to use their nervousness to their advantage. Listen to gymnast Carly Patterson, speaking after she won the women's all-around competition in the 2004 Olympic Games in Athens. Asked by a reporter if she was nervous before her final event, the floor exercise, she said, "I'm not usually too nervous on floor, but I definitely was tonight because I was going for gold." Putting her butterflies to good use, Patterson performed brilliantly and scored a 9.712 to nail down the first all-around gold medal for a U.S. woman since 1984.

Much the same thing happens in speechmaking. Surveys show that 76 percent of experienced speakers have stage fright before taking the floor.[10] But their nervousness is a healthy sign that they are getting "psyched up" for a good effort. Novelist and lecturer I. A. R. Wylie explains, "Now after many years of practice I am, I suppose, really a 'practiced speaker.' But I rarely rise to my feet without a throat constricted with terror and a furiously thumping heart. When, for some reason, I *am* cool and self-assured, the speech is always a failure."[11]

In other words, it is perfectly normal—even desirable—to be nervous at the start of a speech. Your body is responding as it would to any stressful situation—by producing extra *adrenaline.* This sudden shot of adrenaline is what makes your heart race, your hands shake, your knees knock, and your skin perspire. Every public speaker experiences all these reactions to some extent. The question is: How can you control your nervousness and make it work for you rather than against you?

adrenaline
A hormone released into the bloodstream in response to physical or mental stress.

Dealing with Nervousness

Rather than trying to eliminate every trace of stage fright, you should aim at transforming it from a negative force into what one expert calls *positive nervousness*—"a zesty, enthusiastic, lively feeling with a slight edge to it. . . . It's still nervousness, but it feels different. You're no longer victimized by it; instead, you're vitalized by it. You're in control of it."[12] Here are six time-tested ways you can turn your nervousness from a negative force into a positive one.

positive nervousness Controlled nervousness that helps energize a speaker for her or his presentation.

Acquire Speaking Experience

You have already taken the first step. You are enrolled in a public speaking course, where you will learn about speechmaking and gain speaking experience. Think back to your first day at kindergarten, your first date, your first day at a new job. You were probably nervous in each situation because you were facing something new and unknown. Once you became accustomed to the situation, it was no longer threatening. So it is with public speaking. For most students, the biggest part of stage fright is fear of the unknown. The more you learn about public speaking and the more speeches you give, the less threatening speechmaking will become.

Your speech class will provide knowledge and experience to help you speak with confidence. Of course, the road to confidence will sometimes be bumpy. Learning to give a speech is not much different from learning any other skill—it proceeds by trial and error. The purpose of your speech class is to shorten the process, to minimize the errors, to give you a nonthreatening arena—a sort of laboratory—in which to undertake the "trial."

Your teacher recognizes that you are a novice and is trained to give the kind of guidance you need to get started. In your fellow students you have a highly sympathetic audience who will provide valuable feedback to help you improve your speaking skills. As the class goes on, your fears about public speaking will gradually recede until they are replaced by only a healthy nervousness before you rise to speak.[13]

Prepare, Prepare, Prepare

Another key to gaining confidence is to pick speech topics you truly care about—and then to prepare your speeches so thoroughly that you cannot help but be successful. Here's how one student combined enthusiasm for his topic with thorough preparation to score a triumph in speech class:

Jesse Young was concerned about taking a speech class. Not having any experience as a public speaker, he got butterflies in his stomach just thinking about talking in front of an audience. But when the time came for Jesse's first speech, he was determined to make it a success.

Jesse chose Habitat for Humanity as the topic for his speech. He had been a volunteer for the past three years, and he believed deeply in the organization and its mission. The purpose of his speech was to explain the origins, philosophy, and activities of Habitat for Humanity.

As Jesse spoke, it became clear that he was enthusiastic about his subject and genuinely wanted his classmates to share his enthusiasm. Because he was intent on communicating with his audience, he forgot to be nervous. He spoke clearly, fluently, and dynamically. Soon the entire class was engrossed in his speech.

Afterward Jesse admitted that he had surprised even himself. "It was amazing," he said. "Once I passed the first minute or so, all I thought about were those people out there listening. I could tell that I was really getting through to them."

How much time should you devote to preparing your speeches? A standard rule of thumb is that each minute of speaking time requires one to two hours of preparation time—perhaps more, depending on the amount of research needed for the speech. This may seem like a lot of time, but the rewards are well worth it. Like an actor who rehearses a role until it is just right, you will find that your confidence as a speaker increases when you work on a speech until it is just right. One professional speech consultant estimates that proper preparation can reduce stage fright by up to 75 percent.[14]

If you follow the techniques suggested by your teacher and in the rest of this book, you will stand up for every speech fully prepared. Imagine that the day for your first speech has arrived. You have studied your audience and selected a topic you know will interest them. You have researched the speech thoroughly and practiced it several times until it feels absolutely comfortable. You have even tried it out before two or three trusted friends. How can you help but be confident of success?

Think Positively

Confidence is mostly the well-known power of positive thinking. If you think you can do it, you usually can. On the other hand, if you predict disaster and doom, that is almost always what you will get. This is especially true when it comes to public speaking. Speakers who think negatively about themselves and the speech experience are much more likely to be overcome by stage fright than are speakers who think positively. Here are some ways you can transform negative thoughts into positive ones as you work on your speeches:

Negative Thought	Positive Thought
I wish I didn't have to give this speech.	This speech is a chance for me to share my ideas and gain experience as a speaker.
I'm not a great public speaker.	No one's perfect, but I'm getting better with each speech I give.
I'm always nervous when I give a speech.	Everyone's nervous. If other people can handle it, I can too.
No one will be interested in what I have to say.	I have a good topic and I'm fully prepared. Of course they'll be interested.

Many psychologists believe that the ratio of positive to negative thoughts in regard to stressful activities such as speechmaking should be at least five to one. That is, for each negative thought, you should counter with a minimum of five positive ones. Doing so will not make your nerves go away completely, but it will help keep them under control so you can concentrate on communicating your ideas rather than on brooding about your fears and anxieties.

Use the Power of Visualization

visualization
Mental imaging in which a speaker vividly pictures himself or herself giving a successful presentation.

Visualization is closely related to positive thinking. It is a technique used by many people—athletes, musicians, actors, speakers, and others—to enhance their performance in stressful situations. How does it work? Listen to Olympic long-distance runner Vicki Huber:

> Right before a big race, I'll picture myself running, and I will try and put all of the other competitors in the race into my mind. Then I will try and imagine every possible situation I might find myself in . . . behind someone, being boxed in, pushed, shoved or cajoled, different positions on the track, laps to go, and, of course, the final stretch. And I always picture myself winning the race, no matter what happens during the event.[15]

Of course, Huber does not win every race she runs, but research has shown that the kind of mental imaging she describes can significantly increase athletic performance. Research has also shown that the same technique is of great benefit in helping speakers control their stage fright.[16]

The key to visualization is creating a vivid mental blueprint in which you see yourself succeeding in your speech. Picture yourself in your classroom rising to speak. See yourself at the lectern, poised and self-assured, making eye contact with your audience and delivering your introduction in a firm, clear voice. Feel your confidence growing as your listeners get more and more caught up in what you are saying. Imagine your sense of achievement as you conclude the speech knowing you have done your very best.

As you create these images in your mind's eye, be realistic but keep focused on the positive aspects of your speech. Don't allow negative images to eclipse the positive ones. Acknowledge your nervousness, but picture yourself overcoming it to give a vibrant, articulate presentation. If there is one part of the speech that always seems to give you trouble, visualize yourself getting through it without any hitches. And be specific. The more lucid your mental pictures, the more successful you are likely to be.

As with your physical rehearsal of the speech, this kind of mental rehearsal of the speech should be repeated several times in the days before you speak. It doesn't guarantee that every speech will turn out exactly the way you envision it—and it certainly is no substitute for thorough preparation. But used in conjunction with the other methods of combating stage fright, it is a proven way to help control your nerves and to craft a successful presentation.

Know That Most Nervousness Is Not Visible

In addition to being anxious about giving a speech, many novice speakers are worried about appearing nervous to the audience. It's hard to speak with poise and assurance if you think you look tense and insecure. One of the most valuable lessons you will learn as your speech class proceeds is that only a fraction of the turmoil you are feeling inside is visible on the outside.

The need for public speaking arises in many situations. Here Eileen Collins, commander of the space shuttle *Discovery,* speaks at a prelaunch press conference at the Kennedy Space Center.

"Your nervous system may be giving you a thousand shocks," says one experienced speaker, "but the viewer can see only a few of them."[17]

Even though your palms are sweating and your heart is pounding, your listeners probably won't realize how tense you are—especially if you do your best to act cool and confident on the outside. Most of the time when students confess after a speech, "I was so nervous I thought I was going to die," their classmates are surprised. To them the speaker looked calm and assured.

Knowing this should make it easier for you to face your listeners with confidence. As one student stated after watching a videotape of her first classroom speech, "I was amazed at how calm I looked. I assumed everyone would be able to see how scared I was, but now that I know they can't, I won't be nearly so nervous in the future. It really helps to know that you look in control even though you may not feel that way."

Don't Expect Perfection

It may also help you to know that there is no such thing as a perfect speech. At some point in every presentation, every speaker says or does something—no matter how minor—that does not come across exactly as he or she had planned. Fortunately, as with one's nerves, such moments are usually not evident to the audience. Why? Because the audience does not know what the speaker *plans* to say. It hears only what the speaker *does* say. If you momentarily lose your place, reverse the order of a couple statements, or forget to pause at a certain spot, no one need be the wiser. When such moments occur, don't worry about them. Just proceed as if nothing happened.

Even if you do make an obvious mistake during a speech, that is no catastrophe. If you have ever listened to Martin Luther King's famous "I Have a Dream" speech, you may recall that he stumbles over his words twice during the speech. Most likely, however, you don't remember. Why? Because you were focusing on King's message rather than on the fine points of his delivery.

One of the biggest reasons people are concerned about making a mistake in a speech is that they view speechmaking as a kind of performance rather than as an act of communication. They feel the audience is judging them against a scale of absolute perfection in which every misstated word or awkward gesture will count against them. But speech audiences are not like judges in a violin recital or an ice-skating contest. They are not looking for a virtuoso performance, but for a well-thought-out address that communicates the speaker's ideas clearly and directly. Sometimes an error or two can actually enhance a speaker's appeal by making her or him seem more human.[18]

As you work on your speeches, make sure you prepare thoroughly and do all you can to get your message across to your listeners. But don't panic about being perfect or about what will happen if you make a mistake. Once you free your mind of these burdens, you will find it much easier to approach your speeches with confidence and even with enthusiasm.

Besides stressing the six points just discussed, your teacher will probably give you several tips for dealing with nervousness in your first speeches. They may include:

- Be at your best physically and mentally. It's not a good idea to stay up until 4:00 A.M. partying with friends or cramming for an exam the night before your speech. A good night's sleep will serve you better.
- As you are waiting to speak, quietly tighten and relax your leg muscles, or squeeze your hands together and then release them. Such actions help reduce tension by providing an outlet for your extra adrenaline.
- Take a couple slow, deep breaths before you start to speak. Most people, when they are tense, take short, shallow breaths, which only reinforces their anxiety. Deep breathing breaks this cycle of tension and helps calm your nerves.
- Work especially hard on your introduction. Research has shown that a speaker's anxiety level begins to drop significantly after the first 30 to 60 seconds of a presentation.[19] Once you get through the introduction, you should find smoother sailing the rest of the way.
- Make eye contact with members of your audience. Remember that they are individual people, not a blur of faces. And they are your friends.
- Concentrate on communicating with your audience rather than on worrying about your stage fright. If you get caught up in your speech, your audience will too.
- Use visual aids. They create interest, draw attention away from you, and make you feel less self-conscious.[20]

If you are like most students, you will find your speech class to be a very positive experience. As one student wrote on her course evaluation form at the end of the class:

> I was really dreading this class. The idea of giving all those speeches scared me half to death. But I'm glad now that I stuck with it. It's a small class, and I got to know a lot of the students. Besides that, this is one class in which I got to express *my* ideas, instead of spending the whole time listening to the teacher talk. I even came to enjoy giving the speeches. I could tell at times that the audience was really with me, and that's a great feeling.

Over the years thousands of students have developed confidence in their speechmaking abilities. As your confidence grows, you will be better able to stand before other people and tell them what you think and feel and know—and to make them think and feel and know those same things. The best part about confidence is that it nurtures itself. After you score your first triumph, you will be that much more confident the next time. And as you become a more confident public speaker, you will likely become more confident in other areas of your life as well.

Public Speaking and Critical Thinking

> That guy at the party last night really owned me when we were talking about the economy. I know my information is right, and I'm sure his argument didn't make sense, but I can't put my finger on the problem.
>
> I'm in the market for a used car, and the salesperson says every car on the lot is a great deal. But how do I sort the lemons from the peaches?
>
> I worked really hard on my term paper, but it's just not right. It doesn't seem to hang together, and I can't figure out what's wrong.
>
> Political speeches are so one-sided. The candidates sound good, but they all talk in slogans and generalities. It's really hard to decide who has the best stands on the issues.

Do any of these situations sound familiar? Have you ever found yourself in similar situations? If so, you may find help in your speech class. Besides building confidence, a course in public speaking can develop your skills as a critical thinker. Those skills can make the difference between the articulate debater and the pushover, the careful consumer and the easy mark, the A student and the C student, the thoughtful voter and the coin tosser.

critical thinking
Focused, organized thinking about such things as the logical relationships among ideas, the soundness of evidence, and the differences between fact and opinion.

What is critical thinking? To some extent, it's a matter of logic—of being able to spot weaknesses in other people's arguments and to avoid them in your own. It also involves related skills such as distinguishing fact from opinion, judging the credibility of statements, and assessing the soundness of evidence.

In the broadest sense, critical thinking is focused, organized thinking—the ability to see clearly the relationships among ideas. It has often been said that there are few new ideas in the world, only reorganized ideas. The greatest thinkers, scientists, and inventors have often taken information that was readily available and put it together differently to produce new insights. That, too, is critical thinking.[21]

If you are wondering what this has to do with your public speaking class, the answer is quite a lot. As the class proceeds, for example, you will probably spend a good deal of time organizing your speeches. While this may seem like a purely mechanical exercise, it is closely interwoven with critical thinking. If the structure of your speech is disjointed and confused, odds are that your thinking is also disjointed and confused. If, on the other hand, the structure is clear and cohesive, there is a good chance your thinking is too. Organizing a speech is not just a matter of arranging the ideas you already have. Rather, it is an important part of shaping the ideas themselves.

What is true of organization is true of many aspects of public speaking. The skills you learn in your speech class can help you become a more effective thinker in a number of ways. As you work on expressing your ideas in clear, accurate language, you will enhance your ability to think clearly and accurately. As you study the role of evidence and reasoning in speechmaking, you will see how they can be used in other forms of communication as well. As you learn to listen critically to speeches in class, you will be better able to assess the ideas of speakers (and writers) in a variety of situations.[22]

To return to the four examples at the beginning of this section:

The guy at the party last night—would well-honed critical thinking skills help you find the holes in his argument?

Buying a used car—is the salesperson a reliable source of information, or should you check independent reviews of different models?

The term paper—would better organization and a clear outline help pull it together?

Political speeches—once you get past the slogans, are the candidates drawing valid conclusions from sound evidence?

If you take full advantage of your speech class, you will be able to enhance your skills as a critical thinker in many circumstances. This is one reason public speaking has been regarded as a vital part of education since the days of ancient Greece.[23]

The Speech Communication Process

As you begin your first speeches, you may find it helpful to understand what goes on when one person talks to another. Regardless of the kind of speech communication involved, there are seven elements—speaker, message, channel, listener, feedback, interference, and situation. Here we shall focus on how these elements interact when a public speaker addresses an audience.

Speaker

Speech communication begins with a speaker. If you pick up the telephone and call a friend, you are acting as a speaker. (Of course, you will also act as a listener when your friend is talking.) In public speaking, you will usually present your entire speech without interruption.

Your success as a speaker depends on *you*—on your personal credibility, your knowledge of the subject, your preparation of the speech, your manner of speaking, your sensitivity to the audience and the occasion. But successful speaking is more than a matter of technical skill. It also requires enthusiasm. You can't expect people to be interested in what you say unless you are interested yourself. If you are truly excited about your subject, your audience is almost sure to get excited along with you. You can learn all the techniques of effective speechmaking, but before they can be of much use, you must first have something to say—something that sparks your own enthusiasm.

speaker
The person who is presenting an oral message to a listener.

Message

The message is whatever a speaker communicates to someone else. If you are calling a friend, you might say, "I'll be a little late picking you up tonight." That is the message. But it may not be the only message. Perhaps there is a certain tone in your voice that suggests reluctance, hesitation. The underlying message might be "I really don't want to go to that party. You talked me into it, but I'm going to put it off as long as I can."

message
Whatever a speaker communicates to someone else.

Your goal in public speaking is to have your *intended* message be the message that is *actually* communicated. Achieving this depends both on what you say (the verbal message) and on how you say it (the nonverbal message).

Getting the verbal message just right requires work. You must narrow your topic down to something you can discuss adequately in the time allowed for the speech. You must do research and choose supporting details to make your ideas clear and convincing. You must organize your ideas so listeners can follow them without getting lost. And you must express your message in words that are accurate, clear, vivid, and appropriate.

Besides the message you send with words, you send a message with your tone of voice, appearance, gestures, facial expression, and eye contact. Imagine that one of your classmates gets up to speak about student loans. Throughout her speech she slumps behind the lectern, takes long pauses to remember what she wants to say, stares at the ceiling, and fumbles with her visual aids. Her intended message is "We must make more money available for student loans." But the message she actually communicates is "I haven't prepared very well for this speech." One of your jobs as a speaker is to make sure your nonverbal message does not distract from your verbal message.

Channel

The channel is the means by which a message is communicated. When you pick up the phone to call a friend, the telephone is the channel. Public speakers may use one or more of several channels, each of which will affect the message received by the audience.

channel
The means by which a message is communicated.

Consider a speech to Congress by the President of the United States. The speech is carried to the nation by the channels of radio and television. For the radio audience the message is conveyed entirely by the President's voice.

The powers of critical thinking you develop in researching and organizing your speeches can be applied in many forms of communication, including group projects for other classes.

They can hear him, but they can't see him. For the television audience the message is conveyed by both the President's voice and the televised image of the President and his surroundings. The people in Congress have a more direct channel. They not only hear the President's voice as amplified through a microphone, but they see him and the setting firsthand.

In a public speaking class your channel is the most direct of all. Your classmates will see you and hear you without any electronic intervention.

Listener

The listener is the person who receives the communicated message. Without a listener, there is no communication. When you talk to a friend on the phone, you have one listener. In public speaking you will have many listeners.

listener
The person who receives the speaker's message.

Everything a speaker says is filtered through a listener's *frame of reference*—the total of his or her knowledge, experience, goals, values, and attitudes. Because a speaker and a listener are different people, they can never have exactly the same frame of reference. And because a listener's frame of reference can never be exactly the same as a speaker's, the meaning of a message will never be exactly the same to a listener as to a speaker.

frame of reference
The sum of a person's knowledge, experience, goals, values, and attitudes. No two people can have exactly the same frame of reference.

You can easily test the impact of different frames of reference. Ask each of your classmates to describe a chair. If you have 20 classmates, you'll probably get 20 different descriptions. One student might picture a large, overstuffed easy chair, another an elegant straight-backed chair, yet another an office chair, a fourth a rocking chair, and so on. Even if two or more envision the same general type—say, a rocking chair—their mental images of the chair could still be different. One might be thinking of an early American rocker, another of a modern Scandinavian rocker—the possibilities are unlimited. And "chair" is a fairly simple concept. What about "patriotism" or "freedom"?

Because people have different frames of reference, a public speaker must take great care to adapt the message to the particular audience being addressed. To be an effective speaker, you must be *audience-centered.* You must do everything in your speech with your audience in mind. You cannot assume that listeners will be interested in what you have to say. You must understand their point of view as you prepare the speech, and you must work to get them involved. You will quickly lose your listeners' attention if your presentation is either too basic or too sophisticated. You will also lose your audience if you do not relate to *their* experience, interests, knowledge, and values. When you make a speech that causes listeners to say "That is important to *me,*" you will almost always be successful.

Feedback

feedback
The messages, usually nonverbal, sent from a listener to a speaker.

When the President addresses the nation on television, he is engaged in one-way communication. You can talk back to the television set, but the President won't hear you. Most situations, however, involve *two-way* communication. Your listeners don't simply absorb your message like human sponges. They send back messages of their own. These messages are called feedback.

For example, when you phone your friend to say you will be late, you may hear, "Oh, no you don't! I don't care *what* your problem is; you get here on time!" That is feedback.

This kind of verbal give-and-take is unusual in public speaking. Still, there is always plenty of feedback to let you know how your message is being received. Do your listeners lean forward in their seats, as if paying close attention? Do they applaud in approval? Do they laugh at your jokes? Do they have quizzical looks on their faces? Do they shuffle their feet and gaze at the clock? The message sent by these reactions could be "I am fascinated," "I am bored," "I agree with you," "I don't agree with you," or any number of others. As a speaker, you need to be alert to these reactions and adjust your message accordingly.

Like any kind of communication, feedback is affected by one's frame of reference. How would you feel if, immediately after your speech, all your classmates started to rap their knuckles on the desks? Would you run out of the room in despair? Not if you were in a European university. In many parts of Europe, students rap their knuckles on their desks to show admiration for a classroom lecture. You must understand the feedback to be able to deal with it.

There are still two more elements we must consider to understand fully what happens in speech communication.

Interference

Interference is anything that impedes the communication of a message. When you talk on the telephone, sometimes there is static, or wires get crossed so that two different conversations are going on at once. That is a kind of interference.

In public speaking there are two kinds of interference. One, like the static or crossed wires in a phone conversation, is *external* to the audience. Many classrooms are subject to this kind of interference—from traffic outside the building, the clatter of a radiator, students conversing in the hall, a room that is stifling hot or freezing cold. Any of these can distract your listeners from what you are saying.

interference
Anything that impedes the communication of a message. Interference can be external or internal to listeners.

A second kind of interference is *internal* and comes from within your audience rather than from the outside. Perhaps one of your listeners has a bad mosquito bite or a patch of poison ivy. She may be so distracted by the itch that she doesn't pay attention to your speech. Another listener could be worrying about a test coming up in the next class period. Yet another could be brooding about an argument he had with his girlfriend.

As a speaker, you must try to hold your listeners' attention despite these various kinds of interference. In the chapters that follow you will find many ways to do this.

Situation

The situation is the time and place in which speech communication occurs. Conversation always takes place in a certain situation. Sometimes the situation helps—as when you propose marriage over an intimate candlelight dinner. Other times it may hurt—as when you try to speak words of love in competition with a blaring stereo. When you have to talk with someone about a touchy issue, you usually wait until the situation is just right.

situation
The time and place in which speech communication occurs.

Public speakers must also be alert to the situation. Certain occasions—funerals, church services, graduation ceremonies—require certain kinds of speeches. Physical setting is also important. It makes a great deal of difference whether a speech is presented indoors or out, in a small classroom or in a gymnasium, to a densely packed crowd or to a handful of scattered souls. When you adjust to the situation of a public speech, you are only doing on a larger scale what you do every day in conversation.

Now let us look at a complete model of the speech communication process, as shown in Figure 1.1.[24]

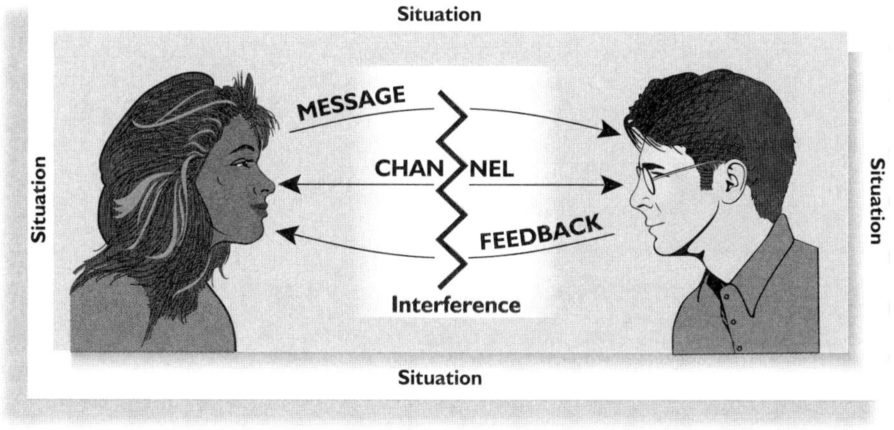

Figure 1.1

The Speech Communication Process: Example with Commentary

The following example shows how the various components of the speech communication process interact:

Situation	It was 5:15 P.M., and the fall sales conference of OmniBrands, Inc., had been going on all day. A series of new-product presentations to buyers from the company's largest customers had taken much longer than expected.
Speaker	Alyson Kaufman was worried. As a marketing manager for fragrances, she was the last speaker of the day. When Alyson rose to address the audience, she knew she faced a difficult situation. She had been allotted 45 minutes to introduce her products, and the meeting was scheduled to end in 15 minutes. What's more, holiday sales of her entire product line depended in large part on this presentation.
Channel Interference	Alyson stepped to the microphone and began to speak. She could see members of the audience looking at their watches, and she knew they were eager to get to dinner after a long day of presentations.
Adapting to Interference	"Good afternoon," Alyson said, "and thanks for your attention. I know everyone is ready for dinner—I certainly am. I was given 45 minutes for my presentation—okay, everybody groan—but with your kind cooperation, I'll do my best to finish in under half an hour. I think you'll find the time well worth your while, because the products I am going to tell you about will seriously boost your holiday sales." Alyson was relieved to see several people smiling as they settled back in their seats.
Message	Now that she had the audience's attention, Alyson presented each new product as briefly as she could. She streamlined her planned presentation to emphasize the features that would be most appealing to the buyers and the ones they would be most likely to remember. She ended by handing out samples of the products and promising to contact anyone who needed more information. She quickly added her e-mail address to her PowerPoint slides and was encouraged to see people writing it down.
Feedback	As promised, Alyson finished in under half an hour. "And that wraps it up!" she concluded. "Let's eat!" Later, the marketing director complimented Alyson on dealing so well with a tough situation. "You did a great job," the marketing director said. "Next year, we'll try to make all the presentations as concise and efficient as yours."

Public Speaking in a Multicultural World

Cultural Diversity in the Modern World

The United States has always been a diverse society. In 1673, more than three centuries ago, a visitor to what is now New York City was astonished to find that 18 languages were spoken among the city's 8,000 inhabitants. By the middle of the nineteenth century, so many people from so many lands had come to the United States that novelist Herman Melville exclaimed, "You cannot spill a drop of American blood without spilling the blood of the whole world."[25]

One can only imagine what Melville would say today! The United States has become the most diverse society on the face of the earth. For more than a century, most immigrants to the U.S. were Europeans—Irish, Germans, English, Scandinavians, Greeks, Poles, Italians, and others. Together with African Americans, they made America the "melting pot" of the world.[26] Today another great wave of immigration—mostly from Asia and Latin America—has transformed the United States into what one writer calls "the first universal nation," a multicultural society of unmatched diversity.[27]

The diversity of life in the United States can be seen in cities and towns, schools and businesses, community groups and houses of worship all across the land. Consider the following:

- There are 215 nations in the world, and every one of them has someone living in the United States.
- New York City has more than 170 distinct ethnic communities.
- Houston has two radio stations that broadcast in Vietnamese and a daily newspaper that prints in Chinese.
- Nearly 61 percent of the people in Miami were born outside the United States.
- More than 34 million people in the U.S. speak a language other than English at home.
- Asian Americans make up 45 percent of first-year students at the University of California, Berkeley.

These kinds of changes are not limited to the United States. We are living in an age of international multiculturalism. The Internet allows for instant communication almost everywhere around the world. CNN is broadcast in more than 200 countries. International air travel has made national boundaries almost meaningless. All nations are becoming part of a vast global village. For example:

- There are 60,000 transnational corporations around the world, and they account for more than a quarter of the world's economic output.
- Restaurants in coastal towns of Queensland, Australia, print their menus in both Japanese and English.
- McDonald's sells more hamburgers and french fries abroad than it does in the United States; Gillette makes 70 percent of its sales through exports.
- In Geneva, Switzerland, there are so many people from around the world that nearly 60 percent of the school population is non-Swiss.
- France has more Muslims than practicing Catholics; radio CHIN in Toronto, Canada, broadcasts in 31 languages.
- Four of every five new jobs in the U.S. are generated as a direct result of international trade.

Cultural Diversity and Public Speaking

"That's all very interesting," you may be saying to yourself, "but what does it have to do with my speeches?" The answer is that diversity and multiculturalism are such basic facts of life that they can play a role in almost any speech you give. Consider the following situations: A business manager briefing employees of a multinational corporation. A lawyer presenting her closing argument to an ethnically mixed jury. A minister sermonizing to a culturally diverse congregation. An international student explaining the customs of his land to students at a U.S. university. A teacher addressing parents at a multiethnic urban school. These are only a few of the countless speaking situations affected by the cultural diversity of modern life.

As experts in intercultural communication have long known, speechmaking becomes more complex as cultural diversity increases. Part of the complexity stems from the differences in language from culture to culture. As we will see in Chapter 11, language and thought are closely linked. So, too, are language and culture. Nothing separates one culture from another more than language. Not only do words change from language to language, but so do ways of thinking and of seeing the world. Language and culture are so closely bound that "we communicate the way we do because we are raised in a particular culture and learn its language, rules, and norms."[28]

The meanings attached to gestures, facial expressions, and other nonverbal signals also vary from culture to culture. Even the gestures for such basic messages as "yes" and "no," "hello" and "goodbye" are culturally based. In the United States people nod their heads up and down to signal "yes" and shake them back and forth to signal "no." In Thailand the same actions have exactly the opposite meaning! To take another example, the North American "goodbye" wave is interpreted in many parts of Europe and South America as the motion for "no," while the Italian and Greek gesture for "goodbye" is the same as the U.S. signal for "come here."[29]

Many stories have been told about the fate of public speakers who fail to take into account cultural differences between themselves and their audiences. Consider the following scenario:[30]

The sales manager of a U.S. electronics firm is in Brazil to negotiate a large purchase of computers by a South American corporation. After three days of negotiations, the sales manager holds a gala reception for all the major executives to build goodwill between the companies.

As is the custom on such occasions, time is set aside during the reception for an exchange of toasts. When it is the sales manager's turn to speak, he praises the Brazilian firm for its many achievements and talks eloquently of his respect for its president and other executives. The words are perfect, and the sales manager can see his audience smiling in approval.

And then—disaster. As the sales manager closes his speech, he raises his hand and flashes the classic U.S. "OK" sign to signal his pleasure at the progress of the negotiations. Instantly the festive mood is replaced with stony silence; smiles turn to icy stares. The sales manager has given his Brazilian audience a gesture with roughly the same meaning as an extended middle finger in the United States.

The next day the Brazilian firm announces it will buy its computers from another company.

Public speaking is a vital mode of communication in most cultures around the world. Here Chinese President Hu Jintao addresses the APEC summit meeting in Santiago, Chile.

As this scenario illustrates, public speakers can ill afford to overlook their listeners' cultural values and customs. This is true whether you are speaking at home or abroad, in Atlanta or Rio de Janeiro, in a college classroom or at a meeting of community volunteers. Because of the increasing diversity of modern life, many—perhaps most—of the audiences you address will include people of different cultural backgrounds.

As you read the rest of this book, you will learn the methods of effective public speaking. Almost all those methods will be helpful to you in speaking to culturally diverse audiences. Here we need to stress the importance of avoiding the ethnocentrism that often blocks communication between speakers and listeners of different cultural, racial, and ethnic backgrounds.

Avoiding Ethnocentrism

Ethnocentrism is the belief that our own group or culture—whatever it may be—is superior to all other groups or cultures. Because of ethnocentrism, we identify with our group or culture and see its values, beliefs, and customs as "right" or "natural"—in comparison to the values, beliefs, and customs of other groups or cultures, which we tend to think of as "wrong" or "unnatural."[31]

ethnocentrism
The belief that one's own group or culture is superior to all other groups or cultures.

Ethnocentrism is part of every culture. If you were born and raised in the United States, you may find it strange that most people in India regard the cow as a sacred animal and forgo using it as a source of food. On the other hand, if you were born and raised in India, you might well be shocked at the use of cows in the United States for food, clothing, and other consumer goods. If you are Christian, you most likely think of Sunday as the "normal" day of worship. But if you are Jewish, you probably regard Saturday as the "correct" Sabbath. And if you are Muslim, you doubtless see both Saturday and Sunday as unusual times for worship. For you, Friday is the "right" day.

THE INTERNET *Connection*

As we shall see throughout this book, there are many resources on the World Wide Web for public speakers. One of those resources is an extensive collection of speeches from U.S. history, which you can access at Douglass: Archives of American Public Address (http://douglassarchives.org/).

Thousands of people in the United States earn their living as professional public speakers. You can learn about their activities at the National Speakers Association Web site (www.nsaspeaker.org/).

ONLINE LEARNING CENTER

You can link to these Web sites at www.mhhe.com/lucas9.

Ethnocentrism can play a positive role in creating group pride and loyalty. But it can also be a destructive force—especially when it leads to prejudice and hostility toward different racial, ethnic, or cultural groups. To be an effective public speaker in a multicultural world, you need to keep in mind that all people have their special beliefs and customs.

Avoiding ethnocentrism does not mean you must agree with the values and practices of all groups and cultures. At times you might try to convince people of different cultures to change their traditional ways of doing things—as speakers from the United Nations seek to persuade farmers in Africa to adopt more productive methods of agriculture, as Muslim parents in the United States urge public school officials to accommodate Muslim customs for children who adhere to Islam, or as delegates from the U.S. and China attempt to influence the other country's trade policies.

If such speakers are to be successful, however, they must show respect for the cultures of the people they address. They cannot assume that their cultural assumptions and practices will be shared—or even understood—by all members of their audience. They need to adapt their message to the cultural values and expectations of their listeners.

When you work on your speeches, keep in mind the diversity of life in the modern world and be alert to how cultural factors might affect the way listeners respond to your speeches. As we shall see in Chapter 5, for classroom speeches you can use audience-analysis questionnaires to learn about the backgrounds and opinions of your classmates in regard to specific speech topics. For speeches outside the classroom, the person who invites you to speak can usually provide information about the audience.

Once you know about any cultural factors that might affect the audience's response to your speech, you can work on adapting the speech to make it as effective and appropriate as possible. As you prepare the speech, try to put yourself in the place of your listeners and to hear your message through their ears. If there is a language difference between you and your audience, avoid any words or phrases that might cause misunderstanding. When researching the speech, keep an eye out for examples, comparisons, and other supporting materials that will relate to a wide range of listeners. Also, consider using visual aids in your speech. As we shall see in Chapter 13, they can be especially helpful in bridging a gap in language or cultural background.

When delivering your speech, be alert to feedback that might indicate the audience is having trouble grasping your ideas. If you see puzzled expressions on the faces of your listeners, restate your point to make sure it is understood. With some audiences, you can encourage feedback by asking, "Am I making myself clear?" or "Did I explain this point fully enough?"

If you pose such questions, however, be aware that listeners from different cultures may respond quite differently. Most Arabs, North Americans, and Europeans will give you fairly direct feedback if you ask for it. Listeners from Asian and Caribbean countries, on the other hand, may not respond, out of concern that doing so will show disrespect for the speaker. (See Chapter 5 for a full discussion of audience analysis and adaptation.)[32]

Finally, we should note the importance of avoiding ethnocentrism when listening to speeches. As we shall see in Chapters 2 and 3, speech audiences have a responsibility to listen courteously and attentively. When you listen to a speaker from a different cultural background, be on guard against the temptation to judge that speaker on the basis of his or her appearance or manner of delivery. Too often we form opinions about people by the way they look or speak rather than by listening closely to what they *say*. No matter what the cultural background of the speaker, you should listen to her or him as attentively as you would want your audience to listen to you.

Summary

Public speaking has been a vital means of personal empowerment and civic engagement throughout history. The need for effective public speaking will almost certainly touch you sometime in your life. When it does, you want to be ready. But even if you never give another speech in your life, you still have much to gain from studying public speaking. Your speech class will give you training in researching topics, organizing your ideas, and presenting yourself skillfully. This training is invaluable for every type of communication.

There are many similarities between public speaking and daily conversation. In conversation, almost without thinking about it, you employ a wide range of skills. You organize your ideas logically. You tailor your message to your audience. You tell a story for maximum impact. You adapt to feedback from your listener. These are among the most important skills you will need for public speaking.

Public speaking is also different from conversation. First, public speaking is more highly structured than conversation. It usually imposes strict time limitations on the speaker, and it requires more detailed preparation than does ordinary conversation. Second, public speaking requires more formal language. Listeners react negatively to speeches loaded with slang, jargon, and bad grammar. Third, public speaking demands a different method of delivery. Effective speakers adjust their voices to the larger audience and work at avoiding distracting physical mannerisms and verbal habits.

One of the major concerns of students in any speech class is stage fright. Actually, most successful speakers are nervous before making a speech. Your speech class will give you an opportunity to gain confidence and make your nervousness work for you rather than against you. You will take a big step toward overcoming stage fright if you think positively, prepare thoroughly, visualize yourself giving a successful speech, keep in mind that most nervousness is not visible to the audience, and think of your speech as communication rather than as a performance in which you must do everything perfectly. Like other students over the years, you too can develop confidence in your speechmaking abilities.

Besides building your confidence, a course in public speaking can help develop your skills as a critical thinker. Critical thinking is the ability to perceive relationships among ideas. It can help you spot weaknesses in other people's reasoning and avoid them in your own. Critical thinking can make a difference in many areas of your life, from your schoolwork to your activities as a consumer to your responsibilities as a citizen.

The speech communication process as a whole includes seven elements—speaker, message, channel, listener, feedback, interference, and situation. The speaker is the person who initiates a speech transaction. Whatever the speaker communicates is the message, which is sent by means of a particular channel. The listener receives the communicated message and provides feedback to the speaker. Interference is anything that impedes the communication of a message, and the situation is the time and place in which speech communication occurs. The interaction of these seven elements is what determines the outcome in any instance of speech communication.

Because of the diversity of modern life, many—perhaps most—of the audiences you address will include people of different cultural, racial, and ethnic backgrounds. When you work on your speeches, be alert to how such factors might affect the responses of your listeners and take steps to adapt your message accordingly. Above all, avoid the ethnocentric belief that your own culture or group—whatever it may be—is superior to every other culture or group. Also keep in mind the importance of avoiding ethnocentrism when listening to speeches. Accord every speaker the same courtesy and attentiveness you would want from your listeners.

Key Terms

ONLINE LEARNING CENTER

Review these terms by doing the Chapter 1 crossword puzzle at www.mhhe.com/lucas9.

stage fright (9)
adrenaline (10)
positive nervousness (11)
visualization (13)
critical thinking (16)
speaker (18)
message (18)
channel (18)
listener (19)
frame of reference (19)
feedback (20)
interference (21)
situation (21)
ethnocentrism (25)

Review Questions

After reading this chapter, you should be able to answer the following questions:

1. In what ways is public speaking likely to make a difference in your life?
2. How is public speaking similar to everyday conversation?

3. How is public speaking different from everyday conversation?
4. Why is it normal—even desirable—to be nervous at the start of a speech?
5. How can you control your nervousness and make it work for you in your speeches?
6. What are the seven elements of the speech communication process? How do they interact to determine the success or failure of a speech?
7. What is ethnocentrism? Why do public speakers need to avoid ethnocentrism when addressing audiences with diverse cultural, racial, or ethnic backgrounds?

CD 1: STUDY QUESTIONS

For further review, go to the Study Questions for this chapter.

Exercises for Critical Thinking

1. Think back on an important conversation you had recently in which you wanted to achieve a particular result. (*Examples:* Asking your employer to change your work schedule; explaining to a friend how to change the oil and filter in a car; attempting to talk your spouse or partner into buying the computer you like rather than the one he or she prefers.) Work up a brief analysis of the conversation.

   In your analysis, explain the following: (1) your purpose in the conversation and the message strategy you chose to achieve your purpose; (2) the communication channels used during the conversation and how they affected the outcome; (3) the interference—internal or external—you encountered during the conversation; (4) the steps you took to adjust to feedback; (5) the strategic changes you would make in preparing for and carrying out the conversation if you had it to do over again.

2. Divide a sheet of paper into two columns. Label one column "Characteristics of an Effective Public Speaker." Label the other column "Characteristics of an Ineffective Public Speaker." In the columns, list and briefly explain what you believe to be the five most important characteristics of effective and ineffective speakers. Be prepared to discuss your ideas in class.
3. On the basis of the lists you developed for Exercise 2, candidly evaluate your own strengths and weaknesses as a speaker. Identify the three primary aspects of speechmaking you most want to improve.

Applying the POWER of PUBLIC SPEAKING

It has been three years since you finished college. After gaining experience as an administrative assistant at a major publishing company, you have just been promoted to marketing manager for a children's book series. Though you have occasionally given brief reports to other members of your work team, you are now facing your first speech to a large audience. At your company's annual sales meeting, you will address the sales force about the company's new books and how to sell them to wholesalers and retail bookstores.

You're pleased to have this opportunity and you know it shows the company's faith in your abilities. Yet the closer you get to the day of the speech, the harder it is to control the butterflies in your stomach. There will be 150 people in your audience, including all the senior editors and regional managers, in addition to the sales force. All eyes will be on you. It's important that you come across as confident and well informed, but you're afraid your stage fright will send the opposite message. What strategies will you use to control your nerves and make them work for you?

Notes

[1]Pericles, quoted in Richard Whately, *Elements of Rhetoric,* 7th ed. London: John W. Parker, 1846), p. 10.

[2]Albert R. Karr, "A Special News Report About Life on the Job and Trends Taking Shape There," *The Wall Street Journal,* December 29, 1998, p. A1; Andrew A. Zekeri, "College Curriculum Competencies and Skills Former Students Found Essential to Their Careers," *College Student Journal,* 38 (2004), pp. 412–422.

[3]Stephanie Armour, "Failure to Communicate Costly for Companies," *USA Today,* April 30, 1998, p. 1B; Midge Costanza quoted in Sharon Nelson, "Address for Success," *Nation's Business* (February 1991), pp. 43–44.

[4]George A. Kennedy, *Comparative Rhetoric: An Historical and Cross-Cultural Introduction* (New York: Oxford University Press, 1998).

[5]For an excellent selection of works from the figures discussed in this and the previous paragraph, see Patricia Bizzell and Bruce Herzberg (eds.), *The Rhetorical Tradition: Readings from Classical Times to the Present,* 2nd ed. (New York: Bedford/St. Martin, 2001). For a comprehensive overview, see Craig R. Smith, *Rhetoric and Human Consciousness,* 2nd ed. (Prospect Heights, IL: Waveland, 2003).

[6]See, for example, Robert L. Heath and Jennings Bryant, *Human Communication Theory and Research,* 2nd ed. (Mahwah, NJ: Erlbaum, 2000); James Price Dillard and Michael Pfau (eds.), *The Persuasion Handbook: Developments in Theory and Practice* (Thousand Oaks, CA: Sage, 2002);

[7]For an overview of that tradition, see David Cohen, "Oratory," and Stephen E. Lucas, "Public Speaking," in Thomas O. Sloane (ed.), *Encyclopedia of Rhetoric* (New York: Oxford University Press, 2001), pp. 538–547, 640–647.

[8]"What Are Americans Afraid Of?" *The Bruskin Report,* 53 (July 1973).

[9]Daniel Goleman, "Social Anxiety: New Focus Leads to Insights and Therapy," *The New York Times*, December 18, 1984. "How Americans Communicate," a 1999 study commissioned by the National Communication Association, found that only 24 percent of Americans are "very comfortable" giving a speech or other formal presentation. The study can be accessed at www.natcom.org/research/Roper/how_americans_communicate.htm.

[10]Jeffrey C. Hahner, Martin A. Sokoloff, and Sandra L. Salisch, *Speaking Clearly: Improving Voice and Diction,* 6th ed. (New York: McGraw-Hill, 2002), p. 12.

[11]Quoted in Bert E. Bradley, *Fundamentals of Speech Communication: The Credibility of Ideas,* 6th ed. (Dubuque, IA: Wm. C. Brown, 1991), p. 36.

[12]Elayne Synder, *Speak for Yourself—With Confidence* (New York: New American Library, 1983), p. 113.

[13]A number of studies have shown that taking a public speaking course is effective in reducing stage fright. See, for example, Ralph R. Behnke and Chris R. Sawyer, "Public Speaking Anxiety as a Function of Sensitization and Habituation Processes," *Communication Education,* 53 (2004), pp. 164–173.

[14]Lilly Walters, *Secrets of Successful Speakers* (New York: McGraw-Hill, 1993), pp. 32–36.

[15]Quoted in Steven Ungerleider, *Mental Training for Peak Performance* (Emmaus, PA: Rodale Press, 1996), p. 9.

[16]Joe Ayres, Tim Hopf, and Debbie M. Ayres, "Visualization and Performance Visualization: Applications, Evidence, and Speculation," in John A. Daly, James C. McCroskey, Joe Ayres, Tim Hopf, and Debbie M. Ayres (eds.), *Avoiding Communication: Shyness, Reticence, and Communication Apprehension,* 2nd ed. (Cresskill, NJ: Hampton Press, 1997), pp. 401–422.

[17]Dick Cavett, quoted in Steve Allen, *How to Make a Speech* (New York: McGraw-Hill, 1986), p. 10.

[18]For more detail on the ideas in this paragraph, see Michael T. Motley, *Overcoming Your Fear of Public Speaking: A Proven Method* (Boston: Houghton Mifflin, 1998).

[19]Chris R. Sawyer and Ralph R. Behnke, "Reduction in Public Speaking State Anxiety During Performance as a Function of Sensitization Processes," *Communication Quarterly,* 50 (2002), pp. 110–121.

[20]For fuller discussion of these and other approaches to controlling stage fright, see Karen Kangas Dwyer, *Conquer Your Speech Anxiety: Learn How to Overcome Your Nervousness About Public Speaking,* 2nd ed. (Belmont, CA: Thomson Wadsworth, 2005).

[21]For more detail on the dimensions of critical thinking, see M. Neil Browne and Stuart M. Keeley, *Asking the Right Questions: A Guide to Critical Thinking,* 7th ed. (Upper Saddle River, NJ: Prentice Hall, 2004).

[22]For the transference of critical thinking skills from public speaking to other activities, see Mike Allen, Sandra Berkowitz, Steve Hunt, and Allen Louden, "A Meta-Analysis of the Impact of Forensics and Communication Education on Critical Thinking," *Communication Education,* 48 (1999), pp. 18–30. Also see Virginia O'Keefe, *Developing Critical Thinking: The Speaking/Listening Connection* (Portsmouth, NH: Boynton/Cook, 2000).

[23]See Bruce A. Kimball, *Orators and Philosophers: A History of the Idea of Liberal Education* (New York: College Board, 1995).

[24]For other models of the speech communication process, see Stephen W. Littlejohn and Karen A. Foss, *Theories of Human Communication,* 8th ed. (Belmont, CA: Thomson Wadsworth, 2005); Em Griffin, *A First Look at Communication Theory,* 6th ed. (New York: McGraw-Hill, 2006).

[25]John Elson, "The Great Migration," *Time* (Fall 1993), p. 30; Melville quoted in Ronald Takaki, *A Different Mirror: A History of Multicultural America* (Boston: Little, Brown, 1993), p. 427.

[26]See Michael Barone, *The New Americans: How the Melting Pot Can Work Again* (New York: Regnery, 2001).

[27]Ben J. Wattenberg, *The First Universal Nation: Leading Indicators and Ideas About the Surge of America in the 1990s* (New York: Free Press, 1991). For a more theoretical perspective, see Stephen B. Croft, "Rethinking Nationality in the Context of Globalization," *Communication Theory,* 14 (2004), pp. 78–96.

[28]William B. Gudykunst and Young Yun Kim, *Communicating with Strangers: An Approach to Intercultural Communication,* 4th ed. (New York: McGraw-Hill, 2003), p. 4.

[29]For more detail on gestures and other aspects of intercultural communication, see Fred E. Jandt, *An Introduction to Intercultural Communication: Identities in a Global Community,* 4th ed. (Thousand Oaks, CA: Sage, 2004).

[30]Adapted from Roger E. Axtell (ed.), *Do's and Taboos Around the World,* 3rd ed. (New York: John Wiley and Sons, 1993), p. 41.

[31]Myron W. Lustig and Jolene Koester, *Intercultural Competence: Interpersonal Communication Across Cultures,* 5th ed. (Boston: Allyn and Bacon, 2006), pp. 145–148.

[32]For a comprehensive review of scholarship on multiculturalism and communication, see William B. Gudykunst and Bella Moody (eds.), *Handbook of International and Intercultural Communication,* 2nd ed. (Thousand Oaks, CA: Sage, 2002).

CHAPTER FOUR

Selecting a Topic and a Purpose

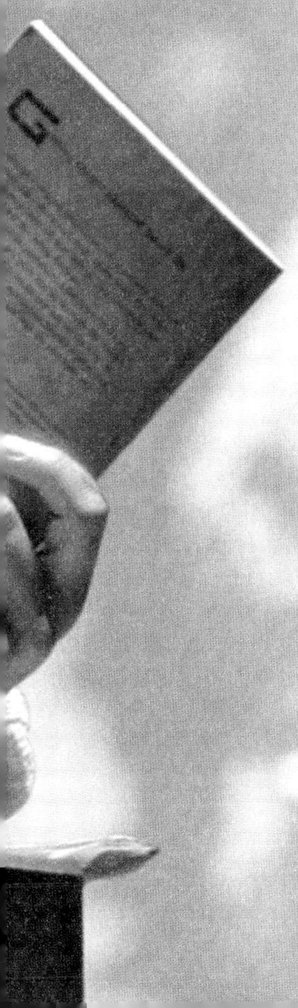

Choosing a Topic

Topics You Know a Lot About

Topics You Want to Know More About

Brainstorming for Topics

Determining the General Purpose

Determining the Specific Purpose

Tips for Formulating the Specific Purpose Statement

Questions to Ask About Your Specific Purpose

Phrasing the Central Idea

What Is the Central Idea?

Guidelines for the Central Idea

As you read through this book, you will find examples of hundreds of speeches that were delivered in classrooms, in the political arena, in community and business situations. Here is a very small sample of the topics they cover:

antibacterial products	Navajo sandpainting
breast cancer	obsessive compulsive disorder
Cesar Chavez	pilates
driving age	Quebec
election reform	reality television
free speech	Supreme Court
genetic engineering	Title IX
Habitat for Humanity	Underground Railroad
Iraq	volunteering
Judaism	women's gymnastics
Koran	x-rays
laser surgery	yoga
Martin Luther King	zoning laws

Undoubtedly you noticed that the list runs from A to Z. This array of topics wasn't planned. It happened naturally in the course of presenting many different kinds of speeches. The list is given here simply to show you that there are literally endless possibilities for speech topics—from A to Z.

Choosing a Topic

topic
The subject of a speech.

The first step in speechmaking is choosing a topic. For speeches outside the classroom this is seldom a problem. Usually the speech topic is determined by the occasion, the audience, and the speaker's qualifications. When Condoleezza Rice lectures on a college campus, she is invited to speak about foreign policy and current events. Christine Amanpour will discuss women and journalism. Roger Ebert might share his views about the latest in filmmaking. The same is true of ordinary citizens. The doctor is asked to inform high-school athletes and their parents about sport injuries, the head of a neighborhood coalition speaks about zoning regulations, the florist discusses how to grow thriving houseplants.

In a public speaking class the situation is different. Most of your speech assignments will not come with a designated topic. Students generally have great leeway in selecting subjects for their speeches. This would appear to be an advantage, since it allows you to talk about matters of personal interest. Yet there may be no facet of speech preparation that causes more gnashing of teeth than selecting a topic.

When you look for a speech topic, keep in mind special expertise you may have or sports, hobbies, travel, and other personal experiences that would make for an interesting presentation.

It is a constant source of amazement to teachers that students who regularly chat with their friends about almost any subject under the sun become mentally paralyzed when faced with the task of deciding what to talk about in their speech class. Fortunately, once you get over this initial paralysis, you should have little trouble choosing a good topic.

There are two broad categories of potential topics for your classroom speeches: (1) subjects you know a lot about and (2) subjects you want to know more about. Let's start with the first.

Topics You Know a Lot About

Most people speak best about subjects with which they are most familiar. When thinking about a topic, you draw on your own knowledge and experience. You may think to yourself, "That's impossible. I've never done anything fascinating. My life is too ordinary to interest other people." Everyone knows things or has done things that can be used in a speech.

Think for a moment about unusual experiences you may have had. Think also about special knowledge or expertise you may have acquired. You are bound to come up with something. One student, who grew up in Pakistan, presented a fascinating speech about daily life in that country. Another used her knowledge as a jewelry store salesperson to prepare a speech on how to judge the value of cut diamonds. A third student, who had lived through a tornado, gave a gripping speech about that terrifying experience.

Too dramatic? Nothing in your life is as interesting? Yet another student, who described herself as "just a housewife who is returning to school to finish the education she started 20 years ago," delivered a witty and highly entertaining speech on the adjustments she had to make in coming back to college. This speaker talked about the strange feelings of sitting in class with students young enough to be her children, the difficulty of balancing her academic work against her family commitments, and the satisfaction of completing the education she had begun years earlier.

Here are a few more examples of speech topics based largely on the students' personal knowledge and experience:

Hong Kong: City of Paradox

The Basics of Backpacking

Making a Difference: The Peace Corps

A Tour of Old Jerusalem

Scuba Diving: A New World Under Water

Performing with the Native American Dance Troupe

Diabetes: You Can Live with It

How to Have a Successful Job Interview

Topics You Want to Know More About

On the other hand, you may decide to make your speech a learning experience for yourself as well as for your audience. You may choose a subject about which you already have some knowledge or expertise but not enough to prepare a speech without doing additional research. You may even select a topic that hasn't touched you at all before but that you want to explore. Say, for example, you've always been interested in extrasensory perception but never knew much about it. This would be a perfect opportunity to research a fascinating subject and turn it into a fascinating speech.

Or suppose you run across a subject in one of your other classes that catches your fancy. Why not investigate it further for your speech class? One student used this approach to develop a speech on a valuable natural resource known as coltan, which commands huge prices and is used in electronic devices such as laptops, cell phones, and pagers. After hearing about the subject in his electrical engineering class, the student checked with his professor for additional readings, which he found in the library. He also arranged an interview with his professor. (See Chapter 6 for information on conducting a research interview.) In the process, the student learned that coltan has also become an object of warfare between Congo and its neighbors in Central Africa. Using what he learned in his research, the student put together a captivating speech that kept everyone's attention from beginning to end.

CD 1: VIDEO 4.1

View an excerpt from "Coltan: Money, Guns, and Cell Phones."

Still another possibility—especially for persuasive speeches—is to think of subjects about which you hold strong opinions and beliefs. Imagine you are at dinner with a friend and find yourself arguing that television broadcasters should not report the projected results of presidential elections until polls have closed throughout the country. Why not give a speech in class on the same topic? Or suppose you believe your school should set up a program to help reduce burglaries on campus. Why not try to convince your classmates and get them to petition for such a program?

Like everyone else, you surely have issues about which you care deeply. They may include national or international concerns such as gun control, protection of the environment, or the threat of terrorism. Or perhaps you are closely involved in a local issue, such as a teachers' strike, the campaign for mayor, or a proposal to increase tuition. Not all such topics must be "political." They can deal with anything from graduation requirements to helping people with physical disabilities, from vegetarianism to preserving a nature sanctuary, from dormitory regulations to building a church recreation center.

Brainstorming for Topics

After all this, you may still be thinking, "I *don't* care about coltan. I've *never* been to Pakistan. I'm *not* active in politics. WHAT am I going to talk about?" If you are having trouble selecting a topic, there are a number of brainstorming procedures you can follow to get started.

brainstorming
A method of generating ideas for speech topics by free association of words and ideas.

Personal Inventory

First make a quick inventory of your experiences, interests, hobbies, skills, beliefs, and so forth. Jot down anything that comes to mind, no matter how silly or irrelevant it may seem. From this list may come a general subject area out of which you can fashion a specific topic. This method has worked for many students.

Clustering

If the first method doesn't work, try the second. It's a technique called clustering. Take a sheet of paper and divide it into nine columns as follows: People, Places, Things, Events, Processes, Concepts, Natural Phenomena, Problems, and Plans and Policies. Then list in each column the first five or six items that come to mind. The result might look like this:

People	Places	Things
George W. Bush	Iraq	robots
Hillary Clinton	Mexico City	cell phones
Oprah Winfrey	Grand Canyon	cartoons
my family	San Francisco	dream catchers
Annika Sorenstam	Alcatraz	Bible
Oscar de la Hoya	my hometown	mosques

Events	Processes
marriage	learning CPR
Passover	cooking Thai food
Chinese New Year	avoiding credit card debt
Super Bowl	taking photographs
Cinco de Mayo	studying abroad
graduation	writing a job resumé

Concepts	**Natural Phenomena**
pacifism	earthquakes
medical ethics	hurricanes
conservatism	global warming
free-speech theories	asteroids
Confucianism	lightning
multiculturalism	tsunami

Problems	**Plans and Policies**
terrorism	homeland security
childhood obesity	protecting civil liberties
election fraud	raising the minimum wage
identity theft	domestic partner benefits
campus crime	homeschooling
illegal business practices	building a new library

Very likely, several items on your lists will strike you as potential topics. If not, take the items you find most intriguing and compose sublists for each. Try to free-associate. Write down a word or idea. What does that trigger in your mind? Whatever it is, write that down next, and keep going until you have six or seven ideas on your list. For example, working from the lists printed above, one student composed sublists for cartoons, campus crime, and lightning:

Cartoons	**Campus Crime**	**Lightning**
television	vandalism	thunder
movies	police	noise
Academy Awards	fingerprints	traffic
prizes	hands	air pollution
lotteries	gloves	gasoline
gambling	cold weather	motorcycles

Can you follow her trail of association? In the first column cartoons made her think of television. Television reminded her of movies. Movies suggest the Academy Awards. The Academy Awards are prizes. Prizes reminded her of lotteries. Lotteries are a form of gambling. Suddenly, this student remembered a magazine article she had read on the growing problem of gambling addiction in America. The idea clicked in her mind. After considerable research she developed an excellent speech entitled "Gambling Addiction: Why You Can't Beat the Odds."

That's a far cry from cartoons! If you started out free-associating from cartoons, you would doubtless end up somewhere completely different. This is what clustering is all about.

Reference Search

By clustering, most people are able to come up with a topic rather quickly. But if you are still stymied, don't despair. There is a third technique you can use. Go to the reference room of the library and browse through an encyclopedia, a periodical database, or some other reference work until you stumble across what might be a good speech topic. As an experiment, one student decided to scan the CD-ROM version of *The American Heritage Dictionary,* limiting herself to the letter *b*. Within 10 minutes she had come up with these potential topics:

Bible	bonsai	Baja California	bar mitzvah
backpacking	blackjack	Braille	backgammon
Bill of Rights	bioethics	bicycle	butterflies
ballet	Beethoven	Beijing	beer
beta-carotene	birthstones	botulism	Buddhism

With proper research and development, any one of these could make an excellent speech.

Internet Search

Yet another possibility is to connect to a subject-based search engine, such as Yahoo or the Librarians' Index to the Internet. You will see a screen much like the one in Figure 4.1, page 92, which lists the major categories of subjects indexed by Yahoo. If you select one of those categories—say, Health—the next screen will show all subcategories indexed under that heading. The result will look something like Figure 4.2, also on page 92, which lists 30 subcategories for Health, any one of which might strike your fancy as a potential speech topic.

One of the advantages of using Yahoo as a brainstorming aid is that you can continue to make your search more and more specific until you find just the right topic. Suppose, for example, that as you look at the subheadings for Health, your attention is grabbed by the first item—Alternative Medicine. If you click on this item, you will get another screen with a detailed list of subheadings for Alternative Medicine. Working from that list, you can link up to other sites that will help you narrow and focus your topic even further. This process is much faster than leafing through reference works in the library, and it can be a great spur to thinking creatively about a topic.

Whatever the means you use for selecting a topic, *start early.* The major reason students have difficulty choosing speech topics is that, like most people, they tend to procrastinate—to put off starting projects for as long as

Figure 4.1

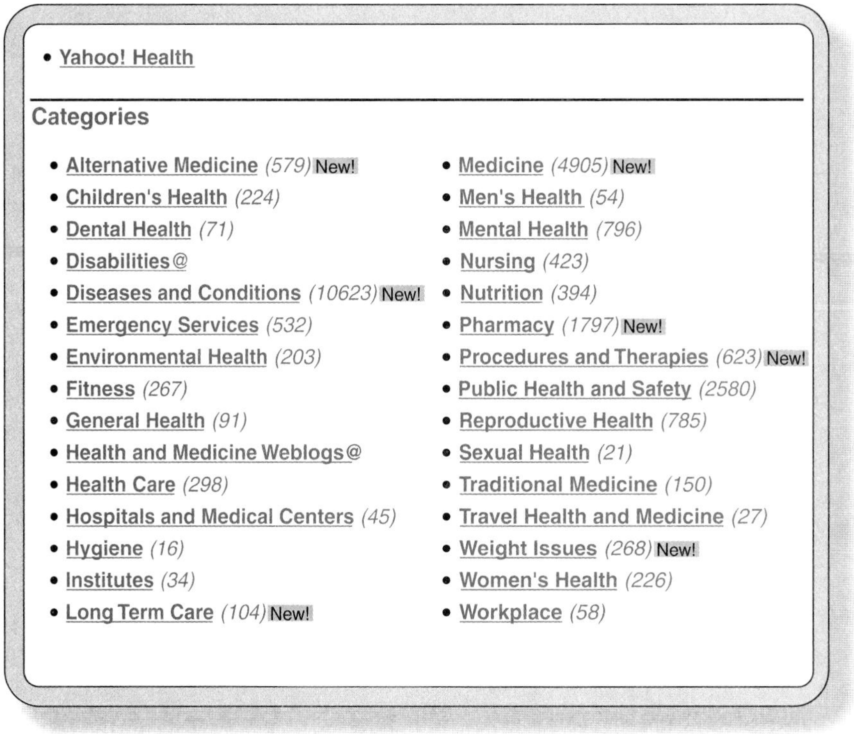

Figure 4.2

possible. Since choosing a topic is your first step in the process of speech preparation, it is only natural to postpone facing up to it. But if you postpone it for too long, you may dig yourself into a hole from which you cannot escape.

Start thinking about your topic as soon as each assignment is announced. Pay attention to interesting subjects in class and conversation, on the radio and television, in newspapers and magazines. Jot down in your notebook ideas for topics as they occur to you. Having an inventory of possible topics to choose from is much better than having to rack your brain for one at the last minute. If you get an early start on choosing a topic, you will have plenty of time to pick just the right one and prepare a first-rate speech.

Determining the General Purpose

Along with choosing a topic, you need to determine the *general purpose* of your speech. Usually it will fall into one of two overlapping categories—to inform or to persuade.

general purpose
The broad goal of a speech

When your general purpose is to *inform,* you act as a teacher or lecturer. Your goal is to convey information—and to do so clearly, accurately, and interestingly. If you describe how to lift weights, narrate the major events of the latest Middle East crisis, give an account of your trip to Spain, report on your sorority's financial position, or explain how the government's forest management plan works, you are speaking to inform. Your aim is to enhance the knowledge and understanding of your listeners—to give them information they did not have before.

When your general purpose is to *persuade,* you act as an advocate or a partisan. You go beyond giving information to espousing a cause. You want to *change* or *structure* the attitudes or actions of your audience. The difference between informing and persuading is the difference between explaining and exhorting. If you try to convince your listeners that they should start a regular program of weight lifting, that the United States should modify its policy in the Middle East, that more students should take advantage of the study-abroad program, that your sorority should start a fund-raising drive to balance its budget, or that the federal government should change its methods of forest management to reduce the incidence of forest fires—then you are speaking to persuade. In doing so, you cannot help but give information; but your primary goal is to win over your listeners to your point of view—to get them to believe something or do something as a result of your speech.

In speech classes, the general purpose is usually specified as part of the speech assignment. For speeches outside the classroom, however, you have to make sure of your general purpose yourself. Usually this is easy to do. Are you going to explain, report, or demonstrate something? Then your general purpose is to inform. Are you going to sell, advocate, or defend something? Then your general purpose is to persuade. But no matter what the situation, you must be certain of exactly what you hope to achieve by speaking. Knowing your general purpose is the first step. The next step is determining your specific purpose.

Determining the Specific Purpose

Once you have chosen a topic and a general purpose, you must narrow your choices to determine the *specific purpose* of your speech. The specific purpose should focus on one aspect of a topic. You should be able to state your specific purpose in a single infinitive phrase (to inform my audience about . . . ; to persuade my audience to . . .) that indicates *precisely* what you hope to accomplish with your speech. Perhaps an example will help clarify the process of choosing a specific purpose.

specific purpose
A single infinitive phrase that states precisely what a speaker hopes to accomplish in his or her speech.

Duane Winfield, a student at a large state university, decided to give his first classroom speech on a topic from his personal experience. For the past two years, he had volunteered his time to perform music for patients in mental hospitals, nursing homes, and residences for disabled adults. He had seen how enthusiastically the patients responded to music, even when they remained unmoved by other kinds of stimuli. Duane's experience had given him a better understanding of the benefits of music therapy, and he wanted to share this understanding with his classmates. This gave him a topic and a general purpose, which he stated like this:

Topic: Music therapy

General Purpose: To inform

So far, so good. But what aspect of his topic would Duane discuss? The kinds of facilities in which he had worked? His specific role as a performer? The evidence that music therapy can improve patients' mental health? The needs of patients with different kinds of illnesses? He had to choose something interesting that he could cover in a six-minute speech. Finally, he settled on describing his most memorable experiences with patients to show how music affected them. He stated his specific purpose this way:

Specific Purpose: To inform my audience about the benefits of music therapy for people with psychological or cognitive disabilities.

This turned out to be an excellent choice, and Duane's speech was among the best in the class.

Notice how clear the specific purpose statement is. Notice also how it relates the topic directly to the audience. That is, it states not only what the *speaker* wants to *say* but also what the speaker wants the *audience* to *know* as a result of the speech. This is very important, for it helps keep the audience at the center of your attention as you prepare your speech.

Look what happens when the specific purpose statement does not include the audience.

Specific Purpose: To explain the benefits of music therapy for people with psychological or cognitive disabilities.

THE INTERNET *Connection*

Having trouble choosing a speech topic? Try browsing through the subject categories at the Librarians' Index to the Internet (www.lii.org). You will find a wealth of high-quality materials that can help get your creative juices flowing.

Another valuable Web site for anyone thinking about speech topics is www.wikipedia.org, which provides a free online encyclopedia with more than 10,000 entries, each of which is cross-referenced and linked to other Wikipedia articles.

ONLINE LEARNING CENTER

You can link to these Web sites at www.mhhe.com/lucas9

Explain to whom? To a group of musicians? To medical students? To social workers? Those would be three different speeches. The musicians would want to know about Duane's audiences and the kinds of music he played. The medical students would want to hear about the research on the benefits of music therapy. The social workers would want to learn how to implement a music program. Communicating effectively with each group would require preparing a different speech.

When the audience slips out of the specific purpose, it may slip out of the speaker's consciousness. You may begin to think your task is the general one of preparing "an informative speech," when in fact your task is the specific one of informing a particular group of people. This may seem like a small point right now, but as we shall see in the next chapter, it is almost impossible to prepare a good speech without keeping constantly in mind the *people* for whom it is intended.

Tips for Formulating the Specific Purpose Statement

Formulating a specific purpose is the most important early step in developing a successful speech. When writing your purpose statement, try to follow the general principles outlined below.

Write the Purpose Statement as a Full Infinitive Phrase, Not as a Fragment

Ineffective: Calendars.

More Effective: To inform my audience about the four major kinds of calendars used in the world today.

Ineffective: Stem cell research.

More Effective: To persuade my audience that the federal government should increase funding for stem cell research.

The ineffective statements above are adequate as announcements of the speech topic, but they are not thought out fully enough to indicate the specific purpose.

Express Your Purpose as a Statement, Not as a Question

Ineffective: What is Día le los Muertos?

More Effective: To inform my audience about the history of Mexico's Día de los Muertos celebration.

Ineffective: Is the U.S. space program necessary?

More Effective: To persuade my audience that the U.S. space program provides many important benefits to people here on earth.

The questions might make adequate titles, but they are not effective as specific purpose statements. They give no indication about what direction the speech will take or what the speaker hopes to accomplish.

Avoid Figurative Language in Your Purpose Statement

Ineffective: To inform my audience that yoga is extremely cool.

More Effective: To inform my audience how yoga can improve their health.

Ineffective: To persuade my audience that the campus policy on student parking really stinks.

More Effective: To persuade my audience that the campus policy on student parking should be revised.

Although the ineffective statements indicate something of the speaker's viewpoint, they do not state concisely what he or she hopes to achieve. Metaphors, analogies, and the like are effective devices for reinforcing ideas within a speech, but they are too ambiguous for specific purpose statements.

Limit Your Purpose Statement to One Distinct Idea

Ineffective: To persuade my audience to become literacy tutors and to donate time to the Special Olympics.

This purpose statement expresses two unrelated ideas, either of which could be the subject of a speech. The easiest remedy is to select one or the other as a focus for your presentation.

More Effective: To persuade my audience to become literacy tutors.

Or:

More Effective: To persuade my audience to donate time to the Special Olympics.

Does this mean you can never use the word "and" in your specific purpose statement? Not at all. Suppose your specific purpose is "To inform my

You can turn to many resources when working on your speeches. Researching in the library can help you brainstorm for topics, as well as provide materials for developing the speech itself.

audience about the causes and effects of epilepsy." In this case, "and" is entirely appropriate because it connects two related parts of a unified topic. What you need to avoid is not simply the word "and," but a specific purpose statement that contains two unrelated ideas, either of which could easily be developed into a speech in its own right.

Make Sure Your Specific Purpose Is Not Too Vague or General

Ineffective: To inform my audience about the Civil War.

More Effective: To inform my audience about the role of African-American soldiers in the Civil War.

The ineffective purpose statement above falls into one of the most common traps—it is too broad and ill-defined. It gives no clues about what aspect of the Civil War the speaker will cover. The more effective purpose statement is sharp and concise. It reveals clearly what the speaker plans to discuss.

Here is another example, thi.s time from a persuasive speech:

Ineffective: To persuade my audience that something should be done about medical care.

More Effective: To persuade my audience that the federal government should adopt a system of national health insurance for all people in the United States.

Again, the ineffective purpose statement is vague and indistinct. It gives no indication of the speaker's stance toward the topic. The "something" that "should be done" could include anything from clamping down on abuses by HMOs to reforming Medicare and Medicaid. The more effective purpose statement is crisp and clear. It does not leave us guessing what the speaker hopes to accomplish.

The more precise your specific purpose, the easier it will be to prepare your speech. Consider this topic and specific purpose:

Topic: Hot-air balloons.

Specific Purpose: To inform my audience about hot-air balloons.

With such a hazy purpose, you have no systematic way of limiting your research or of deciding what to include in the speech and what to exclude. The origins of hot-air balloons, how they work, their current popularity—all could be equally relevant to a speech designed "to inform my audience about hot-air balloons."

In contrast, look at this topic and specific purpose:

Topic: Hot-air balloons.

Specific Purpose: To inform my audience about the scientific uses of hot-air balloons.

Now it is easy to decide what is germane and what is not. The origins of hot-air balloons, how they work, their popularity for recreation—all are interesting, but none is essential to the specific purpose of explaining "the scientific uses of hot-air balloons." Thus you need not worry about researching these matters or about explaining them in your speech. You can spend your preparation time efficiently.

Questions to Ask About Your Specific Purpose

Sometimes you will arrive at your specific purpose almost immediately after choosing your topic. At other times you may do quite a bit of research before deciding on a specific purpose. Much will depend on how familiar you are with the topic, as well as on any special demands imposed by the assignment, the audience, or the occasion. But whenever you settle on your specific purpose, ask yourself the following questions about it.

Does My Purpose Meet the Assignment?

Students occasionally stumble over this question. Be sure you understand your assignment, and shape your specific purpose to meet it. If you have questions, check with your instructor.

Can I Accomplish My Purpose in the Time Allotted?

Most classroom speeches are quite short, ranging from four to ten minutes. That may seem like a lot of time if you have never given a speech before. But you will quickly find what generations of students have discovered, much to their surprise—time flies when you are giving a speech! Most people

SPECIFIC PURPOSE CHECKLIST

yes	no	
☐	☐	1. Is the specific purpose written as a full infinitive phrase?
☐	☐	2. Does the specific purpose include a reference to the audience?
☐	☐	3. Is the specific purpose phrased as a statement rather than a question?
☐	☐	4. Is the specific purpose free of figurative language?
☐	☐	5. Is the specific purpose limited to a distinct subject?
☐	☐	6. Does the specific purpose indicate precisely what I plan to accomplish in the speech?
☐	☐	7. Does the specific purpose meet the requirements of the assignment?
☐	☐	8. Can the specific purpose be accomplished in the time allotted for the speech?
☐	☐	9. Is the specific purpose relevant to my audience?
☐	☐	10. Does the specific purpose deal with a nontrivial subject?
☐	☐	11. Is the specific purpose suitable for a nontechnical audience?

CD 1: SPEECH CHECKLIST

You can print a copy of this checklist from the CD-ROM.

speak at an average rate of 120 to 150 words a minute. This means that a six-minute speech will consist of roughly 720 to 900 words. That is not long enough to develop a highly complex topic. Here are some specific purpose statements that would defy being handled well in the time normally allocated for classroom speeches:

To inform my audience about the role of technology in human history.

To inform my audience about the rise and fall of ancient Rome.

To persuade my audience to convert to Buddhism.

You are much better off with a limited purpose that you have some reasonable hope of achieving in the short span of four to ten minutes.

Is the Purpose Relevant to My Audience?

The price of retirement homes in Palm Beach might be an engrossing topic for older citizens who are in the market for such dwellings. And the quality of hot lunches in the elementary schools is of great concern to the students who eat them and the parents who pay for them. But neither subject has much relevance for an audience of college students. No matter how well you construct your speeches, they are likely to fall flat unless you speak about matters of interest to your listeners.

This is not to say you must select only topics that pertain directly to the college student's daily experience—the grading system, dormitory conditions, parking spaces on campus, and the like. Most students have wide-ranging backgrounds, interests, ideas, and values. And most of them are intellectually curious. They can get involved in an astonishing variety of subjects. Follow your common sense and make sure *you* are truly interested in the topic. Also, when speaking on a subject that is not obviously relevant to your listeners, take time in your speech to tie the subject in with their goals, values, interests, and well-being. We'll discuss how to do this in the next chapter.

Is the Purpose Too Trivial for My Audience?

Just as you need to avoid speech topics that are too broad or complicated, so you need to steer clear of topics that are too superficial. How to build a fire without matches might absorb a group of Cub Scouts, but your classmates would probably consider it frivolous. Unfortunately, there is no absolute rule for determining what is trivial to an audience and what is not. Here are some examples of specific purposes that most people would find too trivial for classroom speeches:

To inform my audience about the parts of a backpack.

To inform my audience how to tie a bow tie.

To persuade my audience that espresso is better than cappuccino.

Is the Purpose Too Technical for My Audience?

Nothing puts an audience to sleep faster than a dry and technical speech. Beware of topics that are inherently technical and of treating ordinary subjects in a technical fashion. Although you may be perfectly familiar with the principles and vocabulary of international finance, physical anthropology, molecular biology, clinical psychology, or constitutional law, most of your classmates probably are not. There are aspects of these and similar subjects that can be treated clearly, with a minimum of jargon. But if you find that you can't fulfill your specific purpose without relying on technical words and concepts, you should reconsider your purpose.

Here are some examples of specific purposes that are overly technical for most classroom speeches:

To inform my audience about the solution to Fermat's Last Theorem.

To inform my audience about the principles of neutrino physics.

To inform my audience about the methods of encryption technology.

We shall discuss the details of audience analysis and adaptation in Chapter 5. For the moment, remember to make sure that your specific purpose is appropriate for your listeners. If you have doubts, ask your instructor, or circulate a questionnaire among your classmates (see pages 128–131).

Phrasing the Central Idea

What Is the Central Idea?

The specific purpose of a speech is what you hope to accomplish. The *central idea* is a concise statement of what you *expect to say*. Sometimes it is called the thesis statement, the subject sentence, or the major thought. Whatever the term, the central idea is usually expressed as a simple, declarative sentence that refines and sharpens the specific purpose statement.

central idea
A one-sentence statement that sums up or encapsulates the major ideas of a speech.

Imagine you run into a friend on your way to speech class. She says, "I have to dash to my history lecture, but I hear you're giving a speech today. Can you tell me the gist of it in one sentence?" "Sure," you reply. "America's prison system suffers from three major problems—overcrowding of inmates, lack of effective rehabilitation programs, and high expense to taxpayers."

Your answer is the central idea of your speech. It is more precise than your topic (America's prison system) or your specific purpose statement ("To inform my audience of the three major problems facing America's prison system"). By stating exactly what the three major problems are, the central idea sums up your speech in a single sentence.

Another way to think of the central idea is as your *residual message*—what you want your audience to remember after they have forgotten everything else in the speech. Most of the time the central idea will encapsulate the main points to be developed in the body of the speech. To show how this works, let's take a few of the examples we saw earlier in this chapter and develop them from the topic, general purpose, and specific purpose to the central idea.

residual message
What a speaker wants the audience to remember after it has forgotten everything else in a speech.

We can start with the speech about music therapy.

Topic:	Music therapy.
General Purpose:	To inform.
Specific Purpose:	To explain the benefits of music therapy for people with psychological or cognitive disabilities.
Central Idea:	Music therapy developed as a formal mode of treatment during the twentieth century, utilizes a number of methods, and is explained by several theories that account for its success.

CD 1: VIDEO 4.2
View the introduction from "The Benefits of Music Therapy."

Look carefully at this example. It shows how the speaker might start with a broad subject (music therapy) that becomes narrower and narrower as the speaker moves from the general purpose to the specific purpose to the central idea. Notice also how much more the central idea suggests about the content of the speech. From it we can expect the speaker to address three main points in the speech—the first summarizing the development of music therapy, the second looking at methods of music therapy, and the third exploring theories that account for the success of music therapy.

This sharpening of focus as one proceeds to the central idea is crucial. Here is another example:

Topic:	Día de los Muertos.
General Purpose:	To inform.
Specific Purpose:	To inform my audience about the history of Mexico's Día de los Muertos celebration.
Central Idea:	Día de los Muertos can be traced to the Aztecs, was moved from summer to fall by Spanish priests, and today is celebrated in a number of ways in different regions of Mexico.

This central idea is especially well worded. We can assume from it that the body of the speech will contain three main points—on the origins of Día de los Muertos among the Aztecs, on how it was changed by the Spanish, and on the ways it is celebrated today.

Much the same is true of the following example:

Topic:	Alternative-fuel vehicles.
General Purpose:	To persuade.
Specific Purpose:	To persuade my audience that the federal government should speed up efforts to develop alternative-fuel vehicles.
Central Idea:	Developing alternative-fuel vehicles will help reduce American dependence on foreign oil and will help reduce air pollution.

From this central idea we can deduce that the speaker will develop two main points in the speech: (1) alternative-fuel vehicles have the potential to reduce America's need for imported oil, and (2) alternative-fuel vehicles will help reduce the air pollution caused by automobile and truck exhaust.

There is something else important about these examples. Notice in each case how much more the central idea reveals about the content of the speech than does the specific purpose. This is not accidental. Often you can settle on a specific purpose statement early in preparing your speech. The central idea, however, usually emerges later—after you have done your research and have decided on the main points of the speech. The process may work like this:

As an environmental science major, Marcia Esposito had learned that many experts fear the world may face a severe water shortage by the year 2020. She decided this would make a good topic for her informative speech. Tentatively, she adopted the following specific purpose statement: "To inform my audience about the seriousness of the growing international water crisis." Then Marcia started her research.

An article in *Newsweek,* which she located through ProQuest, explained how the population in countries such as China, Egypt, and Mexico is outstripping the available supply of fresh water. According to the article, one-third of the wells in Beijing, China's capital, have gone dry, and the water table in Mexico City is dropping at the rate of 11 feet per year.

Next Marcia found a report on the Worldwatch Institute Web site about the impact of pollution on the water supply. The report stated that, in many parts of the world, urban and industrial contamination is creating "a water supply too polluted for their people to drink."

Then Marcia hit upon the idea of interviewing one of her environmental science professors. In addition to confirming Marcia's research about the impact of population growth and pollution, the professor mentioned the problems caused by mismanagement of water supplies. Around the world 65 to 70 percent of the water people use is lost to waste, evaporation, and other inefficiencies; the rate in the United States is about 50 percent.

Marcia digested all this information. Now she was ready to formulate her central idea: "Population growth, pollution, and mismanagement are creating a serious shortage of fresh water in many parts of the world."

Guidelines for the Central Idea

What makes a well-worded central idea? Essentially the same things that make a well-worded specific purpose statement. The central idea should (1) be expressed in a full sentence, (2) should not be in the form of a question, (3) should avoid figurative language, and (4) should not be vague or overly general.

Here, for example, are four poorly written central ideas. See if you can identify the problem with each and figure out how each might be phrased more effectively:

Ineffective: Paying college athletes a salary is a good idea.

Ineffective: Problems of fad diets.

Ineffective: How does indoor soccer differ from outdoor soccer?

Ineffective: Mexico's Yucatán Peninsula is an awesome place for a vacation.

The first, of course, is too general. To say that paying college athletes a monthly salary is a "good idea" does not convey the speaker's viewpoint sharply and clearly. What does the speaker mean by a "good idea"? That paying athletes a monthly salary is justified given the millions of dollars generated for universities by sports such as football and basketball? That the salary should be paid to all athletes, or just to those in major revenue-producing sports? That the salary should be $250 a month? If so, the

CENTRAL IDEA CHECKLIST

yes	no	
☐	☐	1. Is the central idea written as a complete sentence?
☐	☐	2. Is the central idea phrased as a statement rather than a question?
☐	☐	3. Is the central idea free of figurative language?
☐	☐	4. Does the central idea clearly encapsulate the main points to be discussed in the body of the speech?
☐	☐	5. Can the central idea be adequately discussed in the time allotted for the speech?
☐	☐	6. Is the central idea relevant to the audience?
☐	☐	7. Is the central idea appropriate for a nontechnical audience?

CD 1: SPEECH CHECKLIST

You can print a copy of this checklist from the CD-ROM.

central idea should say as much. A revised central idea for this speech might be:

More Effective: Because college athletes in revenue-producing sports such as football and basketball generate millions of dollars in revenue for their schools, the NCAA should allow such athletes to receive a $250 monthly salary as part of their scholarships.

The second ineffective central idea is also too general, but it suffers further from not being written as a complete sentence. "Problems of fad diets" might work as a topic statement, but it does not reveal enough about the content of the speech to serve as the central idea. It should be rewritten as a full sentence that identifies the problems of fad diets to be discussed in the speech:

More Effective: Although fad diets produce quick weight loss, they can lead to serious health problems by creating deficiencies in vitamins and minerals and by breaking down muscle tissue as well as fat.

The third poorly written central idea is phrased as a question rather than as a full declarative sentence. Asking "How does indoor soccer differ from outdoor soccer?" might be a good way to catch the interest of your listeners, but it does not encapsulate the main points to be developed in the speech. A more effective central idea would be:

More Effective: Played on a smaller, enclosed field that resembles a hockey rink with artificial turf, indoor soccer involves

Unlike the specific purpose, which you need to settle on early in the speech preparation process, the central idea usually takes shape later, as a result of your research and analysis of the topic.

faster action, more scoring, and different strategies than outdoor soccer.

The final ineffective central idea is flawed by its use of figurative language. To say that the Yucatán Peninsula is an "awesome" place for a vacation does not state the speaker's central idea clearly and concisely. It does not indicate what characteristics of the Yucatán Peninsula the speaker intends to discuss. Moreover, "awesome" could mean quite different things to different people. A better central idea might be:

More Effective: Mexico's Yucatán Peninsula has many attractions for vacationers, including a warm climate, excellent food, and extensive Mayan ruins.

Notice that in all these examples the more effective central idea encapsulates or sums up the main points of the speech in a single sentence. If you are having trouble phrasing your central idea, the reason may be that you do not yet have a firm grasp on the main points of your speech. Do not worry too much about your central idea until after you have developed the body of your speech (see Chapter 8). If, at that point, you still can't come up with a clear, concise central idea, it may be that your speech itself is not very clear or concise. Keep working on the speech until you can compose a central idea that fits the criteria just discussed. The result will be a sharper central idea and a tighter, more coherent speech.

Summary

The first step in speechmaking is choosing a topic. For classroom speeches it is often best to choose a subject you know well or in which you have personal experience, but you can also succeed with a topic you research especially for the speech. If you have trouble picking a topic, you can follow at least four brainstorming procedures. First, make a quick inventory of your hobbies, interests, skills, experiences, beliefs, and so forth. Second, use the technique of clustering and write down on a sheet of paper the first topics that come to mind in several categories. Third, look through a reference work for ideas. Fourth, use a World Wide Web subject directory such as Yahoo! to help you scan possible topics.

After you choose a topic, you need to settle on the general purpose of your speech. Usually the general purpose will be to inform or to persuade. When your general purpose is to inform, you act as a teacher. Your goal is to communicate information clearly, accurately, and interestingly. When your general purpose is to persuade, you act as an advocate. You go beyond giving information to espousing a cause. Your goal is to win listeners over to your point of view.

Once you know your topic and general purpose, you must focus in on a specific purpose that you can express as a single infinitive phrase. The phrase should indicate precisely what your speech seeks to achieve; for example, "To inform my audience of the major kinds of canoe races." The specific purpose statement should (1) be a full infinitive phrase, not a fragment; (2) be phrased as a statement, not a question; (3) avoid figurative language; (4) concentrate on one distinct idea; (5) not be too vague or too general.

In addition, keep several questions in mind as you formulate your specific purpose statement: Does my purpose meet the assignment? Can I accomplish my purpose in the time allotted? Is the purpose relevant to my audience? Is the purpose too trivial or too technical for my audience?

The central idea refines and sharpens your specific purpose. It is a concise statement of what you will say in your speech, and it usually crystallizes in your thinking after you have done your research and have decided on the main points of your speech. An example of a central idea is, "The three major kinds of canoe races are marathon races, white-water races, and flat-water races." As you can see, the central idea usually encapsulates the main points to be developed in the body of your speech.

Key Terms

ONLINE LEARNING CENTER

Review these terms by doing the Chapter 4 crossword puzzle at www.mhhe.com/lucas9.

topic (86)
brainstorming (89)
general purpose (93)
specific purpose (94)
central idea (101)
residual message (101)

Review Questions

After reading this chapter, you should be able to answer the following questions:

1. What four brainstorming methods can you follow if you are having trouble choosing a topic for your speech?
2. What are the two general purposes of most classroom speeches? How do they differ?
3. Why is determining the specific purpose such an important early step in speech preparation? Why is it important to include the audience in the specific purpose statement?
4. What are five tips for formulating your specific purpose?
5. What are five questions to ask about your specific purpose?
6. What is the difference between the specific purpose and the central idea of a speech? What are four guidelines for an effective central idea?

CD 1: STUDY QUESTIONS

For further review, go to the Study Questions for this chapter.

Exercises for Critical Thinking

1. Using one of the four brainstorming methods described in this chapter, come up with three topics you might like to deal with in your next classroom speech. For each topic, devise two possible specific purpose statements suitable for the speech assignment. Make sure the specific purpose statements fit the guidelines discussed in the chapter.
2. Below is a list of nine topics. Choose three, and for each of the three compose two specific purpose statements—one suitable for an informative speech and one suitable for a persuasive speech.

   Example

Topic:	School buses
Informative:	To inform my audience of the dangerous conditions of many school buses in the United States.
Persuasive:	To persuade my audience that the federal government should impose stronger safety standards for school buses in the United States.

education	technology	crime
sports	politics	prejudice
science	music	health

3. Here are several specific purpose statements for classroom speeches. Identify the problem with each, and rewrite the statement to correct the problem.

To inform my audience how to make perfect popcorn every time.

To inform my audience about the growth of credit card fraud and the methods of sound financial planning.

What is obsessive compulsive disorder?

To inform my audience why square grooves are superior to U-shaped grooves on golf clubs.

To inform my audience about Thailand.

Donate blood.

To persuade my audience that something has to be done about the problem of antibiotic-resistant bacteria.

4. Below are three sets of main points for speeches. For each set, supply the general purpose, specific purpose, and central idea.

General Purpose:

Specific Purpose:

Central Idea:

Main Points:

I. The first step in making pottery is preparing the clay until it is soft and smooth.

II. The second step in making pottery is shaping the clay to the desired form.

III. The third step in making pottery is decorating and glazing the shaped clay.

IV. The fourth step in making pottery is firing the finished product to make it hard and strong.

General Purpose:

Specific Purpose:

Central Idea:

Main Points:

I. You should volunteer as a literacy tutor because it helps children.

II. You should volunteer as a literacy tutor because it strengthens the community.

III. You should volunteer as a literacy tutor because it is personally rewarding.

General Purpose:

Specific Purpose:

Central Idea:

Main Points:

I. As a painter, Leonardo da Vinci produced *The Last Supper,* the *Mona Lisa,* and other masterpieces.

II. As an inventor, Leonardo da Vinci drew plans for such devices as a parachute and a flying machine.

III. As an astronomer, Leonardo da Vinci concluded that the earth revolves around the sun.

Applying the POWER of PUBLIC SPEAKING

Your communication degree has helped you land a job as spokesperson for the mayor of a medium-sized city on the West Coast. A year after starting the job, you are selected to organize an information campaign explaining the benefits of a new youth center proposed by the mayor.

To launch this campaign, you've decided to hold a news briefing at the end of the week. To open the briefing, you will present a short set of comments on the mayor's initiative. You decide to focus on four benefits of the youth center: (1) It will offer a range of activities—from sports to the arts—in a safe environment; (2) It will provide social networks for youths from all walks of life; (3) It will operate most hours of the day and night; and (4) It will be free and open to everyone.

Following the format used in this chapter, state the general purpose, specific purpose, central idea, and main points of your comments.

CHAPTER SEVEN

Supporting Your Ideas

An economics major and a committed free-trader, Doug Chaplin decided to give his first classroom speech on the benefits of outsourcing to the economy. Part of his speech ran like this:

"For the past few years now we've heard that outsourcing jobs is bad for the economy and for individuals. Politicians campaign on the issue, companies create ads around it, and ordinary citizens blame it for all kinds of problems. But do you want to be able to buy high-quality, low-cost manufactured goods? Do you want 24-7 tech support for your computer and better service from your bank? Outsourcing reduces the price of basic goods and services and, contrary to what many people say, it does not cost the U.S. a significant number of jobs. So it's good for all of us."

After the speech, Doug's classmates were polite but skeptical. As one remarked, "Doug raised some interesting points, but he's no expert. A lot of people are talking about outsourcing right now, and it's hard to know exactly what the facts are. Personally, I'd be more convinced if Doug gave some statistics or expert opinion to back up his ideas."

Good speeches are not composed of hot air and generalizations. They need strong supporting materials to bolster the speaker's point of view. In Doug's case, enormous amounts of research have been done on the advantages and disadvantages of outsourcing for the U.S. economy. If there is evidence that outsourcing has reduced the cost of goods and services without reducing jobs in the U.S., then Doug should have cited it instead of making vague, unsupported generalizations.

The problem with generalizations is that they do not answer the three questions listeners always mentally ask of a speaker: "What do you mean?" "Why should I believe you?" "So what?" Consider, for example, the following sets of statements:

General	Less General	Specific
Childhood obesity is a serious problem in the United States.	The incidence of childhood obesity is now so high as to endanger the health of a whole generation of Americans.	At least 15 percent of American children are obese—more than twice the percentage only 25 years ago. The Department of Health and Social Services estimates that in the coming decades the prevalence of obesity will decrease life expectancy in the U.S. by two to five years.
There are a lot of big cities in China.	China has more cities with 1 million people than does any other country in the world.	In China, there are 47 cities with 1 million or more people. Its closest competitor is India, with 32 cities of comparable size. In contrast, Mexico

		has 11 cities with a million or more people, the United States has 9, and England and France have one each.
Coffee is a very popular beverage.	Consumed daily by millions of people, coffee is a major element in the world economy.	With global retail sales of more than $70 billion a year, coffee is second only to oil as the world's most heavily traded legal commodity. Total world coffee consumption exceeds 11 billion pounds annually. Every working day Starbucks opens four new coffeehouses somewhere on the planet.

Which group of statements do you find most interesting? Most convincing? Chances are you will prefer those in the right-hand column. They are sharp and specific, clear and credible—just the sort of thing a speech needs to come alive.

Supporting Materials and Critical Thinking

The skillful use of supporting materials often makes the difference between a poor speech and a good one. It is also closely related to critical thinking. Using supporting materials is not a matter of haphazardly tossing facts and figures into your speech. You must decide which ideas need to be supported given your audience, topic, and specific purpose. You must do research to find materials that will bring your ideas across clearly and creatively. And you must evaluate your supporting materials to make sure they really do back up your ideas.

As you put your speeches together, you will need to make sure your supporting materials are accurate, relevant, and reliable. You will find yourself asking such questions as, "Are my examples representative?" "Am I using statistical measures correctly?" "Am I quoting reputable, qualified sources?" Assessing the supporting materials in your speeches—as well as in the speeches of your classmates—is yet another way in which critical thinking is part of public speaking.

supporting materials
The materials used to support a speaker's ideas. The three major kinds of supporting materials are examples, statistics, and testimony.

In Chapters 14 and 16, we will look at special uses of supporting materials in informative and persuasive speeches. In this chapter, we focus on the basic kinds of supporting materials—examples, statistics, and testimony—and on general principles for using them effectively and responsibly.

Examples

Corina Alamillo is lying on her right side in an operating room at the UCLA Medical Center. There is a pillow tucked beneath her cheek and a steel scaffold screwed into her forehead to keep her head perfectly still. On the other side of a tent of sterile blue paper, two surgeons are hard at work on a saucer-size portion of Corina's brain, which gleams like mother-of-pearl and pulsates gently to the rhythm of her heartbeat.

These lines are from the opening of an article in *National Geographic* magazine about the human brain. It illustrates a device well known to magazine writers—and speechmakers: Get the audience involved.

example
A specific case used to illustrate or to represent a group of people, ideas, conditions, experiences, or the like.

See how skillfully this example accomplishes the goal. It gives us a specific person to focus on (Corina Alamillo). It sets the stage with details of place, color, and the activities of Corina's surgeons. We can almost see ourselves in the operating room, watching the surgeons at work as Corina's brain gleams in the light and pulses in rhythm with her heartbeat. We would not be nearly as involved if the article had merely said, "Brain surgery is a risky and complicated procedure." The *example* touches something in us that no generalization can.

Research has shown that vivid, concrete examples have strong impact on listeners' beliefs and actions.[1] Without examples, ideas often seem vague, impersonal, and lifeless. With examples, ideas become specific, personal, and lively. This is nowhere better illustrated than in the Bible and the Koran, both of which use all manner of stories, parables, and anecdotes to make abstract principles clear and compelling. There are several kinds of examples you may want to try in your speeches.

Brief Examples

brief example
A specific case referred to in passing to illustrate a point.

Brief examples—also called specific instances—may be referred to in passing to illustrate a point. The following excerpt uses a brief example to illustrate the miraculous nature of recent advances in creating artificial limbs for accident victims:

> Changes in technology have made it possible for doctors to work wonders that once seemed impossible. *Roger Charter, for example, lost both his feet when they were crushed in a truck accident. Now he has new feet—made of a springy plastic alloy that duplicates a normal arch. Not only can Roger walk normally, but he can run and play sports again!*

A brief example may also be used to introduce a topic:

> *When archaeologists broke the seal on Tutankhamen's tomb in the autumn of 1922, they uncovered an amazing treasure—a storehouse of ancient Egyptian art of priceless beauty that had lain, untouched and unseen, for more than 3,000 years.* Archaeology is a profession of endless drudgery, painstaking research, and the occasional—very rare—marvelous find.

Another way to use brief examples is to pile them one upon the other until you create the desired impression. Here is how the technique might be used to reinforce the point that Mexican Americans have made many valuable contributions to U.S. life and culture:

Many of us are familiar with prominent Chicanos and Chicanas such as comedian George Lopez, singer Selena, baseball player Luiz Gonzalez, and guitarist Carlos Santana. But you may be less familiar with other Americans of Mexican origin who have made important contributions to U.S. society. Nancy Lopez played a crucial role in popularizing women's professional golf and won 48 tour championships. Dr. Ellen Ochoa is an astronaut who has logged more than 480 hours in space and has invented several optical methods that greatly aid space exploration. Dr. Mario Molina won the 1995 Nobel Prize in Chemistry for his research on the formation and decomposition of the ozone layer.

Extended Examples

Extended examples are often called narratives, illustrations, or anecdotes. They are longer and more detailed than brief examples. By telling a story vividly and dramatically, they pull listeners into the speech. Here is such an example, from a speech by Sun Yan, a student at Fudan University in Shanghai, China. Participating in China's 2001 national English-language speech competition, Sun Yan used an extended example to illustrate the spirit of the Olympic Games:

extended example
A story, narrative, or anecdote developed at some length to illustrate a point.

In the history of the Olympic Games, there have been many shining stars. Among them was a European girl. With the lapse of time, her name has faded from memory, yet her unbending spirit shall never perish. It was she who highlighted the Olympic Creed.

In the lead though she had been, she stumbled near the terminus and her leg was injured. Competitors passed her from behind in succession until finally only her weak and lonely figure remained on the track. Doctors came and offered to take her away. Yet she refused. With the only strength left in her, she managed to get up and shuffled feebly to the endpoint with drops of blood along her trail.

But cheers broke out. Though she failed in the race, the girl won applause from people all over the world. It was she who elucidated the Olympic creed of participation. It was she who instilled perseverance in our minds.[2]

CD 1: VIDEO 7.1
View this portion of Sun Yan's speech on the Olympic spirit.

This long example captures vividly the courage of the Olympic runner and her personification of the Olympic spirit. The speaker could merely have said, "Olympic athletes often display great fortitude," but the story makes the point far more vividly.

Hypothetical Examples

Whether brief or extended, examples can be either factual or hypothetical. All the examples presented up to now have been factual; the incidents they refer to really happened. Sometimes, however, speakers will use a hypothetical example—one that describes an imaginary situation. Usually such examples are brief stories that relate a general principle.

hypothetical example
An example that describes an imaginary or fictitious situation.

Here is how one student used a hypothetical example to illustrate the use of honor codes to reduce cheating:

Imagine this: You're taking your psychology exam when you notice the student sitting next to you is staring at your answers. You also see his open notebook under his desk. You feel your cheeks redden as you become angry that he may get a high score by cheating while you've worked hard to earn your grade. And you feel helpless because you think telling the professor will do nothing.

CD 1: VIDEO 7.2

View this portion of "College Cheating: A National Epidemic."

> But now imagine that you attend a school with an honors system. At the beginning of each exam, you sign a statement that says you will not cheat and that you accept the responsibility to report cheating. After the professor hands out the exam, she leaves the room. In this case, you have the power and the duty to report cheaters rather than feel robbed by them.
>
> Such a system has worked elsewhere and it can work at our school. Professor Donald McCabe, president of the Center for Academic Integrity, has surveyed more than 20,000 students at 70 colleges throughout the country, and his research shows that the level of cheating is significantly lower at schools with honor codes than at schools without them.

This hypothetical example is especially effective. The speaker creates a realistic scenario, relates it directly to her listeners, and gets them involved in the speech. In addition, she uses figures from the president of the Center for Academic Integrity to show that honor codes do help reduce the incidence of cheating on college campuses. Whenever you use a hypothetical example, it is a good idea to follow it with statistics or testimony to show that the example is not far-fetched.

Tips for Using Examples

Use Examples to Clarify Your Ideas

You probably use clarifying examples all the time in everyday conversation. If you were explaining to a friend about different body types, you might say, "Look at Professor Shankar. He's a typical ectomorph—tall, thin, and bony." Examples are an excellent way to clarify unfamiliar or complex ideas. This is why so many teachers use examples in the classroom. Examples put abstract ideas into concrete terms that listeners can easily understand.

This principle works exceptionally well in speeches. Suppose you are talking about suspension bridges. You could give a technical description:

> The suspension bridge has a roadway suspended by vertical cables attached to two or more main cables. The main cables are hung on two towers and have their ends anchored in concrete or bedrock.

If your audience were made up of people familiar with structural systems, they might be able to visualize what a suspension bridge looks like. But for listeners lacking this background, you might want to add a simple example:

> Two well-known suspension bridges are the Golden Gate Bridge in San Francisco and the Brooklyn Bridge in New York.

Because almost everyone has at least seen a picture of the Golden Gate Bridge or the Brooklyn Bridge, using them as examples clarifies your meaning quickly and effectively.

Use Examples to Reinforce Your Ideas

In a speech titled "Coming Home: The Other Side of War," one student focused on the incidence of post-traumatic stress disorder among soldiers returning

No matter what the occasion, personal examples are an excellent way to clarify ideas and to build audience interest. To be most effective, they should be delivered sincerely and with strong eye contact.

to the U.S. after serving in Iraq. He cited figures from the Department of Veterans Affairs noting that 18 percent of American soldiers in Iraq experience post-traumatic stress disorder. He also explained their most common symptoms, including flashbacks, nightmares, depression, anxiety, alcohol or drug abuse, and a sense of social isolation.

To reinforce his ideas, the speaker cited the example of Robert E. Brown, a Marine from Peru, Indiana, who was part of the first wave of troops deployed to Iraq. He talked of how Brown lost his wife and began drinking heavily after returning home. How he recoiled from loud noises and shunned even his friends and family. How his dreams were filled "with ghastly memories that left him a shadow of the strong, confident man he had once been."

CD 1: VIDEO 7.3
View this portion of "Coming Home: The Other Side of War."

This example was especially effective. It put the medical facts about post-traumatic stress disorder in vivid, human terms that everyone could understand. When you use such an example, make sure it is representative—that it does not deal with rare or exceptional cases. Your listeners are likely to feel betrayed if they suspect you have chosen an atypical example to prove a general point.

Use Examples to Personalize Your Ideas

People are interested in people. As social psychologist Eliot Aronson explains, "Most people are more deeply influenced by one clear, vivid, personal example than by an abundance of statistical data."[3] Whenever you talk to a general audience (such as your speech class), you can include examples that will add human interest to your speech. So far in this section we have seen a number of such examples—Corina Alamillo, who underwent brain surgery at the UCLA Medical Center; the heroic Olympic runner;

accident victim Roger Charter; and so on. The abstract becomes more meaningful when applied to a person. Which of the following would you be more likely to respond to?

> There are many hungry families in our community who could benefit from food donations.

Or:

> Let me tell you about Arturo. Arturo is four years old. He has big brown eyes and a mop of black hair and an empty belly. In all his four years on this earth, Arturo has never once enjoyed three square meals in a single day.

Try using examples with human interest in your speeches. You will soon discover why accomplished speakers consider them "the very life of the speech."[4]

Make Your Examples Vivid and Richly Textured

The richly textured example supplies everyday details that bring the example to life. Recall the example on page 179 of the Olympic runner. The speaker provided us with many details about the runner's bravery in the face of adverse conditions. The runner stumbles and injures her leg near the end of the race. She is passed by other competitors until she alone is left on the track. Doctors offer to help, but she refuses their assistance. With drops of blood along her trail, she shuffles to the finish line with all her remaining strength.

How much less compelling the example would have been if the speaker had merely said:

> One Olympic runner courageously completed her race despite being injured and exhausted.

Instead, the details let us *see* the runner as she battles through her pain and misfortune to win the applause of people around the globe. She is much more likely to stay in our minds than a "brave runner who completed her race." The more vivid your examples—brief or extended—the more impact they are likely to have on your audience.

Practice Delivery to Enhance Your Extended Examples

An extended example is just like a story or narrative. Its impact will depend as much on delivery as on content. Many students have discovered this the hard way. After spending much time and energy developing a splendid example, they have seen it fall flat on the day of the speech because they did not take the extra step to make it vivid and gripping for listeners.

Look again at the speaker in CD 1, Video 7.1. Notice how she uses her voice to increase the impact of her story about the Olympic runner. Like that speaker, you should think of yourself as a storyteller when you use an extended example. Don't rush through the example as though you were reading the newspaper; use your voice to get listeners involved. Speak faster here to create a sense of action, slower there to build suspense. Raise your voice in some places; lower it in others. Pause occasionally for dramatic effect.

CHECKLIST FOR USING EXAMPLES

yes	no	
☐	☐	1. Do I use examples to clarify my ideas?
☐	☐	2. Do I use examples to reinforce my ideas?
☐	☐	3. Do I use examples to personalize my ideas?
☐	☐	4. Are my examples representative of what they are supposed to illustrate or prove?
☐	☐	5. Do I reinforce my examples with statistics or testimony?
☐	☐	6. Are my extended examples vivid and richly textured?
☐	☐	7. Have I practiced the delivery of my extended examples to give them dramatic effect?

CD 1: SPEECH CHECKLIST
You can print a copy of this checklist from the CD-ROM.

Most important, maintain eye contact with your audience. The easiest way to ruin a fine example is to read it dully from your notes. As you practice the speech, "talk through" your extended examples without relying on your notes. By the day of your speech, you should be able to deliver your extended examples as naturally as if you were telling a story to a group of friends.

Statistics

We live in an age of statistics. Day in and day out we are bombarded with a staggering array of numbers: U2 has sold over 140 million albums; 12 percent of U.S. children under the age of 18 suffer from some form of psychological illness; Russia produces about 333 million gallons of vodka annually; the adult literacy rate of Brazil is 83 percent; Americans consume more than 4 million pounds of peanut products each day.

statistics
Numerical data.

What do all these numbers mean? Most of us would be hard-pressed to say. Yet we feel more secure in our knowledge when we can express it numerically. According to Lord Kelvin, the 19th-century physicist, "When you can measure what you are speaking about, and express it in numbers, you know something about it. But when you cannot measure it, when you cannot express it in numbers, your knowledge is . . . meager and unsatisfactory." It is this widely shared belief that makes statistics, when used properly, such an effective way to clarify and support ideas.[5]

Like brief examples, statistics are often cited in passing to clarify or strengthen a speaker's points. The following examples show how three students used statistics in their speeches:

> To document the role of community colleges in the U.S. educational system: "According to the *Chronicle of Higher Education,* 45 percent of all undergraduates in America study at a community college."

To illustrate the growing popularity of organic foods: "According to MSNBC News, sales of organic crops now exceed $15 billion a year and are increasing at the rate of 17–20 percent annually."

To quantify the problem of identity theft: "Last year the Federal Trade Commission received more than 635,000 complaints about identity theft, and consumers reported losses of more than $547 million."

Statistics can also be used in combination—stacked up to show the magnitude or seriousness of an issue. We find a good instance of this technique in a student presentation on the economic benefits of opening casinos on Native American tribal land. To demonstrate his point that these businesses provide economic benefits to Native Americans and to the surrounding communities, the speaker cited the following figures:

CD 1: VIDEO 7.4

View this excerpt from "The Economics of Native-American Casinos."

Across the nation, Native American casinos have created more than 100,000 jobs. Four years after a casino opens, employment in the local area has typically increased by 26 percent, and the percentage of working adults who work but are poor has declined by 14 percent. Among some tribes, the decrease in unemployment is truly startling: Among the Ojibwa of Wisconsin, unemployment plummeted from 70 percent to less than 5 percent. Many other tribes have reported similar results.

This is a well-supported argument. But what if the speaker had merely said:

Casinos increase employment among Native Americans.

The second statement is neither as clear nor as convincing as the one containing statistics. The statistics make the speaker's claim credible and specific. Of course, the audience didn't remember all the numbers, but that's all right. The purpose of presenting a series of figures is to create an *overall* impact on listeners. What the audience did recall is that an impressive array of statistics supported the speaker's position.

Understanding Statistics

In his classic book *How to Lie with Statistics,* Darrell Huff exploded the notion that numbers don't lie. Strictly speaking, they don't. But they can be easily manipulated and distorted. For example, which of the following statements is true?

a. Enriched white bread is more nutritious than whole-wheat bread because it contains as much or more protein, calcium, niacin, thiamine, and riboflavin.

b. Whole-wheat bread is more nutritious than white bread because it contains seven times the amount of fiber, plus more iron, phosphorus, and potassium.

As you might expect, *both* statements are true. And you might hear either one of them—depending on who is trying to sell you the bread.

One can play with statistics in all kinds of areas. Which of these statements is true?

When used properly, statistics make us feel more secure in our knowledge. A speech that is supported by statistics is usually more persuasive than an undocumented presentation.

a. The cheetah, clocked at 70 miles per hour, is the fastest animal in the world.

b. The pronghorn antelope, clocked at 61 miles per hour, is the fastest animal in the world.

The cheetah, right? Not necessarily. It's true the cheetah can go faster, but only for short sprints. The antelope can maintain its high speed over a much greater distance. So which is faster? It depends on what you're measuring. Put in terms of human races, the cheetah would win the hundred-yard dash, but the antelope would win the marathon.

When you are dealing with money, statistics become even trickier. For instance, consider the following facts:

a. In 1942 President Franklin D. Roosevelt earned a salary of $75,000.

b. In 1972 President Richard Nixon earned a salary of $200,000.

c. In 2002 President George W. Bush earned a salary of $400,000.

Which President was paid the most money? In purely mathematical terms, Bush is the highest earner. But as we all know, a dollar today does not buy as much as it did when Franklin Roosevelt was President. One measure of the inflation rate is the Consumer Price Index, which allows us to gauge the value of the dollar in any given year against its purchasing power in 1972. If we apply the Consumer Price Index to the three Presidents' salaries, we can see how much each earned in 1972 dollars:

a. In 1942 President Franklin D. Roosevelt earned a salary of $192,000.

b. In 1972 Richard Nixon earned a salary of $200,000.

c. In 2002 George W. Bush earned a salary of $92,800.

In other words, although Bush had the highest salary, the value of his $400,000 was less than half the value of Roosevelt's $75,000.

The point is that there is usually more to statistics than meets the eye.[6] When you track down statistics for your speeches, be sure to evaluate them in light of the following questions.

Are the Statistics Representative?

Say that on your way to class you choose ten students at random and ask them whether they favor or oppose banning recreational vehicles on public lands. Say also that six approve of such a ban and four do not. Would you then be accurate in claiming that 60 percent of the students on your campus favor banning recreational vehicles from public lands?

Of course not. Ten students is not a big enough sample. But even if it were, other problems would arise. Do the ten students interviewed accurately reflect your school's proportion of freshmen, sophomores, juniors, and seniors? Do they mirror the proportion of male and female students? Are the various majors accurately represented? What about part-time and full-time students? Students of different cultural and religious backgrounds?

In short, make sure your statistics are representative of what they claim to measure.

Are Statistical Measures Used Correctly?

Here are two groups of numbers:

Group A	Group B
7,500	5,400
6,300	5,400
5,000	5,000
4,400	2,300
4,400	1,700

Let us apply to each group three basic statistical measures—the mean, the median and the mode.

mean
The average value of a group of numbers.

median
The middle number in a group of numbers arranged from highest to lowest.

mode
The number that occurs most frequently in a group of numbers.

The *mean*—popularly called the average—is determined by summing all the items in a group and dividing by the number of items. The mean for group A is 5,520. For group B it is 3,960.

The *median* is the middle figure in a group once the figures are put in order from highest to lowest. The median for both group A and group B is exactly the same—5,000.

The *mode* is the number that occurs most frequently in a group of numbers. The mode for group A is 4,400. For group B it is 5,400.

Notice the results:

	Group A	Group B
Mean	5,520	3,960
Median	5,000	5,000
Mode	4,400	5,400

All these measures have the same goal—to indicate what is typical or characteristic of a certain group of numbers. Yet see how different the results are, depending on which measure you use.

The differences among the various measures can be striking. For instance, the *mean* salary of local TV news anchorpersons is $72,200 a year. But most anchors don't earn anywhere near that amount. The mean is inflated by the huge salaries (up to $1 million a year) paid to a few star anchors in media centers such as New York, Los Angeles, and Chicago. In contrast, the *median* salary of local news anchors is $59,500—not a sum to scoff at, but still $12,700 less than the average salary.[7]

How might a speaker use these different measures? The owner of a television station would probably cite the *mean* ($72,200) to show that local news anchors are handsomely compensated for their work. An organization of news anchors might emphasize the *median* ($59,500) to demonstrate that salaries are not nearly as high as the station owner makes them out to be. Both speakers would be telling the truth, but neither would be completely honest unless she or he made clear the meaning of the statistics.

Are the Statistics from a Reliable Source?

Which is the more reliable estimate of the environmental dangers of toxic waste in a landfill—one from the U.S. Environmental Protection Agency or one compiled by the company that owns the landfill? Easy—the estimate by the EPA, which does not have a vested interest in what the figures look like. What about nutritional ratings for fast foods offered by Consumers Union (a highly respected nonprofit organization) or by Burger King? That's easy too—Consumers Union, whose claims are not manipulated by advertising executives.

But now things get tougher. What about the competing statistics offered by groups for and against Social Security reform? Or the conflicting numbers tossed out by a school board and the teachers striking against it? In these cases the answer is not so clear, since both sides would present the facts according to their own partisan motives.

As a speaker, you must be aware of possible bias in the use of numbers. Since statistics can be interpreted so many ways and put to so many uses, you should seek figures gathered by objective, nonpartisan sources.

Tips for Using Statistics

Use Statistics to Quantify Your Ideas

The main value of statistics is to give your ideas numerical precision. This can be especially important when you are trying to document the existence of a problem. Examples can bring the problem alive and dramatize it in personal terms. But your listeners may still wonder how many people the problem actually affects. In such a situation, you should turn to statistics. Research has shown that the impact of examples is greatly enhanced when they are combined with statistics that show the examples to be typical.[8]

Suppose you are talking about the need for college students to avoid credit-card debt. Part of your speech deals with the large amount of such debt the typical college student faces by the time he or she graduates. You give an example, you personalize the subject, you provide many details, as follows:

Charles Perkins left college a changed person. Not only had he earned his degree in geography, but he had racked up almost $4,000 in credit-card debt. Charles was sure he would be able to pay off his debt easily once he got a full-time job. But when he received his first paycheck, he found, to his dismay, that after paying taxes and his living expenses, he could only make the minimum monthly payment on his credit cards. Rather than getting rid of his debt, it would take him years to pay it off.

Confronted with this example, a listener might think, "Poor Charles. But I'm not going to end up in his spot because I don't plan to leave college with a lot of credit-card debt." Anticipating just such a response, a sharp speaker would include figures to quantify the extent of credit-card debt among college students in general:

According to the latest issue of *Money* magazine, the average credit-card debt of a graduating college student is $3,700 and new graduates spend almost 25 percent of their income on debt payments. If someone makes only the minimum monthly payment on his or her credit cards—which is what most people do—they will rack up more than $4,200 in interest charges alone before paying off their original $3,700 debt. Perhaps this explains why in the past few years the number of people under 25 filing for bankruptcy has increased by over 50 percent.

Now the audience is much more likely to agree that they need to keep a closer eye on their credit-card balance.

Use Statistics Sparingly

As helpful as statistics can be, nothing puts an audience to sleep faster than a speech cluttered with numbers from beginning to end. Insert statistics only when they are needed, and then make sure they are easy to grasp. Even the most attentive listener would have trouble sorting out this barrage of figures:

According to the *World Factbook,* life expectancy at birth in the United States ranks 18th among 25 industrialized countries. Life expectancy of women in Japan is 84.25 years compared with 80.2 years for American women, and 77.73 years for Japanese men compared with 74.5 years for American men. The United States ranks 23rd among 25 industrialized nations in infant mortality, with a rate almost twice as high as Japan's. Canada ranks 13th. Americans spend more each year on health care than any other nation—$1 trillion dollars, or 13.7 percent of gross domestic product—yet the World Health Organization ranks the U.S. health care system 37th in overall performance among member nations.

Instead of drowning your audience in a sea of statistics, use only those that are most important. For example:

According to the *World Factbook,* people in the United States have one of the lowest life expectancies among industrialized nations. We also have one of the highest rates of infant mortality. Even though we spend more on health care than any other nation, the World Health Organization ranks 36 other nations ahead of us with regard to the overall performance of our health care system.

This second statement makes the same point as the first statement, but now the ideas are not lost in a torrent of numbers.

Identify the Sources of Your Statistics

As we have seen, figures are easy to manipulate. This is why careful listeners keep an ear out for the sources of a speaker's statistics. One student learned this by experience. In a speech titled "Tax Reform: Fact Versus Fiction," he claimed that the wealthiest 1 percent of U.S. taxpayers pay 34 percent of federal income taxes, even though they account for only 19 percent of all earned income. He also noted that the wealthiest 25 percent of Americans pay 83 percent of federal income taxes. These are startling statistics—especially given concerns that upper-income Americans do not pay their fair share of taxes. But because the student did not say where he got the figures, his classmates were not willing to accept them. They were sure he must be wrong.

As it turned out, the figures were quite reliable. They had come from a study by the Internal Revenue Service reported in *The New York Times.* If the speaker had mentioned the source in his speech, he would have been more successful.[9]

Explain Your Statistics

Statistics don't speak for themselves. They need to be interpreted and related to your listeners. Notice how effectively former Secretary of State Colin Powell did this in a speech to the United Nations General Assembly during a special session on the international AIDS crisis:

> Many speakers have noted the dreadful toll that AIDS is taking. . . . But let me try to make it more relevant.
>
> This hall holds about 2,000 people. By the time the three hours of this session elapse, 2,000 people around the world—just about the same number who are here—will be newly infected with HIV/AIDS. That's one for every person in this room. In some countries the infection rate is so high that one in three of us—the delegate to your right, the delegate to your left, or you, yourself—would be HIV positive.[10]

Explaining what statistics mean is particularly important when you deal with large numbers, since they are hard to visualize. How, for example, can we comprehend the $8 trillion U.S. national debt? We could explain that a trillion is a thousand billion and a billion is a thousand million. But that doesn't do much good, since millions and billions are almost as hard to visualize as trillions. Suppose, instead, we translate the huge numbers into terms a listener can relate to. Here is one speaker's solution:

> How much money is a trillion dollars? Think of it this way. If you had $1 million and spent it at the rate of $1,000 a day, you would run out of money in less than three years. If you had $1 billion and spent it at the rate of $1,000 a day, you would not run out of money for almost 3,000 years. And if you had $1 trillion and spent it at the rate of $1,000 a day, you wouldn't run out of money for nearly 3 million years!

Whenever you use statistics in your speeches, think of how you can make them meaningful to your audience. Rather than simply reciting figures about, say, the continuing destruction of the world's rainforests, find a way to bring those figures home to your audience. You might say, as did one speaker:

> According to the Rainforest Action Network, rainforest is disappearing at an alarming rate. Within the next second, we will lose an area of rainforest equal to two football fields. Within the next fifteen minutes, an area the size of this campus will be erased. By this time tomorrow, 214,000 acres, an area equivalent to the size of New York City, will be gone forever.

Or suppose you're discussing the number of people who die from hunger or hunger-related diseases. You could say, "As reported by the Hunger Project Web site, almost 9 million people—including 6.5 million children under the age of five—lose their lives annually to starvation or other hunger-related causes." These are alarming statistics, but they are likely to go in one ear and out the other unless you bring them home to your audience. Here's what one student said in her speech:

CD 1:VIDEO 7.5

View these excerpts from "The Rainforests: Nature's Pharmacy" and "To Save a Child."

> The Hunger Project Web site states that about 24,000 people die from hunger or hunger-related causes every day, and three-fourths of them are children under the age of five. To put this in perspective, 24,000 deaths is equivalent to more than half the students on this campus dying every day. To think of it another way, it means that more children lose their lives to hunger *every week* than the number of Americans who lose their lives to cancer in an *entire year*.

Be creative in thinking of ways to relate your statistics to your audience. This is probably the single most important step you can take to make statistics work in your speeches.

Round Off Complicated Statistics

Mount Kilimanjaro is 19,341 feet high; the official world land speed record is 763.065 miles per hour; the world's highest waterfall has a total drop of 3,212 feet; the population of Saudi Arabia is 23,513,330 people; the moon is 238,855 miles from earth.

These are intriguing figures, but they are too complicated to be readily understood by listeners. Unless there is an important reason to give exact numbers, you should round off most statistics. You might say that Mount Kilimanjaro is 19,300 feet high; the world land speed record is more than 763 miles per hour; the world's highest waterfall has a drop of some 3,200 feet; the population of Saudi Arabia is more than 23 million; and the moon is 239,000 miles from earth.

Use Visual Aids to Clarify Statistical Trends

Visual aids can save you a lot of time, as well as make your statistics easier to comprehend. Suppose you are discussing the number of major strikes by labor unions in the United States since World War II. You could start by explaining that after the war, during the early 1950s, there were a record number of strikes involving 1,000 or more workers—including the 1950 walkout of 370,000 United Mine Workers that crippled the nation's industries. Then, after the start of Dwight Eisenhower's presidency in 1953, the

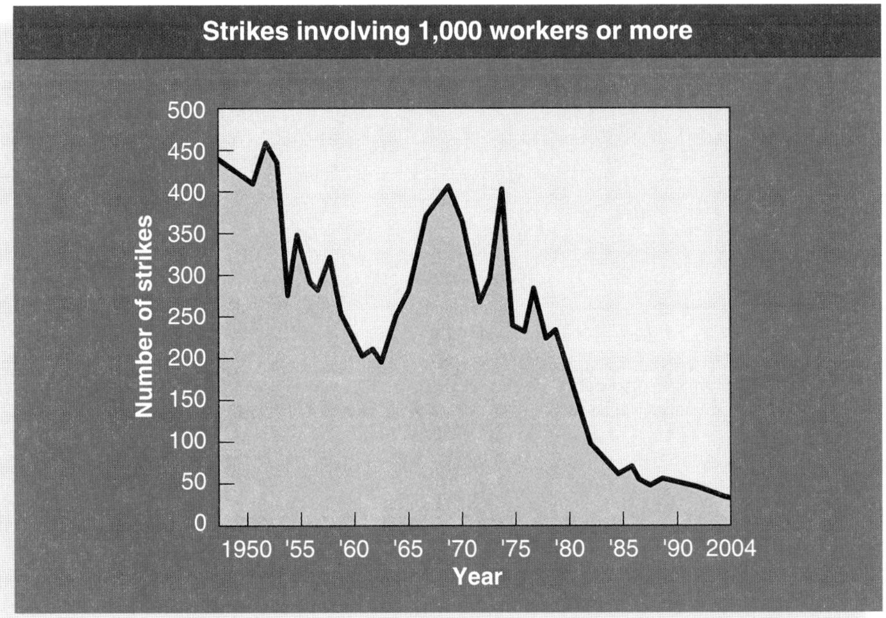

Figure 7.1

number of strikes declined fairly steadily until 1964, when they started climbing to a peak of more than 400 in 1968. After a sharp decline in the early 1970s, they jumped again in 1975 to the highest level in two decades. Finally, the number of strikes took a dramatic turn downward during the Reagan years of the 1980s and reached a record low in 2004 under President George W. Bush.

These are interesting statistics, and you could build a good speech around them. But strung together in a few sentences they are hard to digest. Figure 7.1 shows how much more clearly the points can be made with a simple graph. We shall discuss visual aids in detail in Chapter 13. For the moment, keep in mind that they can be helpful in presenting statistical information.

Where to Find Statistics

Statistics can be found in any kind of reputable publication—books, magazines, newspapers, scholarly journals, government documents, business reports, and so forth. There are also some sources devoted solely to statistics. They include *The World Almanac and Book of Facts* and the United Nations' *Statistical Yearbook.* These works contain statistics on everything from the U.S. economy to world population trends. *Guinness World Records* offers more esoteric information, such as the weight of the world's largest polished diamond, the internal temperature of the sun, and the number of hours of television the average child watches by the age of 18.

You will find these and other handy sources of statistics in the reference section of your library (see Chapter 6). Besides being easy to use, they can be fascinating to look through. This is one reason *The World Almanac* and *Guinness World Records* remain best-sellers year after year.

CD 1: SPEECH CHECKLIST

You can print a copy of this checklist from the CD-ROM.

CHECKLIST FOR USING STATISTICS

yes	no	
☐	☐	1. Do I use statistics to quantify my ideas?
☐	☐	2. Are my statistics representative of what they purport to measure?
☐	☐	3. Are my statistics from reliable sources?
☐	☐	4. Do I cite the sources of my statistics?
☐	☐	5. Do I use statistical measures (mean, median, mode) correctly?
☐	☐	6. Do I round off complicated statistics?
☐	☐	7. Do I use visual aids to clarify statistical trends?
☐	☐	8. Do I explain my statistics and relate them to the audience?

You can also garner a wealth of statistics from the Internet. Many Web sites provide numerical data—much of it more current than that found in printed works. As with any kind of information acquired off the Internet, you need to make sure your statistics come from reliable sources such as universities, government agencies, nonpartisan organizations, and the like. One excellent source is the *Statistical Abstract of the United States* Web site (www.census.gov/statab/www). Another is FedStats, which provides links to more than 70 federal agencies that produce statistics of public interest (www.fedstats.gov). Yet another is the CIA's *World Factbook* site, where you can find figures about every country around the globe (www.cia.gov/cia/publications/factbook).

Testimony

Imagine you are talking with a friend about the classes you plan to take next term. You are not sure whether to sign up for Psychology 230 or Accounting 181. Both are requirements; both meet at the same time of day. Your friend says, "I took those classes last year. They're both good, but Professor Hassam was excellent in Psych 230. She's one of the best teachers on campus. If she's teaching the course next term, I'd take it for sure." You check the timetable and find that Professor Hassam is indeed slated for Psychology 230. You sign up for her course.

testimony Quotations or paraphrases used to support a point.

As this story illustrates, we are often influenced by the *testimony* of other people when making decisions in everyday life. Much the same thing happens in public speaking. Just as you are likely to be swayed by your friend's recommendation about which class to take, so audiences tend to respect the opinions of people who have special knowledge or experience on the topic at hand. By quoting or paraphrasing such people, you can give your ideas greater strength and impact. The two major kinds of testimony are expert testimony and peer testimony.

Citing expert testimony is an excellent way for students to lend credibility to their speeches. It shows that the speaker's views are shared by people who have special knowledge on the topic.

Expert Testimony

expert testimony
Testimony from people who are recognized experts in their fields.

In most speeches you will probably rely on expert testimony—testimony from people who are acknowledged authorities in their fields. Expert testimony is especially helpful for student speakers because students are seldom recognized as experts on their speech topics. Citing the views of people who are experts is a good way to lend credibility to your speeches. It shows that you are not just mouthing your own opinions, but that your position is supported by people who are knowledgeable about the topic.[11]

Expert testimony is even more important when a topic is controversial or when the audience is skeptical about a speaker's point of view. The following story explains how one speaker enlisted expert testimony for a speech on stem-cell research:

As Anna Ciwinski investigated the topic of stem-cell research, she became convinced that the benefits of such research are so great that it should receive full financial support from the federal government. Yet Anna was not an expert on the science of stem cells or on the ethical issues surrounding the use of stem cells. How could she convince the audience to accept her ideas?

Statistics helped, and so did examples. But on such a controversial topic that was not enough. So to reinforce her credibility, Anna cited a wide range of experts who agreed with her—including Harvard medical professor Stuart Orkin, Magdalena Gotz from Germany's Max-Planck Institute of Neurobiology, Catholic theologian Jean Porter of Notre Dame University, and Melissa Little from the Institute for Molecular Bioscience in Australia. She also quoted from reports by the President's Council on Bioethics, the American Association for the Advancement of Science, and the Jewish Rabbinical Society. By citing the views of these experts—some of whom might be expected to disagree with her point of view—Anna made her speech much more persuasive.

Peer Testimony

peer testimony
Testimony from ordinary people with firsthand experience or insight on a topic.

Another type of testimony often used in speeches is peer testimony—opinions of people like ourselves; not prominent figures, but ordinary citizens who have firsthand experience on the topic. This kind of testimony is especially valuable because it gives a more personal viewpoint on issues than can be gained from expert testimony. It conveys the feelings, the knowledge, the insight of people who speak with the voice of genuine experience.

For example, if you were speaking about the barriers faced by people with physical disabilities, you would surely include testimony from doctors and other medical authorities. But in this case, the expert testimony would be limited because it cannot communicate what it really means to have a physical disability. To communicate that, you need statements from people who have physical disabilities—such as the following:

> Itzhak Perlman, the world-renowned violinist whose legs are paralyzed, once said: "When you are in a wheelchair, people don't talk to you. Perhaps they think it is contagious, or perhaps they think crippled legs mean a crippled mind. But whatever the reason, they treat you like a thing."

> Paul Longmore, who lost the use of his legs as a child, notes that most people are uncomfortable in the presence of someone who is handicapped. "It's only when they really go out of their way to get to know us," he says, "that they realize we are just as bright, witty, and companionable as they are."

There is no way expert testimony can express these ideas with the same authenticity and emotional impact.

Quoting Versus Paraphrasing

direct quotation
Testimony that is presented word for word.

The statements from Itzhak Perlman and Paul Longmore are presented as direct quotations. Testimony can also be presented by paraphrasing. Rather than quoting someone verbatim, you present the gist of that person's ideas in your own words—as did one student in her speech about America's potential water crisis:

> Writing in *Audubon* magazine, Dr. Peter Bourne, president of Global Water, a nonpartisan educational group in Washington, D.C., said most Americans do not yet realize the extent and urgency of the water problem. At the present rate, he says, we are headed for a crisis that will change the way we live in every part of the nation.

paraphrase
To restate or summarize a source's ideas in one's own words.

When should you use a direct quotation as opposed to paraphrasing? The standard rule is that quotations are most effective when they are brief, when they convey your meaning better than you can, and when they are particularly eloquent, witty, or compelling. If you find a quotation that fits these criteria, then recite the quotation word for word.

Paraphrasing is better than direct quotation in two situations: (1) when the wording of a quotation is obscure or cumbersome, as is often the case with government documents; (2) when a quotation is longer than two or three sentences. Audiences often tune out partway through lengthy quotations, which tend to interrupt the flow of a speaker's ideas. Since the rest of the speech is in your own words, you should put longer quotations in your own words as well.

Tips for Using Testimony

Quote or Paraphrase Accurately

Accurate quotation involves three things: making sure you do not misquote someone; making sure you do not violate the meaning of statements you paraphrase; making sure you do not quote out of context. Of these, the last is the most subtle—and the most dangerous. By quoting out of context, you can twist someone's remarks so as to prove almost anything. Take movie advertisements. A critic pans a movie with these words:

quoting out of context
Quoting a statement in such a way as to distort its meaning by removing the statement from the words and phrases surrounding it.

> This movie is a colossal bore. From beginning to end it is a disaster. What is meant to be brilliant dialogue is about as fascinating as the stuff you clean out of your kitchen drain.

But when the movie is advertised in the newspapers, what appears in huge letters over the critic's name? "COLOSSAL! FROM BEGINNING TO END—BRILLIANT! FASCINATING!"

This is so flagrant as to be humorous. But quoting out of context can have serious consequences. Consider the following statement by a political candidate:

> Creating a national sales tax would provide needed revenue for programs such as education, health care, and national defense. Several European countries have such a tax, and it could certainly work in the U.S. However, I do not support such a tax here—in fact, I don't support new taxes of any kind.

Now look what happens when the first part of that statement is quoted out of context by a competing candidate:

> Americans already pay too much in taxes. Yet my opponent in this election has stated—and I quote: "Creating a national sales tax would provide needed revenue for programs such as education, health care, and national defense. Several European countries have such a tax, and it could certainly work in the U.S." Well, my opponent may think new taxes are good for Europe, but they're the last thing we need in this country.

By quoting the original statement out of context, the competing candidate has created a false impression of his opponent. Such behavior is highly unethical and has no place in responsible communication of any kind. Be sure, when you quote or paraphrase someone, that you represent their words and ideas with complete accuracy.

Use Testimony from Qualified Sources

We have all become accustomed to the celebrity testimonial in television and magazine advertising. The professional golfer endorses a particular brand of clubs. The movie star praises a certain hair spray or shampoo. The basketball player plugs a type of athletic shoe. So far, so good. These are the tools of the trade for the people who endorse them.

But what happens when an Academy Award winner endorses a cell phone company? A tennis player represents a line of cameras? A college

CD 1: SPEECH CHECKLIST

You can print a copy of this checklist from the CD-ROM.

CHECKLIST FOR USING TESTIMONY

yes	no	
☐	☐	1. Do I use testimony to support my ideas?
☐	☐	2. Do I use testimony from qualified sources?
☐	☐	3. Do I use testimony from unbiased sources?
☐	☐	4. Do I distinguish between expert testimony and peer testimony?
☐	☐	5. Do I identify the sources of all testimony?
☐	☐	6. Do I quote and paraphrase all sources of testimony with complete accuracy?

basketball coach lends his name to a credit-card company? Do they know more about these products than you or I? Probably not. They have been paid large sums of money to be photographed with the product in hopes that their popularity will rub off on it.

Being a celebrity or an authority in one area does not make someone competent in other areas. Listeners will find your speeches much more credible if you use testimony from sources qualified *on the subject at hand.* As we have seen, this may include either recognized experts or ordinary citizens with special experience on the speech topic.

Use Testimony from Unbiased Sources

In a speech about the use of stun guns by police officers to subdue unruly students in public schools, a student said:

> Steve Tuttle, a spokesman for Taser International, said in a statement that "the Taser device has been shown to be medically safe when used on children" and that there is no reason to prohibit its use when necessary to maintain security in the public schools.

As you might expect, the students' classmates were not persuaded. After all, what would you expect someone at Taser International, the leading manufacturer of stun guns, to say—that its product is unsafe and should be banned? One listener reacted this way: "For all I know the statement by Tuttle may be true, but he is hardly an unbiased source. I wish you had cited an impartial expert instead."

Careful listeners are suspicious of testimony from biased or self-interested sources. Be sure to use testimony from credible, objective authorities.

Identify the People You Quote or Paraphrase

The usual way to identify your source is to name the person and sketch his or her qualifications before presenting the testimony. The following excerpt is from a student speech titled "Bursting the Antibacterial Bubble":

> Not only do antibacterial products fail to deliver what they promise, but they can actually increase your chances of getting sick. According to Stuart Levy, professor of

THE INTERNET *Connection*

Do you need supporting materials for your speech? Check out Finding Data on the Internet (www.robertniles.com/data/). Created as a handy resource guide for journalists, this site provides links to facts and figures on dozens of topics of national and international interest.

There are a number of think tanks whose Web sites provide excellent resources for speech materials. They include the Brookings Institution (www.brook.edu/), RAND (www.rand.org/), and the Cato Institute (www.cato.org/).

ONLINE LEARNING CENTER

You can link to these Web sites at www.mhhe.com/lucas9.

microbiology and medicine at Tufts University, excessive use of antibacterial products in the home has been shown to make children more likely to develop allergies and asthma.

Had the speaker not identified Professor Levy, listeners would not have had the foggiest notion who he is or why his opinion should be heeded.

For another example, look at this statement from a speech on the growing use of acupuncture in conjunction with Western medical procedures:

> Another example of the integration of acupuncture with Western medicine is at the Wasser Pain Management Center at Mount Sinai Hospital in Toronto, Canada. Neurologist Allan Gordon, director of the Center, says that introducing acupuncture to the hospital "expands the treatment available to chronic pain sufferers" and provides "multiple options for care to our patients."

CD 1: VIDEO 7.6

View these excerpts from "Bursting the Antibacterial Bubble" and "Acupuncture: New Uses for an Ancient Remedy."

After this statement, there is no doubt about Dr. Gordon's qualifications or why the audience should respect his judgment on the benefits of acupuncture.

Nor are students the only speakers who need to identify their sources. Whether you are speaking in a classroom or a courtroom, at a business meeting or a technical conference, to a community organization or a religious gathering, you will be much more effective if you make clear to your audience why they should accept the testimony of the people you quote or paraphrase.

As we saw in Chapter 2, identifying the source of testimony is also an important ethical responsibility. If you use another person's words or ideas without giving credit to that person, you will be guilty of plagiarism. This is true whether you paraphrase the original source or quote it verbatim.

Examples, statistics, and testimony are all helpful devices for the speaker. Depending on your topic, you may want to use some of them, all of them, or none of them. Remember, they are tools, and they all serve the same purpose—getting your message across to your listeners.

Sample Speech with Commentary

The following speech illustrates how to work supporting materials into a presentation. As you read, study how the speaker uses a variety of examples, statistics, and quotations to make her ideas clear, credible, and convincing.

Suffer the Children

Commentary	*Speech*
The speaker begins with an extended example to gain attention and interest. The example is specific and detailed. We are told Matthew Garvey's name and age, where he lived, the kind of work he did, and how he was injured. These are the kinds of details that bring examples to life and help get listeners involved in a speech.	Matthew Garvey was just 13 years old when he was hired by Quality Car Wash in Laurel, Maryland, to towel-dry cars as they came off the line. Not long after he began working, Matthew lost his right leg when it got caught in an industrial machine used to suck the moisture out of the towels. After investigating, the U.S. Department of Labor fined the car wash for illegally hiring a minor and for operating a machine with a broken safety lid.
The speaker moves into testimony suggesting that the opening story is representative of a major problem in the U.S. When you use an extended example, it is usually a good idea to precede or follow the example with statistics or testimony showing that the example is not unusual or exceptional.	This is just one of the more tragic examples of what Jeffrey Newman of the National Child Labor Committee calls the "crisis" of child-labor law abuses in the United States. In researching this speech, I discovered that employers from New York to California are breaking the law by hiring children from ages 7 to 17 who often put in long, hard hours in dangerous conditions. Today I would like to show you the extent of the problem and how it jeopardizes the education and safety of millions of young people.
In her first main point the speaker explores the problem of child-labor law violations in the United States. She begins by summarizing the provisions of the law. Notice how she identifies the Web site where she acquired the information.	To understand the problem of child-labor law violations, we need to begin by looking at the provisions of the law. As explained on the U.S. Department of Labor Web site, the Fair Labor Standards Act sets a minimum working age of 14. It limits 14-year-olds and 15-year-olds to three hours of work on school days, prohibits them from working after 7 at night, and allows them a total of 18 work hours per week during the school year. The law also restricts employment of children under 18 in dangerous jobs such as construction, meat-cutting, and mining.
Statistics in this and the next paragraph back up the speaker's point that violations of child-labor laws are widespread in the U.S. Rather than giving the exact number of violations, she rounds them off, making them easier to grasp and recall.	Passed in 1938 and amended several times since, the Fair Labor Standards Act was designed to prevent the exploitation of child labor that took place during the 19th century. Yet today violations of the law are shockingly widespread. According to the Associated Press, 148,000 minors in the U.S. are employed illegally in nonagricultural jobs during an average week, working too many hours or in hazardous conditions. In addition, the National Child Labor Committee reports that more than 110,000 children work illegally on U.S. farms.
The speaker uses a combination of statistics and testimony to support her point about child-labor abuses in the garment industry. The statement from Thomas Gubiak is an example of expert testimony; the closing quotation from Faviola Flores is an instance of peer testimony.	Some of the most serious violations occur in garment industry factories known as sweatshops that hire immigrant children at rates well below minimum wage. The Associated Press estimates that as many as 2,600 minors are employed illegally in New York City sweatshops. Thomas Gubiak, head of the city's garment district task force, says "most of the children in these factories are below 18, some as young as 8." Like Faviola Flores, a 15-year-old Mexican girl in a Manhattan sweatshop, they toil

long days in unsafe conditions for as little as $3.50 an hour. "I don't like working here," Flores says, "but I have no choice."

A series of brief examples supports the speaker's claim about the pervasiveness of child-labor law violations. Because the examples deal with companies throughout the U.S. and in different lines of business, they provide strong evidence to reinforce the speaker's point that violations of the law are widespread.

Although the exploitation of child labor has been a problem in the garment trade since the 1800s, it can be found in almost every industry that employs minors. In June 2003, Davy's Locker, a seafood restaurant in New Bedford, Massachusetts, was fined $130,000 by the U.S. Department of Labor for hiring underage workers and threatening employees who cooperated with investigators. In March 2004, the A&P supermarket chain agreed to pay more than $242,000 in penalties for employing minors under the age of 18 in jobs involving hazardous machinery. In January 2005, Wal-Mart was fined $135,000 for violating child-labor laws in Connecticut, New York, and Arkansas.

The speaker begins her second main point—that violations of child-labor laws have serious consequences for the education and physical safety of young workers.

Like other businesses caught breaking child-labor laws, A&P and Wal-Mart denied any wrongdoing, but the growing epidemic of child-labor law violations threatens both the education and physical safety of young workers.

The quotation from Hugh McDaid is a good instance of expert testimony. This quotation, like others in the speech, is short and forceful. There is no reason to use a direct quotation unless it makes the point more clearly and forcefully than you can in your own words.

Here the speaker paraphrases rather than quoting verbatim. Notice that she gives the name of the book she is paraphrasing from and identifies its authors. As we saw in Chapter 2, speakers have an ethical obligation to indicate the sources of paraphrases, as well as of quotations.

The educational consequences are most damaging to illegal underage employees who work instead of attending school. As Hugh McDaid of New York City's garment task force says, illegal underage workers "sacrifice their education and literally commit themselves to a life of working in a sweatshop. They have no future." But even for children who do attend school, too many hours at work can harm their education. In their book *When Teenagers Work,* psychology professors Ellen Greenberger and Laurence Steinberg note that intensive levels of work among youth tend to produce higher truancy and lower grades. According to Greenberger and Steinberg, one study after another has found that working more than a very few hours a week has a negative impact on teenagers' academic performance.

The examples in this paragraph show specific cases in which teenagers were injured or killed by the violation of child-labor laws. The extended example about Michael Hurcone is especially effective. Filled with specific details that make it interesting and credible, it puts the speaker's point in human terms with which the audience can identify.

Not only do child workers harm their education, but they often endanger their physical safety as well. Recall the story I told in my introduction about Matthew Garvey, the 13-year-old who lost his leg while working at a car wash. Even more tragic is the case of Michael Hurcone, a 17-year-old Pennsylvania high-school student. While employed at a supermarket, he was working with a bailer—a machine that crushes and binds cardboard boxes and is supposed to be off-limits to minors. Noticing that some material was stuck in the bailer, Michael tried to free up the jam when he got caught in the machine. It crushed his body for 30 minutes before he suffocated.

In this paragraph the speaker presents testimony and statistics to prove that the

Nor are these isolated examples. The most recent figures from the Bureau of Labor Statistics show that 230,000 examples in the previous paragraph are not atypical. As in other parts of the speech, she is quite specific in identifying the sources of her evidence.

teenagers are injured at work each year. According to former U.S. Labor Secretary Alexis Herman, nearly 70 minors are killed on the job annually—most in accidents involving infractions of child-labor laws.

The speaker begins her conclusion by summarizing the two main points she had made in the body of the speech. She then ends with a dramatic quotation. As we shall see in Chapter 9, this is an effective way to pull a speech together and to reinforce its central idea.

In the light of all this evidence, there can be no doubt that the violation of child-labor laws is a widespread problem with serious consequences. The issue is well summarized by former U.S. Senator Howard Metzenbaum of Ohio, who stated after congressional hearings on the subject, "I shudder to think that children the same age as my own grandchildren are being robbed of an education, their limbs, and indeed, their lives through illegal child labor."

Summary

Good speeches are not composed of hot air and unfounded assertions. They need strong supporting materials to bolster the speaker's point of view. In fact, the skillful use of supporting materials often makes the difference between a good speech and a poor one. The three basic types of supporting materials are examples, statistics, and testimony.

In the course of a speech you may use brief examples—specific instances referred to in passing—and sometimes you may want to give several brief examples in a row to create a stronger impression. Extended examples—often called illustrations, narratives, or anecdotes—are longer and more detailed. Hypothetical examples describe imaginary situations and can be quite effective for relating ideas to the audience. All three kinds of examples help clarify ideas, reinforce ideas, or personalize ideas. To be most effective, though, they should be vivid and richly textured.

Statistics can be extremely helpful in conveying your message as long as you use them sparingly and explain them so that they are meaningful to your audience. Above all, you should understand your statistics and use them fairly. Numbers can easily be manipulated and distorted. Make sure your figures are representative of what they claim to measure, that you use statistical measures correctly, and that you take statistics only from reliable sources.

Testimony is especially helpful for student speakers because students are seldom recognized as experts on their speech topics. Citing the views of people who are experts is a good way to make your ideas more credible. When you include testimony in a speech, you can either quote someone verbatim or paraphrase his or her words. As with statistics, there are guidelines for using testimony. Be sure to quote or paraphrase accurately and to cite qualified, unbiased sources. If the source is not generally known to your audience, be certain to establish his or her credentials.

Key Terms

supporting materials (177)
example (178)
brief example (178)
extended example (179)
hypothetical example (179)
statistics (183)
mean (186)
median (186)
mode (186)
testimony (192)
expert testimony (193)
peer testimony (194)
direct quotation (194)
paraphrase (194)
quoting out of context (195)

ONLINE LEARNING CENTER

Review these terms by doing the Chapter 7 crossword puzzle at www.mhhe.com/lucas9.

Review Questions

After reading this chapter, you should be able to answer the following questions:

1. Why do you need supporting materials in your speeches?
2. What are the three kinds of examples discussed in this chapter? How might you use each kind to support your ideas?
3. What are five tips for using examples in your speeches?
4. Why is it so easy to lie with statistics? What three questions should you ask to judge the reliability of statistics?
5. What are six tips for using statistics in your speeches?
6. What is testimony? Explain the difference between expert testimony and peer testimony.
7. What are four tips for using testimony in your speeches?

CD 1: STUDY QUESTIONS

For further review, go to the Study Questions for this chapter.

Exercises for Critical Thinking

1. Each of the following statements violates at least one of the criteria for effective supporting materials discussed in this chapter. Identify the flaw (or flaws) in each statement.

   a. According to a study conducted by Verizon Wireless, there is no evidence that the use of cell phones is a major cause of automobile accidents.

   b. Figures compiled by the Bureau of Labor Statistics show that the median salary for lawyers in the U.S. is $87,945. This shows that lawyers average almost $88,000 a year in salary.

   c. As Nicole Kidman noted in a recent interview, the United States needs to change its environmental policies or it will soon see a dramatic increase of health problems due to air and water pollution.

   d. I don't know why insurance companies should charge higher rates for drivers under the age of 25. All my friends drive a lot and none of them have been in car accidents.

e. In the words of one expert, "Creating a national health insurance system in the U.S. would be extremely expensive and would not improve the quality of health care for most Americans."

f. In a random survey conducted last month among members of People for the Ethical Treatment of Animals, 99 percent of respondents opposed using animals for medical experiments. Clearly, then, the American people oppose such experiments.

g. According to *The New York Times Almanac*, California has the largest Native-American population of any state in the union—420,501. Arizona is second with 286,680; Oklahoma is third with 278,124; and New Mexico is fourth with a total Native-American population of 183,972.

2. Analyze "Bursting the Antibacterial Bubble" in the appendix of sample speeches following Chapter 18. Identify the main points of the speech and the supporting materials used for each. Evaluate the speaker's use of supporting materials in light of the criteria discussed in this chapter.

Applying the POWER of PUBLIC SPEAKING

After receiving your master's degree in education administration, you took a job at the state department of education. At the request of the governor, your section of the department has developed a new early childhood intervention program for children from impoverished households. Now you have been asked to help publicize the program and to build support for it. You will be speaking to church groups, teachers' associations, family advocacy groups, and others with an interest in children's welfare. You want to prepare a talk that makes good use of statistics and expert testimony to demonstrate the value of early childhood education programs, especially for poor children.

As part of your research, you decide to search the Web for supporting materials. List three reputable Web sites that provide useful statistics or testimony on the value of early childhood education. Explain why each Web site is reputable and list one statistic or expert quotation you obtain from each source.

Notes

[1]See, for example, Nurit Tal-Or, David S. Boninger, Amir Poran, and Faith Gleicher, "Counterfactual Thinking as a Mechanism in Narrative Persuasion," *Human Communication Research,* 30 (2004), pp. 301–328.

[2]Sun Yan's speech was presented in Beijing during the 2001 *21st Century* Cup national English-language public speaking competition. I would like to thank *21st Century* and *China Daily* for permission to include video from the speech on the CD that accompanies this edition of *The Art of Public Speaking.*

[3]Eliot Aronson, *The Social Animal,* 9th ed. (New York: Worth Publishers, 2004), pp. 73–74.

[4]This point was made by James A. Winans in his classic *Speech-Making* (New York: Appleton-Century-Crofts, 1922), p. 141.

[5]Over the years, there has been much debate over whether statistics or examples have more impact on listeners. For a summary of that debate, see Richard M. Perloff, *The Dynamics of Persuasion: Communication and Attitudes in the 21st Century,* 2nd ed. (Mahwah, NJ: Erlbaum, 2003), pp. 182–184.

[6]For two fascinating recent works on the use and misuse of statistics, see Joel Best, *More Damned Lies and Statistics: How Numbers Confuse Public Issues* (Berkeley: University of California Press, 2004); Gerd Gigerenzer, *Calculated Risks: How to Know When the Numbers Deceive You* (New York: Simon and Schuster, 2002).

[7]Bob Papper, "Salaries Soar," *RTNDA Communicator,* 58 (June 2004), pp. 28–32.

[8]M. Allen, R. Bruflat, R. Fucilla, M. Kramer, S. McKellips, D. J. Ryan, and M. Spiegelhoff, "Testing the Persuasiveness of Evidence: Combining Narrative and Statistical Forms," *Communication Research Reports,* 17 (2000), pp. 331–336.

[9]For research confirming the importance of citing sources when presenting evidence, see Rodney A. Reynolds and J. Lynn Reynolds, "Evidence," in James Price Dillard and Michael Pfau (eds.), *The Persuasion Handbook: Developments in Theory and Practice* (Thousand Oaks, CA: Sage, 2002), pp. 429–430.

[10]Colin Powell, "U.N. Special Session on HIV/AIDS," *Vital Speeches,* 67 (2001), pp. 578–580.

[11]See Daniel O'Keefe, *Persuasion: Theory and Research,* 2nd ed. (Thousand Oaks, CA: Sage, 2002), pp. 186–187.

CHAPTER EIGHT

Organizing the Body of the Speech

Organization Is Important

Main Points

Number of Main Points

Strategic Order of Main Points

Tips for Preparing Main Points

Supporting Materials

Connectives

Transitions

Internal Previews

Internal Summaries

Signposts

If you thumb through any mail-order catalogue today, you will discover that many of the items for sale are *organizers*—closet organizers, kitchen organizers, office organizers, audio and video equipment organizers. Read enough catalogues, and you must conclude that if something exists, it can be organized.

Why all this quest for organization? Obviously, when the objects you possess are well organized, they serve you better. There's little point in having multiple possessions if you can't find them when you need them. Organization allows you to see what you have and to put your hands immediately on the garment, the tool, the tape, the piece of paper, the CD you want without a frenzied search.

Much the same is true of your speeches. If they are well organized, they will serve you better. Organization allows you—and your listeners—to see what ideas you have and to put mental "hands" on the most important ones.

Organization Is Important

Several years ago a college professor took a well-organized speech and scrambled it by randomly changing the order of its sentences. He then had a speaker deliver the original version to one group of listeners and the scrambled version to another group. After the speeches, he gave a test to see how well each group understood what they had heard. Not surprisingly, the group that heard the original, unscrambled speech scored much higher than the other group.[1]

A few years later, two professors repeated the same experiment at another school. But instead of testing how well the listeners comprehended each speech, they tested to see what effects the speeches had on the listeners' attitudes toward the speakers. They found that people who heard the well-organized speech believed the speaker to be much more competent and trustworthy than did those who heard the scrambled speech.[2]

These are just two of many studies that show the importance of organization in effective speechmaking.[3] They confirm what most of us know from experience. How many times have you listened to someone who rambled aimlessly from one idea to another? You realize how difficult it is to pay attention to the speaker, much less to understand the message. In fact, when students explain what they hope to learn from their speech class, they almost always put "the ability to organize my ideas more effectively" near the top of the list.

This ability is especially vital for speechmaking. Listeners demand coherence. They have little patience with speakers who bounce wildly from idea to idea. Keep in mind that listeners—unlike readers—cannot flip back to a previous page if they have trouble grasping a speaker's ideas. In this respect a speech is much like a movie. Just as a director must be sure viewers can follow the plot of a film from beginning to end, so must a speaker be sure listeners can follow the progression of ideas in a speech from beginning to end. This requires that speeches be organized *strategically*. They should be put together in particular ways to achieve particular results with particular audiences.

Speech organization is important for other reasons as well. As we saw in Chapter 1, it is closely connected to critical thinking. When you work to organize your speeches, you gain practice in the general skill of establishing clear relationships among your ideas. This skill will serve you well throughout your college days and in almost any career you may choose. In addition, using a clear, specific method of speech organization can boost your confidence as a speaker and improve your ability to deliver a message fluently.

The first step in developing a strong sense of speech organization is to gain command of the three basic parts of a speech—introduction, body, and conclusion—and the strategic role of each. In this chapter we deal with the body of the speech. The next chapter will take up the introduction and the conclusion.

strategic organization
Putting a speech together in a particular way to achieve a particular result with a particular audience.

There are good reasons for talking first about the body of the speech. The body is the longest and most important part. Also, you will usually prepare the body first. It is easier to create an effective introduction after you know exactly what you will say in the body.

The process of organizing the body of a speech begins when you determine the main points.

Main Points

The main points are the central features of your speech. You should select them carefully, phrase them precisely, and arrange them strategically. Here are the main points of a student speech about the medical uses of hypnosis:

Specific Purpose: To inform my audience about the major uses of hypnosis.

Central Idea: The major uses of hypnosis today are to control pain in medical surgery, to help people stop smoking, and to help students improve their academic performance.

Main Points:
I. Hypnosis is used in surgery as an adjunct to chemical anesthesia.
II. Hypnosis is used to help people stop smoking.
III. Hypnosis is used to help students improve their academic performance.

main points
The major points developed in the body of a speech. Most speeches contain from two to five main points.

These three main points form the skeleton of the body of the speech. If there are three major *uses* of hypnosis for medical purposes, then logically there can be three *main points* in the speech.

How do you choose your main points? Sometimes they will be evident from your specific purpose statement. Suppose your specific purpose is "To inform my audience about the origins, philosophy, and results of charter schools." Obviously, your speech will have three main points. The first will deal with the origins of charter schools, the second with the philosophy behind charter schools, the third with the performance of charter schools. Written in outline form, the main points might be:

Specific Purpose: To inform my audience about the origins, philosophy, and performance of charter schools.

Research studies confirm that clear organization is vital to effective public speaking. Listeners must be able to follow the progression of ideas in a speech from beginning to end.

Central Idea: Charter schools provide alternatives to traditional public education by allowing more innovation and independence, but the results are not entirely clear.

Main Points:

I. The idea of charter schools originated among educators in the 1970s and was implemented starting in the late 1980s.
II. Proponents of charter schools hold that some children learn better when they are taught in nontraditional ways.
III. The performance of charter schools is difficult to assess because recent studies of their impact are contradictory.

Even if your main points are not stated expressly in your specific purpose, they may be easy to project from it. Let's say your specific purpose is "To inform my audience of the basic steps in making stained-glass windows." You know each of your main points will correspond to a step in the window-making process. They might look like this in outline form:

Specific Purpose: To inform my audience of the basic steps in making stained-glass windows.

Central Idea: There are four steps in making stained-glass windows.

Main Points:

I. The first step is designing the window.
II. The second step is cutting the glass to fit the design.
III. The third step is painting the glass.
IV. The fourth step is assembling the window.

You will not always settle on your main points so easily. Often they will emerge as you research the speech and evaluate your findings. Suppose your specific purpose is "To persuade my audience that our state should not approve proposals for online voting." You know that each main point in the speech will present a *reason* why online voting should not be instituted in your state. But you aren't sure how many main points there will be or what they will be. As you research and study the topic, you decide there are two major reasons to support your view. Each of these reasons will become a main point in your speech. Written in outline form, they might be:

Specific Purpose: To persuade my audience that our state should not approve proposals for online voting.

Central Idea: Our state should not approve online voting because it will increase voter fraud and disfranchise people without Internet access.

Main Points:

I. Our state should not approve online voting because it will increase voter fraud.
II. Our state should not approve online voting because it will disfranchise people without access to the Internet.

Now you have two broad areas around which to organize your ideas.

Number of Main Points

You will not have time in your classroom speeches to develop more than four or five main points, and most speeches will contain only two or three. Regardless of how long a speech might run, if you have too many main points, the audience will have trouble sorting them out. When everything is equally important, nothing is important.

Imagine, for example, that you have a particularly lenient professor who gives everyone in the class an A. Your A won't have much value for you. But if only three students in the class get an A and you are one of them, then you stand out from the crowd. That is what you must aim to do in your speeches—to make a few main points stand out and be remembered.

If, when you list your main points, you find you have too many, you may be able to condense them into categories. Here is a set of main points for a speech about yoga:

Specific Purpose: To inform my audience about the benefits of yoga.

Central Idea: Yoga provides a large number of benefits.

Main Points:

I. Yoga strengthens muscle tone.
II. Yoga increases flexibility.
III. Yoga reduces blood pressure.
IV. Yoga improves sleep patterns.
V. Yoga decreases anxiety and depression.
VI. Yoga increases concentration and attention.
VII. Yoga improves self-confidence.
VIII. Yoga enhances one's overall sense of well-being.

You have eight main points—which is too many. But if you look at the list, you see that the eight points fall into two broad categories: the physical benefits of yoga and the psychological benefits of yoga. You might, therefore, restate your main points this way:

I. Yoga provides a number of physical benefits.
II. Yoga provides a number of psychological benefits.

Strategic Order of Main Points

Once you establish your main points, you need to decide in what order you will present them in your speech. This is extremely important, for it will affect both the clarity and the persuasiveness of your ideas.

The most effective order depends on three things—your topic, your purpose, and your audience. Chapters 14 and 15 will deal with special aspects of organizing informative speeches and persuasive speeches. Here let us look briefly at the five basic patterns of organization used most often by public speakers.

Chronological Order

chronological order A method of speech organization in which the main points follow a time pattern.

Speeches arranged chronologically follow a time pattern. They may narrate a series of events in the sequence in which they happened. For example:

Specific Purpose: To inform my audience how the Great Wall of China was built.

Central Idea: The Great Wall of China was built in three major stages.

Main Points:
I. Building of the Great Wall began during the Qin dynasty of 221–206 B.C.
II. New sections of the Great Wall were added during the Han dynasty of 206 B.C.–220 A.D.
III. The Great Wall was completed during the Ming dynasty of 1368–1644.

Chronological order is also used in speeches explaining a process or demonstrating how to do something. For example:

Specific Purpose: To inform my audience of the steps in getting a professional tattoo.

Central Idea: There are four main steps in getting a professional tattoo.

Main Points:
I. First, the skin is shaved and sterilized in the area to be tattooed.
II. Second, the main lines of the tattoo are traced on the skin with a machine called an outliner.
III. Third, colored pigments are applied inside the outline with a machine called a shader.
IV. Fourth, the tattoo is sterilized and bandaged.

As this outline shows, chronological order is especially useful for informative speeches.

The main points of a speech should be organized to communicate the speaker's message. Spatial order might work very well for a speech explaining the structure of a hurricane.

Spatial Order

spatial order
A method of speech organization in which the main points follow a directional pattern.

Speeches arranged in spatial order follow a directional pattern. That is, the main points proceed from top to bottom, left to right, front to back, inside to outside, east to west, or some other route. For example:

Specific Purpose: To inform my audience about the structure of a hurricane.

Central Idea: A hurricane is made up of three parts going from inside to outside.

Main Points:

I. At the center of a hurricane is the calm, cloud-free eye.

II. Surrounding the eye is the eyewall, a dense ring of clouds that produces the most intense wind and rainfall.

III. Rotating around the eyewall are large bands of clouds and precipitation called spiral rain bands.

Or:

Specific Purpose: To inform my audience of five major civilizations that existed in different parts of North America centuries before the arrival of Columbus.

Central Idea: Centuries before the arrival of Columbus there were major civilizations in what is today New York, Florida, New Mexico, the Pacific Northwest, and the Mississippi Valley.

Main Points:

I. In New York, the Onondaga were skilled agriculturalists and fierce warriors.
II. In Florida, the Calusa developed one of the most advanced cultures to flourish without agriculture.
III. In New Mexico, the people of Chaco Canyon were sophisticated architectural planners and builders.
IV. In the Pacific Northwest, the Makah were expert mariners and foresters.
V. In the Mississippi Valley, the Cahokia created a complex, prosperous society whose burial mounds are still evident today.

Spatial order, like chronological order, is used most often in informative speeches.

Causal Order

causal order
A method of speech organization in which the main points show a cause-effect relationship.

Speeches arranged in causal order organize main points so as to show a cause-effect relationship. When you put your speech in causal order, you have two main points—one dealing with the causes of an event, the other dealing with its effects. Depending on your topic, you can either devote your first main point to the causes and the second to the effects, or you can deal first with the effects and then with the causes.

Suppose your specific purpose is "To persuade my audience that the widespread use of Ritalin to treat attention deficit hyperactivity disorder (ADHD) is a serious problem." You would begin with the causes for the use of Ritalin and work toward its effects:

Specific Purpose: To persuade my audience that the widespread use of Ritalin to treat attention deficit hyperactivity disorder (ADHD) is a serious problem.

Central Idea: Widely prescribed for young children who suffer from ADHD, Ritalin has a number of serious side effects.

Main Points:

I. Ritalin is widely prescribed for young children who suffer from attention deficit hyperactivity disorder.
II. Ritalin has been linked with a number of serious side effects, including liver damage, heart disease, depression, stunted growth, and Tourette's syndrome.

When the effects you are discussing have already occurred, you may want to reverse the order and talk first about the effects and then about their causes—as in this speech about the Mayan civilization of Central America:

Specific Purpose: To inform my audience about the possible causes for the collapse of Mayan civilization.

Central Idea: The causes for the collapse of Mayan civilization have not yet been fully explained.

Main Points:

I. Mayan civilization flourished for over a thousand years until 900 A.D., when it mysteriously began to disintegrate.

II. Scholars have advanced three major explanations for the causes of this disintegration.

Because of its versatility, causal order can be used both for persuasive speeches and informative speeches.

Problem-Solution Order

Speeches arranged in problem-solution order are divided into two main parts. The first shows the existence and seriousness of a problem. The second presents a workable solution to the problem. For example:

problem-solution order
A method of speech organization in which the first main point deals with the existence of a problem and the second main point presents a solution to the problem.

Specific Purpose: To persuade my audience that legislation is needed to control the abuses of fraudulent charity fund-raisers.

Central Idea: Fraudulent fund-raising for charities is a serious problem that requires action by government and individuals alike.

Main Points:

I. Fraudulent charity fund-raising has become a widespread national problem.

II. The problem can be solved by a combination of government initiative and individual awareness.

Or:

Specific Purpose: To persuade my audience that the electoral college should be abolished.

Central Idea: Because the electoral college does not give equal weight to the vote of each citizen, it should be replaced with direct popular election of the President.

Main Points:

I. The electoral college is a serious problem in the U.S. political system because it does not give equal weight to each citizen's vote in electing the President.

II. The problem can be solved by abolishing the electoral college and electing the President by popular vote.

As these examples indicate, problem-solution order is most appropriate for persuasive speeches.

Topical Order

Speeches that are not in chronological, spatial, causal, or problem-solution order usually fall into topical order. Topical order results when you divide the speech topic into *subtopics*, each of which becomes a main point in the speech. The main points are not part of a chronological, spatial, causal, or problem-solution sequence, but are simply parts of the whole. If this sounds confusing, a few examples should help make it clearer.

topical order
A method of speech organization in which the main points divide the topic into logical and consistent subtopics.

Suppose your specific purpose is "To inform my audience of the major kinds of fireworks." This topic does not lend itself to chronological, spatial, causal, or problem-solution order. Rather, you separate the subject—kinds of fireworks—into its constituent parts, so that each main point deals with a single kind of fireworks. Your central idea and main points might look like this:

Specific Purpose: To inform my audience of the major kinds of fireworks.

Central Idea: The major kinds of fireworks are skyrockets, Roman candles, pinwheels, and lances.

Main Points:

I. Skyrockets explode high in the air, producing the most dramatic effects of all fireworks.
II. Roman candles shoot out separate groups of sparks and colored flames with a series of booming noises.
III. Pinwheels throw off sparks and flames as they whirl on the end of a stick.
IV. Lances are thin, colorful fireworks used in ground displays.

To take another example, let's say your specific purpose is "To inform my audience about the achievements of Ida Wells-Barnett." Wells-Barnett, an African American who lived at the turn of the 20th century, was an outspoken champion of social and political justice for her race. You could organize your speech chronologically—by discussing Wells-Barnett's exploits during each decade of her career. On the other hand, you could arrange the speech topically—by dividing Wells-Barnett's accomplishments into categories. Then your central idea and main points might be:

Specific Purpose: To inform my audience about the achievements of Ida Wells-Barnett.

Central Idea: Ida Wells-Barnett was a multitalented figure in the fight for racial justice.

Main Points:

I. As a teacher, Wells-Barnett spoke out against inferior school facilities for African-American children.
II. As a journalist, Wells-Barnett campaigned against lynching.
III. As a civic organizer, Wells-Barnett helped found the NAACP.

Notice that in both of the preceding examples, the main points subdivide the speech topic logically and consistently. In the first example, each main point deals with a single category of fireworks. In the second example, each main point isolates one aspect of Wells-Barnett's achievements. But suppose your main points look like this:

I. As a teacher, Wells-Barnett spoke out against inferior school facilities for African-American children.

II. As a journalist, Wells-Barnett campaigned against lynching.
III. In the early 20th century, Wells-Barnett expanded her activities and the scope of her influence.

This would *not* be a good topical order because main point III is inconsistent with the rest of the main points. It deals with a *period* in Wells-Barnett's life, whereas main points I and II deal with *kinds* of activism.

All the examples so far refer to informative speeches. But topical order also works for persuasive speeches. Usually the topical subdivisions are the *reasons* why a speaker believes in a certain point of view. Here, for example, are the main points of a speech on why the United States should continue its program of space exploration:

Specific Purpose: To persuade my audience that the United States should continue its program of space exploration.

Central Idea: The United States should continue its program of space exploration because it will open access to vital natural resources, expand scientific knowledge, and further the search for extraterrestrial life.

Main Points:

I. Space exploration will open access to vital natural resources that are in limited supply on earth.
II. Space exploration will produce scientific knowledge that will benefit life on earth.
III. Space exploration will further the search for extraterrestrial life.

Because it is applicable to almost any subject and to any kind of speech, topical order is used more often than any other method of speech organization.

Tips for Preparing Main Points

Keep Main Points Separate

Each main point in a speech should be clearly independent of the other main points. Take care not to lump together what should be separate main points. Compare these two sets of main points for a speech about the process of producing a Broadway play:

Ineffective	More Effective
I. The first step is choosing the play.	I. The first step is choosing the play.
II. The second step is selecting the cast.	II. The second step is selecting the cast.
III. The third step is conducting rehearsals and then performing the play.	III. The third step is conducting the rehearsals.
	IV. The fourth step is performing the play.

The problem with the left-hand list is that point III contains two main points. It should be divided, as shown in the right-hand list.

CD 1: SPEECH CHECKLIST

You can print a copy of this checklist from the CD-ROM.

MAIN POINTS CHECKLIST

yes	no	
☐	☐	1. Does the body of my speech contain two to five main points?
☐	☐	2. Are my main points organized according to one of the following methods of organization? (Check the one that applies.)
☐	☐	Chronological order
☐	☐	Spatial order
☐	☐	Causal order
☐	☐	Topical order
☐	☐	Problem-solution order
☐	☐	3. Are my main points clearly separate from one another?
☐	☐	4. As much as possible, have I used the same pattern of wording for all my main points?
☐	☐	5. Have I roughly balanced the amount of time devoted to each main point?
☐	☐	6. Is each main point backed up with strong, credible supporting materials?
☐	☐	7. Do I use connectives to make sure my audience knows when I am moving from one main point to another?

Try to Use the Same Pattern of Wording for Main Points

Consider the following main points for an informative speech about the benefits of exercise.

Ineffective

I. Regular exercise increases your endurance.
II. Your sleeping pattern is improved by regular exercise.
III. It is possible to help control your weight by regular exercise.

More Effective

I. Regular exercise increases your endurance.
II. Regular exercise improves your sleeping pattern.
III. Regular exercise helps control your weight.

The set of main points on the right follows a consistent pattern of wording throughout. Therefore, it is easier to understand and easier to remember than the set on the left.

You will find that it is not always possible to use this kind of parallel wording for your main points. Some speeches just don't lend themselves to such a tidy arrangement. But try to keep the wording parallel when you can, for it is a good way to make your main points stand out from the details surrounding them.

Balance the Amount of Time Devoted to Main Points

Because your main points are so important, you want to be sure they all receive enough emphasis to be clear and convincing. This means allowing sufficient time to develop each main point. Suppose you discover that the proportion of time devoted to your main points is something like this:

I. 85 percent
II. 10 percent
III. 5 percent

A breakdown of this sort indicates one of two things. Either points II and III aren't really *main* points and you have only one main point, or points II and III haven't been given the attention they need. If the latter, you should revise the body of the speech to bring the main points into better balance.

This is not to say that all main points must receive exactly equal emphasis, but only that they should be roughly balanced. For example, either of the following would be fine:

I. 30 percent	I. 20 percent
II. 40 percent	II. 30 percent
III. 30 percent	III. 50 percent

The amount of time spent on each main point depends on the amount and complexity of supporting materials for each point. Supporting materials are, in effect, the "flesh" that fills out the skeleton of your speech.

Supporting Materials

By themselves, main points are only assertions. As we saw in Chapter 7, listeners need supporting materials to accept what a speaker says. When the supporting materials are added, the body of a speech looks like the following in outline form:

I. Hypnosis is used in surgery as an adjunct to chemical anesthesia.
    A. Hypnosis reduces both the physical and psychological aspects of pain.
        1. Hypnosis can double a person's pain threshold.
        2. It also reduces the fear that intensifies physical pain.
    B. Hypnosis is most useful in cases when the patient is known to have problems with general anesthesia.
        1. Quotation from Dr. Harold Wain of Walter Reed Army Hospital.
        2. Story of Linda Kuay.
        3. Statistics from *Psychology Today.*

II. Hypnosis is used to help people stop smoking.
   A. Many therapists utilize hypnosis to help people break their addiction to cigarettes.
      1. The U.S. Department of Health and Human Services considers hypnosis a safe and effective means of stopping smoking.
      2. Success rates are as high as 70 percent.
         a. Story of Alex Hamilton.
         b. Quotation from New York psychiatrist Dr. Herbert Spiegel.
   B. Hypnosis does not work for all smokers.
      1. A person must want to stop smoking for hypnosis to work.
      2. A person must also be responsive to hypnotic suggestion.
III. Hypnosis is used to help students improve their academic performance.
   A. Hypnosis enables people to use their minds more effectively.
      1. The conscious mind uses about 10 percent of a person's mental ability.
      2. Hypnosis allows people to tap more of their mental power.
   B. Studies show that hypnosis can help people overcome many obstacles to academic success.
      1. It improves ability to concentrate.
      2. It increases reading speed.
      3. It reduces test anxiety.

supporting materials
The materials used to support a speaker's ideas. The three major kinds of supporting materials are examples, statistics, and testimony.

In Chapter 7 we discussed the major kinds of supporting materials and how to use them. Here, we need stress only the importance of *organizing* your supporting materials so they are directly relevant to the main points they are supposed to support. Misplaced supporting materials are confusing. Here's an example:

I. There are several reasons why people immigrate to the United States.
   A. Over the years, millions of people have immigrated to the United States.
   B. Many people immigrate in search of economic opportunity.
   C. Others immigrate to attain political freedom.
   D. Still others immigrate to escape religious persecution.

The main point deals with the reasons immigrants come to the United States, as do supporting points B, C, and D. Supporting point A ("Over the years, millions of people have immigrated to the United States") does not. It is out of place and should not be included with this main point.

If you find such a situation in your own speeches, try to reorganize your supporting points under appropriate main points, like this:

I. Over the years, millions of people have immigrated to the United States.
   A. Since the American Revolution, an estimated 80 million people have immigrated to the U.S.
   B. Today there are 30 million Americans who were born in other countries.

II. There are several reasons why people immigrate to the United States.
    A. Many people immigrate in search of economic opportunity.
    B. Others immigrate to attain political freedom.
    C. Still others immigrate to escape religious persecution.

Now you have two supporting points to back up your "millions of people" point and three supporting points to back up your "reasons" point.

Once you have organized your main points and supporting points, you must give attention to the third element in the body of a speech—connectives.

Connectives

Carla Maggio was speaking to her class about the need for medical malpractice reform. She had rehearsed the speech several times, had a well-defined central idea, three sharp main points, and strong evidence to support her position. But when Carla delivered the speech, she said "All right" every time she moved from one thought to the next. All told, she said "All right" 10 times in six minutes. After a while, her classmates started counting. By the end of the speech, most had stopped listening to Carla's message. They were too busy waiting for the next "All right." Afterward, Carla said, "I never even thought about saying 'All right.' I guess it just popped out when I didn't know what else to say."

This experience is not unusual. We all have stock phrases that we habitually use to fill the space between thoughts. In casual conversation they are seldom troublesome. But in speechmaking they create a problem—particularly when they call attention to themselves.

What Carla's speech lacked were strong *connectives*—words or phrases that join one thought to another and indicate the relationship between them. Connectives in the body of a speech are like ligaments and tendons in a human body. Without connectives, a speech is disjointed and uncoordinated—much as a person would be without ligaments and tendons to join the bones and hold the organs in place. Four types of speech connectives are transitions, internal previews, internal summaries, and signposts.

connective
A word or phrase that connects the ideas of a speech and indicates the relationship between them.

Transitions

Transitions are words or phrases that indicate when a speaker has just completed one thought and is moving on to another. Technically, the transitions state both the idea the speaker is leaving and the idea she or he is coming up to. In the following examples, the transitional phrases are underlined:

transition
A word or phrase that indicates when a speaker has finished one thought and is moving on to another.

Now that we have a clear understanding of the problem, let me share the solution with you.

I have spoken so far of bravery and patriotism, but it is the sacrifice of the Massachusetts 54th that has etched them into the pages of history.

Now that we've seen how drinking too much is a serious problem for students and their communities, let's look at some causes.

CD 1: VIDEO 8.1

View these transitions from student speeches.

Keeping these points in mind about sign language, let's return to the sentence I started with and see if we can learn the signs for "You are my friend."

Now that we've taken a look at what feng shui is, let's put this ancient art into practice.

Notice how these phrases remind the listener of the thought just completed, as well as reveal the thought about to be developed.

Internal Previews

internal preview
A statement in the body of the speech that lets the audience know what the speaker is going to discuss next.

Internal previews let the audience know what the speaker will take up next, but they are more detailed than transitions. In effect, an internal preview works just like the preview statement in a speech introduction, except that it comes in the body of the speech—usually as the speaker is starting to discuss a main point. For example:

> In discussing how Asian Americans have been stereotyped in the mass media, we'll look first at the origins of the problem and second at its continuing impact today.

After hearing this, the audience knows exactly what to listen for as the speaker develops the "problem" main point.

Internal previews are often combined with transitions. For example:

> [*Transition*]: Now that we have seen how serious the problem of faulty credit reports is, let's look at some solutions. [*Internal Preview*]: I will focus on three solutions—instituting tighter government regulation of credit bureaus, holding credit bureaus financially responsible for their errors, and giving individuals easier access to their credit reports.

You will seldom need an internal preview for each main point in your speech, but be sure to use one whenever you think it will help listeners keep track of your ideas.

Internal Summaries

internal summary
A statement in the body of the speech that summarizes the speaker's preceding point or points.

Internal summaries are the reverse of internal previews. Rather than letting listeners know what is coming up next, internal summaries remind listeners of what they have just heard. Such summaries are generally used when a speaker finishes a complicated or particularly important main point or set of main points. Rather than moving immediately to the next point, the speaker takes a moment to summarize the preceding point or points. For example:

> In short, palm reading is an ancient art. Developed in China more than five thousand years ago, it was practiced in classical Greece and Rome, flourished during the Middle Ages, survived the Industrial Revolution, and remains popular today in many parts of the world.

When organizing your speeches, be sure to include transitions and other connectives to help listeners keep track of your ideas. The result will be a crisp presentation that moves clearly from point to point.

I hope I've made clear the benefits of walking as a form of exercise. Unlike running, which often causes as many injuries as it prevents, walking is a gentle but no less effective way to keep in shape. Regular walking at a brisk pace strengthens the heart, increases lung capacity, improves blood circulation, and burns calories—all without the strain on the knees and ankles caused by running.

Such internal summaries are an excellent way to clarify and reinforce ideas. By combining them with transitions, you can also lead your audience smoothly into your next main point:

[*Internal Summary*]: So far we have seen that the normal individual's need for a three-minute burst of stimuli has produced a growing demand for thrill rides and has helped launch a coaster war between amusement parks. Then we looked at the roller coaster's past and present. [*Transition*]: Now I'd like to show you what's in store for us in the future.

[*Internal Summary*]: Let's pause for a moment to summarize what we have found so far. First, we have seen that America's criminal justice system is less effective than it should be in deterring crime. Second, we have seen that prison programs to rehabilitate prisoners have been far from successful. [*Transition*]: We are now ready to explore solutions to these problems.

Signposts

Signposts are very brief statements that indicate exactly where you are in the speech. Frequently they are just numbers. Here is how one student used simple numerical signposts to help her audience keep track of the major causes for the continuing problem of famine in Africa:

signpost
A very brief statement that indicates where a speaker is in the speech or that focuses attention on key ideas.

> The first cause of this problem is inefficient agricultural production.
>
> The second cause is recurrent drought in the affected countries.
>
> The final cause is mismanagement of available food resources by local leaders.

Another way to accomplish the same thing is to introduce your main points with a question, as did one student in his speech titled "Protecting Yourself Against Mail-Order Fraud." His first main point showed that mail-order fraud continues to be a serious problem despite the growth of the Internet. He introduced it this way:

> So just how serious is the problem of mail-order fraud? Is it just a few isolated cases, or is it widespread enough to require serious measures to protect consumers?

His second point explored the causes for the persistence of mail-order fraud. He introduced it like this:

CD 1: VIDEO 8.2

View these signposts from "Protecting Yourself Against Mail-Order Fraud."

> Why is it that mail-order fraud continues to be such a major problem? Why do people keep falling for outrageous gimmicks that are obviously too good to be true?

His third main point dealt with ways to curb mail-order fraud. He introduced it by saying:

> So how can we solve this problem? Is there a way to protect the rights of legitimate mail-order companies while attacking the fraudulent ones?

Questions are particularly effective as signposts because they invite subliminal answers and thereby get the audience more involved with the speech.

Besides using signposts to indicate where you are in the speech, you can use them to focus attention on key ideas. You can do this with a simple phrase, as in the following example:

> The most important thing to remember about abstract art is that it is always based on forms in the natural world.

The underlined words alert the audience to the fact that an especially significant point is coming up. So do phrases such as these:

> Be sure to keep this in mind . . .
>
> This is crucial to understanding the rest of the speech . . .
>
> Above all, you need to know . . .
>
> Let me repeat that last statement . . .

Depending on the needs of your speech, you may want to use two, three, or even all four kinds of connectives in combination. You needn't worry too much about what they are called—whether this one is a signpost and that a transition. In fact, many people lump them all together as "transitions." The important thing is to be aware of their functions. Properly applied, connectives can make your speeches much more unified and coherent.

Summary

Clear organization is vital to speechmaking. Listeners demand coherence. They get only one chance to grasp a speaker's ideas, and they have little patience for speakers who ramble aimlessly from one idea to another. A well-organized speech will enhance your credibility and make it easier for the audience to understand your message.

Speeches should be organized strategically. They should be put together in particular ways to achieve particular results with particular audiences. The first step in organizing speeches is to gain command of the three basic parts of a speech—introduction, body, conclusion—and the strategic role of each. In this chapter we have dealt with the body of the speech.

The process of planning the body of a speech begins when you determine the main points. These are the central features of your speech. You should choose them carefully, phrase them precisely, and organize them strategically. Because listeners cannot keep track of a multitude of main points, most speeches should contain no more than two to five main points. Each main point should focus on a single idea, should be worded clearly, and should receive enough emphasis to be clear and convincing.

You can organize main points in various ways. The strategic order will be determined by your topic, your purpose, and your audience. Chronological order means that your speech follows a time pattern. Speeches arranged in spatial order follow a directional pattern. To put your speech in causal order, you organize main points according to their cause-effect relationship. Topical order results when you divide your main topic into subtopics, each of which covers one aspect of the main topic. For problem-solution order you break the body of your speech into two main parts—the first showing a problem, the second giving a solution.

Supporting materials are the backup ideas for your main points. When organizing supporting materials, make sure they are directly relevant to the main points they are supposed to support.

Once you have organized your main points and supporting materials, you are ready to work out the third element in the body of your speech: connectives. Connectives help tie a speech together. They are words or phrases that join one thought to another and indicate the relationship between them. The four major types of speech connectives are transitions, internal previews, internal summaries, and signposts. Using them effectively will make your speeches more unified and coherent.

Key Terms

strategic organization (207)
main points (207)
chronological order (210)
spatial order (211)
causal order (212)
problem-solution order (213)
topical order (213)
supporting materials (218)
connective (219)
transition (219)
internal preview (220)
internal summary (220)
signpost (222)

ONLINE LEARNING CENTER

Review these terms by doing the Chapter 8 crossword puzzle at www.mhhe.com/lucas9.

Review Questions

CD 1: STUDY QUESTIONS

For further review, go to the Study Questions for this chapter.

After reading this chapter, you should be able to answer the following questions:

1. Why is it important that speeches be organized clearly and coherently?
2. How many main points will your speeches usually contain? Why is it important to limit the number of main points in your speeches?
3. What are the five basic patterns of organizing main points in a speech? Which are appropriate for informative speeches? Which is used only in persuasive speeches? Which is used most often?
4. What are three tips for preparing your main points?
5. What is the most important thing to remember when organizing supporting materials in the body of your speech?
6. What are the four kinds of speech connectives? What role does each play in a speech?

Exercises for Critical Thinking

1. Identify the organizational method used in each of the following sets of main points.

   I. Cesar Chavez is best known for his efforts to protect the rights of Mexican-American farmworkers in California.
   II. Cesar Chavez was also a tireless advocate for Mexican-American racial and cultural pride in general.

   I. The game we know as golf originated in Scotland during the 15th century.
   II. Most of golf's rules and traditions developed during the 19th century.
   III. Professional golf tours for men and women emerged during the 20th century.
   IV. Today golf is at a peak of popularity among everyday players and as a spectator sport.

   I. Caused by the bite of infected mosquitos, West Nile virus is spreading throughout the United States.
   II. The effects of West Nile virus include flulike symptoms, convulsions, swelling of the brain, and, in some cases, death.

   I. The outer layer of the skin, the epidermis, is about as thick as a sheet of paper.
   II. The middle layer of the skin, the dermis, is 15 to 40 times thicker than the epidermis.
   III. The innermost layer of the skin, the subcutaneous tissue, is by far the thickest layer.

   I. Childhood obesity has reached crisis proportions in the United States.
   II. Solving the problem will require changes in attitudes, eating habits, and exercise.

2. What organizational method (or methods) might you use to arrange main points for speeches with the following specific purpose statements?

   To inform my audience about the major events in the development of the civil rights movement from 1955 to 1970.

   To inform my audience of the causes and effects of the erosion of America's seacoasts.

   To inform my audience about the nonviolent philosophy of Mahatma Gandhi.

   To inform my audience about the geographical regions of the Philippines.

   To persuade my audience that our state legislature should enact tougher laws to deal with the problem of motorists who run red lights.

   To inform my audience about the major kinds of symbols used in traditional Native American art.

3. Turn to the outline of main points and supporting materials for the speech about hypnosis on pages 217–218. Create appropriate transitions, internal previews, internal summaries, and signposts for the speech.

Applying the POWER of PUBLIC SPEAKING

You are in the purchasing department of a large clothing manufacturer. The company's design team has come up with an idea for a new shirt requiring a lightweight, stretchable fabric. The fabric cannot be provided by your company's usual suppliers, so you were sent to visit a number of textile firms in the U.S. and abroad to see what they can offer. You were asked to evaluate their products for quality, availability, and cost.

You have just returned from a 10-day trip to textile manufacturers in North Carolina, Italy, India, and China. You will present your findings and recommendations to the purchasing and design departments, but you're not sure how best to organize your speech. Your major choices are chronological order, problem-solution order, and topical order. What might be the main points of your speech with each of these methods of organization? Explain which method you think would be most effective for your presentation.

Notes

[1]Ernest C. Thompson, "An Experimental Investigation of the Relative Effectiveness of Organizational Structure in Oral Communication," *Southern Speech Journal,* 26 (1960), pp. 59–69.

[2]Harry Sharp, Jr., and Thomas McClung, "Effects of Organization on the Speaker's Ethos," *Speech Monographs,* 33 (1966), pp. 182–183.

[3]For two recent studies, see B. Scott Titsworth, "Students' Notetaking: The Effects of Teacher Immediacy and Clarity," *Communication Education,* 53 (2004), pp. 305–320; Joseph L. Chesebro, "Effects of Teacher Clarity and Nonverbal Immediacy on Student Learning, Receiver Apprehension, and Affect," *Communication Education,* 52 (2003), pp. 135–147.

WEL

CHAPTER NINE

Beginning and Ending the Speech

On the night of April 19, 2001, a conductor stepped up to the podium at the St. James Theater in New York City, tapped his baton, raised his arms, and signaled the orchestra to play. Moments later the public first heard the rollicking opening chords of the hit musical *The Producers.*

Like most musical stage plays, *The Producers* begins with an overture—an orchestral introduction that captures the audience's attention and gives them a preview of the music they are going to hear. Without such an introduction—if the characters simply walked onstage and began singing or speaking—the beginning of the play would seem too abrupt, and the audience would not be suitably "primed" for the entertainment.

Similarly, nearly all musicals end with a finale, when the whole cast is onstage, elements of the dramatic plot are resolved, portions of the principal songs are recalled, and the music is brought to a dramatic climax. If there were no such conclusion, if the actors merely stopped and walked offstage, the audience would be left unsatisfied.

Just as musical plays need appropriate beginnings and endings, so do speeches. The beginning, or introduction, prepares listeners for what is to come. The conclusion ties up the speech and alerts listeners that the speech is going to end. Ideally, it is a satisfying conclusion.

In this chapter we explore the roles played by an introduction and a conclusion in speechmaking. We also discuss techniques aimed at fulfilling those roles. If you apply these techniques imaginatively, you will take a big step toward elevating your speeches from the ordinary to the splendid.

The Introduction

First impressions are important. A poor beginning may so distract or alienate listeners that the speaker can never fully recover. Moreover, getting off on the right foot is vital to a speaker's self-confidence. What could be more encouraging than watching your listeners' faces begin to register interest, attention, and pleasure? The hardest part of any presentation is the beginning. If you get through the opening stages of your speech without blundering, the rest will go much more smoothly. A good introduction, you will find, is an excellent confidence booster.

In most speech situations, there are four objectives you need to accomplish at the outset:

- Get the attention and interest of your audience.
- Reveal the topic of your speech.
- Establish your credibility and goodwill.
- Preview the body of the speech.

We'll look at each of these objectives in turn.

Get Attention and Interest

"Unless a speaker can interest his audience at once, his effort will be a failure." So said the great lawyer Clarence Darrow. If your topic is not one of extraordinary interest, your listeners are likely to say to themselves, "So what? Who cares?" No matter how famous the speaker or how vital the topic, the speaker can quickly lose an audience if she or he doesn't use the introduction to get their attention and quicken their interest.

Getting the initial attention of your audience is usually easy to do—even before you utter a single word. After you are introduced and step to the lectern, your audience will normally give you their attention. If they don't, merely wait patiently. Look directly at the audience without saying a word. In a few moments all talking and physical commotion will stop. Your listeners will be attentive. You will be ready to start speaking.

Keeping the attention of your audience once you start talking is more difficult. Here are the methods used most often. Employed individually or in combination, they will help get the audience caught up in your speech.

Relate the Topic to the Audience

People pay attention to things that affect them directly. If you can relate the topic to your listeners, they are much more likely to be interested in it.

Suppose, for example, one of your classmates begins her speech like this:

> Today I am going to talk about collecting postcards—a hobby that is both fascinating and financially rewarding. I would like to explain the basic kinds of collectible postcards, why they are so valuable, and how collectors buy and sell their cards.

This is certainly a clear introduction, but it is not one to get you hooked on the speech. Now what if your classmate were to begin her speech this way—as one student actually did.

> It's Saturday morning, and you are helping clean out your grandmother's attic. After working a while, you stumble upon a trunk, open it, and discover inside hundreds of old postcards. Thinking about getting to the football game on time, you start tossing the cards into the trash can. Congratulations! You have just thrown away a year's tuition.

This time the speaker has used just the right bait. Chances are you will be hooked.

Even when you use other interest-arousing lures, you should *always* relate your topic to the audience. At times this will test your ingenuity, but it pays dividends. Here are two excellent examples. The first is from a speech entitled "Making Campus Accessible for Disabled Students." Notice how the speaker gets her classmates to put themselves in the place of people who are unable to get to class on time because they can't get their wheelchairs or scooters through the snow.

CD 1: VIDEO 9.1
View the beginning of "Making Campus Accessible for Disabled Students."

> I'd like to ask you to use your imaginations and think how it would feel if you'd spent an evening studying for an exam, you get up in the morning all set to go to class, you go down, you get to your door, and it won't open. You think, "Oh, I can just use my back door." But you go to your back door, and that won't open either.
>
> It would be pretty frustrating, wouldn't it? That's the kind of frustration handicapped students feel when they can't get to class because of the snow.

A good introduction will get your speech off to a strong start. To be most effective, it should relate the topic to the audience and be delivered from a minimum of notes.

The second example is from a student speech about dreams. This is how the speaker began his remarks:

> You are being chased by an object of unspeakable horror, yet your legs can only move in slow motion. Each step takes unbearably long, and your frantic struggle to run faster is hopeless. Your pursuer gets closer, and your desperation turns to terror. You know you are not going to escape. You can't breathe, and you gulp for air that isn't there. You are completely helpless—eye to eye with death.
>
> Then you wake up, gasping for air, your heart pounding, your face clammy with sweat. It takes a few minutes for you to reorient yourself to reality, for your heart and breathing to slow down. You reassure yourself that it was "just a dream." Soon you drift back to sleep.

By using vivid language to describe something all his classmates had experienced at some point in their lives, the speaker made sure of an attentive audience.

State the Importance of Your Topic

Presumably, you think your speech is important. Tell your audience why they should think so too. Here is how Susan Paddack, President of the American Medical Association Alliance, used this method to involve her audience in a speech about youth violence to the AMA National Leadership Conference:

> Of the many threats to our public health, youth violence is the one that threatens not only each of us an individuals, but also the very fabric of our nation. . . .

I'd like you to imagine some 300 students from our public high schools among us now. Three hundred students would fill about one-third of this room. That's how many students will be attacked or robbed in our country during the 10 minutes I'll be speaking to you. More than 17,000 every day—more than half a million every month. . . . And adolescents in our country suffer the highest rates of murder and suicide among the 26 wealthiest nations.[1]

These are striking statistics. By citing them in the introduction, Paddack emphasized the importance of her topic and captured the attention of her audience.

Clearly this technique is easy to use when discussing social and political issues such as youth violence, endangered species, terrorism, and stem-cell research, but it is appropriate for other topics as well. Here is how one student handled it in a speech about starting a home aquarium:

It is very hard to cuddle a fish. Fish won't roll over or fetch the morning paper. You won't find them curling up on your lap, chasing a ball of string, or rescuing a child from a burning building.

Yet despite these shortcomings, 250 million tropical fish have found their way into 10 million American homes. Tropical fish make up 50 percent of all live animal sales in the United States, and they have earned a spot next to the all-American dog and the cuddly kitten in the hearts of millions of people. Today I would like to explain how you can start a home aquarium and discover the pleasures of owning tropical fish.

The first paragraph—with its clever opening line—grabs the listener's attention. But it is the second paragraph that keeps the attention. Indeed, whenever you discuss a topic whose importance may not be clear to the audience, you should think about ways to demonstrate its significance in the introduction.

Startle the Audience

One surefire way to arouse interest quickly is to startle your listeners with an arresting or intriguing statement. Everyone in the audience paid close attention after this speaker's introduction:

Take a moment and think of the three women closest to you. Who comes to mind? Your mother? Your sister? Your girlfriend? Your wife? Your best friend? Now guess which one will be sexually assaulted during her lifetime. It's not a pleasant thought, but according to the U.S. Department of Justice, one of every three American women will be sexually assaulted sometime during her life.

Notice the gradual buildup to the speaker's arresting statement, "Now guess which one will be sexually assaulted during her lifetime." This statement startles the audience—especially the men—and drives home at a personal level the problem of sexual assault against women. The effect would have been much less if the speaker had said, "Sexual assault against women is a serious problem."

Sometimes you may want to startle your audience in the very first sentence of your speech. Here is how one student began her speech opposing the use of Native American names for sports teams:

> In tonight's games, the San Antonio Spics are playing the New Jersey Japs, while the Los Angeles Jews will take on the Minnesota Polacks.

Here is a longer example of the same technique, used by a speaker at a professional development seminar on privacy and the Internet:

> Three of you in this room have spent time in jail. Two of you were late on your mortgage payment last month; three more of you didn't make the latest payment on your student loans. Two of the males and three of the females were recently diagnosed with cancer. Five of you are behind in the number of credits needed to maintain your professional certification.
>
> How did I find out all of this? Simply by plugging your first and last names into my computer and searching through specialized sources. I did not enter your addresses, Social Security numbers, driver's license numbers, or any other specific information.

This technique is highly effective and easy to use. Just be sure the startling introduction relates directly to the subject of your speech. The example cited above worked perfectly for a speech on how the Internet is undermining our personal privacy. It would not work for a speech about electronic commerce. If you choose a strong opening simply for its shock value and then go on to talk about something else, your audience will be confused and possibly annoyed.

Arouse the Curiosity of the Audience

People are curious. One way to draw them into your speech is with a series of statements that progressively whet their curiosity about the subject of the speech. For example:

> It is the most common chronic disease in the United States. Controllable but incurable, it is a symptomless disease. You can have it for years and never know until it kills you. Some 40 million Americans have this disease, and 300,000 will die from it before the year is out. Odds are that five of us in this class have it.
>
> What am I talking about? Not cancer. Not AIDS. Not heart disease. I am talking about hypertension—high blood pressure.

For another example, look at this splendid opening from a student speech entitled "The Gift of Life":

> Each of you has a gift. What kind of gift is it? It's not a Christmas gift or a birthday gift. It's not some special talent or skill. It's a gift that could save a life—maybe more than one. If you decide to give it, you lose nothing.
>
> Some people bury their gift. Others burn it. All but one of you who completed my questionnaire would gladly receive the gift, but only 20 percent of you have decided to give it. This gift is the donation of your vital organs when you die.

Not only does this speaker relate the topic directly to his classmates, he gets them further involved by building suspense about the "gift" that each of us has. Notice how much less effective the introduction would have been if he had simply said, "Today I am going to talk about organ donation." When used appropriately, arousing curiosity is a surefire way to capture and hold your listeners' interest.

Question the Audience

Asking a *rhetorical question* is another way to get your listeners thinking about your speech. Sometimes a single question will do:

rhetorical question
A question that the audience answers mentally rather than out loud.

How would you respond if a loved one was the victim of terrorism?

What would you think if you went to the doctor because you were ill and she told you to watch *The Simpsons* as part of your treatment?

Do you know how many small businesses are started each year in the United States?

In other circumstances, you may want to pose a series of questions, each of which draws the audience deeper and deeper into the speech. Here is how one speaker used this method:

Have you ever spent a sleepless night studying for an exam? Can you remember rushing to finish a term paper because you waited too long to start writing it? Do you often feel overwhelmed by all the things you have to get done at school? At work? At home?

If so, you may be the victim of poor time management. Fortunately, there are proven strategies you can follow to use your time more effectively and to keep control of your life.

Like beginning with a startling statement, opening with a question works best when the question is meaningful to the audience and firmly related to the content of the speech. It also works most effectively when you pause

As you research your speeches, keep an eye out for quotations, stories, and other materials you can use to craft an introduction that will capture the attention of your listeners.

for just a moment after each question. This adds dramatic impact and gives the question time to sink in. The audience, of course, will answer mentally—not out loud.

Begin with a Quotation

Another way to arouse the interest of your audience is to start with an attention-getting quotation. You might choose your quotation from Shakespeare or Confucius, from the Bible or Talmud, from a poem, song, or film. Here is how one student used a quotation to begin a speech about scientist Jonas Salk, who developed the first polio vaccine:

> "If one is lucky, a solitary fantasy can totally transform one million realities." These words from poet and writer Maya Angelou could apply easily to the dedicated researcher Jonas Salk, who created a vaccine for polio. A half century ago this crippling disease struck indiscriminately, but today widespread use of the vaccine has virtually wiped out polio. In my talk I would like to describe how Salk persevered and triumphed in his quest despite doubts and major setbacks.

You need not use a well-known or famous quotation. The following made an effective introduction for a speech about bird-watching:

> "Even to this day I cannot describe what happened without feeling the excitement of the moment. I glimpsed a flash of color in the thicket. I raised my binoculars to my eyes, and then I saw it—a Bachman's Warbler, one of the rarest birds in all of America. For me, this was the equivalent of a coin collector discovering a rare silver dollar, or of a football player scoring a touchdown in the Super Bowl."
>
> This statement was made by my father. He is just one of the millions of people who have discovered the joys and thrills of bird-watching.

A humorous quotation can afford double impact, as in this speech about the need for political reform in the U.S. Congress:

> Mark Twain once said, "It could probably be shown by facts and figures that there is no distinctly American criminal class except Congress."

By opening with Twain's words, the speaker not only got the audience's attention but also foreshadowed a central theme of her speech. Notice, too, that all the quotations used here as examples are relatively short. Opening your speech with a lengthy quotation is a sure way to set your audience yawning.

Tell a Story

We all enjoy stories—especially if they are provocative, amusing, dramatic, or suspenseful. To work well as introductions, they should also be clearly relevant to the main point of the speech. Used in this way, stories are perhaps the most effective way to begin a speech.

Consider, for example, the story one student told to open his speech about the strengths and weaknesses of the current Social Security system:

> Shirley Malone is a 69-year-old woman who lives on $912 dollars a month—$700 from Social Security and $212 from a volunteer program that pays low-income senior citizens to work in public schools. She has no savings, no investments, and no private pension, although she worked until she turned 62.
>
> Social Security provides the vast majority of Shirley's income. She is not unusual in this regard. Two-thirds of all retirees get the majority of their income from Social Security. But even with Social Security, Shirley has a hard time getting by. She's unable to buy presents for her grandchildren, and she's thinking of stopping her cable TV subscription, even though it's her only form of entertainment.
>
> Shirley's story, reported in *The New York Times,* shows the importance of Social Security for many retirees—as well as the limitations of the current program.

Like many good introductions, this one does a double job—it arouses the interest of the audience and gets listeners emotionally involved in the subject of the speech.

You can also use stories based on your personal experience. Here is how one student used such a story in his commencement speech at the University of Richmond. The student had come from Bombay, India, to attend college in the United States. He began by explaining the questions and uncertainties that were running through his mind as he prepared to leave his native land:

CD 1: VIDEO 9.2

View the beginning of Sajjid Zahir Chinoy, "Questions of Culture."

> I can visualize the scene again and again: 11:30 P.M., Saturday night, the 15th of August, Bombay International Airport, India. I was leaving home for the University of Richmond. And as I said that final goodbye to my parents, my family, and my friends; and as I saw hope, expectation, even a tinge of sadness, in their eyes; and as I stepped aboard the Boeing 747 in front, I knew my life had changed forever.

Telling a story is an excellent way of gaining attention in a speech introduction. The story should be clearly relevant to the topic and should be delivered expressively with strong eye contact.

ONLINE LEARNING CENTER

You can link to these Web sites at www.mhhe.com/lucas9.

THE INTERNET *Connection*

Looking for a quotation to use in the introduction or conclusion of your speech? Visit Yahoo (http://dir.yahoo.com/Reference/Quotations/) for a comprehensive roster of links to collected quotations on the Web.

Are you interested in reading introductions and conclusions from important speeches in U.S. history? You can find them at Douglass: Archives of American Public Address (http://douglassarchives.org/).

The effectiveness of any story—especially a personal one—hinges as much on the speaker's delivery as on the content of the story. As you can see from the clip of this speech on CD 1, Video 9.2, the speaker used pauses, eye contact, and changes in his tone of voice to heighten the impact of his words and draw his audience into the speech. See if you can do the same in your speech introductions.

The seven methods discussed above are the ones used most often by student speakers to gain attention and interest. Other methods include referring to the occasion, inviting audience participation, using audio equipment or visual aids, relating to a previous speaker, and beginning with humor. For any given speech, try to choose the method that is most suitable for the topic, the audience, and the occasion.

Reveal the Topic

In the process of gaining attention, be sure to state clearly the topic of your speech. If you do not, your listeners will be confused. And once they are confused, your chances of getting them absorbed in the speech are almost nil.

This is a basic point—so basic that it may hardly seem worth mentioning. Yet you would be surprised how many students need to be reminded of it. You may hear speeches in your own class in which the topic is not clear by the end of the introduction. So you will know what to avoid, here is such an introduction, presented in a public speaking class.

Everyone knows that former Vice President Al Gore claimed to have invented the Internet. This caused a furor during the 2000 presidential campaign and inspired lots of great comedy routines. Of course, Gore did not create the Internet. The Internet came from the Arpanet, a consortium of university computers dating from the late 1960s. Today almost 1 billion people use the Internet—but it is showing its age. How long does it take you to download music or open-source code? How often do you get fed up with the poor quality of streaming video? You must wonder if there isn't a better way.

What is the topic of this speech? Al Gore and political comedy? No. The history of the Internet? No. The limitations of the Internet? No. The student was speaking about a "better way," an alternative to the current Internet known as Internet2. But she did not make that clear to her audience.

This student found an interesting introduction, but she ignored the fact that it didn't relate properly to her speech. Certainly Al Gore's legendary statement is a good attention getter. But in this case it was wasted. Suppose, instead, the student had begun her speech differently:

> How long does it take you to download music or open-source code from the Internet? When you view streaming video on your computer, does the movement remind you of the robots in a bad 1950s science fiction movie? You may wonder if there isn't a better way. Well, there is. It's called Internet2, a network made up entirely of high-speed fiber-optic cables. Right now it's used only by about 200 universities, but it will be available to all of us soon. When it is, it will make as big a difference in our lives as today's Internet has.

This opening would have provided a way to get the audience's attention, but it also would have related directly to the speech topic.

If you beat around the bush in your introduction, you may lose your listeners. Even if they already know your topic, you should restate it clearly and concisely at some point in the introduction.

Establish Credibility and Goodwill

Besides getting attention and revealing the topic, there is a third objective you may need to accomplish in your introduction—establishing your credibility and goodwill.

Credibility is mostly a matter of being qualified to speak on a given topic—and of being *perceived* as qualified by your listeners. If, for instance, Brad Pitt got up before an audience to speak about nuclear physics, he would have to take drastic steps to establish his credibility on the subject.

credibility
The audience's perception of whether a speaker is qualified to speak on a given topic.

Here is how one student established her credibility on the subject of weight lifting without sounding like a braggart:

> What is the fastest-growing sport today among American women? If you answered weight lifting, you are absolutely correct. Once seen as an exclusively male activity, weight lifting has crossed the gender barrier—and with good reason. Regardless of whether you are male or female, weight lifting can give you a sense of strength and power, enhance your self-esteem, and make you look and feel better.
>
> I started lifting weights when I was in high school, and I have kept at it for the past eight years. I have also taught weight lifting in several health clubs, and I am a certified instructor through the Aerobics and Fitness Association of America.
>
> Using some of my experience, I would like to explain the basic kinds of weights and how to use them properly.

Whether or not you lift weights, you will probably be more interested in the speech when you realize the speaker knows what she is talking about.

Your credibility need not be based on firsthand knowledge and experience. It can come from reading, from classes, from interviews, from friends—as in these cases:

> I have been interested in the history of the civil rights movement for several years, and I have read a number of books and articles about it.

The information I am going to share with you today comes mostly from my biology class and an interview with Reyna Vasquez of the local Audubon Society.

I've learned a great deal about the problems of early childhood education from my mother, who is a teacher in the San Francisco school system.

Whatever the source of your expertise, be sure to let the audience know.

goodwill
The audience's perception of whether the speaker has the best interests of the audience in mind.

Establishing your *goodwill* is a slightly different problem. It is often crucial outside the classroom, where speakers have well-established reputations and may be identified with causes that arouse hostility among listeners. In such a situation, the speaker must try to defuse that hostility right at the start of the speech.[2]

Occasionally you may have to do the same thing in your classroom speeches. Suppose you advocate a highly unpopular position. You will need to make a special effort at the outset to ensure that your classmates will at least consider your point of view. This is how one student tried to minimize his classmates' opposition at the start of a speech in favor of building more nuclear power plants to meet America's energy needs during the 21st century.

The development of new nuclear power plants in the United States came to a standstill during the 1980s. As *Discover* magazine stated just last month, however, the time has come to look again at the benefits of nuclear power. Unlike fossil fuels, it does not contribute to the greenhouse effect; it does not leave America at the mercy of foreign oil; and, with advances in technology, it is much safer than before.

That is why I am speaking in favor of building more nuclear power plants to meet our future energy needs. I know that most of you oppose nuclear power—I did, too, until I started researching this speech. Today I would like to share with you some of the facts I have found. I know I can't change all your minds. But I do ask you to listen with an open mind and to consider the merit of my arguments.

What reasonable listener could ignore such a sincere, forthright plea?

Preview the Body of the Speech

As we saw in Chapter 3, most people are poor listeners. Even good listeners need all the help they can get in sorting out a speaker's ideas. One way to help your listeners is to tell them in the introduction what they should listen for in the rest of the speech. Here is an excellent example, from a speech by biotechnologist Tony L. White at the Columbia University School of Public Health:

I'm pleased to be here with you, and I'm honored to have been asked to deliver this year's Weiss lecture. . . .

Today I'd like to talk about some of the promises associated with the mapping of the human genome. I'll explain some of the opportunities that have emerged from reaching this milestone, and the impact I think it will have on public health. Finally, I'll call your attention to some of the challenges and issues that accompany this achievement.[3]

After this introduction, there was no doubt about White's topic or the main points he would cover in his lecture.

Using the introduction to establish goodwill is often a major concern for speakers who deal with controversial public issues—as in the case of Japanese Prime Minister Junichiro Koizumi.

In some types of persuasive speeches, you may not want to reveal your central idea until later in the speech. But even in such a situation you must be sure your audience is not left guessing about the main points they should listen for as the speech unfolds. Nearly always, you should include some *preview statement* similar to the following:

preview statement
A statement in the introduction of a speech that identifies the main points to be discussed in the body of the speech.

Today I will share part of what I have learned by explaining what happens when you receive an acupuncture treatment, how acupuncture works, the kinds of medical conditions that can be treated with acupuncture, and the growing use of acupuncture in combination with Western medical techniques.

To understand the importance of Frederick Douglass in African-American history, we will look first at the years he spent in slavery before escaping to the North, then at his battle against slavery during the Civil War, and finally at his contributions as a race spokesman during the final years of his life.

CD 1:VIDEO 9.3
View these preview statements from student speeches.

I'm here to tell you that, try as we might, we cannot build a bubble between ourselves and germs with antibacterial products and that these products actually create more problems than they solve. After looking at the problems created by antibacterial products, we'll explore some solutions.

Preview statements such as these serve another purpose as well. Because they usually come at the very end of the introduction, they provide a smooth lead-in to the body of the speech. They signal that the body of the speech is about to begin.

There is one other aspect you may want to cover in previewing your speech. You can use your introduction to give specialized information—definitions or

CD 1: SPEECH CHECKLIST

You can print a copy of this checklist from the CD-ROM.

SPEECH INTRODUCTION CHECKLIST

yes	no	
☐	☐	1. Do I gain the attention and interest of my audience by using one or more of the methods discussed in this chapter?
☐	☐	2. Do I relate the speech topic to my audience?
☐	☐	3. Do I clearly reveal the topic of my speech?
☐	☐	4. Do I establish my credibility to speak on this topic?
☐	☐	5. If my topic is controversial, do I take steps to establish my goodwill toward the audience?
☐	☐	6. Do I define any key terms that will be necessary for the audience to understand the rest of my speech?
☐	☐	7. Do I provide a preview statement of the main points to be covered in the body of the speech?
☐	☐	8. Is the introduction limited to 10–20 percent of my entire speech?
☐	☐	9. Have I worked out the language of my introduction in detail?
☐	☐	10. Have I practiced the delivery of my introduction so I can present it fluently, confidently, and with strong eye contact?

background—that your listeners will need if they are to understand the rest of the speech. Often you can do this very quickly, as in the following examples:

> "Cryonics" is the science of freezing human organs or body parts in liquid nitrogen to preserve them for later use.
>
> A "triathlon" is a race made up of three different events completed in succession. The events are usually swimming, biking, and running, though canoeing is sometimes substituted for one of these.

In other circumstances, you may have to explain an important term in more detail. Here is how one student handled the problem in a speech about the Underground Railroad used by slaves to escape from the South before the Civil War. Although most people have heard the phrase "Underground Railroad," many are not sure exactly what it means. Knowing this, the speaker took time in her introduction to give a precise definition:

> The term "Underground Railroad" was first used about 1830. But in fact, the Underground Railroad was neither underground nor a railroad. It was an informal network that provided runaway slaves food, clothing, directions, and places to hide on their escape routes to the North and to Canada.

Why was it called the Underground Railroad? Because of its secrecy and because many of the people involved used railroad terms as code words. Hiding places, for example, were called "stations," and people who helped the slaves were called "conductors." Over the years, the Underground Railroad helped thousands of slaves make their way from bondage to freedom.

Sample Introduction with Commentary

So far we have seen many excerpts showing how to fulfill the various objectives of an introduction. Now here is a complete introduction from a student speech. The side comments indicate the principles used in developing the introduction.

The Miracle of Bone Marrow Transplants

Commentary	*Introduction*
The speaker uses a story to gain attention. This story works particularly well because it is richly detailed and is high in human interest.	Katy Hubbell was four years old when she was diagnosed with a severe case of aplastic anemia, a disease in which the bone marrow stops producing new blood cells. After several types of treatment failed, Katy underwent a bone marrow transplant. Her donor was a 40-year-old airline manager who lived thousands of miles away. His generosity saved the life of a little girl he had never met. Today Katy is an active preteen girl who loves Harry Potter books and wants to be a cheerleader.
Now the speaker reveals her topic. Calling bone marrow transplants a "medical miracle" reinforces the importance of the subject, while explaining her personal involvement shows the speaker's goodwill and helps establish her credibility.	Bone marrow transplants have been called a medical miracle because of their life-saving capability. I first became interested in the subject when a 12-year-old member of my church was diagnosed with leukemia. I joined a committee to publicize Greg's case and to seek potential donors. Eventually a suitable donor was found and Greg is now a healthy high-school sophomore.
Here the speaker relates the topic directly to her audience and shows why they should care about it. The combination of statistics with the quotation from the Food and Drug Administration reinforces the importance of the topic.	Because of Greg's illness, I learned that anyone can get sick and need a bone marrow donation. It could be any of us in this room, a close friend, or even a family member. An estimated 15,000 bone marrow transplants are performed in the U.S. each year. According to the U.S. Food and Drug Administration, these transplants give patients "a chance to beat diseases once believed to have no cure."
By mentioning her research, the speaker further bolsters her credibility. She then ends the introduction by previewing the main points to be discussed in the body of the speech.	Through my research for this speech, I have learned much more about this remarkable procedure. Today I would like to talk with you about bone-marrow donation—how simple a process it is for the donor, how absolutely vital it is for the recipient, and how donors and recipients find one another.

Tips for Preparing the Introduction

1. Keep the introduction relatively brief. Under normal circumstances it should not constitute more than about 10 to 20 percent of your speech.

2. Be on the lookout for possible introductory materials as you do your research. File them with your notes, so they will be handy when you are ready for them.

3. Be creative in devising your introduction. Experiment with two or three different openings and choose the one that seems most likely to get the audience interested in your speech. (Don't hesitate to discard a "great" introduction that doesn't quite fit your speech. You'll think of another great one.)

4. Don't worry about the exact wording of your introduction until you have finished preparing the body of the speech. After you have determined your main points, it will be much easier to make final decisions about how to begin the speech.

5. Work out your introduction in detail. Some teachers recommend that you write it out word for word; others prefer that you outline it. Whichever method you use, practice the introduction over and over until you can deliver it smoothly from a minimum of notes and with strong eye contact. This will get your speech off to a good start and give you a big boost of confidence.

The Conclusion

"Great is the art of beginning," said Longfellow, "but greater the art is of ending." Longfellow was thinking of poetry, but his insight is equally applicable to public speaking. Many a speaker has marred an otherwise fine speech by a long-winded, silly, or antagonistic conclusion. Your closing remarks are your last chance to drive home your ideas. Moreover, your final impression will probably linger in your listeners' minds. Thus you need to craft your conclusion with as much care as your introduction.

No matter what kind of speech you are giving, the conclusion has two major functions:

- To let the audience know you are ending the speech.
- To reinforce the audience's understanding of, or commitment to, the central idea.

Let us look at each.

Signal the End of the Speech

It may seem obvious that you should let your audience know you are going to stop soon. However, you will almost certainly hear speeches in your class in which the speaker concludes so abruptly that you are taken by surprise. Even in casual conversation you expect some signal that the talk is coming to an end. You are taken aback when the person you are talking with suddenly walks off without warning. The same is true of speechmaking. Too sudden an ending leaves the audience puzzled and unfulfilled.

How do you let an audience know your speech is ending? One way is through what you say. "In conclusion," "One last thought," "In closing," "My purpose has been," "Let me end by saying"—these are all brief cues that you are getting ready to stop.

You can also let your audience know the end is in sight by your manner of delivery. The conclusion is the climax of a speech. A speaker who has carefully built to a peak of interest and involvement will not need to say anything like "in conclusion." By use of the voice—its tone, pacing, intonation, and rhythm—a speaker can build the momentum of a speech so there is no doubt when it is over.

crescendo ending
A conclusion in which the speech builds to a zenith of power and intensity.

One method of doing this has been likened to a musical crescendo. As in a symphony in which one instrument after another joins in until the entire orchestra is playing, the speech builds in force until it reaches a zenith of power and intensity.[4] (This does *not* mean simply getting louder and louder. It is a combination of many things, including vocal pitch, choice of words, dramatic content, gestures, pauses—and possibly loudness.)

A superb example of this method is the memorable conclusion to Martin Luther King's "I've Been to the Mountaintop," the speech he delivered the night before he was assassinated in April 1968. Speaking to an audience of 2,000 people in Memphis, Tennessee, he ended his speech with a stirring declaration that the civil rights movement would succeed despite the many threats on his life:

> Like anybody, I would like to live a long life. Longevity has its place, but I'm not concerned about that now. I just want to do God's will, and he's allowed me to go up to the mountain, and I've looked over and I've seen the Promised Land. I may not get there with you, but I want you to know tonight that we as a people will get to the Promised Land. So I'm happy tonight. I'm not worried about anything; I'm not fearing any man. Mine eyes have seen the glory of the coming of the Lord.

CD 1: VIDEO 9.4
View the ending of Martin Luther King's "I've Been to the Mountaintop."

Another effective method might be compared to the dissolve ending of a concert song that evokes deep emotions: "The song seems to fade away while the light on the singer shrinks gradually to a smaller and smaller circle until it lights only the face, then the eyes. Finally, it is a pinpoint, and disappears with the last note of the song."[5] Here is a speech ending that does much the same thing. It is from General Douglas MacArthur's moving farewell to the cadets at the U.S. Military Academy:

dissolve ending
A conclusion that generates emotional appeal by fading step-by-step to a dramatic final statement.

> In my dreams I hear again the crash of guns, the rattle of musketry, the strange, mournful mutter of the battlefield. But in the evening of my memory always I come back to West Point. Always there echoes and re-echoes: duty, honor, country.
>
> Today marks my final roll call with you. But I want you to know that when I cross the river, my last conscious thoughts will be of the Corps, and the Corps, and the Corps.
>
> I bid you farewell.

The final words fade like the spotlight, bringing the speech to an emotional close.

The conclusion is your last chance to drive home your ideas. Successful speakers such as Michigan Governor Jennifer Granholm craft their endings with great care to leave a strong final impression.

ONLINE LEARNING CENTER

To read these speeches by King and MacArthur, log on to the Top 100 American Speeches of the 20th Century at www.mhhe.com/lucas9.

You may think that you couldn't possibly end a speech with that much pathos—and you'd be right. MacArthur was an eloquent speaker discussing a grave issue with extraordinary poignance. This combination rarely occurs. But that doesn't mean you can't use the dissolve ending effectively. One student used it with great effect in a speech about the immigrant experience in the United States. During the body of the speech, the student spoke about the numbers of immigrants and the challenges they faced once they arrived. Then, in her conclusion, she created a moving dissolve ending by evoking the emotional images of her grandfather's arrival in the United States:

> On a recent trip to Ellis Island, where my grandfather first stepped on American soil, I saw his name etched into the wall along with the names of tens of thousands of other immigrants. I saw the entry hall where he lined up to process his forms. I saw the room where he underwent a physical examination. I sensed the fear and the insecurity he must have felt. But I could also sense his excitement as he looked forward to life in a land of opportunity—a land he came to think of as home.

Both the crescendo and the dissolve endings must be worked out with great care. Practice until you get the words and the timing just right. The benefits will be well worth your time.

Reinforce the Central Idea

The second major function of a conclusion is to reinforce the audience's understanding of, or commitment to, the central idea. There are many ways to do this. Here are the ones you are most likely to use.

Summarize Your Speech

Restating the main points is the easiest way to end a speech. One student used this technique effectively in his persuasive speech about the AIDS epidemic in Africa:

> In conclusion, we have seen that the AIDS epidemic is having a devastating effect on African society. An entire adult generation is slowly being wiped out. An entirely new generation of AIDS orphans is being created. Governments in the nations most afflicted have neither the resources nor the expertise to counter the epidemic. Many African economies are being crippled by the loss of people in the workplace.
>
> Before it's too late, the United Nations and developed countries need to increase their efforts to halt the epidemic and bring it under control. The lives and well-being of tens of millions of people hang in the balance.

CD 1: VIDEO 9.5

View the conclusion of "AIDS in Africa: A World Crisis."

The value of a summary is that it explicitly restates the central idea and main points one last time. But as we shall see, there are more imaginative and compelling ways to end a speech. They can be used in combination with a summary or, at times, in place of it.

End with a Quotation

A quotation is one of the most common and effective devices to conclude a speech. Here is a fine example, from a speech on the misuse of television advertisements in political campaigns:

> We cannot ignore the evils of television commercials in which candidates for the highest offices are sold to the voters in 30-second spots. These ads cheapen the elective process and degrade our political institutions. In the words of historian Arthur Schlesinger, Jr., "You cannot merchandise candidates like soap and hope to preserve a rational democracy."

The closing quotation is particularly good because its urgency is exactly suited to the speech. When you run across a *brief* quotation that so perfectly captures your central idea, keep it in mind as a possible conclusion.

Make a Dramatic Statement

Rather than using a quotation to give your conclusion force and vitality, you may want to devise your own dramatic statement. Some speeches have become famous because of their powerful closing lines. One is Patrick Henry's legendary "Liberty or Death" oration. It takes its name from the final sentences Henry uttered on March 23, 1775, as he exhorted his audience to resist British tyranny:

> Is life so dear, or peace so sweet, as to be purchased at the price of chains and slavery? Forbid it, Almighty God! I know not what course others may take; but as for me, give me liberty, or give me death.

Although your classroom speeches are not likely to become famous, you can still rivet your listeners—as Henry did—with a dramatic concluding statement. What follows is a particularly striking example, from a speech on suicide prevention. Throughout the speech, the student referred to a friend who had tried to commit suicide the previous year. Then, in the conclusion, she said:

> My friend is back in school, participating in activities she never did before—and enjoying it. I'm happy and proud to say that she's still fighting for her life and even happier that she failed to kill herself. Otherwise, I wouldn't be here today trying to help you. You see, I am my "friend," and I'm more than glad to say, I've made it.

As you can imagine, the audience was stunned. The closing lines brought the speech to a dramatic conclusion.

Here is another example of the same technique—this time from a less unusual situation:

> So there you have it—a rundown on the use and enjoyment of a home aquarium. I suppose some people will say that fish are not for them. But picture this: You have invited a special friend over for dinner. The dishes are soaking in the sink. The stereo is whispering softly. The lights are out except for the one on the aquarium. There are only the two of you and the fish. And they won't say a word!

This conclusion works because it takes the listener slightly by surprise and yet seems exactly right. Here the speaker made it even more effective by pausing just a moment before the last words and by using her voice to give them just the right inflection.

Refer to the Introduction

An excellent way to give your speech psychological unity is to conclude by referring to ideas in the introduction. This is an easy technique to use, and it may give your speech an extra touch of class. Here is how one student used the method in her speech about the Special Olympics:

Introduction: In Seattle, nine young athletes assembled at the starting line for the 100-yard dash. At the gun, they all started off—not exactly in a dash, but with a desire to run the race to the finish and win. All except one little boy who stumbled on the asphalt, tumbled over a couple of times, and began to cry. The other runners heard the boy cry. They stopped; they looked back. Then they all went back to the boy's side—every single one of them. One girl with Down syndrome kissed him and said, "This will make it better." Then all nine linked arms and walked to the finish line—together.

These athletes were not competing on national television; they were not sponsored or idolized. But they were given an opportunity to flourish under the glow of their own spotlights, to feel the brush of the ribbon cross their chests as they ran through their own finish line in their own Olympics—the Special Olympics.

In the body of her speech, the student explained the origins of the Special Olympics, the need for volunteers, and its benefits for athletes and volunteers

SPEECH CONCLUSION CHECKLIST

yes	no	
☐	☐	1. Do I signal that my speech is coming to an end?
☐	☐	2. Do I reinforce my central idea by (check all that apply):
☐	☐	Summarizing the main points of my speech
☐	☐	Ending with a quotation
☐	☐	Making a dramatic statement
☐	☐	Referring to the introduction
☐	☐	3. Is the conclusion limited to 5–10 percent of my entire speech?
☐	☐	4. Have I worked out the language of my conclusion in detail?
☐	☐	5. Have I practiced the delivery of my conclusion so I can present it fluently, confidently, and with strong eye contact?

CD 1: SPEECH CHECKLIST

You can print a copy of this checklist from the CD-ROM.

alike. She also called on members of the audience to become volunteers in whatever capacity and for whatever amount of time they could afford. Then, in her closing words, she tied the whole speech together by returning to the story described in her introduction:

Conclusion: Remember the nine children I mentioned at the beginning of this speech. Think of their happiness and their support for one another. Think of how much they gained from running in that race. And think how you can help others experience the same benefits as they strive to fulfill the motto of the Special Olympics: "Let me win. But if I can't win, let me be brave in the attempt."

CD 1: VIDEO 9.6

View the beginning and ending of "Making a Difference Through the Special Olympics."

Summarizing the speech, ending with a quotation, making a dramatic statement, referring to the introduction—all these techniques can be used separately. But you have probably noticed that speakers often combine two or more in their conclusions. Actually, all four techniques can be fused into one—for example, a dramatic quotation that summarizes the central idea while referring to the introduction.

One other concluding technique is making a direct appeal to your audience for action. This technique applies only to a particular type of persuasive speech, however, and will be discussed in Chapter 15. The four methods covered in this chapter are appropriate for all kinds of speeches and occasions.

Sample Conclusion with Commentary

How do you fit these methods together to make a conclusion? Here is an example, from the speech about bone marrow transplants whose introduction we looked at earlier (page 241).

Commentary	Conclusion
The speaker gives an excellent summary of her speech. This is particularly important when speaking to inform because it gives you one last chance to make sure the audience remembers your main points.	We have seen, then, that becoming a bone marrow donor is safe and relatively painless. We have also seen the immense benefits to the people who receive bone marrow transplants. Finally, we have seen how donors and recipients are matched up through a national network of bone marrow organizations.
By referring to Greg, whom she had mentioned in her introduction, the speaker unifies the entire speech. The quotation from Greg and the speaker's final sentence end the speech on a strong note.	It is now more than three years since Greg received his bone marrow transplant. In that time, he has changed from a very sick young boy to a busy, healthy, active young man. Greg says of his donor, "Without her, I wouldn't be here today. I owe my whole life, and everything I ever accomplish, to her." Through bone marrow donation, all of us have the opportunity to make that kind of contribution.

Tips for Preparing the Conclusion

1. As with the introduction, keep an eye out for possible concluding materials as you research and develop the speech.

2. Conclude with a bang, not a whimper. Be creative in devising a conclusion that hits the hearts and minds of your audience. Work on several possible endings, and select the one that seems likely to have the greatest impact.

3. Don't be long-winded. The conclusion will normally make up no more than about 5 to 10 percent of your speech. Nothing aggravates audiences more than a speaker who says "In conclusion" and then drones on interminably.

4. Don't leave anything in your conclusion to chance. Work it out in detail, and give yourself plenty of time to practice delivering it. Many students like to write out the conclusion word for word to guarantee it is just right. If you do this, make sure you can present it smoothly, confidently, and with feeling—without relying on your notes or sounding wooden. Make your last impression as forceful and as favorable as you can.

Summary

First impressions are important. So are final impressions. This is why speeches need strong introductions and conclusions.

In most speech situations you need to accomplish four objectives with your introduction—get the attention and interest of the audience, reveal the topic of your speech, establish your credibility and goodwill, and preview the body of the speech. Gaining attention and interest can be done in several ways. You can show the importance of your topic, especially as it relates to your audience. You can startle or question your audience or arouse their curiosity. You can begin with a quotation or a story.

Be sure to state the topic of your speech clearly in your introduction; otherwise, your audience may be confused and wonder where the speech is going. Establishing credibility means that you tell the audience why you are qualified to speak on the topic at hand; establishing goodwill, although less important for classroom speeches than for speeches outside the classroom, may be necessary if your point of view is unpopular. Previewing the body of the speech helps the audience listen effectively and provides a smooth lead-in to the body of the speech.

The conclusion of a speech is particularly important, because the final impression is often what will stick in your listeners' minds. The conclusion has two major objectives—to let the audience know you are ending the speech, and to reinforce their understanding of, or commitment to, your central idea. Too sudden an ending may leave your audience puzzled; it is always a good idea to alert them that you are finishing. You can do this either by your words or by your manner of delivery.

You can use a number of techniques to reinforce your central idea in the conclusion. They include summarizing the speech, ending with a pertinent quotation, making a dramatic statement, and referring to the introduction. Sometimes you may want to combine two or more of these techniques. Be creative in devising a vivid, forceful conclusion.

Key Terms

rhetorical question (233)
credibility (237)
goodwill (238)
preview statement (239)
crescendo ending (243)
dissolve ending (243)

ONLINE LEARNING CENTER

Review these terms by doing the Chapter 9 crossword puzzle at www.mhhe.com/lucas9.

Review Questions

After reading this chapter, you should be able to answer the following questions:

1. What are four objectives of a speech introduction?
2. What are seven methods you can use in the introduction to get the attention and interest of your audience?
3. Why is it important to establish your credibility at the beginning of your speech?
4. What is a preview statement? Why should you nearly always include a preview statement in the introduction of your speech?

CD 1: STUDY QUESTIONS

For further review, go to the Study Questions for this chapter.

5. What are five tips for preparing your introduction?
6. What are the major functions of a speech conclusion?
7. What are two ways you can signal the end of your speech?
8. What are four ways to reinforce the central idea when concluding your speech?
9. What are four tips for preparing your conclusion?

Exercises for Critical Thinking

1. Here are six speech topics. Explain how you might relate each to your classmates in the introduction of a speech.

Social Security	laughter
illiteracy	steroids
soap operas	blood donation

2. Think of a speech topic (preferably one for your next speech in class). Create an introduction for a speech dealing with any aspect of the topic you wish. In your introduction be sure to gain the attention of the audience, to reveal the topic and relate it to the audience, to establish your credibility, and to preview the body of the speech.
3. Using the same topic as in Exercise 2, create a speech conclusion. Be sure to let your audience know the speech is ending, to reinforce the central idea, and to make the conclusion vivid and memorable.

Applying the POWER of PUBLIC SPEAKING

Your degree in civil engineering has served you well and you are now the chief city planner for a major metropolis. After studying the issue for more than a year, you and the planning commission have decided that the best way to relieve the city's growing traffic congestion is to build a new downtown freeway. Unfortunately, there is no way to build the freeway without knocking down a number of houses and businesses. You are not happy about this, and you know it will create difficulty for the people affected, but your research and computer simulations show that it is by far the most effective long-range option for improving the city's traffic flow.

Not surprisingly, the neighborhood association that represents the area through which you plan to build the freeway has expressed a number of concerns about the proposal. Because of your excellent public speaking skills, you have been chosen to represent the city at a meeting of the neighborhood association. Your job at the meeting will be to address the audience's concerns and provide a convincing explanation of the city's decision to build the freeway. You know that if your speech is to be persuasive, you must use the introduction to establish your credibility and goodwill so your listeners will be willing to listen receptively to what you say in the body.

Write a draft of your introduction. In it be sure to address all four functions of a speech introduction discussed in this chapter.

Notes

[1]Susan Paddack, "Campaigning for Peace: Preventing Youth Violence in America," *Vital Speeches,* 67 (2001), pp. 468–470.

[2]For research on the importance of goodwill to speakers in a variety of situations, see James C. McCroskey and Jason J. Teven, "Goodwill: A Reexamination of the Construct and Its Measurement," *Communication Monographs,* 66 (1999), pp. 90–103.

[3]Tony White, "Smart Medicine Is Coming: Making Intelligent Choices," *Vital Speeches,* 68 (2002), p. 326.

[4]Dorothy Sarnoff, *Speech Can Change Your Life* (Garden City, NY: Doubleday, 1970), p. 189.

[5]Sarnoff, *Speech Can Change Your Life,* p. 190.

CHAPTER TEN

Outlining the Speech

Think what might happen if you tried to build a house without a floor plan or an architect's blueprint. You build the kitchen next to the driveway to make it convenient for carrying in groceries. But the dining room turns up at the other end of the house. When you cook and serve a meal, you have to run with the plates to keep the food from getting cold. You put the bathroom at the head of the stairs to make it accessible to visitors. But the door opens in such a way that the unwary guest is catapulted down the steps. You think it's a wonderful idea to have almost no interior walls. After all, the modern living space is supposed to be free and open. But when the first snowfall comes, your (unsupported) roof collapses.

Plans and blueprints are essential to architecture. So, too, are outlines essential to effective speeches. An outline is like a blueprint for your speech. It allows you to see the full scope and content of your speech at a glance. By outlining, you can judge whether each part of the speech is fully developed, whether you have adequate supporting materials for your main points, and whether the main points are properly balanced. An outline helps you make sure that related items are together, that ideas flow from one to another, that the structure of your speech will "stand up"—and not collapse.

Probably you will use two kinds of outlines for your speeches—one very detailed, for the planning stage, and one very brief, for the delivery of the speech.

The Preparation Outline

The preparation outline is just what its name implies—an outline that helps you prepare the speech. Writing a preparation outline means actually putting your speech together. It is the stage at which you decide what you will say in the introduction, how you will organize the main points and supporting materials in the body of the speech, and what you will say in the conclusion.

Guidelines for the Preparation Outline

preparation outline
A detailed outline developed during the process of speech preparation that includes the title, specific purpose, central idea, introduction, main points, subpoints, connectives, conclusion, and bibliography of a speech.

Over the years, a relatively uniform system for preparation outlines has developed. It is explained below and is exemplified in the sample outline on pages 260–262. You should check with your teacher to see exactly what format you are to follow.

State the Specific Purpose of Your Speech

The specific purpose statement should be a separate unit that comes before the text of the outline itself. Including the specific purpose with the outline makes it easier to assess how well you have constructed the speech to accomplish your purpose.

Identify the Central Idea

Some teachers prefer that the central idea be given immediately after the purpose statement. Others prefer that it be given and identified in the text of the outline itself. Check to see which your teacher wants.

Label the Introduction, Body, and Conclusion

If you label the parts of your speech, you will be sure that you indeed *have* an introduction and conclusion and have accomplished the essential objectives of each. Usually the names of the speech parts are placed in the middle of the page or in the far left margin. They are technical labels only and are not included in the system of symbolization used to identify main points and supporting materials.

Use a Consistent Pattern of Symbolization and Indentation

In the most common system of outlining, main points are identified by Roman numerals and are indented equally so as to be aligned down the page. Subpoints (components of the main points) are identified by capital letters and are also indented equally so as to be aligned with each other. Beyond this, there may be sub-subpoints and even sub-sub-subpoints. For example:

I. Main point
    A. Subpoint
    B. Subpoint
        1. Sub-subpoint
        2. Sub-subpoint
            a. Sub-sub-subpoint
            b. Sub-sub-subpoint
II. Main point
    A. Subpoint
        1. Sub-subpoint
        2. Sub-subpoint
    B. Subpoint

The clear *visual framework* of this outline immediately shows the relationships among the ideas of the speech. The most important ideas (main points) are farthest to the left. Less important ideas (subpoints, sub-subpoints, and so on) are progressively farther to the right. This pattern reveals the structure of your entire speech.

visual framework
The pattern of symbolization and indentation in a speech outline that shows the relationships among the speaker's ideas.

Once you have organized the body of your speech (see Chapter 8), you should have identified the main points. You need only flesh out your outline with subpoints and sub-subpoints, as necessary, to support the main points. But suppose, as sometimes happens, you find yourself with a list of statements and are not sure which are main points, which are subpoints, and so forth. Such a list might look like this:

There were 13 people at the Last Supper—Jesus and his 12 disciples.

One of the most common sources of superstition is numbers.

In the United States, 13 is often omitted in the floor numbering of hotels and skyscrapers.

The number 13 has meant bad luck as long as anyone can remember.

Which statement is the main point? The second statement ("One of the most common sources of superstition is numbers"), which is broader in scope than any of the other statements. This would be one of the main ideas of your speech. The fourth statement is the subpoint; it immediately supports the main point. The other two statements are sub-subpoints; they illustrate the subpoint. Rearranged properly, they look like this:

I. One of the most common sources of superstition is numbers.
  A. The number 13 has meant bad luck as long as anyone can remember.
    1. There were 13 people at the Last Supper—Jesus and his 12 disciples.
    2. In the United States, 13 is often omitted in the floor numbering of hotels and skyscrapers.

Above all, remember that all points at the same level should immediately support the point that is just above and one notch to the left in your outline. If this sounds confusing, think of it as a business organization chart:

I. President
  A. Vice president—Operations
    1. Manager—Domestic Operations
      a. Assistant manager—East
      b. Assistant manager—West
    2. Manager—Foreign Operations
      a. Assistant manager—Europe and Asia
      b. Assistant manager—Africa
      c. Assistant manager—Americas
  B. Vice president—Administration
    1. Manager—Finance
    2. Manager—Personnel

As you can see, every person on this chart reports to the person who is above and one notch to the left—except, of course, the president, who is the "main point."

State Main Points and Subpoints in Full Sentences

Below are two sets of main points and subpoints for the same speech on the life of Martin Luther King.

Ineffective	More Effective
I. Montgomery	I. King began his civil rights career in the Montgomery bus boycott of 1955–1956.
II. 1960s	II. King's greatest triumphs came during the early 1960s.
A. Birmingham	A. In 1963 he campaigned against segregation in Birmingham, Alabama.

As blueprints are essential to architecture, so outlines are essential to speechmaking. Developing an outline helps ensure that the structure of your speech is clear and coherent.

B. March	B. Later that year he participated in the famous march on Washington, D.C.
1. 200,000	1. More than 200,000 people took part.
2. "Dream"	2. King gave his "I Have a Dream" speech.
C. Prize	C. In 1964 he received the Nobel Peace Prize.
III. Final years	III. King faced great turmoil during his final years.
A. Criticized	A. He was criticized by more militant blacks for being nonviolent.
B. Vietnam	B. He protested against the war in Vietnam.
C. Assassination	C. He was assassinated in Memphis, Tennessee, on April 4, 1968.

The sample at left might serve adequately as a speaking outline, but it is virtually useless as a preparation outline. It gives only vague labels rather than distinct ideas. It does not indicate clearly the content of the main points and subpoints. Nor does it reveal whether the speaker has thought out his or her ideas. But there is no concern about any of these matters with the outline on the right.

In sum, a skimpy preparation outline is of little value. Stating your main points and subpoints in full sentences will ensure that you develop your ideas fully.

Label Transitions, Internal Summaries, and Internal Previews

One way to make sure you have strong transitions, internal summaries, and internal previews is to include them in the preparation outline. Usually they are not incorporated into the system of symbolization and indentation, but are labeled separately and inserted in the outline where they will appear in the speech.

Attach a Bibliography

bibliography
A list of all the sources used in preparing a speech.

You should include with the outline a list of the sources you consulted in preparing the speech. The bibliography will show all the books, magazines, newspapers, and Internet sources you consulted, as well as any interviews or field research you conducted.

The two major bibliographic formats are those developed by the Modern Language Association (MLA) and the American Psychological Association (APA). Both are widely used by communication scholars; ask your instructor which he or she prefers. No matter which format you adopt, make sure your statement of sources is clear, accurate, and consistent. For help, check the Bibliography Formats on CD 1, where you will find a complete set of MLA and APA sample citations for a wide range of sources, from books and articles to personal interviews and Internet materials.

CD 1: BIBLIOGRAPHY FORMATS

Go to the Bibliography Formats for a complete set of sample MLA and APA citations.

Give Your Speech a Title, If One Is Desired

In the classroom you probably do not need a title for your speech unless your teacher requires one. In some other situations, however, a speech title is necessary—as when the speech is publicized in advance, when the group inviting you to speak requests a title, or when the speech is going to be published. Whatever the reason, if you do decide to use a title, it should (1) be brief, (2) attract the attention of your audience, and (3) encapsulate the main thrust of your speech.

A good title need not have what Madison Avenue would call "sex appeal"—lots of glitter and pizzazz. By the same token, there is certainly nothing wrong with a catchy title—as long as it is germane to the speech. Here are two groups of titles. Those on the left are straightforward and descriptive. Those on the right are figurative alternatives to the ones on the left.

Group I	Group II
Unsafe Drinking Water	Toxins on Tap
Living with Deafness	The Sounds of Silence
The Rage to Diet	The Art of Wishful Shrinking
The United States Mint	The Buck Starts Here
Gambling Addiction	Against All Odds

Which group do you prefer? Neither is perfect. There are advantages and disadvantages to both. Those in the first group clearly reveal the topic

PREPARATION OUTLINE CHECKLIST

yes	no	
☐	☐	1. Does my speech have a title, if one is required?
☐	☐	2. Do I state the specific purpose before the text of the outline itself?
☐	☐	3. Do I state the central idea before the text of the outline itself?
☐	☐	4. Are the introduction, body, and conclusion clearly labeled?
☐	☐	5. Are main points and subpoints written in full sentences?
☐	☐	6. Are transitions, internal summaries, and internal previews clearly labeled?
☐	☐	7. Does the outline follow a consistent pattern of symbolization and indentation?
☐	☐	8. Does the outline provide a clear visual framework that shows the relationships among the ideas of my speech?
☐	☐	9. Does the bibliography identify all the sources I consulted in preparing the outline?
☐	☐	10. Does the bibliography follow the format required by my instructor?

CD 1: SPEECH CHECKLIST

You can print a copy of this checklist from the CD-ROM.

of the speech, but they are not as provocative as those in the second group. Those in the second group are sure to arouse interest, but they do not give as clear an idea of what the speeches are about.

There is one other kind of title you should consider—the question. Phrasing your title as a question can be both descriptive and provocative. Using this method, we can construct a third set of titles combining the virtues of groups I and II:

Group III

Is Your Water Safe to Drink?

Can You See What I'm Saying?

Diets: How Effective Are They?

Where Is Making Money a Way of Life?

Do You Really Think You Can Beat the Odds?

CD 1: SPEECH OUTLINER

The Speech Outliner will guide you through the steps in creating a preparation outline.

Sometimes you will choose a title for your speech very early. At other times you may not find one you like until the last minute. Either way, try to be resourceful about creating titles for your speeches. Experiment with several and choose the one that seems most appropriate.

Sample Preparation Outline with Commentary

The following outline for a six-minute informative speech illustrates the principles just discussed. The commentary explains the procedures used in organizing the speech and writing the outline. (Check with your teacher to see if she or he wants you to include a title with your outline.)

Panic Attacks

Commentary	*Outline*
Stating your specific purpose and central idea as separate units before the text of the outline makes it easier to judge how well you have constructed the outline to achieve your purpose and to communicate your central idea.	*Specific Purpose*: To inform my audience about the nature, extent, and symptoms of panic attacks. *Central Idea*: Panic attacks are serious medical conditions whose fearful symptoms affect millions of people.
Labeling the introduction marks it as a distinct section that plays a special role in the speech	*Introduction*
The opening story gets attention and, as it progresses, reveals the topic of the speech.	I. I can't breathe, my arms are tingling, I'm really dizzy, and it feels as if my heart is about to fly out of my chest. II. When this happened to me three years ago at an outdoor concert, I was really frightened. A. At the time, I had no idea what was going on. B. My doctor told me later that I had experienced a panic attack.
Here the speaker establishes her credibility and previews the main points to be discussed in the body of the speech.	III. I have learned a lot about my condition during the past three years, and I did additional research for this speech. IV. Today I would like to inform you about the nature of panic attacks, the people affected most often by them, and the options for treatment.
Including transitions ensures that the speaker has worked out how to connect one idea to the next. Notice that the transition is not included in the system of symbolization and indentation used for the rest of the speech.	(Transition: Let's start with the nature of panic attacks.)

Labeling the body marks it as a distinct part of the speech

Body

Main point I is phrased as a full sentence. As the outline progresses, notice that the main points are arranged in topical order.

I. Panic attacks are a severe medical condition with a number of physical and mental symptoms.
   A. As defined by the National Institute of Mental Health, panic attacks involve "unexpected and repeated episodes of intense fear accompanied by physical symptoms."
      1. The attacks usually come out of nowhere and strike when least expected.
      2. Their length can vary from a few minutes to several hours.

The two subpoints of main point I are shown by the capital letters A and B and are written out in full sentences to ensure that the speaker has thought them out fully. Points below the level of subpoint are indicated by Arabic numerals and lowercase letters. Sometimes they are not written as full sentences. Check to see what your teacher prefers.

   B. There are a number of symptoms common to most panic attacks.
      1. Physical symptoms include a pounding heart, shortness of breath, lightheadedness, and numbness or tingling sensations in the arms and legs.
      2. Mental symptoms include acute fear, a sense of disaster or helplessness, and a feeling of being detached from one's own body.

The transition shows how the speaker will move from main point I to main point II.

(*Transition*: Now that you know something about the nature of panic attacks, let's look at how widespread they are.)

Like main point I, main point II is phrased as a full sentence.

The progressive indentation shows visually the relationships among main points, subpoints, and sub-subpoints.

II. Panic attacks affect millions of people.
   A. According to the American Psychiatric Association, 2.5 million Americans suffer from panic attacks.
   B. Some groups have a higher incidence of panic attacks than do other groups.
      1. The National Institute of Mental Health reports that panic attacks strike women twice as often as men.
      2. Half the people who suffer from panic attacks develop symptoms before the age of 24.

The transition indicates that the speaker is moving to her next main point.

(*Transition*: Given the severity of panic attacks, I'm sure you are wondering how they can be treated.)

This main point, like the first two, is stated as a full sentence.

III. There are two major options for treating panic attacks.
   A. One option is medication.
      1. Antidepressants are the most frequently prescribed medication for panic attacks.
      2. They rearrange the brain's chemical levels so as to get rid of unwanted fear responses.

Notice the pattern of subordination in this section. Subpoint B notes that cognitive-behavioral therapy is one of the options for treating panic attacks. Sub-subpoint 1 identifies the kinds of techniques involved in this therapy. Because items a and b expand upon the techniques point, they are subordinated to it.

   B. Another option is cognitive-behavioral therapy.
      1. This therapy involves techniques that help people with panic attacks gain control of their symptoms and feelings.
         a. Some techniques involve breathing exercises.
         b. Other techniques target thought patterns that can trigger panic attacks.

2. According to Dr. David Carbonell, author of the *Panic Attacks Workbook,* cognitive-behavioral therapy can be highly effective.

Labeling the conclusion marks it as a distinct part of the speech.

Conclusion

Summarizing the main points is usually standard procedure in an informative speech.

I. As we have seen, panic attacks affect millions of people.
II. Fortunately, there are treatment options to help prevent panic attacks and to deal with them when they occur.

Referring back to the speaker's personal experience mentioned in the introduction gives the speech a sense of unity and provides an effective ending.

III. In my case, the combination of medication and cognitive-behavioral therapy has been extremely helpful.
IV. I don't know if I will ever be completely free of panic attacks, but at least I understand now what they are and what I can do about them.

This is the final bibliography. It lists the sources actually used in writing the speech and is shorter than the preliminary bibliography compiled in the early stages of research. (See Chapter 6 for a discussion of the preliminary bibliography.)

This bibliography follows the Modern Language Association (MLA) format. Check with your instructor to see what format you should use for your bibliography.

Bibliography

Books

Carbonell, David. *Panic Attacks Workbook: A Guided Program for Breaking the Panic Cycle*. Berkeley, CA: Ulysses Press, 2004.

Swede, Shirley, and Jaffe Seymour. *The Panic Attack Recovery Book,* rev. ed. New York: New American Library, 2001.

Articles

Leskin, Gregory A., and Sheikh, Javaid I. "Gender Differences in Panic Disorders." *Psychiatric Times* Jan. 2004: 65.

Wilkinson, Donna. "Anxiety Disorders: Living on a Thin Line." *The New York Times* 5 June 2005: A9.

Internet Sources

American Psychiatric Association. "Panic Disorder." 27 Jan. 2005. 26 Sept. 2005 <www.psych.org/public_info/panic.cfm>.

National Institute of Mental Health. "Panic Disorder." 2 Feb. 2005. 26 Sept. 2005 <www.nimh.nih.gov/HealthInformation/panicmenu.cfm>.

The Speaking Outline

"I was never so excited by public speaking before in my life," wrote one listener in 1820 after listening to Daniel Webster. "Three or four times I thought my temples would burst with the gush of blood. . . . I was beside myself, and am so still."[1]

Such reactions were not unusual among Webster's audiences. He thrilled two generations of Americans with his masterful orations. Incredible as it seems today, he did so while speaking for three, four, even five hours at a time. Equally incredible, he often spoke without using any notes! A reporter once asked how he managed this. "It is my memory," Webster said. "I can prepare a speech, revise and correct it in my memory, then deliver the corrected speech exactly as finished."[2]

Few people have Webster's remarkable powers of memory. Fortunately, it is no longer customary to speak from memory. Today most people speak extemporaneously—which means the speech is thoroughly prepared and carefully practiced in advance, but much of the exact wording is selected while the speech is being delivered (see Chapter 12). Your speeches will probably be of this type. You should know, then, about the *speaking outline*—the most widely recommended form of notes for extemporaneous speeches.

The aim of a speaking outline is to help you remember what you want to say. In some ways it is a condensed version of your preparation outline. It should contain key words or phrases to jog your memory, as well as essential statistics and quotations that you don't want to risk forgetting. But it should also include material *not* in your preparation outline—especially cues to direct and sharpen your delivery.

speaking outline
A brief outline used to jog a speaker's memory during the presentation of a speech.

Most speakers develop their own variations on the speaking outline. As you acquire more experience, you, too, should feel free to experiment. But for now, your best bet is to follow the basic guidelines below and to use the sample speaking outline on pages 266–267 as your model.

Guidelines for the Speaking Outline

Follow the Visual Framework Used in the Preparation Outline

Your speaking outline should use the same visual framework—the same symbols and the same pattern of indentation—as your preparation outline. This will make it much easier to prepare the speaking outline. More important, it will allow you to see instantly where you are in the speech at any given moment while you are speaking. You will find this a great advantage. As you speak, you will look down at your outline periodically to make sure you are covering the right ideas in the right order. It will be of little help if you have to hunt around to find where you are every time you look down.

Compare the following two versions of a partial speaking outline. They are from an informative speech about the history of the U.S. women's rights movement.

Accomplished speakers such as former New York Mayor Rudy Giuliani often use a brief set of notes, which allows them to maintain eye contact and to communicate directly with the audience.

Ineffective

I. 1840–1860
A. World Anti-Slavery Convention
B. Seneca Falls convention
1. Lucretia Mott
2. Elizabeth Cady Stanton
3. Declaration of Sentiments
II. 1900–1920
A. National American Woman Suffrage Association
1. Founding
2. Objectives
B. Nineteenth Amendment
1. Campaign
2. Ratification

More Effective

I. 1840–1860
   A. World Anti-Slavery Convention
   B. Seneca Falls convention
      1. Lucretia Mott
      2. Elizabeth Cady Stanton
      3. Declaration of Sentiments
II. 1900–1920
   A. National American Woman Suffrage Association
      1. Founding
      2. Objectives
   B. Nineteenth Amendment
      1. Campaign
      2. Ratification

The wording of both outlines is exactly the same. But the visual framework of the one on the right makes it easier to take in at a glance and reduces the odds of the speaker losing her or his place.

Make Sure the Outline Is Legible

You would be surprised how many students try to speak from messy, scribbled notes that would be hard to decipher at leisure, much less under the pressures of a speech situation. Your speaking outline is all but worthless unless it is instantly readable at a distance. When you make your outline, use large lettering, leave extra space between lines, provide ample margins, and write or type on one side of the paper only.

Some speakers put their notes on index cards. Most find the 3 × 5 size too cramped and prefer the 4 × 6 or 5 × 8 size instead. Other people write their speaking outlines on regular paper. Either practice is fine, as long as your notes are immediately legible to you while you are speaking.

Keep the Outline as Brief as Possible

If your notes are too detailed, you will have difficulty maintaining eye contact with your audience. A detailed outline will tempt you to look at it far too often, as one student discovered:

Angela Granato was speaking about the benefits of Pilates. She had prepared the speech thoroughly and practiced it until it was nearly perfect. But when she delivered the speech in class, she referred constantly to her detailed notes. As a result, her delivery was choppy and strained. After the speech, Angela's classmates remarked on how often she had looked at her notes, and she was amazed. "I didn't even know I was doing it," she said. "Most of the time I wasn't even paying attention to the outline. I knew the speech cold."

Many students have had the same experience. Having lots of notes is a psychological security blanket against the possibility that something will go terribly wrong. The feeling seems to be, "As long as I have plenty of notes, disaster will not strike." In fact, most beginning speakers use far too many notes. Like Angela, they find they don't need all of them to remember the speech. They also discover that too many notes can actually interfere with good communication.

To guard against having too many notes, keep your speaking outline as brief as possible. It should contain key words or phrases to help you remember major points, subpoints, and connectives. If you are citing statistics, you will probably want to include them in your notes. Unless you are good at memorizing quotations, write them out fully as well. Finally, there may be two, three, or four key ideas whose wording is so important that you want to state them in simple complete sentences. The best rule is that your notes should be the *minimum* you need to jog your memory and keep you on track. At first you may find it risky to speak from a brief outline, but you will soon become more comfortable with it.

Give Yourself Cues for Delivering the Speech

A good speaking outline reminds you not only of *what* you want to say but also of *how* you want to say it. As you practice the speech, you will decide that certain ideas and phrases need special emphasis—that they should be spoken more loudly, softly, slowly, or rapidly than other parts of the speech. You will also determine how you want to pace the speech—how you will control its timing, rhythm, and momentum. But no matter how you work these things out ahead of time, no matter how often you practice, it is easy to forget them once you get up in front of an audience.

delivery cues
Directions in a speaking outline to help a speaker remember how she or he wants to deliver key parts of the speech.

The solution is to include in your speaking outline *delivery cues*—directions for delivering the speech. One way to do this is by underlining or otherwise highlighting key ideas that you want to be sure to emphasize. Then, when you reach them in the outline, you will be reminded to stress them. Another way is to jot down on the outline explicit cues such as "pause," "repeat," "slow down," "louder," and so forth. Both techniques are good aids for beginning speakers, but they are also used by most experienced speakers.

Sample Speaking Outline with Commentary

Below is a sample speaking outline for a six-minute informative talk about panic attacks. By comparing it with the preparation outline for the same speech on pages 260–262, you can see how a detailed preparation outline is transformed into a concise speaking outline.

Commentary	Outline
These comments remind the speaker to establish eye contact and not to race through the speech.	*Eye Contact!!* *Slow Down*
	I. Can't breathe, arms tingling, dizzy, heart flying.
The word "pause" reminds the speaker to pause after her opening lines.	—*Pause*—
Including the main ideas of the introduction helps keep the speaker on track at the start of the speech.	II. Happened three years ago—told later I had a panic attack. III. Learned about condition and researched for speech. IV. Today—nature of panic attacks, people affected, and treatment options. (Let's start with nature of panic attacks.)
It's usually a good idea to pause briefly before launching into the first main point. This is another way of signaling that you are moving from the introduction to the body.	—*Pause*—
Most speakers find it helpful to demarcate the body of the speech in the speaking outline as well as in the preparation outline.	*Body*
Quotations are usually written out in full in the speaking outline.	I. Severe condition with physical and mental symptoms. A. Defined by NIMH: "unexpected and repeated episodes of intense fear accompanied by physical symptoms." 1. Come out of nowhere. 2. Few minutes to several hours.
Notice how the body of the speech follows the same visual format as the preparation outline. This makes the outline easy to read at a glance.	B. Common symptoms. 1. Physical—heart, breath, dizziness, numbness or tingling. 2. Mental—fear, disaster or helplessness, detached from body.
Inserting transitions makes sure the speaker doesn't forget them.	(Now you know nature . . . look at people affected.)
Underlining reminds the speaker to stress key words or ideas.	II. Affect <u>millions</u> of people. A. American Psychiatric Assn—2.5 million. B. Groups with higher incidence. 1. NIMH: Women <u>twice as often</u> as men 2. Most people develop symptoms <u>before age 24.</u>

Throughout the outline, key words are used to jog the speaker's memory. Because the final wording of an extemporaneous speech is chosen at the moment of delivery, it will not be exactly the same as that in the preparation outline.

Sources of statistics or testimony should be included in the speaking outline to make sure the speaker identifies them during the speech.

It's usually a good idea to pause before entering the conclusion.

Most speakers label the conclusion in the speaking outline as well as in the preparation outline.

Including key ideas and phrases from the conclusion jogs the speaker's memory and ensures that the speech will end as planned.

(Given severity . . . wonder how treated.)

III. Two major options for treatment.
   A. Medication.
      1. Antidepressants most prescribed.
      2. Rearrange brain's chemical levels.
   B. Cognitive-behavioral therapy.
      1. Techniques to control symptoms and feelings.
         a. Breathing.
         b. Thought patterns.
      2. Effective says David Carbonall, author of *Panic Attacks Workbook*.

—*Pause*—

Conclusion

I. As we have seen, panic attacks affect millions of people.
II. Fortunately, there are treatments for preventing and dealing with attacks.
III. In my case, both medication and cognitive-behavioral therapy have helped.
IV. May never be free of attacks, but now I know what they are and what I can do about them.

Summary

Outlines are essential to effective speeches. By outlining, you make sure that related ideas are together, that your thoughts flow from one to another, and that the structure of your speech is coherent. You will probably use two kinds of outlines for your speeches—the detailed preparation outline and the brief speaking outline.

The preparation outline helps you prepare your speech. In this outline you state your specific purpose and central idea; label the introduction, body, and conclusion; and designate transitions, internal summaries, and internal previews. You should identify main points, subpoints, and sub-subpoints by a consistent pattern of symbolization and indentation. It is usually advisable to state at least main points and subpoints in full sentences. Your teacher may require a bibliography with your preparation outline.

The speaking outline consists of brief notes to help you while you deliver the speech. It should contain key words or phrases to jog your memory, as well as essential statistics and quotations. In making up your speaking outline, follow the same visual framework used in your preparation outline. Keep the speaking outline as brief as possible, and be sure it is legible. You can also give yourself cues for delivering the speech—when to speak more softly or more slowly, when to pause, and so forth.

Key Terms

ONLINE LEARNING CENTER

Review these terms by doing the Chapter 10 crossword puzzle at www.mhhe.com/lucas9.

preparation outline (254)
visual framework (255)
bibliography (258)
speaking outline (263)
delivery cues (265)

Review Questions

CD: STUDY QUESTIONS

For further review, go to the Study Questions for this chapter.

After reading this chapter, you should be able to answer the following questions:

1. Why is it important to outline your speeches?
2. What is a preparation outline? What are the eight guidelines discussed in the chapter for writing a preparation outline?
3. What is a speaking outline? What are four guidelines for your speaking outline?

Exercises for Critical Thinking

1. In the left-hand column below is a partially blank outline from a speech about Weblogs (blogs). In the right-hand column, arranged in random order, are the subpoints to fill in the outline. Choose the appropriate subpoint for each blank in the outline.

Outline

I. Blogs have become an important part of the Internet in recent years.
   A.
   B.
II. Blogs have acquired significant political and economic influence in a short period of time.
   A.
      1.
      2.
   B.
      1.
      2.

Subpoints

Bloggers helped turn Howard Dean into an early frontrunner for the 2004 Democratic nomination.

Large companies have begun paying bloggers to start word-of-mouth advertising.

As many as 10 million blogs have already been created.

The political influence of blogs was felt in the 2004 U.S. presidential campaign.

Small companies are starting their own blogs as promotional tools.

In addition, more than 40,000 new blogs are created every day.

Also in 2004, bloggers revealed that a CBS News story on President Bush's military service included falsified documents.

The economic influence of blogs has been recognized by large and small companies alike.

2. Following the format used in the sample preparation outline on pages 260–262, outline "Acupuncture: New Uses for an Ancient Remedy," the sample speech at the end of Chapter 14. Be sure to include a specific purpose statement; to identify the central idea; to label the introduction, body, and conclusion; to use a consistent pattern of symbolization and indentation; to state the main points and subpoints in full sentences; and to label transitions and internal summaries.

CD I: OUTLINE EXERCISES

Check your outlining skills by doing the Outline Exercises.

3. From the preparation outline you constructed in Exercise 2, create a speaking outline that you might use in delivering the speech. Follow the guidelines for a speaking outline discussed in this chapter.

Applying the POWER of PUBLIC SPEAKING

As the defense attorney in a car theft case, you need to prepare your closing argument to the jury before it begins its deliberations. After reviewing evidence from the trial, you decide to stress the following points to demonstrate the innocence of your client:

a. The stolen car was found abandoned three hours after the theft with the engine still warm; at the time the car was found, your client was at the airport to meet the flight of a friend who was flying into town.
b. Lab analysis of muddy shoe prints on the floor mat of the car indicates that the prints came from a size 13 shoe; your client wears a size 10.
c. Lab analysis shows the presence of cigarette smoke in the car, but your client does not smoke.
d. The only eyewitness to the crime, who was 50 feet from the car, said the thief "looked like" your client; yet the eyewitness admitted that at the time of the theft she was not wearing her corrective lenses, which had been prescribed for improving distance vision.
e. The car was stolen at about 1 P.M.; your client testified that he was in a small town 175 miles away at 11 A.M.
f. In a statement to police, the eyewitness described the thief as blond; your client has red hair.

As you work on the outline of your speech, you see that these points can be organized into three main points, each with two supporting points. Compose an outline that organizes the points in this manner.

Notes

[1]Robert T. Oliver, *History of Public Speaking in America* (Boston: Allyn and Bacon, 1965), p. 143.

[2]Oliver, *History of Public Speaking*, p. 145.

CHAPTER ELEVEN

Using Language

Language Is Important

Meanings of Words

Using Language Accurately

Using Language Clearly

Use Familiar Words

Choose Concrete Words

Eliminate Clutter

Using Language Vividly

Imagery

Rhythm

Using Language Appropriately

Appropriateness to the Occasion

Appropriateness to the Audience

Appropriateness to the Topic

Appropriateness to the Speaker

A Note on Inclusive Language

Have you ever played *Pictionary?* The point of the game is to draw words so people watching you can guess them. Some words are easy—"house," "bird," and "television," for instance. Even people without artistic talent can draw these in such a way that observers catch on immediately. But other kinds of words are more challenging. Try drawing "numb," "embarrass," or "dehydrated." The more abstract the word, the more difficult it is to represent visually. How would you draw "improvement" or "appropriate"?

This is why language has evolved. Human beings need to communicate at a level far above what can be shown by pictures. But for language to work there must be a common understanding of what words mean. In effect, we've all made a pact that a certain collection of letters and sounds will mean the same thing to everybody. If you say "book," everybody who speaks English will picture something like what you're holding right now. On the other hand, when you don't use words properly, you "break the pact" and communication breaks down. Suppose you say to a friend, "Abby, you're so pedestrian." You may mean she walks a lot; but Abby is likely to become angry, because you actually called her boring and ordinary.

Language Is Important

Good speakers respect language and how it works. How well do you use language? Do you say Kobe Bryant plays basketball *good,* when you mean he plays *well*? Do you say *in the eventuality of* when *if* will do? Do you describe a hurricane as a *terrible disaster,* as if there were such a thing as a *good disaster*? Do you litter your speech with such meaningless words as *you know, like,* and *really*?

If you do these things, you are bound to be less effective as a speaker. And, unfortunately, you are not alone. Much American speech is turning into the linguistic equivalent of junk food. For example:

Gib Lewis, Speaker of the Texas state House of Representatives: "This is unparalyzed in state history." (I'm sure it's unparalleled, too!)

From the Technical Support Working Group, a U.S. government agency: "Mission: Identify, prioritize, and execute research and development projects that satisfy interagency requirements for existing and emerging technology in the area of explosives detection and diagnostics." (In plain English: "Our job is to find and defuse bombs.")

Sign in an eyeglass shop: "Eyes examined while you wait." (Definitely more comfortable than the alternative.)

University of Nebraska football coach Bill Callahan, after his team failed to win a game in which they were ahead: "We didn't close the book when we had a chance to put a nail in the coffin." (Maybe closing the coffin or putting a nail in the book would have helped!)

The problem with these statements is not that they violate elitist standards of "good English." People in the United States have always talked casually.

Our language has grown with as much vigor and variety as our population. We have borrowed words from other languages. We have coined new words and dropped old ones.[1] The first edition of *Webster's Collegiate Dictionary*, published in 1898, contained about 70,000 words. The 11th edition, published in 2003, has 225,000 words—and these are just the words deemed necessary for a college education. One expert has estimated that the English language has more than 2 million words, with a thousand new ones being added each year.[2]

There is a big difference, however, between the natural growth of a living language and the misuse of that language. To misuse our language is much more than a matter of mere words. Contrary to popular belief, language does not mirror reality. It does not simply describe the world as it is. Instead, language helps create our sense of reality by giving meaning to events. Language is not neutral. The words we use to label an event determine to a great extent how we respond to it.

Consider the public debate over doctor-assisted suicide. If you see doctor-assisted suicide as "immoral," as a form of "murder," as "a violation of the doctor's duty to save lives," you will likely oppose efforts to allow it in any form. But if you see doctor-assisted suicide as "moral," as a way to provide "death with dignity," as "an acceptable alternative to needless pain and suffering" for the terminally ill, you will likely support efforts to permit it in some circumstances.

What separates these two viewpoints? Not the capabilities of modern medicine; not the conditions of terminally ill patients; not even the act of doctor-assisted suicide itself. All those are the same for both sides. The difference is in the *meaning* given to them by the words that label them. This is why, as one writer has said, a choice of words is also a choice of worlds.[3]

Words are vital to thinking itself. Thought and language are closely linked. We do not get an idea and then come up with words to express it. Rather, we usually think in words. How often have you said, "I know what I want to say, but I just don't know how to say it." In fact, if you truly knew what you wanted to say, you probably would be able to say it. On most occasions when we are looking for "just the right word," what we are really looking for is just the right *idea*.[4]

As a speaker, once you get the right idea, you must decide how best to *communicate* it to listeners. To do this, you need to be especially conscious of what language can do. Unless you use language accurately and clearly, no one will understand your ideas.

Words are the tools of a speaker's craft. They have special uses, just like the tools of any other profession. Have you ever watched a carpenter at work? The job that would take you or me a couple of hours is done by the carpenter in 10 minutes—with the right tools. You can't drive a nail with a screwdriver or turn a screw with a hammer. It is the same with public speaking. You must choose the right words for the job you want to do.

Good speakers are aware of the meanings of words—both their obvious and their subtle meanings. They also know how to use language accurately, clearly, vividly, and appropriately. The balance of this chapter will explore each of these aspects of language use. We will also give special attention to inclusive language in public speaking.

Meanings of Words

denotative meaning
The literal or dictionary meaning of a word or phrase.

connotative meaning
The meaning suggested by the associations or emotions triggered by a word or phrase.

Words have two kinds of meanings—denotative and connotative. *Denotative* meaning is precise, literal, and objective. It simply describes the object, person, place, idea, or event to which the word refers. One way to think of a word's denotative meaning is as its dictionary definition. For example, denotatively, the noun "school" means "a place, institution, or building where instruction is given."

Connotative meaning is more variable, figurative, and subjective. Put simply, the connotative meaning of a word is what the word suggests or implies. For instance, the connotative meaning of the word "school" includes all the feelings, associations, and emotions that the word touches off in different people. For some people, "school" might connote personal growth, childhood friends, and a special teacher. For others, it might connote frustration, discipline, and boring homework assignments.

Connotative meaning gives words their intensity and emotional power. It arouses in listeners feelings of anger, pity, love, fear, friendship, nostalgia, greed, guilt, and the like. Speakers, like poets, often use connotation to enrich their meaning. For example:

> Terrorists neither listen to reason nor engage in reasoning with others. Their aim is to generate fear—to frighten people into submission. They measure success by the magnitude of the fear they generate through brutal, savage acts of violence. Terrorists are prepared to kill to further whatever cause they claim to be pursuing. And the heinousness of these murders is accentuated by the fact that terrorists murder without passion. They murder with cool deliberation and deliberate planning. They are utterly amoral.

The underlined words in this passage have powerful connotations that are almost certain to produce a strong emotional revulsion to terrorism.

Here, in contrast, is another version of the same statement—this time using words with a different set of connotations:

> Terrorists do not seek to negotiate with their opponents. They seek victory by using political and psychological pressure, including acts of violence that may endanger the lives of some people. To the terrorist, ultimate objectives are more important than the means used to achieve them.

With the exception of "terrorist," the words in this statement are less likely to evoke an intensely negative response than those in the first statement.

Which statement is preferable? That depends on the audience, the occasion, and the speaker's purpose. Do you want to stir up your listeners' emotions, rally them to some cause? Then select words with more intense connotative meanings. Or are you addressing a controversial issue and trying to seem completely impartial? Then stick with words that touch off less intense reactions. Choosing words skillfully for their denotative and connotative meanings is a crucial part of the speaker's craft.

Using Language Accurately

Using language accurately is as vital to a speaker as using numbers accurately is to an accountant. One student found this out the hard way. In a speech about America's criminal justice system, he referred several times to "criminal *persecution*." What he meant, of course, was "criminal *prosecution*." This one error virtually ruined his speech. As one of his classmates said, "How can I believe what you say about our courts when you don't even know the difference between prosecution and persecution?"

Sometimes inaccuracy results from a misguided attempt to be elegant. This happened to the business manager of a magazine.

Mary Jo Hundt had a special fondness for adding "istic" to the end of a word. Addressing the magazine's editorial staff one day, she said, "We are going to streamline our paperwork to make it more *simplistic*. That's the *modernistic* way to do things. With less paperwork, we'll have more time to devote to the magazine, and that will be *impressionistic* to management."

Mary Jo clearly did not realize that "simplistic" doesn't mean simple or easy but instead refers to *over*simplification on shaky grounds. And "modernistic" refers to a particular style of design, not the general condition of being modern. "Impressionistic," of course, has nothing to do with making an impression on someone; it describes a

Words are the tools of the speaker's craft. Good speakers use them accurately and correctly. They also use language that will be clear, vivid, and appropriate for their listeners.

certain type of art or music. But the editorial staff knew all these things, and they were embarrassed for Mary Jo.

The moral of this story is obvious. Don't use a word unless you are sure of its meaning. If you are not sure, look up the word in a dictionary.

Fortunately, such outright blunders are relatively rare among college students. However, we all commit more subtle errors—especially using one word when another will capture our ideas more precisely. Every word has shades of meaning that distinguish it from every other word. As Mark Twain said, "The difference between the right word and the almost right word is the difference between lightning and the lightning bug."

thesaurus
A book of synonyms.

If you look in a thesaurus, you'll find the following words given as synonyms:

success	accomplishment
victory	triumph

All mean roughly the same thing—a favorable outcome. But all these words have different shades of meaning. See if you can fill in the best word to complete each of the sentences below:

1. My most important ____________ this year was getting an A in calculus.
2. Priya's business ____________ results from a combination of hard work and street smarts.
3. The critics agreed that Denyce Graves's brilliant performance in *Carmen* was a ____________.
4. Paul's ____________on the parallel bars gave him confidence to pursue the gold medal for best all-around gymnast.

The best answers for the four statements are

1. accomplishment	3. triumph
2. success	4. victory

Each of the words means something a little different from the others, and each says something special to listeners.

As you prepare your speeches, ask yourself constantly, "What do I *really* want to say? What do I *really* mean?" Choose words that are precise, exact, accurate. When in doubt, consult a dictionary or thesaurus to make sure you have the best words to express your ideas.

If you have serious aspirations as a speaker, you should work out a systematic plan to improve your vocabulary. Years ago Malcolm X, the famous African-American leader, did this by copying the dictionary, word by word! This method is extreme, and few people would take the time for it. A less arduous plan might be to try using one new word every day—and using the word correctly. The purpose of this is not to learn a lot of big words, but to "learn when certain words should be used, . . . to use the proper word at the proper time."[5]

Using Language Clearly

Suppose you are standing on a street corner and you see a careless pedestrian about to step into the path of an oncoming car. Do you say, "It would appear from available empirical evidence as if an unsuspecting person is in danger of being struck and injured by an approaching automotive vehicle"? Of course not. You yell, "Look out!"

As many people have discovered, much to their dismay, it is possible to use language accurately without using it clearly. Here is a well-known story that shows how much trouble can be caused by not communicating clearly. A plumber wrote to a government agency to ask whether there was any harm in using hydrochloric acid to clean out drain pipes. The agency replied:

> The efficacy of hydrochloric acid is indisputable, but the corrosive effect is incompatible with metallic permanence.

The plumber thanked the agency for approving the use of hydrochloric acid. The agency wrote back, saying:

> We cannot assume responsibility for the production of toxic and noxious residue with hydrochloric acid and suggest you use an alternative procedure.

Once more the plumber thanked the agency for its approval. Finally, the agency, alarmed at the prospect of hundreds of ruined drain pipes, called in another scientist. He wrote:

> Don't use hydrochloric acid. It eats holes in the pipes!

Remember, people are different. What makes perfect sense to some may be gobbledygook to others. You cannot assume that what is clear to you is clear to your audience. This is particularly true in speechmaking. Listeners, unlike readers, cannot turn to a dictionary or reread an author's words to discover their meaning. A speaker's meaning must be *immediately* comprehensible; it must be so clear that there is virtually no chance of misunderstanding. You can ensure this by using familiar words, by choosing concrete words over abstract words, and by eliminating verbal clutter.

Use Familiar Words

It may seem obvious that familiar words are better than unfamiliar ones. But you would be amazed at how many speakers persist in bombarding listeners with complicated words—usually out of the mistaken belief that such words sound impressive. In truth, filling a speech with long, multisyllabic words only marks the speaker as stuffy and pretentious. Worse, it usually destroys understanding. One of the greatest barriers to clear speech is using big, bloated words where short, sharp ones will do the job better.[6]

Here, for example, are two passages expressing much the same idea. Which is easier to understand?

THE INTERNET *Connection*

Looking for just the right word to express your ideas? There's a good chance you will find it at the Merriam-Webster Online Language Center (www.m-w.com). In addition to a providing a dictionary and thesaurus, this site contains links to a number of language-related items from Merriam-Webster.

Are you a non-native speaker of English? If so, you will find many helpful resources on the Web. One of the best is Ohio University's Grammar for English Language Learners ([illegible] grammar/index.html), which provides several dozen language activities, as well as links to sites with additional resources.

ONLINE LEARNING CENTER

You can link to these Web sites at www.mhhe.com/lucas9.

Is this a genuine affirmation that the utterances you anticipate communicating during the time period immediately succeeding the present shall be entirely veracious and devoid of deception, complete in all pertinent minutiae and particularities, and absent of all misleading obfuscation or superfluous and undocumentable specificities, on the authority of your allegiance and fidelity to the supreme deity?

Or,

Do you swear that the testimony you are about to give shall be the truth, the whole truth, and nothing but the truth, so help you God?

The second passage is the standard oath taken by a witness before testifying in a court of law. It consists of short, simple, familiar words that are easy to comprehend. Its meaning comes across without forcing you to perform complex mental gymnastics. The first passage says essentially the same thing as the second, but is full of stuffy, ostentatious words that make its meaning almost impossible to decipher.

When speaking about technical subjects, you may not be able to avoid unfamiliar words. If this happens, keep the technical terms to a minimum and define clearly those that your audience may not understand. If you work at it, you will almost always be able to translate even the most specialized topic into clear, familiar language.

Here, for instance, are three passages explaining the devastating effects of a pregnant woman's drinking on her unborn child. The first passage is in medical jargon, and it defies comprehension by ordinary listeners:

Alcohol consumption by the pregnant woman seriously influences the intrauterine milieu and therefore contributes to the morbidity and mortality of children born to these mothers. In regard to the pathophysiology of this syndrome, genetic polymorphism of enzymes for ethanol metabolism may alter fetal susceptibility. There may also be poor microsomal or mitochondrial function or decreased ATP activity.

Even an educated person without a medical background would have trouble with "pathophysiology" and "polymorphism" and "mitochondrial," much less be able to put them all together.

The second passage represents an attempt to adapt to a nonmedical audience. It is in more familiar language but retains enough obscure words to be difficult:

The deleterious effects of alcohol on the unborn child are very serious. When a pregnant mother consumes alcohol, the ethanol in the bloodstream easily crosses the placenta from mother to child and invades the amniotic fluid. This can produce a number of abnormal birth syndromes, including central-nervous-system dysfunctions, growth deficiencies, a cluster of facial aberrations, and variable major and minor malformations.

Well-informed listeners could probably figure out "deleterious effects," "central-nervous-system dysfunctions," and "facial aberrations." But these terms don't create a sharp mental image of what the speaker is trying to say. We still need to go one step further away from medical jargon toward ordinary language.

So we come to the third passage, which is utterly clear. It shows what can be done with work, imagination, and a healthy respect for everyday words:

When the expectant mother drinks, alcohol is absorbed into her bloodstream and distributed throughout her entire body. After a few beers or a couple of martinis, she begins to feel tipsy and decides to sober up. She grabs a cup of coffee, two aspirin, and takes a little nap. After a while she'll be fine.

Even when discussing technical subjects, effective speakers such as biologist Paul Ewald look for ways to communicate their ideas in clear, familiar language.

But while she sleeps, the fetus is surrounded by the same alcoholic content as its mother had. After being drowned in alcohol, the fetus begins to feel the effect. But it can't sober up. It can't grab a cup of coffee. It can't grab a couple of aspirin. For the fetus's liver, the key organ in removing alcohol from the blood, is just not developed. The fetus is literally pickled in alcohol.[7]

This kind of plain talk is what listeners want. You cannot go wrong by following the advice of Winston Churchill to speak in "short, homely words of common usage." If you think big words (or a lot of words) are needed to impress listeners, bear in mind that the Gettysburg Address—considered the finest speech in the English language—contains 271 words, of which 251 have only one or two syllables.

Choose Concrete Words

concrete words
Words that refer to tangible objects.

abstract words
Words that refer to ideas or concepts.

Concrete words refer to tangible objects—people, places, and things. They differ from abstract words, which refer to general concepts, qualities, or attributes. "Carrot," "pencil," "nose," and "door" are concrete words. "Humility," "science," "progress," and "philosophy" are abstract words.

Of course, few words are completely abstract or concrete. Abstractness and concreteness are relative. "Apple pie" is concrete, but in the United States, the phrase also has abstract values of patriotism and conventional morals. Usually, the more specific a word, the more concrete it is. Let us say you are talking about golf. Here are several words and phrases you might use:

physical activity	abstract/general
sports	↓
golf	↓
professional golf	↓
Tiger Woods	concrete/specific

As you move down the list, the words become less abstract and more concrete. You begin with a general concept (physical activity), descend to one type of activity (sports), to a particular sport (golf), to a division of that sport (professional golf), to one specific professional golfer (Tiger Woods).

The more abstract a word, the more ambiguous it will be. Although abstract words are necessary to express certain kinds of ideas, they are much easier to misinterpret than are concrete words. Also, concrete words are much more likely to claim your listeners' attention. Suppose you make a speech about fire ants, which have long plagued the South and are now attacking western states. Here are two ways you could approach the subject—one featuring abstract words, the other concrete words:

Abstract Words

Fire ants have been a problem ever since they arrived in the United States. They have spread across the South and now threaten various parts of the West as well. This is a serious problem because fire ants are highly aggressive. There have even been human casualties from fire ant stings.

Concrete Words

Since fire ants came here from South America sometime before World War II, they have spread like a biblical plague across 11 states from Florida to Texas. Now they are invading New Mexico, Arizona, and California. Fire ants attack in swarms and they will climb any foot that is left in the wrong spot for a few seconds. They have even turned up indoors, in clothes hampers, beds, and closets. Fortunately, fewer than 1 percent of people who are stung have to see a doctor, but toddlers who have fallen on fire ant mounds have sometimes died from stings, as have highly allergic adults.[8]

Notice how much more persuasive the second version is. A speech dominated by concrete words will almost always be clearer, more interesting, and easier to recall than one dominated by abstract words.

Eliminate Clutter

Cluttered speech has become a national epidemic. Whatever happened to such simple words as "before," "if," and "now"? When last seen they were being routed by their cluttered counterparts—"prior to," "in the eventuality of," and "at this point in time." By the same token, why can't weather forecasters say, "It's raining," instead of saying, "It appears as if we are currently experiencing precipitation activity"? And why can't politicians say, "We have a crisis," instead of saying, "We are facing a difficult crisis situation that will be troublesome to successfully resolve"?

This type of clutter is deadly to clear, compelling speech. It forces listeners to hack through a tangle of words to discover the meaning. When you make a speech, keep your language lean and lively. Beware of using several words where one or two will do. Avoid flabby phrases. Let your ideas emerge sharply and firmly. Above all, watch out for redundant adjectives and adverbs. Inexperienced speakers (and writers) tend to string together two or three synonymous adjectives, such as "a learned and educated person," or "a hot, steamy, torrid day."

clutter
Discourse that takes many more words than are necessary to express an idea.

Here is part of a student speech that has been revised to eliminate clutter:

Sitting Bull was one of the most important ~~and significant of all~~ Native American leaders. He was born in ~~the year of~~ 1831 near Grand River, in ~~an area that is now part of the state of~~ *present-day* South Dakota. A fearless ~~and courageous~~ warrior, he ~~ended up being~~ *was* elected chief of the Hunkpapa Sioux in 1867. In the following years, he also attracted a large ~~and numerous~~ following among the ~~tribes of the~~ Cheyenne and Arapaho. He is best known ~~to people in this day and age~~ *today* for his ~~instrumental~~ role in ~~helping to lead the defeat of~~ *defeating* General Custer at the Battle of Little Big Horn in 1876. Although eventually ~~required against his will~~ *forced* to live ~~his life~~ on the Standing Rock Reservation in South Dakota, he never surrendered ~~to anyone~~ his dignity or his ~~personal~~ devotion to the Sioux way of life.

Notice how much cleaner and easier to follow the revised version is. No longer are the speaker's ideas hidden in a thicket of wasted words.

This kind of pruning is easy once you get the knack of it. The hardest part—and it is often very hard—is recognizing clutter for what it is and then forcing yourself to throw away the unnecessary words. Watch for clutter when you write your speech outlines. Be prepared to revise the outline until your ideas emerge as clearly and crisply as possible. As with revising an essay or a term paper, this will take extra time. But if you keep at it, you will become a much more effective speaker—and writer.

You can also help eliminate clutter by practicing your speeches with a digital recorder. As you play the speech back, keep an ear out not just for flabby phrases but for verbal fillers such as "you know," "like," and "really." Practice delivering the speech again, this time making a special effort to trim it of wasted or distracting words. At first you may feel awkward and unnatural because you are forcing yourself to break old habits. But if you keep at it, you will gradually develop a new habit of speaking naturally without all that clutter. This will not only make you a better public speaker, but it will help you present ideas more effectively in meetings, conversations, and group discussions.

Using Language Vividly

Just as you can be accurate without being clear, so you can be both accurate and clear without being interesting. Here, for example, is how Martin Luther King *might have* phrased part of his great "I Have a Dream" speech:

> Turning back is something we cannot do. We must continue to work against police brutality, segregated housing, disfranchisement, and alienation. Only when these problems are solved will we be satisfied.

Here is what King *actually* said:

> We cannot turn back. There are those who ask the devotees of civil rights, "When will you be satisfied?" We can never be satisfied as long as the Negro is the victim of the unspeakable horrors of police brutality. We can never be satisfied as long as our bodies, heavy with the fatigue of travel, cannot gain lodging in the motels of the highways and the hotels of the cities. . . . We cannot be satisfied as long as a Negro in Mississippi cannot vote and a Negro in New York believes he has nothing for which to vote. No, no, we are not satisfied, and we will not be satisfied until justice rolls down like waters and righteousness like a mighty stream.

Much more stirring, isn't it? If you want to move people with your speeches, use moving language. Dull, dreary words make for dull, dreary speeches. Bring your speeches to life by using vivid, animated language. Although there are several ways to do this, here are two of the most important—imagery and rhythm.

Clear, vivid, uncluttered language is a hallmark of Julian Bond's speeches. Bond gives a great deal of thought to finding just the right words to express his ideas.

Imagery

One sign of a good novelist is the ability to create word pictures that get you totally involved with a story. These word pictures let you "see" the haunted house, or "feel" the bite of the snow against your face, or "hear" the birds chirping on a warm spring morning, or "smell" the bacon cooking over an open campfire, or "taste" the hot enchiladas at a Mexican restaurant.

Speakers can use imagery in much the same way to make their ideas come alive. Three ways to generate imagery are by using concrete words, simile, and metaphor.

imagery
The use of vivid language to create mental images of objects, actions, or ideas.

Concrete Words

As we saw earlier in this chapter, choosing concrete words over abstract words is one way to enhance the clarity of your speeches. Concrete words are also the key to effective imagery. Consider the following excerpt from Ronald Reagan's famous address commemorating the 40th anniversary of D-Day. Speaking at the scene of the battle, Reagan dramatically recounted the heroism of the U.S. Rangers who scaled the cliffs at Pointe du Hoc to help free Europe from Hitler's stranglehold:

> We stand on a lonely, windswept point on the northern shore of France. The air is soft, but 40 years ago at this moment, the air was dense with smoke and the cries of men, and the air was filled with the crack of rifle fire and the roar of cannon.
>
> At dawn, on the morning of the 6th of June, 1944, 225 Rangers jumped off the British landing craft and ran to the bottom of these cliffs. . . . The Rangers looked up and saw the enemy soldiers—at the edge of the cliffs shooting down at them

CD 1: VIDEO 11.1
View this excerpt from Ronald Reagan's speech at Pointe du Hoc.

> with machine guns and throwing grenades. And the American Rangers began to climb. They shot rope ladders over the face of these cliffs and began to pull themselves up.
>
> When one Ranger fell, another would take his place. When one rope was cut, a Ranger would grab another and begin his climb again. They climbed, shot back, and held their footing. Soon, one by one, the Rangers pulled themselves over the top, and in seizing the firm land at the top of these cliffs, they began to seize back the continent of Europe.

ONLINE LEARNING CENTER
For the full text of Reagan's speech, log on to the Top 100 American Speeches of the 20th Century at www.mhhe.com/lucastop100.

Concrete words call up mental impressions of sights, sounds, touch, smell, and taste. In the speech just quoted, we do not merely learn that the U.S. Rangers helped win the battle of D-Day. We visualize the Rangers landing at the foot of the cliffs. We see them fighting their way up the cliffs in the face of enemy grenades and machine guns. We hear the crack of rifle fire and the cries of the soldiers. The concrete words create images of sights and sounds, feelings and emotions that pull us irresistibly into the speech.

Simile

Another way to create imagery is through the use of simile. Simile is an explicit comparison between things that are essentially different yet have something in common. It always contains the words "like" or "as." Here are some examples from student speeches:

simile
An explicit comparison, introduced with the word "like" or "as," between things that are essentially different yet have something in common.

> Walking into my grandparents' home when I was a child was like being wrapped in a giant security blanket.

> Air pollution is eating away at the monuments in Washington, D.C., like a giant Alka-Seltzer tablet.

These are bright, fresh similes that clarify and vitalize ideas. Some similes, however, have become stale through overuse. Here are a few:

fresh as a daisy	hungry as a bear
fit as a fiddle	busy as a bee
strong as an ox	big as a mountain
stubborn as a mule	happy as a lark
blind as a bat	light as a feather

cliché
A trite or overused expression.

Such *clichés* are fine in everyday conversation, but you should avoid them in speechmaking. Otherwise, you are likely to be "dull as dishwater" and to find your audience "sleeping like a log"!

Metaphor

You can also use metaphor to create imagery in your speeches. Metaphor is an implicit comparison between things that are essentially different yet have something in common. Unlike simile, metaphor does not contain the words "like" or "as." For example:

America's cities are the windows through which the world looks at American society. (Henry Cisneros)

With globalization, the same sea washes all of humankind. We are all in the same boat. There are no safe islands. (Kofi Annan)

metaphor
An implicit comparison, not introduced with the word "like" or "as," between two things that are essentially different yet have something in common.

These are both brief metaphors. Sometimes, however, a speaker will develop a longer metaphor. Here is an excellent example, from China's 2002 national English-language speech competition. The speaker is Zhang Jiexuan, a student at Fudan University in Shanghai:

Globalization should not be a huge melting pot into which people of uniqueness go only to come out all the same. It should not be a process in which countries gradually lose their identities.

To my understanding, globalization should be a grand orchestra—an orchestra in which every player has his particular position and function; an orchestra where the uniqueness of every member is so cherished that anyone's role is irreplaceable by anyone else; an orchestra based on the joint contribution of every participant, which can and will produce the most beautiful symphony of tomorrow's peace and prosperity.[9]

CD 1: VIDEO 11.2
View this excerpt from Zhang Jiexuan's speech on globalization.

The subject of this metaphor—globalization—is the same as the subject of the metaphor by U.N. Secretary General Kofi Annan quoted earlier in this section. Though different in length, both metaphors convey the speaker's thoughts vividly and memorably. When used effectively, metaphor—like simile—is an excellent way to bring color to a speech, to make abstract ideas concrete, to clarify the unknown, and to express feelings and emotions.[10]

Rhythm

Language has a rhythm created by the choice and arrangement of words. Sometimes the appeal of a statement depends almost entirely on its rhythm—as in this children's verse:

rhythm
The pattern of sound in a speech created by the choice and arrangement of words

Pease porridge hot,
  Pease porridge cold,
Pease porridge in the pot,
  Nine days old.

There is little meaning here. The appeal comes from the combination of sounds, which gives the passage an almost musical cadence.[11]

Speakers, like poets, sometimes seek to exploit the rhythm of language. By catching up their listeners in an arresting string of sounds, speakers can enhance the impact of their words—and therefore of their ideas. Winston Churchill was a master at this. Here is a passage from one of his famous speeches during World War II. To emphasize its cadence, the passage has been printed as if it were poetry rather than prose:

We cannot tell what the course
  of this fell war will be
as it spreads remorseless
  through ever-wider regions.

We know it will be hard;
 we expect it will be long.
We cannot predict or measure
 its episodes or its tribulations. . . .
We cannot yet see
 how deliverance will come,
or when it will come.
 But nothing is more certain
than that every trace of Hitler's footsteps,
 every stain of his infected and corroding fingers,
will be sponged and purged
 and, if need be,
blasted from the surface of the earth.[12]

CD 1:VIDEO 11.3
View this excerpt from Winston Churchill's speech of June 12, 1941.

The impact of the passage was heightened by Churchill's superb delivery; but even by themselves the words take on an emphatic rhythm that reinforces the message. You can see why one observer said that Churchill "mobilized the English language and sent it into battle."[13]

A speech, however, is not a poem. You should never emphasize sound and rhythm at the expense of meaning. The aim is to think about ways you can use the rhythm and flow of language to enhance your meaning. Although you may never have paid much conscious attention to this subject, you can develop an ear for vocal rhythms by study and practice. What's more, you can easily begin now to use four basic stylistic devices employed by Churchill and other fine speakers to improve the rhythm of their prose.

Parallelism

parallelism
The similar arrangement of a pair or series of related words, phrases, or sentences.

The first device is parallelism—the similar arrangement of a pair or series of related words, phrases, or sentences. For example:

Rich and poor, intelligent and ignorant, wise and foolish, virtuous and vicious, man and woman—it is ever the same, each soul must depend wholly on itself. (Elizabeth Cady Stanton)

We defeated communism. *We defeated* fascism. *We defeated them on the field of* battle, and *we defeated them on the field of* ideas. (Colin Powell)

The effects of parallelism are perhaps best illustrated by seeing what happens when it is absent. For instance, compare this statement:

I speak as a Republican. I speak as a woman. I speak as a United States Senator. I speak as an American. (Margaret Chase Smith)

with this one:

I speak as a Republican. I speak as a woman. I speak as a United States Senator. And I am also addressing you as an American.

The first statement is clear, consistent, and compelling. The second is not. By violating the principle of parallel structure, its final sentence ("And

I am also addressing you as an American") destroys the progression begun by the preceding three sentences ("I speak as a Republican. I speak as a woman. I speak as a United States Senator"). It thereby turns a strong, lucid, harmonious statement into one that is fuzzy and jarring.

Repetition

The second device you can use to lend rhythm to your speeches is repetition. This means repeating the same word or set of words at the beginning or end of successive clauses or sentences. For example:

repetition
Reiteration of the same word or set of words at the beginning or end of successive clauses or sentences.

When you see your street, *see my* street. *When you see your* house, *see my* house. *When you see your* children, *see my* children. (Whitney Young, Jr.)

We will not tire, *we will not* falter, and *we will not* fail. (George W. Bush)

As you can see, repetition usually results in parallelism. In addition to building a strong cadence, it also unifies a sequence of ideas, emphasizes an idea by stating it more than once, and helps create a strong emotional effect.

Alliteration

The third device you can use to enhance the rhythm of your speeches is alliteration. The most common method of alliteration is repeating the initial consonant sound of close or adjoining words. For example:

alliteration
Repetition of the initial consonant sound of close or adjoining words.

*P*eace is essential for *p*rogress, but *p*rogress is no less essential for *p*eace. (Liaquat Ali Khan)

In a nation founded on the promise of human dignity, our *c*olleges, our *c*ommunities, our *c*ountry should *c*hallenge hatred wherever we find it. (Hillary Rodham Clinton)

By highlighting the sounds of words, alliteration catches the attention of listeners and can make ideas easier to remember. Used sparingly, it is a marvelous way to spruce up your speeches. Used to excess, however, it can be laughable and draw too much attention, so that listeners get more involved in listening for the next alliteration than in absorbing the content of the speech.

Antithesis

Finally, you might try using antithesis—the juxtaposition of contrasting ideas, usually in parallel structure. For example:

antithesis
The juxtaposition of contrasting ideas, usually in parallel structure.

Ask not what your country can do for you; ask what you can do for your country. (John F. Kennedy)

Your success as a family, our success as a society, depends not on what happens at the White House, but on what happens inside your house. (Barbara Bush)

Antithesis has long been a favorite device of accomplished speakers. Because it nearly always produces a neatly turned phrase, it is a fine way to give your speeches a special touch of class.

You may be thinking that imagery and rhythm are fine for famous people but are too fancy for ordinary speeches like yours. This is not true. Imagery and rhythm are easy to use and can enliven even the most routine of speeches. As an example, take a look at the following excerpt from one student's speech about the Massachusetts 54th, the regiment of African-American soldiers during the Civil War featured in the movie *Glory:*

CD 1: VIDEO 11.4

View this excerpt from "The Massachusetts 54th."

> To join an army that didn't believe in you. To fight with an army who didn't like you. To die for an army that didn't respect you. This was the Massachusetts 54th. Today they lay where they died, on the beaches of South Carolina. Colonel Shaw and his men were piled together in a mass grave, which has since been covered by the shifting tides of the Atlantic. A small statue stands in Boston—a reminder of their sacrifice.
>
> Bravery, patriotism, and sacrifice. These are qualities of the Massachusetts 54th. With the help of their efforts, along with all the other black regiments that followed them, slavery did eventually come to an end.

This is vivid, moving language. The imagery is sharp and poignant, the rhythm strong and insistent. Think of how you can do similar things in your own speeches.

Using Language Appropriately

Here is part of a famous oration given by John Hancock in 1774, during the American Revolution. Speaking of the British soldiers who killed five Americans in the Boston Massacre, Hancock exclaimed:

> Ye dark designing knaves, ye murderers, parricides! How dare you tread upon the earth, which has drank in the blood of slaughtered innocents shed by your wicked hands? How dare you breathe that air which wafted to the ear of heaven the groans of those who fell a sacrifice to your accursed ambition? . . . Tell me, ye bloody butchers, ye villains high and low, ye wretches . . . do you not feel the goads and stings of conscious guilt pierce through your savage bosoms?[14]

This is certainly vivid language—and Hancock's audience loved it. But can you imagine speaking the same way today? In addition to being accurate, clear, and vivid, language should be appropriate—to the occasion, to the audience, to the topic, and to the speaker.

Appropriateness to the Occasion

Language that is appropriate for some occasions may not be appropriate for others. "There is a time for dialect, a place for slang, an occasion for literary form. What is correct on the sports page is out of place on the op-ed page; what is with-it on the street may well be without it in the classroom."[15] As a simple example, a coach might address the football team as "you guys" (or worse!), whereas the speaker in a more formal situation would begin with "distinguished guests." Try reversing these two situations, and see how ridiculous it becomes. It's only common sense to adjust your language to different occasions.

Language needs to be appropriate to a speaker's topic, as well as to the audience. A speech on snowboarding would use more action-oriented words than a speech about theories of psychology.

Appropriateness to the Audience

Appropriateness also depends on the audience. If you keep this in mind, it will help you greatly when dealing with technical or scientific topics. When addressing an audience of physicians, you might use the word "parotitis" to refer to a viral disease marked by the swelling of the parotid glands. Your audience would know just what you meant. But when talking to a nonmedical audience, such as your classmates, a word like "parotitis" would not be appropriate. The appropriate word in this case would be "mumps."

You should be especially careful to avoid language that might offend your audience. If you were a stand-up comedian, off-color humor or profanity might be appropriate in a nightclub routine, but most listeners would find it offensive in a formal public speech. Remember, speakers are expected to elevate and polish their language when addressing an audience.

They are also expected to avoid name-calling and other forms of abusive language. As we saw in Chapter 2, such language is ethically suspect because it demeans the basic human worth of the people against whom it is directed. In addition, most listeners take offense at statements that denounce people on the basis of their religious beliefs or ethnic heritage. If you include such statements in your speeches, you will not only violate an important ethical responsibility, but you will almost surely alienate a good portion of your audience.

Of course, you cannot always be sure of how listeners will respond to what you say. As a general rule, bend over backward to avoid language that may confuse or offend your listeners. When it comes to appropriateness, you will seldom go wrong by erring on the side of caution. (Put simply, "erring on the side of caution" means "when in doubt—don't.")

Appropriateness to the Topic

Language should also be appropriate to the topic. You would not use metaphor, antithesis, and alliteration when explaining how to change a bicycle tire or how to perform routine maintenance on a car. But you might use all three in a speech celebrating the genius of Leonardo da Vinci or honoring U.S. soldiers who have died in defense of their country. The first two topics call for straightforward description and explanation. The latter two call for special language skills to evoke emotion, admiration, and appreciation.

Appropriateness to the Speaker

No matter what the occasion, audience, or topic, language should also be appropriate to the speaker. Imagine the effect if Dick Cheney tried to adopt the religious imagery and rhythmical cadence of Al Sharpton. The results would be comical. Every public speaker develops his or her own language style.

"Terrific," you may be thinking. "I have my own style too. I feel more comfortable using abstract words, slang, and technical jargon. That's just me. It's *my* way of speaking." But to say that language should be appropriate to the speaker does not justify ignoring the other needs for appropriateness. There is a difference between one's everyday style and one's *developed* style as a public speaker. Accomplished speakers have developed their speaking styles over many years of trial, error, and practice. They have *worked* at using language effectively.

You can do the same if you become language-conscious. One way to develop this consciousness is to read and listen to the speeches of effective speakers, whether they are current public figures such as Colin Powell and Hillary Clinton or historical figures such as Barbara Jordan and Martin Luther King. Study their techniques for achieving accuracy, clarity, and vividness, and try to adapt those techniques to your own speeches. But do not try to "become" someone else when you speak. Learn from other speakers, blend what you learn into your own language style, and seek to become the best possible you.

A Note on Inclusive Language

"When a soldier goes to war, he should have the best possible equipment."

"Improving education has always been a high priority for Negro leaders."

"Any discrimination against crippled people is completely unacceptable."

Forty years ago, most people in the United States who heard these statements in a speech would not have given them a second thought. Today the same statements would raise more than a few eyebrows—and perhaps tempers—in almost any audience. Here's why:

Soldiers in the U.S. military include women as well as men. To say, "When a soldier goes to war, he should have the best possible equipment," ignores the existence of female soldiers. It can also be interpreted as meaning that only male soldiers should go to war with the finest possible equipment—hardly a comforting thought to female soldiers or their loved ones!

The word "Negro" has fallen out of common usage and has changed in meaning. While this term was considered acceptable through the 1960s and was used by civil rights leaders such as Martin Luther King, it is now considered offensive. Today the preferred terms are "black" and "African American."

Historically "crippled" was used as a word of ridicule and disparagement. It was replaced some years ago by "handicapped," which has itself been supplanted by "people with disabilities." This last phrase is preferable because it is not judgmental and includes the full range of functional limitations that interfere with a person's ability to see, walk, hear, or learn.

inclusive language
Language that does not stereotype, demean, or patronize people on the basis of gender, race, religion, disability, sexual orientation, or other factors.

For centuries, the English language has contained countless words and phrases that favor men and convey stereotyped, misleading, or demeaning views of women and minority groups. Today that is changing—not as fast, perhaps, as some people might like, and doubtless too fast for other people—but changing nonetheless. As the United States has become more diverse, our language has evolved to reflect that diversity. Regardless of the situation, audiences today expect public speakers to use inclusive language that is respectful of the different groups that make up American society.

We saw in Chapter 2 that name-calling and other forms of abusive language is ethically suspect because it demeans the dignity of the individuals or groups being attacked and can undermine the right of all groups in a democratic society to be fairly heard. But using inclusive language involves more than avoiding name-calling. Even speakers with the best of intentions can inadvertently use language that stereotypes, demeans, or patronizes people on the basis of gender, race, religion, disabilities, sexual orientation, or other factors.

In addition to its ethical implications, using inclusive language is important as a matter of accuracy. To speak as if all soldiers (or doctors, or lawyers, or firefighters) are men is incorrect—just as it is erroneous to speak as if all secretaries, nurses, or flight attendants are women. Being accurate in such matters is no less important than being accurate in other aspects of your language.

As we saw in Chapter 5, conveying respect for various groups in society is also a vital part of being an audience-centered public speaker. Even if you do not care about inclusive language yourself, you can be sure that almost any audience you address will contain people who do care and who will be upset if you use language that does not reflect a spirit of inclusiveness. This is one reason why governments, businesses, and professional groups invest millions of dollars each year in workshops that help employees and associates understand the importance of respecting diversity and of reflecting that respect in their language.

When editors, linguists, social advocates, and others first proposed inclusive alternatives to traditional words and phrases, some people reacted with shock and indignation. You cannot change the language, they said, without destroying its beauty and purity. But the English language has been changing for centuries—just as it will continue to change in the future. Today a number of principles for inclusive language have become so widespread that no aspiring speaker (or writer) can afford to ignore them. Let's look at several of these principles.

Avoid the Generic "He"

generic "he"
The use of "he" to refer to both women and men.

Ineffective: Each time a surgeon walks into the operating room, *he* risks being sued for malpractice.

More Effective: Each time a surgeon walks into the operating room, *she or he* risks being sued for malpractice.

Often, a more graceful alternative is to pluralize. For example:

More Effective: Whenever surgeons walk into the operating room, *they* risk being sued for malpractice.

Avoid the Use of "Man" When Referring to Both Men and Women

Ineffective: If a large comet struck the Earth, it could destroy all of mankind.

More Effective: If a large comet struck the Earth, it could destroy all human life.

Ineffective: No matter how popular cats have become, the dog is still man's best friend.

More Effective: No matter how popular cats have become, the dog is still a person's best friend.

Avoid Stereotyping Jobs and Social Roles by Gender

Ineffective: Being a small businessman in the current economic climate is not easy.

More Effective: Being a small businessperson in the current economic climate is not easy.

Sometimes you can solve this problem with a simple twist in sentence construction. For example:

More Effective: Owning a small business is not easy in the current economic climate.

Avoid Identifying Personal Traits That Are Unrelated to the Topic

Ineffective: Patrick Spiegel, a stay-at-home father, proposed a bike path plan to the City Council.

More Effective: Patrick Spiegel proposed a bike path plan to the City Council.

Ineffective: Condoleezza Rice, an African-American woman, has had a major impact on U.S. foreign policy.

More Effective: Condoleezza Rice has had a major impact on U.S. foreign policy.

Use Names That Groups Use to Identify Themselves

One of the most fundamental ways of showing respect for others is to refer to them by the names they use to identify themselves and to avoid names they consider offensive.[16]

Ineffective: Despite progress in recent years, homosexuals still face many forms of discrimination.

More Effective: Despite progress in recent years, lesbians and gay men still face many forms of discrimination.

Ineffective: Michelle Kwan is one of many Orientals who have had a major impact on U.S. life.

More Effective: Michelle Kwan is one of many Asians who have had a major impact on U.S. life.

Most Effective: Michelle Kwan is one of many Chinese Americans who have had a major impact on U.S. life.

As this last example suggests, there is currently a trend away from broad words such as "Asian" to more precise terms that do not lump people of distinct nationalities and cultures under one label. Until very recently, "Hispanic" was considered the correct way to designate someone from Latin America, which includes Mexico, Central America, South America, Cuba, and the Carribean Islands. Today, however, many Mexican Americans wish to be called "Chicano" or "Chicana," while people from other Latin American countries frequently prefer the terms "Latino" or "Latina."

The use of specific identifiers is often preferred by other groups as well. For example:

Ineffective: Indian code talkers were vital to the U.S. armed forces during World War II.

More Effective: Native American code talkers were vital to the U.S. armed forces during World War II.

Most Effective: Navajo code talkers were vital to the U.S. armed forces during World War II.

Like many other aspects of American life, questions of inclusive language can sometimes be confusing. Language is alive and constantly evolving, so what is considered inclusive at one point in time may shift down the road. If you do a lot of public speaking (or writing), you should consider purchasing a guidebook such as Rosalie Maggio's *Talking About People:*

A Guide to Fair and Accurate Language. Using inclusive and respectful language is not a matter of political correctness, but it is a matter of P.C.—personal courtesy.[17]

Summary

Of all human creations, language may be the most remarkable. Through language we share experiences, formulate values, exchange ideas, transmit knowledge, and sustain culture. Indeed, language is vital to thinking itself. Contrary to popular belief, language does not simply mirror reality, but helps create our sense of reality by giving meaning to events.

Good speakers have respect for language and how it works. Words are the tools of a speaker's craft. They have special uses, just like the tools of any other profession. As a speaker, you should be aware of the meanings of words and know how to use language accurately, clearly, vividly, and appropriately.

Words have two kinds of meanings—denotative and connotative. Denotative meaning is precise, literal, and objective. One way to think of a word's denotative meaning is as its dictionary definition. Connotative meaning is more variable, figurative, and subjective. It is whatever the word suggests or implies. Connotative meaning includes all the feelings, associations, and emotions that a word touches off in different people.

Using language accurately is as vital to a speaker as using numbers accurately is to an accountant. Never use a word unless you are sure of its meaning. If you are not sure, look up the word in a dictionary. As you prepare your speeches, ask yourself constantly, "What do I *really* want to say? What do I *really* mean?" Choose words that are precise and accurate.

Using language clearly allows listeners to grasp your meaning immediately. You can ensure this by using words that are known to the average person and require no specialized background; by choosing concrete words in preference to more abstract ones; and by eliminating verbal clutter.

Using language vividly helps bring your speech to life. One way to make your language more vivid is through imagery, or the creation of word pictures. You can develop imagery by using concrete language, simile, and metaphor. Simile is an explicit comparison between things that are essentially different yet have something in common; it always contains the words "like" or "as." Metaphor is an implicit comparison between things that are different yet have something in common; it does not contain the words "like" or "as."

Another way to make your speeches vivid is by exploiting the rhythm of language. Four devices for creating rhythm are parallelism, repetition, alliteration, and antithesis. Parallelism is the similar arrangement of a pair or series of related words, phrases, or sentences. Repetition is the use of the same word or set of words at the beginning or end of successive clauses or sentences. Alliteration is the repetition of the initial consonant sounds of close or adjoining words. Antithesis is the juxtaposition of contrasting ideas, usually in parallel structure.

Using language appropriately means adapting to the particular occasion, audience, and topic at hand. It also means developing your own language style instead of trying to copy someone else's. If your language is appropriate in all respects, your speech is much more likely to succeed.

You will also be more likely to succeed if you use inclusive language in your speeches. Although the subject of inclusive language is complex and controversial, a number of inclusive usages have become so widely accepted that no aspiring speaker can afford to ignore them. They include avoiding the generic "he," dropping the use of "man" when referring to both men and women, refraining from stereotyping jobs and social roles by gender, avoiding identifying personal traits that are unrelated to the topic, and using names that groups use to identify themselves.

Key Terms

denotative meaning (274)
connotative meaning (274)
thesaurus (274)
concrete words (280)
abstract words (280)
clutter (281)
imagery (283)
simile (284)
cliché (284)
metaphor (285)
rhythm (285)
parallelism (286)
repetition (287)
alliteration (287)
antithesis (287)
inclusive language (291)
generic "he" (292)

ONLINE LEARNING CENTER

Review these terms by doing the Chapter 11 crossword puzzle at www.mhhe.com/lucas9.

Review Questions

After reading this chapter, you should be able to answer the following questions:

1. How does language help shape our sense of reality?
2. What is the difference between denotative and connotative meaning? How might you use each to convey your message most effectively?
3. What are the four criteria for using language effectively in your speeches?
4. What are three things you should do to use language clearly in your speeches?
5. What are two ways to bring your speeches to life with vivid, animated language?
6. What does it mean to say you should use language appropriately in your speeches?
7. Why is it important for a public speaker to use inclusive language? What are five usages of inclusive language which have become so widely accepted that no speaker can afford to ignore them?

CD 1: STUDY QUESTIONS

For further review, go to the Study Questions for this chapter.

Exercises for Critical Thinking

1. Arrange each of the sequences below in order, from the most abstract word to the most concrete word.
   a. housing complex, building, dining room, structure, apartment
   b. *Mona Lisa,* art, painting, creative activity, portrait
   c. automobile, vehicle, Ferrari, transportation, sports car
2. Rewrite each of the following sentences using clear, familiar words.
   a. My employment objective is to attain a position of maximum financial reward.
   b. All professors at this school are expected to achieve high standards of excellence in their instructional duties.
   c. In the eventuality of a fire, it is imperative that all persons evacuate the building without undue delay.
3. Each of the statements below uses one or more of the following stylistic devices: metaphor, simile, parallelism, repetition, alliteration, antithesis. Identify the device (or devices) used in each statement.
   a. "We are a people in a quandary about the present. We are a people in search of our future. We are a people in search of a national community." (Barbara Jordan)
   b. "The vice presidency is the sand trap of American politics. It's near the prize, and designed to be limiting." (Howard Fineman)
   c. "We should not demean our democracy with the politics of distraction, denial, and despair." (Al Gore)
   d. "America is not like a blanket—one piece of unbroken cloth, the same color, the same texture, the same size. America is more like a quilt—many patches, many sizes, and woven and held together by a common thread." (Jesse Jackson)
4. Analyze Martin Luther King's "I Have a Dream" in the appendix of sample speeches that follows Chapter 18. Identify the methods King uses to make his language clear, vivid, and appropriate. Look particularly at King's use of familiar words, concrete words, imagery, and rhythm.

Applying the POWER of PUBLIC SPEAKING

Since graduating from college, you have developed a successful business that is located near the campus. As part of its plan to involve more alumni and community members in college affairs, the school has asked you to speak with new students during registration week for the fall term. In the opening section of your speech, you want the audience to feel what you felt the first few days you were on campus as a new student. The best strategy, you decide, is to present two or three similes that complete the sentence, "Beginning college is like . . ." Write your similes.

Notes

[1]For two highly readable works on the natural evolution of language, see David Crystal, *The Cambridge Encyclopedia of the English Language,* 2nd ed. (Cambridge: Cambridge University Press, 2003), and John McWhorter, *The Power of Babel: A Natural History of Language* (New York: Perennial, 2003).

[2]Richard Lederer, *The Miracle of Language,* rev. ed. (New York: Pocket Books, 1999), p. 32.

[3]James R. Andrews, *A Choice of Worlds: The Practice and Criticism of Public Discourse* (New York: Harper and Row, 1973).

[4]The relationship between thought and language has been explored by many writers. For a recent work, see Steven Pinker, *Words and Rules: The Ingredients of Language* (New York: HarperCollins, 2000).

[5]Edward P. J. Corbett and Robert J. Connors, *Classical Rhetoric for the Modern Student,* 4th ed. (New York: Oxford University Press, 1999), p. 372.

[6]Dorothy Sarnoff, *Speech Can Change Your Life* (New York: Doubleday, 1970), p. 71.

[7]Annmarie Mungo, "A Child Is Born," *Winning Orations, 1980* (Mankato, MN: Interstate Oratorical Association, 1980), pp. 49–50.

[8]Adapted from Richard Conniff, "You Never Know What the Fire Ant Is Going to Do Next," *Smithsonian,* July 1990, p. 49.

[9]I would like to thank *China Daily* and *21st Century* for permission to include video from Zhang Jiexuan's speech on the CD that accompanies this edition of *The Art of Public Speaking.*

[10]For an informative recent study on the functions of metaphor in public address, see Pradeep Sopory and James Price Dillard, "The Persuasive Effects of Metaphor: A Meta-Analysis," *Human Communication Research,* 28 (2002), pp. 382–419.

[11]Thomas R. Arp and Greg Johnson, *Perrine's Sound and Sense: An Introduction to Poetry,* 11th ed. (Boston: Thomson Wadsworth, 2005), p. 222.

[12]Winston Churchill, Speech at St. James Palace, London, June 12, 1941, in Lloyd Rohler and Roger Cook (eds.), *Great Speeches for Analysis and Criticism,* 4th ed. (Greenwood, IN: Alistair Press, 2001), p. 94.

[13]Edward Bliss, Jr. (ed)., *In Search of Light: The Broadcasts of Edward R. Murrow, 1938–1961* (New York: Knopf, 1967), p. 276.

[14]John Hancock, Boston Massacre Oration, March 5, 1774, in Ronald F. Reid and James F. Klumpp (eds.), *American Rhetorical Discourse,* 3rd ed. (Long Grove, IL: Waveland Press, 2005), pp. 103.

[15]William Safire, *On Language* (New York: Times Books, 1980), p. xiv.

[16]Rosalie Maggio, *Talking About People: A Guide to Fair and Accurate Language* (Phoenix, AZ: Oryx Press, 1997), p. 16.

[17]Maggio, *Talking About People,* p. 26.

CHAPTER TWELVE

Delivery

If you were to record one of David Letterman's comedy routines, memorize it word for word, and stand up before your friends to recite it, would you get the same response Letterman does? Not very likely. And why not? Because you would not *deliver* the jokes as Letterman does. Of course, the jokes are basically funny. But David Letterman brings something extra to the jokes—his manner of presentation, his vocal inflections, his perfectly timed pauses, his facial expressions, his gestures. All these are part of an expert delivery. It would take you years of practice—as it took Letterman—to duplicate his results.

No one expects your speech class to transform you into a multimillion-dollar talk show host. Still, this example demonstrates how important delivery can be to any public speaking situation. Even a mediocre speech will be more effective if it is presented well, whereas a wonderfully written speech can be ruined by poor delivery.

This does not mean dazzling delivery will turn a mindless string of nonsense into a triumphant oration. You cannot make a good speech without having something to say. But having something to say is not enough. You must also know *how* to say it.

nonverbal communication
Communication based on a person's use of voice and body, rather than on the use of words.

Speech delivery is a matter of *nonverbal communication.* It is not based on your words, but on how you use your voice and body to convey the message expressed by your words. There is a great deal of research on nonverbal communication in general and on speech delivery in particular. That research shows that the impact of a speaker's words—whether in a formal speech or in daily conversation—is powerfully influenced by the speaker's nonverbal communication.[1] In this chapter, we will explain how you can use your nonverbal communication to deliver your speeches effectively and to increase the impact of your verbal message.[2]

What Is Good Delivery?

Wendell Phillips was a leader in the movement to abolish slavery in the United States during the 1800s. Some people considered him the greatest speaker of his time. The following story suggests one reason why:

> Shortly before the Civil War an Andover student, learning that Phillips was to lecture in Boston, made a 22-mile pilgrimage on foot to hear him. At first the trip seemed hardly worthwhile, for the student discovered that Phillips was not an orator in the grand manner, but spoke in an almost conversational style. He stood on the platform, one hand lightly resting on a table, talked for what seemed to be about 20 minutes, concluded, and sat down. When the student looked at his watch, he found to his astonishment that he had been listening for an hour and a half![3]

Good delivery does not call attention to itself. It conveys the speaker's ideas clearly, interestingly, and without distracting the audience. If you mumble your words, shuffle your feet, gaze out the window, or talk in a monotone, you will not get your message across. Nor will you be effective if you show off, strike a dramatic pose, or shout in ringing tones. Most audiences prefer delivery that combines a certain degree of formality with the best attributes of good conversation—directness, spontaneity, animation, vocal and facial expressiveness, and a lively sense of communication.

When you begin speaking in public, you will probably have many questions about delivery: "Should I be strong and aggressive or low-key?" "Where should I stand?" "How should I gesture?" "How should I handle my notes?" "How fast should I speak?" "When should I pause?" "Where should I look?" "What do I do if I make a mistake?"

There are no hard-and-fast answers to these questions. Speech delivery is an art, not a science. What works for one speaker may fail for another. And what succeeds with today's audience may not with tomorrow's. You cannot become a skilled speaker just by following a set of rules in a textbook. In the long run, there is no substitute for experience. But take heart! A textbook *can* give you basic pointers to get you started in the right direction.

When you plan your first speech (or your second or third), you should concentrate on such basics as speaking intelligibly, avoiding distracting mannerisms, and establishing eye contact with your listeners. Once you get these elements under control and begin to feel fairly comfortable in front of an audience, you can work on polishing your delivery to enhance the impact of your ideas. Eventually, you may find yourself able to control the timing, rhythm, and momentum of a speech as skillfully as a conductor controls an orchestra.

Methods of Delivery

There are four basic methods of delivering a speech: (1) reading verbatim from a manuscript; (2) reciting a memorized text; (3) speaking impromptu; and (4) speaking extemporaneously. Let us look at each.

Reading from a Manuscript

Certain speeches *must* be delivered word for word, according to a meticulously prepared manuscript. Examples include a Pope's religious proclamation, an engineer's report to a professional meeting, or a President's message to Congress. In such situations, absolute accuracy is essential. Every word of the speech will be analyzed by the press, by colleagues, perhaps by enemies. In the case of the President, a misstated phrase could cause an international incident.

manuscript speech
A speech that is written out word for word and read to the audience.

Timing may also be a factor in manuscript speeches. Much of today's political campaigning is done on radio and television. If the candidate buys a one-minute spot and pays a great deal of money for it, that one minute of speech must be just right.

Although it looks easy, delivering a speech from a manuscript requires great skill. Some people do it well. Their words "come alive as if coined on the spot."[4] Others seem to ruin it every time. Instead of sounding vibrant and conversational, they come across as wooden and artificial. They falter over words, pause in the wrong places, read too quickly or too slowly, speak in a monotone, and march through the speech without even glancing at their audience. In short, they come across as *reading to* their listeners, rather than *talking with* them.

If you are in a situation where you must speak from a manuscript, do your best to avoid these problems. Practice aloud to make sure the speech sounds natural. Work on establishing eye contact with your listeners. Be certain the final manuscript is legible at a glance. Above all, reach out to your audience with the same directness and sincerity that you would if you were speaking extemporaneously.

Reciting from Memory

Among the feats of the legendary orators, none leaves us more in awe than their practice of presenting even the longest and most complex speeches entirely from memory. Nowadays it is no longer customary to memorize any but the shortest of speeches—toasts, congratulatory remarks, acceptance speeches, introductions, and the like. If you are giving a speech of this kind and want to memorize it, by all means do so. However, be sure to memorize it so thoroughly that you will be able to concentrate on communicating with the audience, not on trying to remember the words. Speakers who gaze at the ceiling or stare out the window trying to recall what they have memorized are no better off than those who read dully from a manuscript.

Speaking Impromptu

impromptu speech
A speech delivered with little or no immediate preparation.

An impromptu speech is delivered with little or no immediate preparation. Few people choose to speak impromptu, but sometimes it cannot be avoided. In fact, many of the speeches you give in life will be impromptu. You might be called on suddenly to "say a few words" or, in the course of a class discussion, business meeting, or committee report, want to respond to a previous speaker.

When such situations arise, don't panic. No one expects you to deliver a perfect speech on the spur of the moment. If you are in a meeting or discussion, pay close attention to what the other speakers say. Take notes of major points with which you agree or disagree. In the process, you will automatically begin to formulate what you will say when it is your turn to speak.

Whenever you are responding to a previous speaker, try to present your speech in four simple steps: First, state the point you are answering. Second, state the point you wish to make. Third, support your point with appropriate statistics, examples, or testimony. Fourth, summarize your point. This four-step method will help you organize your thoughts quickly and clearly.

If time allows, sketch a quick outline of your remarks on a piece of paper before you rise to speak. Use the same method of jotting down key words and phrases followed in a more formal speaking outline (see Chapter 10). This will help you remember what you want to say and will keep you from rambling.

In many cases, you will be able to speak informally without rising from your chair. But if the situation calls for you to speak from a lectern, walk to it calmly, take a deep breath or two (not a visible gasp), establish eye contact with your audience, and begin speaking. No matter how nervous you are inside, do your best to look calm and assured on the outside.

Once you begin speaking, maintain strong eye contact with the audience. If you are prone to talking rapidly when you are nervous, concentrate on speaking at a slower pace. Help the audience keep track of your ideas with signposts such as "My first point is . . . ; second, we can see that . . . ; in conclusion, I would like to say. . . . " If you have had time to prepare notes, stick to what you have written. By stating your points clearly and concisely, you will come across as organized and confident.

Whether you realize it or not, you have given thousands of impromptu "speeches" in daily conversation—as when you informed a new student how to register for classes, or explained to your boss why you were late for work, or answered questions in a job interview, or tried to persuade your roommate to lend you $20 until next week. There is no reason to fall apart when you are asked to speak impromptu in a more formal situation. If you keep cool, organize your thoughts, and limit yourself to a few remarks, you should do just fine.

As with other kinds of public speaking, the best way to become a better impromptu speaker is to practice. If you are assigned an impromptu speech in class, do your best to follow the guidelines discussed here. You can also practice impromptu speaking on your own. Simply choose a topic on which you are already well informed, and give a one- or two-minute impromptu talk on some aspect of that topic. Any topic will do—no matter how serious or frivolous it may be. Nor do you need an audience—you can speak to an empty room. Better yet, you can speak to a digital recorder and play the speech back to hear how you sound. The purpose is to gain experience in pulling your ideas together quickly and stating them succinctly. Over the years, many people have found this an effective way to improve their skills of impromptu speaking.

Extemporaneous speeches are prepared ahead of time, but the exact words are chosen at the moment of presentation. This allows for more direct delivery than does reading from a manuscript.

Speaking Extemporaneously

extemporaneous speech
A carefully prepared and rehearsed speech that is presented from a brief set of notes.

In popular usage, "extemporaneous" means the same as "impromptu." But technically the two are different. Unlike an impromptu speech, which is totally off-the-cuff, an extemporaneous speech is carefully prepared and practiced in advance. In presenting the speech, the extemporaneous speaker uses only a set of brief notes or a speaking outline to jog the memory (see Chapter 10). The exact wording is chosen at the moment of delivery.

This is not as hard as it sounds. Once you have your outline (or notes) and know what topics you are going to cover and in what order, you can begin to practice the speech. Every time you run through it, the wording will be slightly different. As you practice the speech over and over, the best way to present each part will emerge and stick in your mind.

conversational quality
Presenting a speech so it sounds spontaneous no matter how many times it has been rehearsed.

The extemporaneous method has several advantages. It gives more precise control over thought and language than does impromptu speaking; it offers greater spontaneity and directness than does speaking from memory or from a full manuscript; and it is adaptable to a wide range of situations. It also encourages the conversational quality audiences look for in speech delivery. "Conversational quality" means that no matter how many times a speech has been rehearsed, it still *sounds* spontaneous to the audience. When you speak extemporaneously—and have prepared properly—you have full control over your ideas, yet you are not tied to a manuscript. You are free to establish strong eye contact, to gesture naturally, and to concentrate on talking *with* the audience rather than declaiming *to* them.

CD 1: VIDEO 12.1
View excerpts from Elizabeth Dole's speech at the Republican National Convention.

There is no better example of the power of extemporaneous delivery than Elizabeth Dole's renowned speech to the 1996 Republican National Convention in support of her husband's bid for the White House. Speaking to the delegates assembled in San Diego and to a national television audience, Dole broke 150 years of tradition by leaving the lectern and presenting her speech while walking among her listeners on the floor of the auditorium. Speaking extemporaneously, with no notes (and no teleprompter), she was able to break through the physical and psychological barriers that would otherwise have separated her from the audience. As numerous observers commented, it was more like listening to a conversation than to a formal speech.

Dole, of course, is one of the most accomplished speakers in the United States. You can't be expected in your speech class to reach the same mastery that she has worked years to achieve. Yet like thousands of previous students, you can become quite adept at speaking extemporaneously by the end of the term and have a solid foundation to build on in the future. As one student commented in looking back on his speech class, "At the start, I never thought I'd be able to give my speeches without a ton of notes, but I'm amazed at how much progress I made. It's still a bit nerve-racking to speak extemporaneously, but I'm confident I can do it, and I know I'll connect better with the audience as a result. This is one of the most valuable things I learned in the entire class."

Most experienced speakers prefer the extemporaneous method, and most teachers emphasize it. Later in this chapter (pages 317–318), we'll look at a step-by-step program for practicing your extemporaneous delivery.

The Speaker's Voice

What kind of voice do you have? Is it rich and resonant like James Earl Jones's? Thin and nasal like Willie Nelson's? Deep and raspy like Al Sharpton's? Soft and alluring like Catherine Zeta Jones's? Loud and irritating like Dick Vitale's?

Whatever the characteristics of your voice, you can be sure it is unique. Because no two people are exactly the same physically, no two people have identical voices. This is why voiceprints are sometimes used in criminal trials as guides to personal identity. The human voice is produced by a complex series of steps that starts with the exhalation of air from the lungs. (Try talking intelligibly while inhaling and see what happens.) As air is exhaled, it passes through the larynx (or voice box), where it is vibrated to generate sound. This sound is then amplified and modified as it resonates through the throat, mouth, and nasal passages. Finally, the resonated sound is shaped into specific vowel and consonant sounds by the movement of the tongue, lips, teeth, and roof of the mouth. The resulting sounds are combined to form words and sentences.

The voice produced by this physical process will greatly affect the success of your speeches. A golden voice is certainly an asset, but you can manage without. Some of the most famous speakers in history had undistinguished voices. Abraham Lincoln had a harsh and penetrating voice; Winston Churchill suffered from a slight lisp and an awkward stammer. Like them, you can overcome natural disadvantages and use your voice to the best effect. If you speak too softly to be heard, constantly stumble over words, spit out your ideas at machine-gun speed, or plod along as if you were reading a grocery list, your speeches will fail. Lincoln and Churchill learned to *control* their voices. You can do the same thing.

The aspects of voice you should work to control are volume, pitch, rate, pauses, variety, pronunciation, articulation, and dialect.

Volume

volume
The loudness or softness of the speaker's voice.

At one time a powerful voice was all but essential for an orator. Today, electronic amplification allows even a soft-spoken person to be heard in any setting. But in the classroom you will speak without a microphone. When you do, be sure to adjust your voice to the acoustics of the room, the size of the audience, and the level of background noise. If you speak too loudly, your listeners will think you boorish. If you speak too softly, they will not understand you. Remember that your own voice always sounds louder to you than to a listener. Soon after beginning your speech, glance at the people farthest away from you. If they look puzzled, are leaning forward in their seats, or are otherwise straining to hear, you need to talk louder.

Pitch

pitch
The highness or lowness of the speaker's voice.

Pitch is the highness or lowness of the speaker's voice. The faster sound waves vibrate, the higher their pitch; the slower they vibrate, the lower their pitch. Pitch distinguishes the sound produced by the keys at one end of a piano from that produced by the keys at the other end.

In speech, pitch can affect the meaning of words or sounds. Pitch is what makes the difference between the "Aha!" triumphantly exclaimed by Sherlock Holmes upon discovering a seemingly decisive clue and the "Aha" he mutters when he learns the clue is not decisive after all. If you were to read the preceding sentence aloud, your voice would probably go up in pitch on the first "Aha" and down in pitch on the second.

inflections
Changes in the pitch or tone of a speaker's voice.

Changes in pitch are known as *inflections.* They give your voice luster, warmth, and vitality. It is the inflection of your voice that reveals whether you are asking a question or making a statement; whether you are being sincere or sarcastic. Your inflections can also make you sound happy or sad, angry or pleased, dynamic or listless, tense or relaxed, interested or bored.

monotone
A constant pitch or tone of voice.

In ordinary conversation we instinctively use inflections to convey meaning and emotion. People who do not are said to speak in a *monotone*—a trait whose only known benefit is to cure insomnia in one's listeners. Few people speak in an absolute monotone, with no variation whatever in pitch, but many fall into repetitious pitch patterns that are just as hypnotic as a monotone. You can guard against this problem by recording your speeches as you practice them. If all your sentences end on the same inflection—either upward or downward—work on varying your pitch patterns to fit the meaning of your words. As with breaking any other habit, this may seem awkward at first, but it is guaranteed to make you a better speaker.

Rate

rate
The speed at which a person speaks.

Rate refers to the speed at which a person speaks. People in the U.S. usually speak at a rate between 125 and 150 words per minute, but there is no uniform rate for effective speechmaking. Daniel Webster spoke at roughly 90 words per minute, Franklin Roosevelt at 110, John Kennedy at 180. Martin Luther King opened his "I Have a Dream" speech at a pace of 92 words per minute and finished it at 145. The best rate of speech depends on several things—the vocal attributes of the speaker, the mood she or he is trying to create, the composition of the audience, and the nature of the occasion.

For example, if you wanted to convey the excitement of the Daytona 500 car race, you would probably speak rather quickly, but a slower rate would be more appropriate to describe the serenity of the Alaskan wilderness. A fast rate helps create feelings of happiness, fear, anger, and surprise, while a slow rate is better for expressing sadness or disgust. A slower tempo is called for when you explain complex information, a faster tempo when the information is already familiar to the audience.

Two obvious faults to avoid are speaking so slowly that your listeners become bored or so quickly that they lose track of your ideas. Novice speakers are particularly prone to racing through their speeches at a frantic rate. Fortunately, once a speaker begins to work on it, this is usually an easy habit to break, as is the less common one of crawling through one's speech at a snail's pace.

The best rate of speech depends partly on the mood a speaker wants to create. To communicate the excitement of surfing, you would probably speak at a faster-than-normal rate.

The key in both cases is becoming aware of the problem and concentrating on solving it. Use a digital recorder to check how fast you speak. Pay special attention to rate when practicing your speech. Finally, be sure to include reminders about delivery on your speaking outline so you won't forget to make the adjustments when you give your speech in class.

Pauses

pause
A momentary break in the vocal delivery of a speech.

Learning how and when to pause is a major challenge for most beginning speakers. Even a moment of silence can seem like an eternity. As you gain more poise and confidence, however, you will discover how useful the pause can be. It can signal the end of a thought unit, give an idea time to sink in, and lend dramatic impact to a statement. "The right word may be effective," said Mark Twain, "but no word was ever as effective as a rightly timed pause."

As Twain knew, the crucial factor is timing. "For one audience," he cautioned, "the pause will be short, for another a little longer, for another a shade longer still." Looking back on his own career as a speaker, he recalled: "When the pause was right the effect was sure; when the pause was wrong . . . the laughter was only mild, never a crash."

Developing a keen sense of timing is partly a matter of common sense, partly a matter of experience. You will not always get your pauses just right at first, but keep trying. Listen to accomplished speakers to see how they use pauses to modulate the rate and rhythm of their messages. Work on pauses when you practice your speeches.

vocalized pause
A pause that occurs when a speaker fills the silence between words with vocalizations such as "uh," "er," and "um."

When you do pause, make sure you pause at the end of thought units and not in the middle. Otherwise, you may distract listeners from your ideas. Most important, do not fill the silence with "uh," "er," or "um." These *vocalized pauses,* as they are called, are always annoying, and they can be devastating. Not only do they create negative perceptions about a speaker's intelligence, but they often make a speaker appear deceptive.[5]

Vocal Variety

Just as variety is the spice of life, so is it the spice of public speaking. A flat, listless, unchanging voice is just as deadly to speechmaking as a flat, listless, unchanging routine is to daily life.

Try reading this limerick aloud:

> I sat next to the Duchess at tea.
> It was just as I feared it would be:
> Her rumblings abdominal
> Were simply abominable
> And everyone thought it was me!

Now recite this passage from James Joyce's "All Day I Hear the Noise of Waters":

> The gray winds, the cold winds are blowing
> Where I go.
> I hear the noise of many waters
> Far below.
> All day, all night, I hear them flowing
> To and fro.[6]

Certainly you did not utter both passages the same way. You instinctively varied the rate, pitch, volume, and pauses to distinguish the light-hearted limerick from the solemn melancholy of Joyce's poem. When giving a speech, you should modulate your voice in just this way to communicate your ideas and feelings.

vocal variety
Changes in a speaker's rate, pitch, and volume that give the voice variety and expressiveness.

For an excellent example of vocal variety, look at CD 1, Video 12.2. The speaker is Sajjid Zahir Chinoy, who was born and raised in Bombay, India, before coming to the United States to attend college at the University of Richmond. At the end of his senior year, Chinoy was selected as the student commencement speaker in a campuswide competition. He spoke of the warm reception he received at Richmond and of how cultural differences can be overcome by attempting to understand other people.

At the end of his speech, Chinoy received thunderous applause—partly because of what he said, but also because of how he said it. Addressing the audience of 3,000 people without notes, he spoke extemporaneously with strong eye contact and excellent vocal variety. The speech was so inspiring that the main speaker, Harvard psychiatrist Robert Coles, began his presentation by paying tribute to Chinoy. "I've been to a number of commencements," said Coles, "but I've never heard a speech quite like that!"

CD 1: VIDEO 12.2
View an excerpt from Sajjid Zahir Chinoy, "Questions of Culture."

How can you develop a lively, expressive voice? Above all, by approaching every speech as Chinoy approached his—as an opportunity to share with your listeners ideas that are important to you. Your sense of conviction and your desire to communicate will help give your voice the same spark it has in spontaneous conversation.

Diagnose your present speaking voice to decide which aspects need improvement. Record your speeches to hear how they sound. Try them out on members of your family, a friend, or a roommate. Check with your teacher

THE INTERNET *Connection*

Do you want to learn more about speech delivery? Perhaps gain additional experience after your speech class is over? You can do both by joining an organization such as Toastmasters International, which has more than 200,000 members and 10,000 clubs in 90 countries around the world. For information about Toastmasters, log on to its Web site at www.toastmasters.org.

If you are a non-native speaker of English and want to work on your skills of spoken English, you will find a number of excellent resources at the English as a Second Language student Web site (http://owl.english.purdue.edu/handouts/esl/eslstudent.html).

ONLINE LEARNING CENTER

You can link to these Web sites at www.mhhe.com/lucas9.

for suggestions. Practice the vocal variety exercise at the end of this chapter. Vocal variety is a natural feature of ordinary conversation. There is no reason it should not be as natural a feature of your speeches.

Pronunciation

We all mispronounce words now and again. Here, for example, are six words with which you are probably familiar. Say each one aloud.

genuine	err
arctic	nuclear
theater	February

Very likely you made a mistake on at least one, for they are among the most frequently mispronounced words in the English language. Let's see:

Word	Common Error	Correct Pronunciation
genuine	gen-u-wine	gen-u-win
arctic	ar-tic	arc-tic
theater	thee-ate′-er	thee′-a-ter
err	air	ur
nuclear	nu-cu-lar	nu-cle-ar
February	Feb-u-ary	Feb-ru-ary

Every word leads a triple life: it is read, written, and spoken. Most people recognize and understand many more words in reading than they use in ordinary writing, and about three times as many as occur in spontaneous speech.[7] This is why we occasionally stumble when speaking words that are part of our reading or writing vocabularies. In other cases, we may mispronounce the most commonplace words out of habit.

pronunciation The accepted standard of sound and rhythm for words in a given language.

The problem is that we usually don't *know* when we are mispronouncing a word; otherwise we would say it correctly. If we are lucky, we learn the right pronunciation by hearing someone else say the word properly or by having someone gently correct us in private. If we are unlucky, we mispronounce the word in front of a roomful of people, who may raise their eyebrows, groan, or laugh. Even experienced speakers sometimes fall into this trap. In reporting about a recent presidential election, a local TV news anchor referred several times to the number of votes needed to capture a majority in the e-lec-tor′-*e*-al college. When he had finished, his coanchor said (on the air!), "And it also takes 270 votes to win a majority in the e-lec′-tor-al college." The first announcer tried to shrug it off, but he was noticeably embarrassed.

All of this argues for practicing your speech in front of as many trusted friends and relatives as you can corner. If you have any doubts about the proper pronunciation of certain words, be sure to check a dictionary.

Articulation

articulation The physical production of particular speech sounds.

Articulation and pronunciation are not identical. Sloppy articulation is the failure to form particular speech sounds crisply and distinctly. It is one of several causes of mispronunciation; but not all errors in pronunciation stem from poor articulation. You can articulate a word sharply and still mispronounce it. For example, if you say the "s" in "Illinois" or the "p" in "pneumonia," you are making a mistake in pronunciation, regardless of how precisely you articulate the sounds.

Errors in articulation can be caused by a cleft palate, by an overly large tongue, by a misaligned jaw, even by a poorly fitted dental plate or braces on the teeth. Serious problems require the aid of a certified speech therapist. But most of the time poor articulation is caused by laziness—by failing to manipulate the lips, tongue, jaw, and soft palate so as to produce speech sounds clearly and precisely. People in the U.S. seem particularly prone to poor articulation. We habitually chop, slur, and mumble our words, rather than enunciating them plainly.

Among college students, poor articulation is more common than ignorance of correct pronunciation. We know that "let me" is not "lemme," that "going to" is not "gonna," that "did you" is not "didja," yet we persist in articulating these words improperly. Here are some other common errors in articulation you should work to avoid:

Word	Misarticulation
ought to	otta
didn't	dint
for	fur
don't know	dunno
have to	hafta
them	em
want to	wanna
will you	wilya

If you have sloppy articulation, work on identifying and eliminating your most common errors. Like other bad habits, careless articulation can be broken only by persistent effort—but the results are well worth it. Not only will your speeches be more intelligible, but employers will be more likely to hire you, to place you in positions of responsibility, and to promote you. As Shakespeare advised, "Mend your speech a little, lest you may mar your fortunes."

Dialect

Most languages have dialects, each with a distinctive accent, grammar, and vocabulary. Dialects are usually based on regional or ethnic speech patterns. The United States has four major regional dialects—Eastern, New England, Southern, and General American. These dialects affect the way people talk in different parts of the country. In Boston people may get "idears" about "dee-ah" friends. In Alabama parents tell their children to stop "squinching" their eyes while watching television and to go clean up their rooms "rat" now. In Utah people praise the "lard" and put the "lord" in the refrigerator.[8]

dialect
A variety of a language distinguished by variations of accent, grammar, or vocabulary.

There are also several well-established ethnic dialects in the United States, including Black English, Jewish English, Hispanic English, and Cajun English. In recent years we have also seen the emergence of newer dialects such as Haitian English and Cuban English. As the United States becomes more diverse culturally, it is also becoming more diverse linguistically.

Over the years linguists have done a great deal of research on dialects. They have concluded that no dialect is inherently better or worse than another. There is no such thing as a right or wrong dialect. Dialects are not linguistic badges of superiority or inferiority. They are usually shaped by our regional or ethnic background, and every dialect is "right" for the community of people who use it.

Good speakers use a lively voice to help bring their ideas to life. They also use gestures, eye contact, and facial expressions to create a strong bond with members of the audience.

When is a given dialect appropriate in public speaking? The answer depends above all on the composition of your audience. Heavy use of any dialect—regional or ethnic—can be troublesome for a speaker when the audience does not share that dialect. In such a situation, the dialect may cause listeners to make negative judgments about the speaker's personality, intelligence, and competence. This is why professional speakers have been known to invest large amounts of time (and money) to master the General American dialect used by most television news broadcasters. This dialect has become so widely accepted throughout the United States that it is suitable for almost any audience.

Does this mean you must talk like a television news broadcaster if you want to be successful in your speeches? Not at all. Regional or ethnic dialects do not pose a problem as long as the audience is familiar with them and finds them appropriate to the occasion. When speaking in the North, for example, a southern politician will probably avoid heavy use of regional dialect. But when addressing audiences in the South, the same politician may intentionally include regional dialect as a way of creating common ground with his or her listeners.

Although not strictly speaking a matter of dialect, the proficiency of non-native speakers of English often arises in the speech classroom. Fortunately, teachers and students alike usually go out of their way to be helpful and encouraging to international students and others for whom English is not the primary language. Over the years many non-native speakers of English have found speech class a supportive environment in which to improve their proficiency in spoken English.[9]

The Speaker's Body

Imagine you are at a party. During the evening you form impressions about the people around you. Jonte seems relaxed and even-tempered, Nicole tense and irritable. Kyndra seems open and straightforward, Bekah hostile and evasive. Amin seems happy to see you; Seth definitely is not.

How do you reach these conclusions? To a surprising extent, you reach them not on the basis of what people say with words, but because of what they say with their posture, gestures, eyes, and facial expressions. Suppose you are sitting next to Amin, and he says, "This is a great party. I'm really glad to be here with you." However, his body is turned slightly away from you, and he keeps looking at someone across the room. Despite what he says, you know he is *not* glad to be there with you.

Much the same thing happens in speechmaking. Here is the story of one student's first two classroom speeches and the effect created by his physical actions on each occasion:

Sean O'Connor's first speech did not go very well. Even though he had chosen an interesting topic, researched the speech with care, and practiced it faithfully, he did not take into account the importance of using his body effectively. When the time came for him to speak, a stricken look crossed his face. He got up from his chair like a condemned man and plodded to the lectern as though going to the guillotine. His vocal delivery was good enough, but all the while his hands were living a life of their own. They fidgeted with his notes, played with the buttons of his shirt, and drummed on the lectern. Throughout the speech Sean kept his head down, and he looked at his watch repeatedly. Regardless of what his *words* were saying, his *body* was saying, "I don't want to be here!"

Finally it was over. Sean rushed to his seat and collapsed into it, looking enormously relieved. Needless to say, his speech was not a great success.

Fortunately, when Sean's problem was pointed out to him, he worked hard to correct it. His next speech was quite a different story. This time he got up from his chair and strode to the lectern confidently. He kept his hands under control and concentrated on making eye contact with his listeners. This was truly an achievement, because Sean was just as nervous as the first time. However, he found that the more he made himself *look* confident, the more confident he *became*. After the speech his classmates were enthusiastic. "Great speech," they said. "You really seemed to care about the subject, and you brought this caring to the audience."

In fact, the wording of Sean's second speech wasn't much better than that of the first. It was his physical actions that made all the difference. From the time he left his seat until he returned, his body said, "I am confident and in control of the situation. I have something worthwhile to say, and I want you to think so too."

Posture, facial expression, gestures, eye contact—all affect the way listeners respond to a speaker. How we use these and other body motions to communicate is the subject of a fascinating area of study called kinesics. One of its founders, Ray Birdwhistell, estimated that more than 700,000 physical signals can be sent through bodily movement. Studies have shown that these signals have a significant impact on the meaning communicated by speakers. Research has also confirmed what the Greek historian Herodotus observed more than 2,400 years ago: "People trust their ears less than their eyes." When a speaker's body language is inconsistent with his or her words, listeners often believe the body language rather than the words.[10]

kinesics
The study of body motions as a systematic mode of communication.

Here are the major aspects of physical action that will affect the outcome of your speeches.

Personal Appearance

If you were Jennifer Lopez, you could show up to make an Academy Award presentation speech wearing a bizarre creation that left little to the imagination. If you were Albert Einstein, you could show up to address an international science conference wearing wrinkled trousers, a sweater, and tennis shoes. While the members of your audience would certainly comment on your attire, your reputation would not be harmed. In fact, it might be enhanced. You would be one of the few, the very few, who live outside the rules, who are expected to be unusual.

Now imagine what would happen if the president of a corporation showed up to address a stockholders' meeting attired like Jennifer Lopez, or if the President of the United States spoke on national television wearing wrinkled clothes and tennis shoes. Both presidents would soon be looking for work. Barring the occasional eccentric, every speaker is expected by her or his audience to exhibit a personal appearance in keeping with the occasion of the speech.

The President of the United States can be photographed in hiking clothes for a quick weekend interview at Camp David, but that same president will don a conservative suit and tie to address a joint session of Congress. Similarly, a business executive speaking at a winter sales conference in Acapulco would probably wear slacks and a casual shirt or blouse because a business suit, in this atmosphere, would seem too formal. But back home in San Francisco, Chicago, or New York, the same executive will be immaculately dressed in a well-tailored suit.

A number of studies have confirmed that personal appearance plays an important role in speechmaking.[11] Listeners always see you before they hear you. Just as you adapt your language to the audience and the occasion, so should you dress and groom appropriately. Although the force of your speech can sometimes overcome a poor impression created by personal appearance, the odds are against it. Regardless of the speaking situation, you should try to evoke a favorable first impression—an impression that is likely to make listeners more receptive to what you say.

Movement

Novice speakers are often unsure about what to do with their body while giving a speech. Some pace nonstop back and forth across the podium, fearing that if they stop, they will forget everything. Others are perpetual-motion machines, constantly shifting their weight from one foot to the other, bobbing their shoulders, fidgeting with their notes, or jingling coins in their pockets. Still others turn into statues, standing rigid and expressionless from beginning to end.

Such quirks usually stem from nervousness. If you are prone to distracting mannerisms, your teacher will identify them so you can work on controlling them in later speeches. With a little concentration, these mannerisms should disappear as you become more comfortable speaking in front of an audience.

As important as how you act during the speech is what you do just *before* you begin and *after* you finish. As you rise to speak, try to appear calm, poised, and confident, despite the butterflies in your stomach. When you reach the lectern, don't lean on it, and don't rush into your speech. Give yourself time to get set. Arrange your notes just the way you want them. Stand quietly as you wait to make sure the audience is paying attention. Establish eye contact with your listeners. Then—and only then—should you start to talk.

When you reach the end of your speech, maintain eye contact for a few moments after you stop talking. This will give your closing line time to sink in. Unless you are staying at the lectern to answer questions, collect your notes and return to your seat. As you do so, maintain your cool, collected demeanor. Whatever you do, don't start to gather your notes before you have finished talking; and don't cap off your speech with a huge sigh of relief or some remark like, "Whew! Am I glad that's over!"

All this advice is common sense; yet you would be surprised how many people need it. When practicing your speeches, spend a little time rehearsing how you will behave at the beginning and at the end. It is one of the easiest—and one of the most effective—things you can do to improve your image with an audience.

Gestures

Few aspects of delivery seem to cause students more anguish than deciding what to do with their hands. "Should I clasp them behind my back? Let them hang at my sides? Put them in my pockets? Rest them on the lectern? And what about gesturing? When should I do that—and how?" Even people who normally use their hands expressively in everyday conversation seem to regard them as awkward appendages when speaking before an audience.

Over the years, more nonsense has been written about gesturing than about any other aspect of speech delivery. Adroit gestures *can* add to the impact of a speech; but there is nothing to the popular notion that public speakers must have a vast repertoire of graceful gestures. Some accomplished speakers gesture frequently, others hardly at all. The primary rule is this: Whatever gestures you make should not draw attention to themselves and distract from your message. They should *appear* natural and spontaneous, help clarify or reinforce your ideas, and be suited to the audience and occasion.

gestures
Motions of a speaker's hands or arms during a speech.

At this stage of your speaking career, you have many more important things to concentrate on than how to gesture. Gesturing tends to work itself out as you acquire experience and confidence. In the meantime, make sure your hands do not upstage your ideas. Avoid flailing them about, wringing them together, cracking your knuckles, or toying with your rings. Once you have eliminated these distractions, forget about your hands. Think about communicating with your listeners, and your gestures will probably take care of themselves—just as they do in conversation.

Eye Contact

The eyeball itself expresses no emotion. Yet by manipulating the eyeball and the areas of the face around it—especially the upper eyelids and the eyebrows—we are able to convey an intricate array of nonverbal messages. So revealing are these messages that we think of the eyes as "the windows of the soul." We look to them to help gauge the truthfulness, intelligence, attitudes, and feelings of a speaker.

eye contact
Direct visual contact with the eyes of another person.

Like many aspects of communication, eye contact is influenced by cultural background. When engaged in conversation, Arabs, Latin Americans, and Southern Europeans tend to look directly at the person with whom they are talking. People from Asian countries and parts of Africa tend to engage in less eye contact. In Kenya a discussion between a woman and her son-in-law may well be conducted with each person turning her or his back to the other![12]

When it comes to public speaking, there appears to be fairly wide agreement across cultures on the importance of some degree of eye contact.[13] In most circumstances, one of the quickest ways to establish a communicative bond with your listeners is to look at them personally and pleasantly. Avoiding

Research shows that eye contact is one of the most important elements in effective speech delivery. No matter what the situation, you want your eyes to convey confidence, sincerity, and conviction.

their gaze is one of the surest ways to lose them. There is a great deal of research to show that speakers in the United States who refuse to establish eye contact are perceived as tentative or ill at ease and may be seen as insincere or dishonest. It is no wonder, then, that teachers urge students to look at the audience 80 to 90 percent of the time they are talking.

You may find this disconcerting at first. But after one or two speeches, you should be able to meet the gaze of your audience fairly comfortably. As you look at your listeners, be alert for their reactions. Can they hear you? Do they understand you? Are they awake? Your eyes will help you answer these questions.

It isn't enough just to look at your listeners; *how* you look at them also counts. A blank stare is almost as bad as no eye contact at all. So is a fierce, hostile glower or a series of frightened, bewildered glances. Also beware of the tendency to gaze intently at one part of the audience while ignoring the rest. In speech class some students look only at the section of the room where the teacher is sitting. Others avoid looking anywhere near the teacher and focus on one or two sympathetic friends. You should try to establish eye contact with your whole audience.

CD 1: VIDEO 12.3

View an excerpt from "A Family Tradition."

Look at CD 1, Video 12.3 for an excellent example of eye contact. The speech is by Kristin Berg, a student in a beginning speech course. Kristin's assignment was to interview one of her classmates, Reva, and to give a brief talk introducing her to the rest of the class. In her speech, Kristin explained how Reva's parents had worked to help their growing family adapt to a new culture after immigrating to the United States. As you can see from the CD, the impact of Kristin's speech was greatly enhanced by her strong eye contact (as well by her vocal variety and communicative gestures).

When addressing a small audience such as your class, you can usually look briefly, as Kristin did, from one person to another. For a larger group, you will probably scan the audience rather than try to engage the eyes of each person individually. No matter what the size of your audience, you want your eyes to convey confidence, sincerity, and conviction. They should say, "I am pleased to be able to talk with you. I believe deeply in what I am saying, and I want you to believe in it too."

Practicing Delivery

Popular wisdom promises that practice makes perfect. This is true, but only if we practice properly. No matter how long and hard you practice playing the piano, you will never make beautiful music if you don't know the difference between a sharp and a flat. By the same token, you will do little to improve your speech delivery unless you practice the right things in the right ways. Here is a five-step method that has worked well for many students:

1. Go through your preparation outline *aloud* to check how what you have written translates into spoken discourse. Is it too long? Too short? Are the main points clear when you speak them? Are the supporting materials distinct, convincing, interesting? Do the introduction and conclusion come across well? As you answer these questions, revise the speech as needed.

2. Prepare your speaking outline. In doing so, be sure to follow the guidelines discussed in Chapter 10. Use the same visual framework as in the preparation outline. Make sure the speaking outline is easy to read at a glance. Keep the outline as brief as possible. Give yourself cues on the outline for delivering the speech.

3. Practice the speech aloud several times using only the speaking outline. Be sure to "talk through" all examples and to recite in full all quotations and statistics. If your speech includes visual aids, use them as you practice. The first couple of times you will probably forget something or make a mistake, but don't worry about that. Keep going and complete the speech as well as you can. Concentrate on gaining control of the *ideas;* don't try to learn the speech word for word. After a few tries you should be able to get through the speech extemporaneously with surprising ease.

4. Now begin to polish and refine your delivery. Practice the speech in front of a mirror to check for eye contact and distracting mannerisms. Record the speech to gauge volume, pitch, rate, pauses, and vocal variety. Most important, try it out on friends, roommates, family members—anyone who will listen and give you an honest appraisal. Don't be shy about asking. Most people love to give their opinion about something. Since your speech is designed for people rather than for mirrors or recorders, you need to find out ahead of time how it goes over with people.

5. Finally, give your speech a dress rehearsal under conditions as close as possible to those you will face in class. Some students like to try the speech a couple of times in an empty classroom the day before the speech is due.

No matter where you hold your last practice session, you should leave it feeling confident and looking forward to speaking in your class.

If this or any practice method is to work, you must start early. Don't wait until the day of your speech, or even the night before, to begin working on delivery. A single practice session—no matter how long—is rarely enough. Allow yourself *at least* a couple of days, preferably more, to gain command of the speech and its presentation. No matter how brilliant your preparation outline, what counts is how the speech comes across when you deliver it. Give yourself plenty of time to make sure it comes across well.

Answering Audience Questions

As superintendent of the city's municipal building, Delia Sedano was responsible for presenting a new security plan to the public. Employees, citizens, and reporters gathered in the auditorium to hear her plan. After briefly setting forth her main points, Delia offered to answer questions about the plan.

Because the plan was expensive and potentially controversial, Delia had anticipated a large number of questions, so she was not surprised to see many hands go up. First, an employee asked, "Will the new system create long lines to get into the building, like the lines at airport security checks?" Delia had anticipated this question. She explained that enough security guards would be working at peak hours to avoid long lines.

The next question was more confrontational: "Where will the money come from to pay for all this?" The reporter who asked the question seemed hostile, but Delia was careful not to sound defensive. She stated that money would come from the city's general budget. "I know these are tough times," she added, "but everyone agrees that it's important to safeguard our employees and the citizens who come into the building."

The third question was about the training of security guards. After clarifying the question, Delia introduced the city's director of security and asked him to provide a detailed answer.

Near the end of the time she had allotted for her presentation, Delia announced that she would take two more questions. When those were finished, she concluded with a brief restatement of how the new system would improve the security of the municipal building.

After Delia closed, Art Shafer, a member of the security committee, congratulated her on a successful briefing. "Your presentation was great," he said, "but the Q&A was especially impressive. It showed the audience that we've looked at this from all angles."

If you have ever watched a press conference or heard a speaker answer questions after a talk, you know the question-and-answer session can make or break a presentation. A speaker who handles questions well, as Delia Sedano did, can enhance her credibility and strengthen the impact of her speech. On the other hand, a speaker who evades questions or shows annoyance will almost certainly create the opposite effect.

The question-and-answer session is a common part of public speaking, whether the occasion is a press conference, business presentation, public hearing, or classroom assignment. Depending on the situation, questioning may take place throughout the presentation, or it may be reserved until after the speaker has completed his or her remarks. In either case, an answer to a question is often the final word an audience hears and is likely to leave a lasting impression.

Preparing for the Question-and-Answer Session

The first step to doing well in a question-and-answer session is to take it as seriously as the speech itself. Even experienced speakers have been known to stumble if they fail to prepare thoroughly for the question-and-answer part of their presentation. The two major steps in preparing are working out answers to possible questions and practicing the delivery of those answers.

Formulate Answers to Possible Questions

Once you know your presentation will include questions from the audience, you should be thinking about possible questions even as you are writing your speech. If you practice your speech in front of friends, family, or coworkers, ask them to jot down any questions they may have. Keep track of all the questions and take the time to formulate answers. Write your answers in full to make sure you have thought them through completely.

If you are giving a persuasive speech, be sure to work out answers to objections the audience may have to your proposal. No matter how careful you are to deal with those objections in your speech, you can be sure they will come up at some point in the question-and-answer session.

If you are speaking on a topic with technical aspects, be ready to answer specialized inquiries about them, as well as questions that seek clarification in nontechnical terms. You might even prepare a handout that you can distribute afterward for people who want more information than you can provide in the question-and-answer period.

Practice the Delivery of Your Answers

You would not present a speech to a room full of people without rehearsing. Neither should you go into a question-and-answer session without practicing the delivery of your answers. As many speakers have discovered, writing out answers in the privacy of your home or office and vocalizing them coherently under the pressure of an open forum are two different matters. Since you will be presenting your answers out loud, you should rehearse them out loud.

One possibility is to have a friend or colleague listen to your presentation, ask questions, and critique your answers. This method is used by political candidates and business leaders, whose staff members grill them with questions before debates or press conferences. Another possibility is to record your answers to anticipated questions, play them back, and revise your answers until you get them just right.

As you rehearse, work on making your answers brief and to the point. Many simple questions can be answered in 30 seconds, and even complex ones should be answered in a minute or two. If you practice answering questions beforehand, you will find it much easier to keep to these time limits.

Of course, no matter how much you work ahead of time, there is no way to predict every question you will receive. Some people will ask questions you had not anticipated, and some of the questions you did anticipate may not get asked at all. But if you go into the question-and-answer period fully prepared, you will find it much easier to adapt to whatever occurs.

Many speeches are followed by a question-and-answer session. Here Secretary of State Condoleezza Rice responds to questions from the press after her prepared remarks on U.S. foreign policy.

Managing the Question-and-Answer Session

If you have ever watched a skillful speaker field questions from the audience, you know there is an art to managing a question-and-answer session. Entire books have been written on this subject, but the following suggestions will help get you started on the right foot.

Clarify the Format

If there is any doubt about when you will entertain questions, take time early in your speech to clarify the format you prefer. You can do this by saying something like, "Feel free to ask questions throughout my speech," or "I'll be happy to answer questions at the end of my talk." Of course, if the ground rules are already clear, there is no need to say anything about them.

Approach Questions with a Positive Attitude

A positive attitude will help you answer questions graciously and respectfully. Try to view questions from the audience as signs of genuine interest and a desire to learn more about your subject. If someone asks a question about material you feel you have covered or a point that seems clear to you, don't respond by saying, "I discussed that at the beginning of my talk," or "The answer seems obvious." Instead, use moments like these to reiterate or expand upon your ideas. If you insult a questioner by dismissing his or her inquiry, the audience is likely to make negative judgments about your character.

Similarly, a speaker who adopts a sharp or defensive tone while answering questions will alienate many people in the audience. Think of the question-and-answer session as another opportunity to communicate your ideas rather than as a challenge to your competence or personhood.

Even if you are asked a hostile question, keep your cool. Avoid the temptation to answer defensively, sarcastically, or argumentatively. Most people in the audience will respect you for trying to avoid a quarrel.

Listen Carefully

It's hard to answer a question well if you don't listen carefully to it. Give the questioner your full attention. Look directly at her or him rather than glancing around the room, at the floor, or at the ceiling. If an audience member is having a difficult time stating the question, you might even nod in encouragement to help him or her along.

When faced with an unclear or unwieldy question, try to rephrase it by saying something like, "If I understand your question, it seems to me that you are asking . . . " Another option is simply to ask the audience member to repeat the question. Most people will restate it more succinctly and clearly. If you still don't understand, ask the questioner to give an example of what he or she means.

Direct Answers to the Entire Audience

When you are being asked a question, look at the questioner. Direct your answer, however, to the entire audience. Make occasional eye contact with the questioner as you answer, but speak primarily to the audience as a whole. This will help you keep everyone's attention. If you speak just to the questioner, you may well find the rest of your audience drifting off.

When speaking to a large audience, be sure to repeat or paraphrase each question after it is asked. This helps ensure that you understand the question properly. It also involves the entire audience and guarantees that they know the question you are addressing. In addition, repeating or paraphrasing the question gives you a moment to frame an answer before you respond.

Be Honest and Straightforward

Some speakers dread question-and-answer sessions because they fear being derailed by a question they can't answer. The world won't end if you can't answer every possible question. If you don't know the answer, say so. Don't apologize, don't evade, and most important, don't try to bluff. Do, however, let the questioner know that you take the question seriously. Offer to check into the answer as soon as possible after the speech. If a more knowledgeable person is at hand, ask if she or he knows the answer.

Stay on Track

It's easy to get diverted or lose control of time in the give-and-take of a lively question-and-answer session. Unless there is a moderator for the session, the speaker is responsible for keeping things on track. Sometimes that means preventing a single questioner from dominating the session. Allow one follow-up question from each person, and don't let yourself be dragged into a personal debate with any questioner. If someone attempts to ask more than two questions, respond graciously yet firmly by saying, "This is an interesting line of questioning, but we need to give other people a chance to ask questions."

Sometimes, a listener will launch into an extended monologue instead of posing a question. When this happens, you can regain control of the situation by saying something like, "Those are very interesting ideas, but do you have a specific question I can answer?" If the person continues, offer to talk individually with him or her after the session.

On some occasions, the length of the question-and-answer session is predetermined by the moderator or by the schedule of the audience. On other occasions, it's up to the speaker to decide how much time to devote to answering questions. Often this requires adapting to the kind and number of questions you are receiving. Make sure you allow enough time to get through issues of major importance, but don't let things drag on after the momentum of the session has started winding down. As the end approaches, offer to respond to another question or two. After answering them, wrap things up by thanking the audience for its time and attention.[14]

Summary

Speech delivery is a matter of nonverbal communication. It is based on how you use your voice and body to convey the message expressed by your words. You can't make a good speech without having something to say, but you also need to know *how* to say it. Rather than calling attention to itself, effective delivery conveys the speaker's ideas clearly, engagingly, and without distracting the audience.

There are four basic methods of delivering a speech: reading verbatim from a manuscript, reciting a memorized text, speaking impromptu, and speaking extemporaneously. The last of these—speaking extemporaneously—is the method you probably will use for classroom speeches and for most speeches outside the classroom. When speaking extemporaneously, you will have a brief set of notes or a speaking outline. You will choose the exact wording of your speech at the moment of delivery.

To use your voice effectively you should work on controlling your volume, pitch, rate, pauses, vocal variety, pronunciation, articulation, and dialect. Volume is the relative loudness of your voice, and pitch is the relative highness or lowness. Rate refers to the speed at which you talk. Pauses, when carefully timed, can add great impact to your speech, but you should avoid vocalized pauses ("er," "um," and the like). Vocal variety refers to changes in volume, pitch, rate, and pauses, and is crucial to making your voice lively and animated. Most of us speak casually in everyday conversation, but for public speaking you should be sure to pronounce words correctly and to articulate them distinctly. You should also avoid heavy use of dialect in situations where the audience does not share the dialect or will find it inappropriate to the occasion.

Posture, personal appearance, facial expression, gestures, and eye contact also affect the way listeners respond to speakers. You can do little to change your face or body, but you can dress and groom appropriately for the situation at hand. You can also learn to control gestures and bodily movements so they enhance your message, rather than distract from it. Making eye contact with listeners is one of the quickest ways to establish a communicative bond with them.

You should practice all these aspects of delivery along with the words of your speech. Start your practice sessions early so you will have plenty of time to gain command of the speech and its presentation.

If your speech includes a question-and-answer session, you will need to prepare for that as well, since it can have a strong impact on the audience's final impression. Anticipate the most likely questions, prepare answers to them, and practice delivering those answers. Once the question-and-answer period is underway, listen carefully to the questions, approach them positively, and respond to them briefly, graciously, and straightforwardly. Direct your answers to the full audience, rather than to the questioner alone, and make sure to end the session in a timely fashion.

Key Terms

nonverbal communication (300)
manuscript speech (301)
impromptu speech (302)
extemporaneous speech (304)
conversational quality (304)
volume (305)
pitch (305)
inflections (306)
monotone (306)
rate (306)
pause (307)
vocalized pause (307)
vocal variety (308)
pronunciation (310)
articulation (310)
dialect (311)
kinesics (313)
gestures (315)
eye contact (315)

ONLINE LEARNING CENTER

Review these terms by doing the Chapter 12 crossword puzzle at www.mhhe.com/lucas9.

Review Questions

After reading this chapter, you should be able to answer the following questions:

1. What is nonverbal communication? Why is it important to effective public speaking?
2. What are the elements of good speech delivery?
3. What are the eight aspects of voice usage you should concentrate on in your speeches?
4. What are four aspects of bodily action you should concentrate on in your speeches?
5. What are the five steps you should follow when practicing your speech delivery?
6. What steps should you take when preparing for a question-and-answer session? What should you concentrate on when responding to questions during the session?

CD 1: STUDY QUESTIONS

For further review, go to the Study Questions for this chapter.

Exercises for Critical Thinking

1. An excellent way to improve your vocal variety is to read aloud selections from poetry that require emphasis and feeling. Choose one of your favorite poems that falls into this category, or find one by leafing through a poetry anthology. Practice reading the selection aloud. As you read, use your voice to make the poem come alive. Vary your volume, rate, and pitch. Find the appropriate places for pauses. Underline the key words or phrases you think should be stressed. Modulate your tone of voice; use inflections for emphasis and meaning.

   For this to work, you must overcome your fear of sounding affected or "dramatic." Most beginning speakers do better if they exaggerate changes in volume, rate, pitch, and expression. This will make you more aware of the many ways you can use your voice to express a wide range of moods and meanings. Besides, what sounds overly "dramatic" to you usually does not sound that way to an audience. By adding luster, warmth, and enthusiasm to your voice, you will go a long way toward capturing and keeping the interest of your listeners.

   If possible, practice reading the selection into a digital recorder. Listen to the playback. If you are not satisfied with what you hear, practice the selection some more and record it again.

2. Watch a 10-minute segment of a television drama with the sound turned off. What do the characters say with their dress, gestures, facial expressions, and the like? Do the same with a television comedy. How do the nonverbal messages in the two shows differ? Be prepared to report your observations in class.

3. Attend a speech on campus. You may choose either a presentation by a guest speaker from outside the college or a class session by a professor who has a reputation as a good lecturer. Prepare a brief report on the speaker's vocal and nonverbal communication.

   In your report, first analyze the speaker's volume, pitch, rate, pauses, vocal variety, pronunciation, and articulation. Then evaluate the speaker's personal appearance, bodily action, gestures, and eye contact. Explain how the speaker's delivery added to or detracted from what the speaker said. Finally, note at least two techniques of delivery used by the speaker that you might want to try in your next speech.

Applying the POWER of PUBLIC SPEAKING

Utilizing your business degree and computer savvy, you have made a success of the online marketing company you started after graduating from college. Now in its third year, the company has prepared a proposal to design the e-commerce site for a major sporting goods retailer. In your 30-minute presentation to the retailer's management team, you will review the homepage designs, site maps, and security protocols.

You notice on the agenda that another 30 minutes has been allotted after your presentation for questions and answers. Knowing from your previous experience with clients how important the Q&A session can be, you want to be sure you are ready for it. What steps will you take to prepare?

Notes

[1]For two recent studies, see Aldert Vrij, Lucy Akehurst, Stavroula Soukara, and Ray Bull, "Detecting Deceit Via Analyses of Verbal and Nonverbal Behavior in Children and Adults," *Human Communication Research,* 30 (2004), pp. 8–41; and Joseph L. Chesebro, "Effects of Teacher Clarity and Nonverbal Immediacy on Student Learning, Receiver Apprehension, and Affect," *Communication Education,* 52 (2003), pp. 135–147.

[2]For a recent look at research on the impact of nonverbal communication in the full spectrum of communication situations, see Ronald E. Riggio and Robert S. Feldman (eds.), *Applications of Nonverbal Communication* (Mahwah, NJ: Erlbaum, 2005).

[3]Irving Bartlett, *Wendell Phillips: Boston Brahmin* (Boston: Beacon Press, 1961), p. 192.

[4]A. Craig Baird, *Rhetoric: A Philosophical Inquiry* (New York: Ronald Press, 1965), p. 207.

[5]Daniel J. O'Keefe, *Persuasion: Theory and Research,* 2nd ed. (Thousand Oaks, CA: Sage, 2002), p. 185.

[6]James Joyce, "Chamber Music XXXV," from *Collected Poems,* ed. Harry Levin (New York: Viking, 1946–1947). Reprinted by permission of Penguin Putnam, Inc.

[7]Dorothy Sarnoff, *Speech Can Change Your Life* (Garden City, NY: Doubleday, 1970), p. 73.

[8]The most authoritative guide to regional dialects in the United States is Frederic G. Cassidy and Joan H. Hall, eds. *Dictionary of American Regional English,* 4 vols. to date (Cambridge, MA: Harvard University Press, 1985–2002).

[9]For a more detailed guide on vocal communication, consult Jeffrey C. Hahner, Martin A. Sokoloff, and Sandra L. Salisch, *Speaking Clearly: Improving Voice and Diction,* 6th ed. (New York: McGraw-Hill, 2002).

[10]See Mark L. Knapp and Judith A. Hall, *Nonverbal Communication in Human Interaction,* 5th ed. (Belmont, CA: Wadsworth, 2002), pp. 13–16.

[11]Richard M. Perloff, *The Dynamics of Persuasion: Communication and Attitudes in the 21st Century,* 2nd ed. (Mahwah, NJ: Erlbaum, 2003), pp. 170–174.

[12]Knapp and Hall, *Nonverbal Communication in Human Interaction,* p. 365.

[13]See, for example, Scott D. Johnson and Ann N. Miller, "A Cross-Cultural Study of Immediacy, Credibility, and Learning in the U.S. and Kenya," *Communication Education,* 51 (2002), pp. 280–292.

[14]For more on managing question-and-answer sessions, consult Natalie H. Rogers, *The New Talk Power: The Mind-Body Way to Speak Without Fear* (Sterling, VA: Capital Books, 2000), pp. 195–210.

CHAPTER THIRTEEN

Using Visual Aids

A former lifeguard with training in a number of life-saving techniques, Meg Fugate decided to give her informative speech on the steps one should follow in responding to an emergency situation. Part of her speech was devoted to explaining how to administer cardiopulmonary resuscitation, better known as CPR.

A week before her speech, Meg called the local Red Cross chapter and arranged to borrow a life-size dummy of a human torso on which she could demonstrate CPR. She used the dummy in her practice sessions to make sure she knew exactly what maneuvers she was going to perform and how to coordinate them with her words. By the day of her speech, she was able to move effortlessly between explaining her ideas and performing the procedures of CPR without breaking eye contact or stumbling in her delivery.

CD 1: VIDEO 13.1

View an excerpt from "CPR."

By *showing* her classmates how to perform CPR, rather than just telling them about it, Meg made her speech more interesting and communicated her ideas much more effectively. Afterward, one of her classmates commented that the speech was better than the CPR demonstration he had seen at the Red Cross!

As the old saying tells us, one picture is worth a thousand words. People find a speaker's message more interesting, grasp it more easily, and retain it longer when it is presented visually as well as verbally. Can you picture the steps involved in using CPR to save a life? You could if you had watched Meg's speech. Her visual demonstration brought home her ideas more effectively than would have been possible with words alone.

Advantages of Visual Aids

Visual aids offer several advantages. The primary advantage is *clarity.* If you are discussing an object, you can make your message clearer by showing the object or some representation of it. If you are citing statistics, showing how something works, or demonstrating a technique, a visual aid will make your information more vivid to your audience. After all, we live in a visual age. Television and movies have conditioned us to expect a visual image. By using visual aids in your speeches, you often will make it easier for listeners to understand exactly what you are trying to communicate.[1]

Another advantage of visual aids is *interest.* The interest generated by visual images is so strong that visual aids are now used routinely in many areas, not just speechmaking. A generation or so ago, most college textbooks were rather dry—page after page of words. Today they are enlivened with photographs, drawings, and other visual aids that clarify the material and make it more interesting. Encyclopedias have blossomed with photographs and maps; even dictionaries contain small drawings to highlight word definitions. You can do the same thing with your speeches.

Still another advantage of visual aids is *retention.* Visual images often stay with us longer than verbal ones. The people who saw Meg Fugate's speech about CPR may not remember everything she said about the details of responding to an emergency, but they will probably remember her demonstration of how to perform CPR. And perhaps they will remember that demonstration if they are ever in a situation where they need to provide CPR for someone who has been in an accident or has suffered a heart attack. We've all heard that words can "go in one ear and out the other." Visual images tend to last.[2]

In fact, when used properly, visual aids can enhance almost *every* aspect of a speech. One study showed that an average speaker who uses visual aids will come across as better prepared, more credible, and more professional than a dynamic speaker who does not use visual aids. According to the same study, visual aids can increase the persuasiveness of a speech by more than 40 percent.[3] Another study found that business speakers who use multimedia in their presentations are significantly more effective than speakers who do not.[4]

Visual aids can even help you combat stage fright. They heighten audience interest, shift attention away from the speaker, and give the speaker greater confidence in the speech as a whole.

For all these reasons, you will find visual aids of great value in your speeches. In this chapter we will concentrate primarily on visual aids suitable for classroom speeches. However, the principles outlined here are true for all circumstances. For speeches outside the classroom—in business or community situations, for instance—you should have no difficulty applying the general suggestions given here.

Let us look first at the kinds of visual aids you are likely to use, then at guidelines for preparing visual aids, and finally at guidelines for using visual aids effectively.

Kinds of Visual Aids

Objects

Tracy Collins is an avid downhill skier. When it came time for her informative speech, she chose as her specific purpose "To inform my audience how to choose the right ski equipment." On the day of her speech, she brought to class a pair of skis, boots, bindings, and ski clothing. It was then easy for her to explain exactly what to look for in each item.

By *showing* her classmates the equipment, Tracy presented her ideas more effectively than she could have by using words alone. She also made her speech more interesting to nonskiers. As one of her classmates said afterward, "I don't ski, but I found your speech fascinating. Using the skis and other equipment as visual aids really helped get me involved. Now I have a little better idea of what my friends who ski are talking about. Without the visual aids I would have been lost."

As in Tracy's speech, bringing the object of your talk to class can be an excellent way to clarify your ideas and give them dramatic impact. If you talk about guitars, why not bring one to class to show your listeners? If you plan to explain the different kinds of golf clubs, what could be better than showing a sample of each kind? Or suppose you want to inform your audience about the Peruvian art of doll making. You could bring several dolls to class and explain to your classmates how they were made.

Photographs make excellent visual aids if they are large enough to be seen easily. Check CD-1, Clip 13.3, to see how one speaker used this photograph of the famous Incan ruins at Machu Picchu.

In certain situations you might use living objects as visual aids. This worked well for a high-school wrestling coach who returned to college to take a night class in public speaking. Not surprisingly, the coach gave one of his speeches about wrestling. On the night of his speech he brought along two of his high-school students, who demonstrated each of the basic holds as the coach discussed them.

Many objects, however, cannot be used effectively in classroom speeches. Some are too big to be hauled into a classroom. Others are too small to be seen clearly by the audience. Still others may not be available to you. If you were speaking about a rare suit of armor in the local museum, you could, theoretically, transport it to class, but it is most unlikely that the museum would let you borrow it. You would have to look for another kind of visual aid.

Models

model
An object, usually built to scale, that represents another object in detail.

If the item you want to discuss is too large, too small, or unavailable, you may be able to work with a model. One option is a life-size model, such as that used by Meg Fugate in the speech on CPR we discussed at the start of this chapter. Another student, an anthropology major, used a full-scale model of a human skull to show how archaeologists use bone fragments to reconstruct the forms of early humans.

You might also be able to use a small-scale model of a large object. One speaker used such a model to help explain the structural factors that contributed to the collapse of the World Trade Center after the attacks of September 11. Another speaker brought to class a scaled-down model of a hang glider to illustrate the equipment and techniques of hang gliding.

A third kind of model is a large-scale representation of a small object. Science teachers use such models to help students visualize molecules and other minuscule structures. A good example of this kind of model came in a speech about extended-wear contact lenses. The speaker wanted to demonstrate the differences in flexibility among hard contact lenses, soft lenses, and extended-wear lenses. Since the lenses themselves were too small for his classmates to see, he used a glass, a paper plate, and a sheet of clear plastic wrap to illustrate the differences among the three kinds of lenses. As you can see from CD 1, Video 13.2, it worked to perfection and allowed the speaker to communicate his ideas more effectively than he could have by words alone.

CD 1:VIDEO 13.2
View the use of visual aids in "Extended-Wear Contact Lenses."

Photographs

In the absence of an object or a model, you may be able to use photographs. Lawyers often employ photographs in trials to show the crime scene; architects to show prospective clients other buildings the firm has designed; drunk-driving activists to demonstrate the tragic results of combining alcohol with driving.

Photographs will not work effectively, however, unless they are large enough for the audience to view without straining. Normal-size photos are not big enough to be seen clearly without being passed around—which only diverts the audience from what you are saying. The same is true of photographs in a book. Even oversize books are too small to be seen clearly by all members of an audience.

How can you get large-scale photos for a speech? One student used art posters to illustrate her points in a speech about the painter Frida Kahlo. Another speaker used enlargements produced by a color copier to show the spectacular markings of various species of saltwater tropical fish. The enlargements were 18 × 24 inches, and the speaker mounted them on white poster board to make them easier to see.

Another option is to take your photographs to a copy service and have them converted to transparencies that can be shown with an overhead projector. The cost is minimal, and the results can be dramatic.

Finally, PowerPoint and other multimedia programs are excellent vehicles for incorporating photographs into a speech. You can use your own photographs or ones you have downloaded from the Web, and you can easily adjust the size and placement of the photos for maximum clarity and impact. Notice, for example, the way the speaker in CD 1: Video 13.3 used PowerPoint to present a photograph of the famous Incan ruins at Machu Picchu. No other method of showing the photograph would have worked as well.

CD 1:VIDEO 13.3
View an excerpt from "Machu Picchu: City of the Gods."

Drawings

Diagrams, sketches, and other kinds of drawings are superb alternatives to photographs. They are inexpensive to make. Moreover, since they are drawn specifically for one speech, they can be designed to illustrate your points exactly. This more than compensates for what they may lack in realism.

For example, Figure 13.1 (page 332) is a drawing used by a student in a speech about Navajo sandpainting. The student wanted to show his audience what sandpainting looks like and to explain its symbolism and

Figure 13.1

religious significance. As you can imagine, it would have been almost impossible for him to do so without some kind of visual aid.

Figure 13.2 (below) shows a drawing used in a speech about the kinds of problems faced by people who suffer from dyslexia. This aid was particularly effective because it allowed the speaker to translate complex ideas into visual terms the audience could grasp almost immediately.

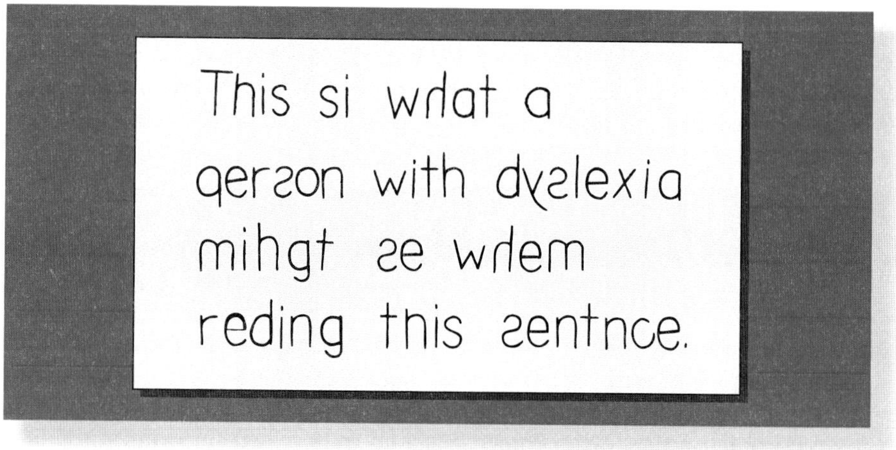

Figure 13.2

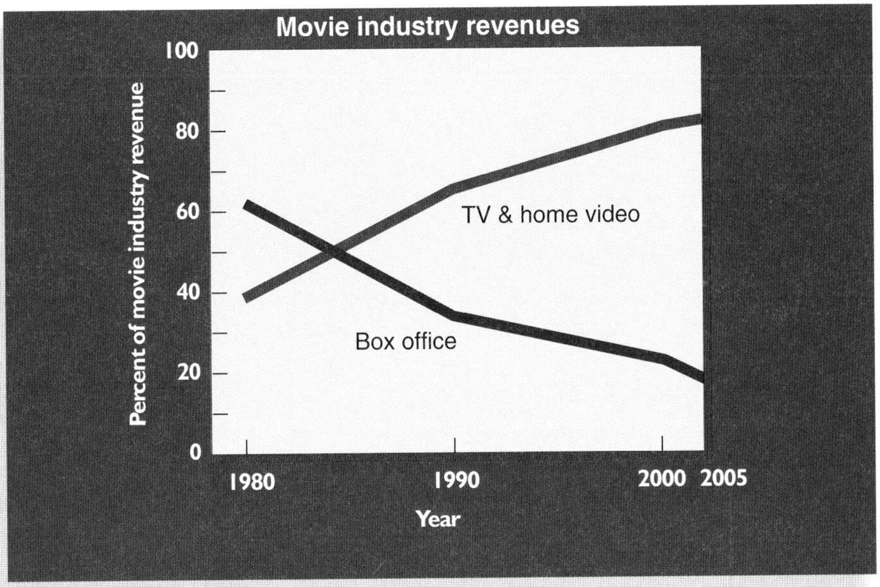

Figure 13.3

CD 1:VIDEO 13.4

View the presentation of this graph in "American Movies: From the Studio System to the Video Age."

Graphs

Graphs are a good way to simplify and clarify statistics. Audiences often have trouble grasping a complex series of numbers. You can ease their difficulty by using graphs to show statistical trends and patterns.

The most common type is the *line graph*. Figure 13.3 (above) shows such a graph, used in a speech about the American movie industry. If you look at CD 1, Video 13.4, you can see how the speaker explained the graph. He said:

> As you can see from this graph based on figures in *Newsweek* magazine, the video revolution has had a profound impact on the American movie industry. From 1980 to 2005, the percent of movie revenues generated by box office receipts fell dramatically—from 61 percent to 21 percent. At the same time, the percent of movie industry revenues generated by DVD, VHS, and television more than doubled—from 39 percent in 1981 to 79 percent in 2005.

graph
A visual aid used to show statistical trends and patterns.

line graph
A graph that uses one or more lines to show changes in statistics over time or space.

The *pie graph* is best suited for illustrating simple distribution patterns. You will see such a graph in your newspaper each year to show the division of the national budget. Figure 13.4 (page 334) shows how one speaker used a pie graph to help listeners visualize changes in marital status among working women in the past century. The graph on the left shows the percentages of working women who were single, married, and widowed or divorced in 1900. The graph on the right shows percentages for the same groups in 2005.

These pie graphs helped the speaker make three points: (1) The percentage of working women who are widowed or divorced has remained relatively stable since 1900; (2) the percentage of working women who are single has declined greatly during the past century; (3) the percentage of working women who are married has more than tripled, to the point that they are now far and away the largest group of working women in the United States.

pie graph
A graph that highlights segments of a circle to show simple distribution patterns.

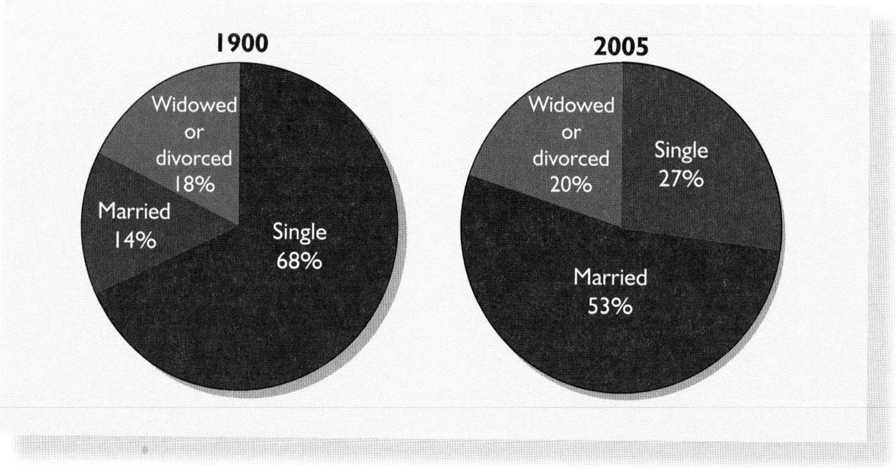

Figure 13.4

Because a pie graph is used to dramatize relationships among the parts of a whole, you should keep the number of different segments in the graph as small as possible. A pie graph should ideally have from two to five segments; under no circumstances should it have more than eight.

bar graph
A graph that uses vertical or horizontal bars to show comparisons among two or more items.

The *bar graph* is a particularly good way to show comparisons between two or more items. It also has the advantage of being easy to understand, even by people who have no background in reading graphs. Figure 13.5

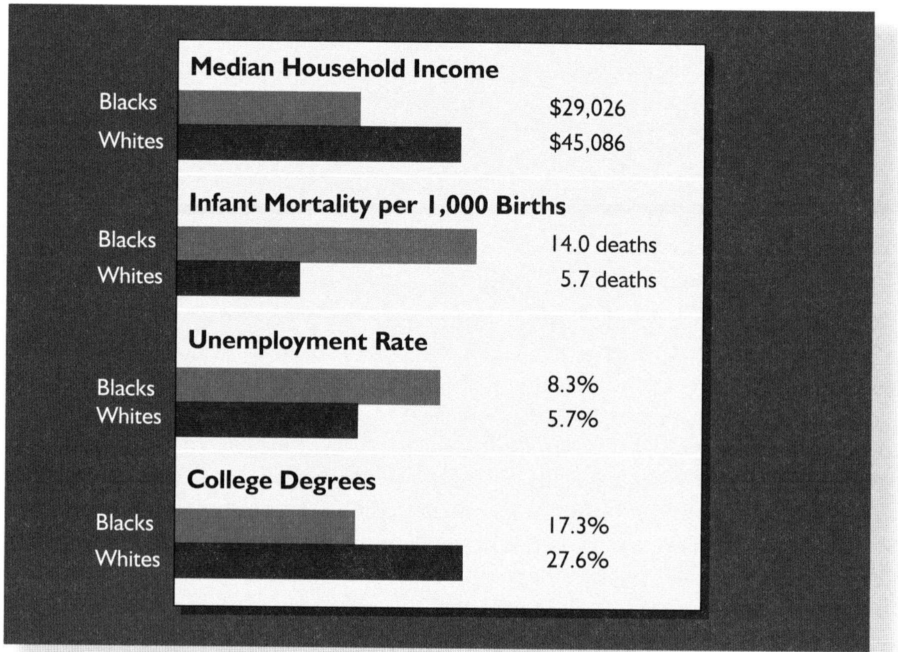

Figure 13.5

Region of Birth	Percent of U.S. Immigrants
Asia	33 percent
Mexico	19 percent
Europe	15 percent
Caribbean	10 percent
Central America	7 percent
South America	7 percent
Africa	6 percent
Other	3 percent

CD 1: VIDEO 13.5

View the presentation of this chart in "The United States: A Nation of Immigrants."

Figure 13.6

is an example of a bar graph from a speech entitled "The Politics of Race in America." It shows visually the relative standing of whites and blacks with respect to median household income, infant mortality, unemployment, and college education. By using a bar graph, the speaker made her points much more vividly than if she had just cited the numbers orally.[5]

Charts

chart
A visual aid that summarizes a large block of information, usually in list form.

Charts are particularly useful for summarizing large blocks of information. One student, in a speech titled "The United States: A Nation of Immigrants," used a chart to show the leading regions of the world for U.S. immigrants (Figure 13.6, above). These are too many categories to be conveyed effectively in a pie graph or a bar graph. By listing them on a chart, the speaker made it easier for listeners to keep the information straight. Look at CD 1: Video 13.5 to see how the student presented the chart during her speech.

Charts are also valuable for showing the steps of a process. One speaker used several charts in a speech about survival techniques in the wilderness, including one outlining the steps in emergency treatment of snakebites. Another speaker used charts effectively to help her listeners keep track of the steps involved in making cappuccino and other specialty coffee drinks.

You can also use charts to present information that your audience may want to write down. In a speech about consumer protection organizations, for example, a speaker might use a chart to let the audience know exactly where to write or phone for consumer services.

The biggest mistake made by beginning speakers when using a chart is to include so much information that the chart is jumbled and hard to read. As we will discuss later, visual aids should be clear, simple, and uncluttered. Lists on a chart should rarely exceed seven or eight items, with generous spacing between items. If you cannot fit everything on a single chart, make a second one.

Video

Video can be extremely effective as a visual aid. If you are talking about the impact caused by even a low-speed automobile accident, what could be more effective than showing slow-motion video of crash tests? Or suppose you are explaining the different kinds of roller coasters found in amusement parks. Your best visual aid would be a video showing those coasters in action. The detail, immediacy, and vividness of video are hard to match.

Despite its advantages, using video in a speech can be complicated. It requires cumbersome equipment, distracts attention from the speaker, and may do more harm than good if used carelessly. If you decide to use video in one of your speeches, you need to follow the lead of the student who gave the speech on roller coasters mentioned in the previous paragraph. He sent away to Arrow Dynamics, Inc., the leading manufacturer of custom roller coasters, for a videotape of their rides. He then went to the audiovisual center on campus and edited several snippets from that tape onto his own tape, which he then showed during his speech.

Knowing that a sloppily edited video is of less value than no video at all, he made sure his editing was clean and expert and would not distract from his ideas. He also included the video every time he rehearsed the speech so it would be smoothly integrated with the rest of his presentation. He even made a special trip to campus to practice with the playback equipment in the classroom so he would be able to use it flawlessly on the day of the speech. The result was a memorable presentation that took full advantage of the benefits of video without falling prey to its potential drawbacks.

Transparencies

transparency
A visual aid drawn, written, or printed on a sheet of clear acetate and shown with an overhead projector.

Earlier in this chapter we mentioned the possibility of converting photographs to transparencies, which can be shown with an overhead projector. You can also use transparencies to present drawings, graphs, and charts. Transparencies are inexpensive, easy to create, and produce a strong visual image. For all these reasons, they are one of the most widely used methods of presenting visual aids.

If you use transparencies, don't try to write or draw on them while you are speaking. Prepare them well in advance and make sure any text is large enough to be seen from the back of the room. A good rule is that all numbers and letters—whether typed or handwritten—should be at least one-quarter inch high (about three times as large as the print on this page).

In addition, check your overhead projector ahead of time to make sure it's working and that you know how to operate it. If possible, arrange to practice with a projector when you rehearse the speech. This will help ensure that your transparencies are well coordinated with the rest of your presentation.

Multimedia Presentations

Multimedia presentations allow you to integrate a variety of visual aids—including charts, graphs, photographs, and video—in the same talk. Presentation software programs include Microsoft PowerPoint, Corel Presentations, and Apple Keynote. Depending on the technological resources at your school, you may be able to give multimedia presentations in your speech class. If so, it will provide training for speeches outside the classroom—especially in business settings, where multimedia presentations are made every day.

In the appendix that follows this chapter, you will find a full discussion of how to use PowerPoint in your speeches. And if you visit *The Art of Public Speaking* Online Learning Center at www.mhhe.com/lucas9, you will find detailed, how-to guides for the use of PowerPoint 2002 and PowerPoint 2003. Here we will take a brief look at multimedia presentations in general.

multimedia presentation
A speech that combines several kinds of visual and/or audio aids in the same talk.

Although each multimedia presentation program operates a bit differently, all give you the tools to incorporate a wide range of material into your speech. Suppose you want to create a graph showing the number of terrorist incidents in different parts of the world. You can use the presentation software's graph program to generate a professional-looking graph tailored specifically to your needs. Or suppose you are talking about the growth of modern skyscrapers. You might follow the lead of one student who used pictures downloaded from the Internet to lend extra impact to his discussion of the world's tallest buildings. As you can see from CD 1, Video 13.6, the results were much more impressive than would have been possible without a multimedia program.

CD 1: VIDEO 13.6
View an excerpt from "The Ups and Downs of Skyscrapers."

Once you have created all the aids you need for your speech and have them stored on your computer, you can call them up in any order. During the speech, you use a computer to control the presentation of your aids. The computer is usually connected to a television monitor or a large-screen video projector. Some systems have a wireless mouse that lets you move through your presentation with a minimum of fuss.

For all their advantages, multimedia presentations do have some drawbacks—not the least of which is the high cost of the equipment required to show them. It also takes considerable time to learn how to use the software, to design graphs and charts, to edit sound and video clips, and to organize and rehearse a presentation so it is smooth and professional. If you plan to make a multimedia presentation, be sure to give yourself plenty of time to make sure it comes off just right.

With any complex technology, there is always the chance of faulty equipment. Set up your computer, projection unit, and so forth early enough that you can double-check them before the audience arrives. Make sure you know the equipment well enough to handle any basic technical difficulties that may arise. Always carry a backup disk of your presentation just in case you should happen to need it.

Most important, be prepared to give your speech even if all the multimedia equipment were to fall apart. It may not be as dazzling as the speech you had planned, but it will be much better than no speech at all. Your audience will sympathize with your predicament, and they will give you credit for adapting to the situation.

The Speaker

Sometimes you can use your own body as a visual aid—by showing how a conductor directs an orchestra, by demonstrating the skills of modern dance, by doing magic tricks, and so forth. One student gave an informative speech on the art of mime. Throughout the speech she illustrated her points by performing mime routines. In addition to clarifying her ideas, the demonstration kept her classmates deeply engrossed in the speech. Many students have also found that doing some kind of demonstration reduces their nervousness during a speech by providing an outlet for their extra adrenaline.

Doing a demonstration well requires special practice to coordinate your actions with your words and to control the timing of your speech. You can see an excellent example on CD 1, Video 13.7. The subject of the speech is sign language. After providing background about the different kinds of sign language used today, the speaker taught her classmates how to sign the phrase "You are my friend." As you watch, notice how clearly the speaker explains each step along the way and how she gives her classmates time to work on each step before she moves to the next one. Also notice how she communicates directly with the audience and maintains eye contact throughout her demonstration.

CD 1: VIDEO 13.7

View an excerpt from "Sign Language."

Special care is required if you are demonstrating a process that takes longer to complete than the time allocated for your speech. If you plan to show a long process, you might borrow the techniques of television personalities such as Emeril Lagasse and Martha Stewart. They work through most of the steps in making a perfect enchilada or holiday decoration, but they have a second, finished enchilada or decoration ready to show you at the last minute.

Guidelines for Preparing Visual Aids

Whether you are creating visual aids by hand or designing them on a computer, there are six basic guidelines you should follow to make your aids clear and visually appealing. These guidelines apply whether you are speaking in or out of the classroom, at a business meeting or a political forum, to an audience of 20 or of 200.

Prepare Visual Aids in Advance

No matter what visual aids you plan to use, prepare them well before the day your speech is due. This has two advantages. First, it means you will have the time and resources to devise creative, attractive aids that will truly enhance your speech. Audiences respond much more favorably to speakers who have obviously put a great deal of thought and effort into their visual aids.

Second, preparing your visual aids ahead of time means you can use them while practicing your speech. Visual aids are effective only when they are integrated smoothly with the rest of the speech. If you lose your place, drop your aids, or otherwise stumble around when presenting them, you will distract your audience and shatter your concentration. You can avoid such disasters by preparing your visual aids far enough in advance.

Keep Visual Aids Simple

The purpose of a visual aid is to communicate your ideas, not to display your virtuosity as an artist or wizardry with computer graphics. Visual aids should be simple, clear, and to the point. Limit each aid to a manageable amount of information, and beware of the tendency to go overboard when using programs such as PowerPoint. It is possible to create a graphic that displays two charts, a photograph, and 10 lines of text in five different typefaces with 250

CHECKLIST FOR PREPARING VISUAL AIDS

yes	no	
☐	☐	1. Have I prepared my visual aids well in advance?
☐	☐	2. Are my visual aids clear and easy to comprehend?
☐	☐	3. Does each visual aid contain only the information needed to make my point?
☐	☐	4. Are my visual aids large enough to be seen clearly by the entire audience?
☐	☐	5. Do the colors on my visual aids work well together?
☐	☐	6. Is there a clear contrast between the lettering and background on my charts, graphs, and drawings?
☐	☐	7. Do I use line graphs, pie graphs, and bar graphs correctly to show statistical trends and patterns?
☐	☐	8. Do I limit charts to no more than eight items?
☐	☐	9. Do I use fonts that are easy to read?
☐	☐	10. Do I use a limited number of fonts?
☐	☐	11. If I am using multimedia equipment, am I prepared to give my speech even if the equipment were to fail?

CD 1: SPEECH CHECKLIST

You can print a copy of this checklist from the CD-ROM.

colors on the same visual aid. But who would be able to read it? Rather than enhancing your speech, such an aid would detract from it.

The basic rule is to include in your visual aid only what you need to make your point. If you look back at the aids presented earlier in this chapter, you will see that all of them are clear and uncluttered. They contain enough information to communicate the speaker's point, but not so much as to confuse or distract the audience.[6]

Make Sure Visual Aids Are Large Enough

A visual aid is useless if no one can see it. This is one of those points that seems so obvious as to need no comment. But as many speakers have discovered, it is one thing to nod your head in agreement and another to prepare a visual aid properly. Beginning speakers in particular tend to design visual aids that are too small.

When you design a visual aid, keep in mind the size of the room in which you will be speaking. Make sure the aid is big enough to be seen easily by everyone in the room. If you compose a diagram, chart, or graph by hand, guard against the tendency to write and draw too small. As you prepare the aid, check its visibility by moving to a point as far away from it as your most distant listener will be sitting. If you have trouble making out the

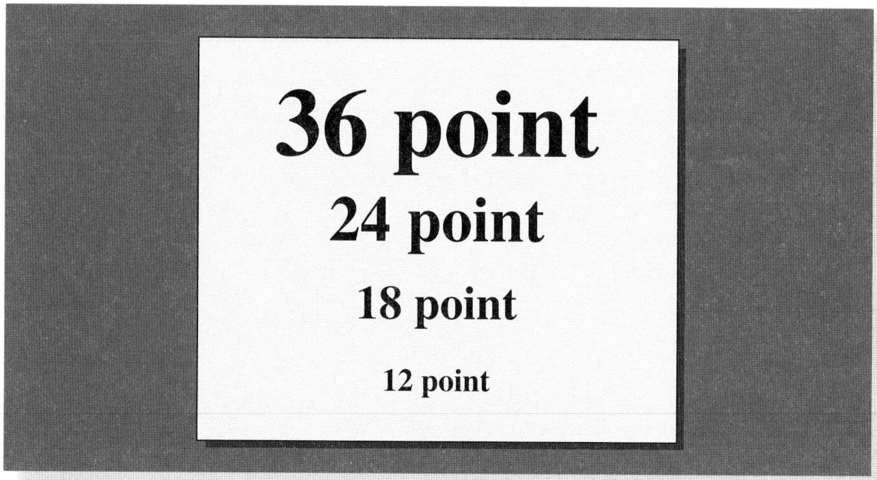

Figure 13.7

words or drawings, your audience will too. By making sure your visual aid is large enough, you will avoid having to introduce it with the comment, "I know some of you can't see this, but . . . "

If you are creating your visual aid by computer, remember that regular-size type (such as that in this book) may be easy to read from two feet away on a computer screen, but it is much too small for a visual aid—even for one that is enlarged with a video unit or an overhead projector. Most experts recommend printing all words and numbers in bold and using at least 36-point type for titles, 24-point type for subtitles, and 18-point type for other text. Figure 13.7 (above) shows these type sizes in comparison to standard 12-point type.

What about using all capital letters? That might seem a great way to ensure that your print is large enough to be read easily. But research has shown that a long string of words in ALL CAPS is actually harder to read than is normal text. Reserve ALL CAPS for titles or for individual words that require special emphasis.

Use Fonts That Are Easy to Read

font
A complete set of type of the same design.

Most computer programs come with a large number of fonts, which you can use to vary the style of your visual aids. Although it can be fun to experiment with the fonts, not all are suitable for visual aids. For the most part, you should avoid decorative fonts such as those on the left in Figure 13.8 (page 341). They are hard to read and can easily distract the attention of listeners.

In contrast, look at the fonts on the right in Figure 13.8. They are less exciting than those on the left, but they are clear and easy to read. If you use fonts such as these, your visual aids will be audience-friendly.

Use a Limited Number of Fonts

Some variety of fonts in a visual aid is appealing, but too much can be distracting—as in the aid on the left in Figure 13.9 (page 341), which uses a different font for each line. Most experts recommend using no more than two fonts in a single visual aid—one for the title or major headings, another for subtitles or other text. Standard procedure is to use a block typeface for

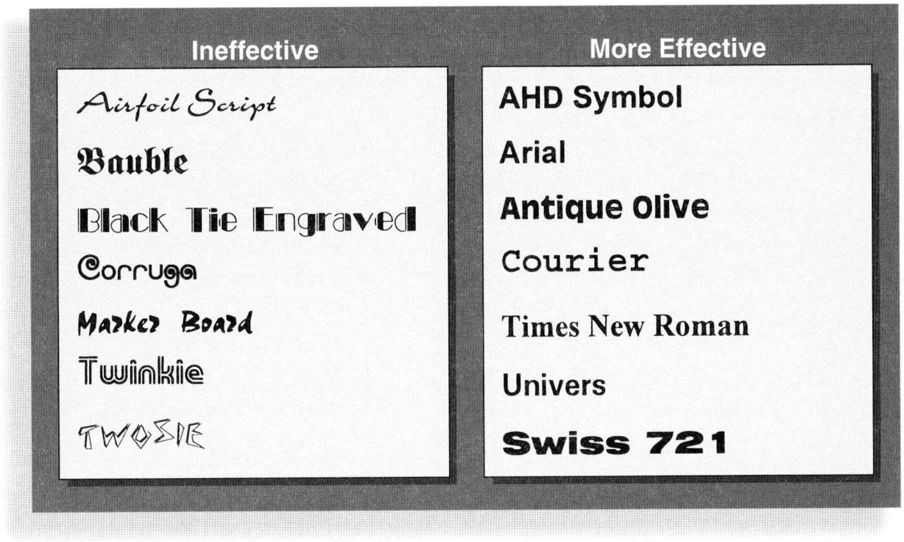

Figure 13.8

the title and a rounder typeface for subtitles and text—as in the aid on the right in Figure 13.9.

Use Color Effectively

Color adds clout to a visual aid. When used effectively, it increases recognition by 78 percent and comprehension by 73 percent.[7] The key words, of course, are "when used effectively." Some colors do not work well together. Red and green are a tough combination for anyone to read, and they look the same to people who are color-blind. Many shades of blue and green are too close to each other to be easily differentiated—as are orange and red, blue and purple.

It is also possible to have too many colors on a visual aid. In most circumstances, charts and graphs should be limited to a few colors that are used consistently and solely for functional reasons. The usual procedure is to use dark print or lettering on a light background—especially if you are using poster board or an overhead transparency. If you are using a video projector

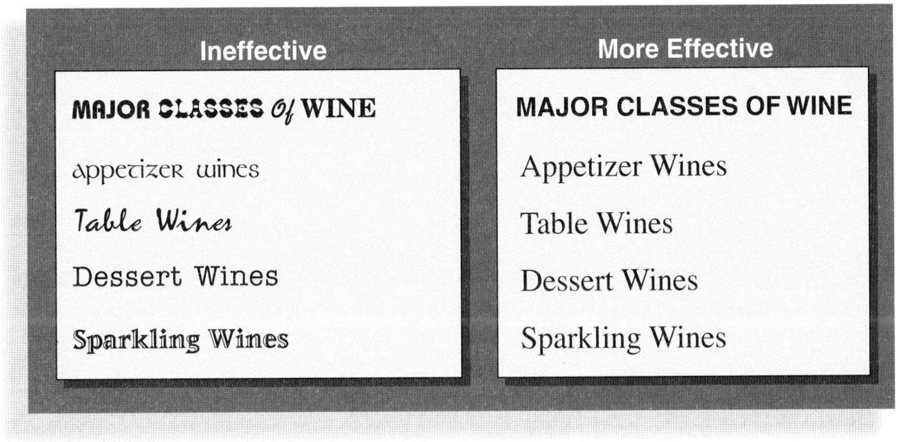

Figure 13.9

IMPACT ON HEARING	DECIBEL LEVEL	TYPE OF NOISE
Harmful	140	Firecracker
to	130	Jackhammer
hearing	120	Jet engine
Risk	110	Rock concert
hearing	100	Chain saw
loss	90	Motorcycle
Loud	80	Alarm clock
but	70	Busy traffic
safe	60	Air conditioner

Figure 13.10

as part of a multimedia presentation, you may find that light print on a dark background works better. In either case, make sure there is enough contrast between the background and the text so listeners can see everything clearly.

You can also use color to highlight key points in a visual aid. One student, in a speech about noise pollution, used a chart to summarize the sound levels of everyday noise and to indicate their potential danger for hearing loss (Figure 13.10). Notice, when you look at the chart, how the speaker used color to emphasize the different levels. He put sounds that are definitely harmful to hearing in red, sounds that may cause hearing loss in blue, and sounds that are loud but safe in green. These colors reinforced the speaker's ideas and, at the same time, made his chart easier to read.

Guidelines for Presenting Visual Aids

In addition to selecting and preparing your visual aids with care, you need to give attention to how you will *present* the aids in your speech. No matter how well designed your visual aids may be, they will be of little value unless you display them properly, discuss them clearly, and integrate them effectively with the rest of your presentation. Here are seven guidelines that will help you get the maximum impact out of your visual aids.

Avoid Using the Chalkboard for Visual Aids

At first thought, using the chalkboard in your classroom to present visual aids seems like a splendid idea. Usually, however, it is not. You have too much to do during a speech to worry about drawing or writing legibly on the board. Many students have marred an otherwise fine speech by turning their backs on the audience to use the chalkboard. Even if your visual aid is put on the chalkboard ahead of time, it will not be as vivid or as neat as one composed on poster board or a transparency.

Display Visual Aids Where Listeners Can See Them

Check the speech room ahead of time to decide exactly where you will display your visual aids. If you are using poster board, make sure it is sturdy enough to be displayed without curling up or falling over. Another choice is foamcore, a thin sheet of styrofoam with graphics-quality paper on both sides.

If you are displaying an object or a model, be sure to place it where it can be seen easily by everyone in the room. Setting it on a table next to the lectern may be fine for listeners seated in front, but the table may be too low for the aid to be visible to people seated farther back. If necessary, hold up the object or model while you are discussing it.

Once you have set the aid in the best location, don't undo all your preparation by standing where you block the audience's view of the aid. Stand to one side of the aid, and point with the arm nearest it. If possible, use a pencil, a ruler, or some other pointer. Using a pointer will allow you to stand farther away from the visual aid, thereby reducing the likelihood that you will obstruct the view of people sitting on the same side of the room as you are standing.

Avoid Passing Visual Aids Among the Audience

Once visual aids get into the hands of your listeners, you are in trouble. At least three people will be paying more attention to the aid than to you—the person who has just had it, the person who has it now, and the person waiting to get it next. By the time the visual aid moves on, all three may have lost track of what you are saying.

Nor do you solve this problem by preparing a handout for every member of the audience. There is no guarantee they will pay attention to it only when you want them to. In fact, they are likely to spend a good part of the speech looking over the handout at their own pace, rather than listening to you. Although handouts can be valuable, they usually just create competition for beginning speakers.

Every once in a while, of course, you will want listeners to have copies of some material to take home. When such a situation arises, keep the copies until after you've finished talking and can distribute them without creating a distraction. Keeping control of your visual aids is essential to keeping control of your speech.

Display Visual Aids Only While Discussing Them

Just as circulating visual aids distracts attention, so does displaying them throughout a speech. Whenever an aid is visible, at least some people will spend their time looking at it rather than listening to you.

If you are using an object or a model, keep it out of sight until you are ready to discuss it. When you finish your discussion, place the object or model back out of sight.

The same is true of charts, graphs, drawings, or photographs prepared on poster board. If you are using an easel, put a blank sheet of poster board in front of the sheet with the visual aid. When the time comes, remove the blank sheet to show the aid. When you are finished with the aid, remove it

CHECKLIST FOR PRESENTING VISUAL AIDS

yes	no	
☐	☐	1. Can I present my visual aids without writing or drawing on the chalkboard?
☐	☐	2. Have I checked the speech room to decide where I can display my visual aids most effectively?
☐	☐	3. Have I practiced presenting my visual aids so they will be clearly visible to everyone in the audience?
☐	☐	4. Have I practiced setting up and taking down my visual aids so I can do both smoothly during the speech?
☐	☐	5. Have I practiced keeping eye contact with my audience while presenting my visual aids?
☐	☐	6. Have I practiced explaining my visual aids clearly and concisely in terms my audience will understand?
☐	☐	7. If I am using handouts, have I planned to distribute them after the speech rather than during it?
☐	☐	8. Have I double-checked all equipment to make sure it works properly?
☐	☐	9. Have I rehearsed my speech with the equipment I will use during the final presentation?

CD 1: SPEECH CHECKLIST

You can print a copy of this checklist from the CD-ROM.

from the easel or cover it back up with a blank piece of poster board so it will not divert the attention of your listeners.

If you are using a multimedia program, you can achieve the same effect by inserting a blank slide that you can project when you are not discussing a visual aid. Regardless of the kind of visual aid you employ or the technology you use to present it, the principle remains the same: Display the aid *only* while you are discussing it.

Talk to Your Audience, Not to Your Visual Aid

When explaining a visual aid, it is easy to break eye contact with your audience and speak to the aid. Of course, your listeners are looking primarily at the aid, and you will need to glance at it periodically as you talk. But if you keep your eyes fixed on the visual aid, you may lose your audience. By keeping eye contact with your listeners, you will also pick up feedback about how the visual aid and your explanation of it are coming across.

Explain Visual Aids Clearly and Concisely

Visual aids don't explain themselves. Like statistics, they need to be translated and related to the audience. For example, Figure 13.11 (page 345) is an excellent visual aid, but do you know what it represents? You may if you suffer from migraine headaches, since it shows the different regions of

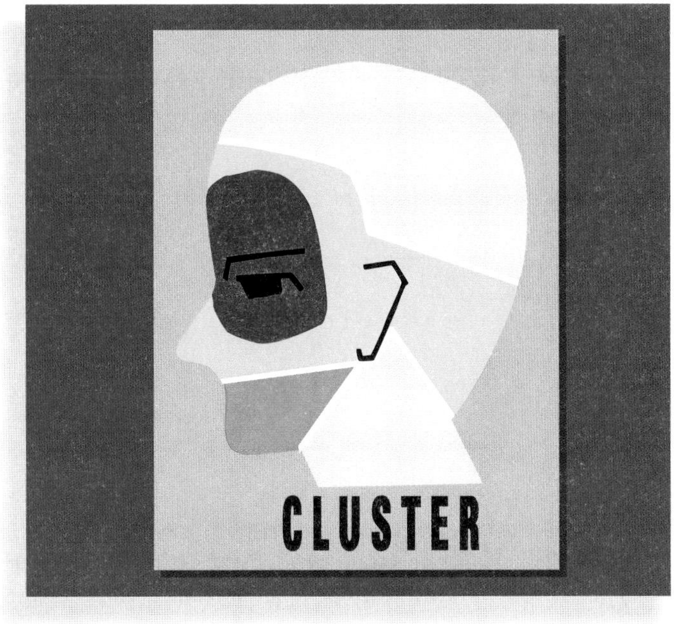

Figure 13.11

pain experienced during a cluster migraine attack. But even then, the full meaning of the drawing may not be clear until it is explained to you. And it certainly will not be clear to a person who knows little about migraines.

A visual aid can be of enormous benefit—but only if the viewer knows what to look for and why. Unfortunately, beginning speakers often rush over their visual aids without explaining them clearly and concisely. Be sure to adapt your visual aids to the audience. Don't just say, "As you can see . . . " and then pass quickly over the aid. Tell listeners what the aid means. Describe its major features. Spell out the meaning of charts and graphs. Interpret statistics and percentages. Remember, a visual aid is only as useful as the explanation that goes with it.

As you can see from CD 1, Video 13.8, the speaker who used the diagram of the migraine headache discussed above did an excellent job of explaining how each color on the drawing corresponds with an area of intense pain suffered during a cluster migraine. Having used the drawing during her practice sessions, she was able to integrate it into the speech smoothly and skillfully—and to maintain eye contact with her listeners throughout her discussion of it. You should strive to do the same when you present visual aids in your speeches.

CD 1: VIDEO 13.8

View an excerpt from "The Agony of Migraines."

Practice with Your Visual Aids

This chapter has mentioned several times the need to practice with visual aids, but the point bears repeating. You do not want to suffer through an experience like the one that follows:

> Several years ago, a young engineer came up with a cutting-edge design for a new machine. He then needed to explain the machine to his supervisors and convince them it was a worthwhile investment. He was told to plan his speech carefully, to prepare slides and other visual aids, and to practice in the conference room, using its complex lectern and projection system.

Unfortunately, although he had done a brilliant job designing the machine, the engineer failed to plan his presentation with similar care. His worst mistake was not practicing with the equipment he now needed to operate. When he dimmed the lights, he couldn't read his text. When the first slide came on, it wasn't his but belonged to a previous speaker. When he reached the first correct slide, the type was too small for anyone past the first row to see.

Unable to turn on the light-arrow indicator to point out the line he was talking about, he walked away from the lectern to point things out directly on the screen. But he left the microphone behind, so people in the back rows could neither see nor hear.

When a slide of his design appeared, he was too close to see the critical parts. Since he couldn't check his text because of the darkness, he lost track of what he was supposed to say. Reaching for a steel-tipped pointer because he couldn't operate the optical one, he managed to punch a hole through the screen.

In desperation, he abandoned his slides, turned up the lights, and raced through the rest of his speech so fast that he was almost unintelligible. Finally, in embarrassment both for himself and the audience, he sat down.[8]

This sounds like a routine from *Saturday Night Live,* but it is a true story. What makes the story especially sad is that it didn't have to happen. With some effort, thought, and preparation, the engineer could have made a success of his presentation instead of turning it into a fiasco.

You can avoid following in his footsteps if you practice with the visual aids you have chosen. Rehearse with your equipment to be sure you can present your aids with a minimum of fuss. Run through the entire speech several times, practicing how you will show the aids, the gestures you will make, and the timing of each move. In using visual aids, as in other aspects of speechmaking, there is no substitute for preparation.[9]

Summary

There are many kinds of visual aids. Most obvious is the object about which you are speaking, or a model of it. Diagrams, sketches, and other kinds of drawings are valuable because you can design them to illustrate your points exactly. Graphs are an excellent way to illustrate any subject dealing with numbers, while charts are used to summarize large blocks of information. Although video can be useful as a visual aid, it needs to be carefully edited and integrated into the speech. Photographs need to be large enough to be seen clearly by all your listeners. If you have access to the right equipment, you may be able to combine several kinds of visual aids—plus sound—in a multimedia presentation. Finally, you can act as your own visual aid by performing actions that demonstrate processes or ideas.

No matter what kind of visual aid you use, you need to prepare it carefully. You will be most successful if you prepare your aids in advance, keep them simple, make sure they are large enough to be seen clearly, and use color effectively for emphasis and visual appeal. If you are creating visual aids on a computer, use a limited number of fonts and make sure the ones you select will be easy for your audience to read.

In addition to being designed with care, visual aids need to be presented skillfully. Avoid writing or drawing visual aids on the chalkboard. Nor should you pass visual aids among the audience. Instead, display each aid only while you are talking about it, and be sure to display it where everyone can see it without straining. When presenting a visual aid, maintain eye contact with your listeners. Talk to the audience, not to the aid, and explain the aid clearly and concisely. Above all, practice with your visual aids so they fit into your speech smoothly and expertly.

Key Terms

model (330)
graph (333)
line graph (333)
pie graph (333)
bar graph (334)
chart (335)
transparency (336)
multimedia presentation (337)
font (340)

ONLINE LEARNING CENTER

Review these terms by doing the Chapter 13 crossword puzzle at www.mhhe.com/lucas9.

Review Questions

After reading this chapter, you should be able to answer the following questions:

1. What are the major advantages of using visual aids in your speeches?
2. What kinds of visual aids might you use in a speech?
3. What guidelines are given in the chapter for preparing visual aids?
4. What guidelines are given in the chapter for presenting visual aids?

CD 1: STUDY QUESTIONS

For further review, go to the Study Questions for this chapter.

Exercises for Critical Thinking

1. Watch a how-to television program (a cooking or gardening show, for example) or the weather portion of a local newscast. Notice how the speaker uses visual aids to help communicate the message. What kinds of visual aids are used? How do they enhance the clarity, interest, and retainability of the speaker's message? What would the speaker have to do to communicate the message effectively without visual aids?
2. Consider how you might use visual aids to explain each of the following:
   a. How to perform the Heimlich maneuver to help a choking victim.
   b. The proportion of the electorate that votes in major national elections in the United States, France, Germany, England, and Japan, respectively.
   c. Where to obtain information about student loans.
   d. The wing patterns of various species of butterflies.
   e. The increase in the amount of money spent by Americans on health care since 1985.
   f. How to change a bicycle tire.
   g. The basic equipment and techniques of rock climbing.

3. Plan to use visual aids in at least one of your classroom speeches. Be creative in devising your aids, and be sure to follow the guidelines discussed in the chapter for using them. After the speech, analyze how effectively you employed your visual aids, what you learned about the use of visual aids from your experience, and what changes you would make in using visual aids if you were to deliver the speech again.

Applying the POWER of PUBLIC SPEAKING

As a veterinarian and owner of a small-animal practice, you work closely with your local humane society to help control a growing population of unwanted dogs and cats. You and your staff devote many hours annually in free and reduced-cost medical services to animals adopted from the society. Now you have been asked to speak to the city council in support of legislation proposed by the society for stronger enforcement of animal licensing and leash laws.

In your speech, you plan to include statistics that (1) compare estimates of the city's dog population with the number of licenses issued during the past five years and (2) show the small number of citations given by local law enforcement for unleashed pets during the same period of time. Knowing from your college public speaking class how valuable visual aids can be in presenting statistics, you decide to illustrate one set of statistics with a chart and the other with a graph.

For which set of statistics will a chart be more appropriate? For which set will a graph be more appropriate? Of the three kinds of graphs discussed in this chapter (bar, line, pie), which will work best for your statistics and why?

Notes

[1]Joseph L. Chesebro, "Effects of Teacher Clarity and Nonverbal Immediacy on Student Learning, Receiver Apprehension, and Affect," *Communication Education,* 52 (2003), pp. 135–147.

[2]See Timothy A. Borchers, *Persuasion in the Media Age* (New York: McGraw-Hill, 2002), pp. 138–166.

[3]Douglas R. Vogel, Gary W. Dickson, and John A Lehman, *Persuasion and the Role of Visual Presentation Support: The UM/3M Study* (Minneapolis: University of Minnesota School of Management, 1986).

[4]Tad Simons, "Multimedia or Bust," *Presentations* (February 2000), pp. 40–50.

[5]For an authoritative look at the art of statistical graphics, see Stephen Few, *Show Me the Numbers: Designing Tables and Graphs to Enlighten* (Oakland, CA: Analytics Press, 2004).

[6]For research on this point, see Richard E. Mayer, Julie Heiser, and Steve Lonn, "Cognitive Constraints on Multimedia Learning: When Presenting More Material Results in Less Understanding," *Journal of Educational Psychology,* 93 (2001), pp. 187–198.

[7]Claudyne Wilder, *The Presentations Kit: 10 Steps for Selling Your Ideas*, rev. ed (New York: Wiley, 1994), p. 101.

[8]Adapted from Eric A. Walker, "About the 'Death' of an Engineer," *Centre Daily Times,* April 25, 1972.

[9]For additional information on the effective use of visual aids, see Thomas Leech, *How to Prepare, Stage, and Deliver Winning Presentations,* 3rd ed. (New York: American Management Association, 2004), pp. 121–204.

APPENDIX

Using PowerPoint

What do a business meeting, a courtroom presentation, a military briefing, and a college lecture have in common? In all four situations there is a good chance you will encounter a speaker using PowerPoint to help communicate her or his ideas. A survey of 300 professional speakers showed that 94 percent use PowerPoint during at least part of their talks.[1] Another study revealed that 90 percent of the multimedia presentations in the United States are developed with PowerPoint.[2] Depending on the technology at your school, you may have an opportunity to use PowerPoint in one or more of your classroom speeches.

In Chapter 13, we discussed general principles for effective multimedia presentations. Here we focus specifically on PowerPoint. As with any method of presenting visual or audio aids, PowerPoint has its pluses and minuses. We'll begin by looking at both, as well as at the major factors to consider when planning to use PowerPoint in a speech.

Pluses and Minuses of PowerPoint

When used well, PowerPoint is a great boon to communication. It allows you to employ all the kinds of visual aids discussed in Chapter 13 without having to juggle poster board and overhead transparencies while also trying to operate a CD player, slide projector, and/or video playback unit. Instead, you can use PowerPoint to incorporate text, photographs, charts, graphs, sound, even video into your speech—all with the click of a mouse.

Unfortunately, PowerPoint is not always used well. Too often speakers allow it to dominate their presentations, wowing the audience with their technical proficiency while causing listeners to lose sight of the message in a flurry of spectacular—but haphazard—sounds and images.[3] As technology expert Herb Lovelace states, it sometimes seems that "the fancier the PowerPoint presentation, the less valuable the ideas being presented."[4]

At the other extreme are speakers who throw their presentations together carelessly, assuming that using PowerPoint—no matter how badly—will magically produce a superb speech. Plodding through one poorly designed visual after another with little or no eye contact with an audience seated in a darkened room, these speakers would be better off if they had never heard of PowerPoint.

Another problem is that some speakers use PowerPoint to illustrate every point of their talk, so the speaker is virtually reading the speech to the audience as the words appear on screen. This is no more effective than reading dully from a manuscript, and it seldom produces genuine communication.

Planning to Use PowerPoint

If you are going to employ PowerPoint effectively, you need a clear idea of exactly why, how, and when you are going to use it in your speech. Rather than falling into the trap of putting everything you say on screen for the audience to read, you need to make choices about which aspects of your speech you will illustrate with visual or audio aids. This requires careful planning.

One of the most surprising aspects of PowerPoint to people who have not used it before is how much time and effort are required to put together a first-rate presentation. Not only are you responsible for all the other activities involved in speechmaking, but you face the additional tasks of deciding where to use PowerPoint in the speech, of gathering images and/or sounds for your presentation, of designing first-rate PowerPoint aids, and of mastering the equipment and PowerPoint commands needed to deliver your speech smoothly and expertly.

The first step is deciding where in the speech you can use PowerPoint to greatest advantage. After you have finished developing the speech, go through it and think about where you might employ PowerPoint to clarify or strengthen your ideas. Rather than using PowerPoint to illustrate every thought, look for spots where it will genuinely enhance your message.

For example, if you're talking about the history of woman's suffrage in the United States, you might include the text of the Nineteenth Amendment, which granted women the vote in 1920; photographs of famous suffrage leaders such as Elizabeth Cady Stanton, Susan B. Anthony, and Carrie Chapman Catt; and a chart with the major events and dates of the suffrage crusade. If you are speaking about West Nile virus, it would make sense to include a diagram showing how the virus is spread, a list of its symptoms, a graph demonstrating the increase in the number of cases in recent years, and a map illustrating the spread of the virus through different regions of the United States.

As you plan your presentation, think about how you can use the tools provided by PowerPoint to go beyond what you might be able to do with traditional visual aids. At the same time, remember that too many visuals—not to mention visuals that are badly designed or poorly explained—can do more harm than good. Be creative and resourceful without allowing PowerPoint to overwhelm your entire speech.

Getting Started in PowerPoint

Once you have decided which aspects of your speech to illustrate with PowerPoint, it's time to start working on your presentation. When you work in PowerPoint, you will be creating *slides* that consist of words, images, and/or sounds that help communicate your ideas to the audience. In the language of PowerPoint, all the slides for a given speech are called a *presentation.* You might think of a PowerPoint slide as equivalent to an individual visual aid, and of a PowerPoint presentation as equivalent to a file folder that holds all the aids for a speech.

slide
A single frame in a PowerPoint presentation.

presentation
A PowerPoint file containing all the slides for a given speech.

Screen Elements

If you have not used PowerPoint before, you should take a moment to familiarize yourself with its screen elements. Figure A.1 (page 352) shows these elements as they appear in PowerPoint 2003. At the top, just below

Figure A.1
PowerPoint 2003
Screen Elements

the Microsoft PowerPoint title, is the menu bar, which helps you perform major functions such as opening and closing presentations, choosing fonts, inserting images, and viewing slides. When you click the boxes on the menu bar, drop-down menus appear with more choices. Just below the menu bar is the upper toolbar, which provides shortcuts for such tasks as creating new slides, adding bold or italicized text, undoing your previous action, and saving your work.

Another toolbar stretches across the bottom of the screen. Among the items on this bar are three buttons with icons just above Draw in the lower left-hand corner. These buttons allow you to shift among different views of your presentation. The lower toolbar also includes shortcuts for such functions as adding text boxes, charts, clip art, and color.

The main part of the screen appears in what PowerPoint calls Normal view. This view is divided into three areas. The center area displays your current slide. On the left is a pane that allows you to switch between viewing an outline of all your slides and thumbnails of the slides. On the right is a task pane that provides tools for creating new presentations and for formatting slides.

Templates

PowerPoint gives you three methods for creating a presentation: AutoContent Wizard, Blank Presentation, and Design Templates.

Designed primarily for business speakers, AutoContent Wizard provides templates with predetermined outlines and sample text for 17 kinds of

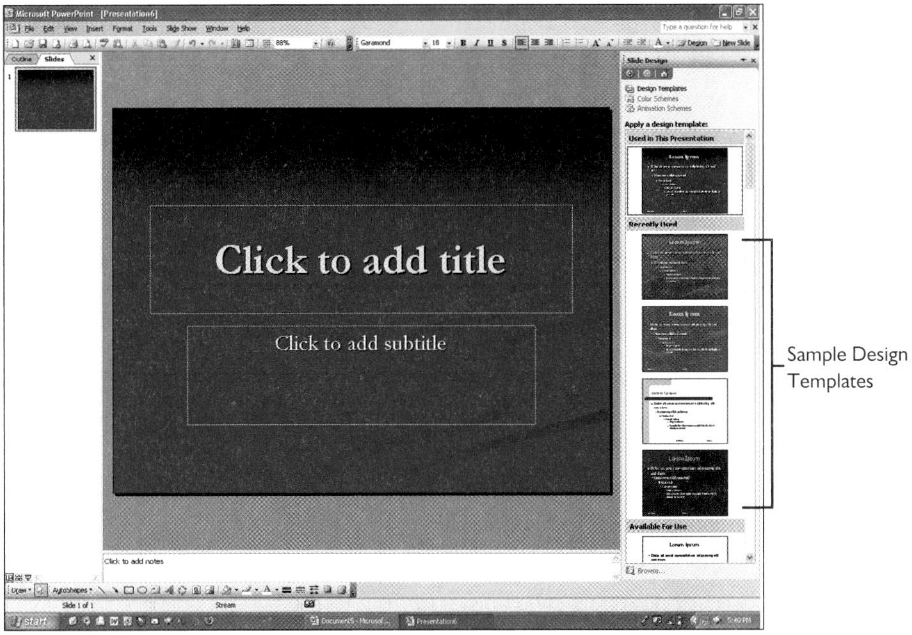

Figure A.2 Design Templates

presentations, such as Employee Orientation, Recommending a Strategy, and Selling a Product or Service. Although helpful in some situations, it is seldom used for speeches outside a business setting.

As its name implies, Blank Presentation does not come with any preset designs. Some experienced speakers prefer the flexibility it provides in designing slides, but it can be daunting for novices.

Most students prefer to start with the Design Template option, which generates a presentation in which all the slides are unified by a preselected combination of colors, fonts, and graphics. When you choose Design Template, sample templates appear on the right of the screen. By clicking any template, you can view it in the main part of your screen. (See Figure A.2, above.)

If you use Design Template, be sure to avoid templates with busy backgrounds that may distract from your message. Fortunately, you can easily switch templates partway through a presentation if you decide you don't like your original choice.

Slide Layouts

Both Design Templates and Blank Presentation provide more than two dozen slide layouts for arranging the items on your slides. Thumbnails of these layouts can be viewed in the right pane on your computer screen. (See Figure A.3, page 354.) Click any layout, and it will appear in the middle of your screen.

Once you know your way around the basic elements of PowerPoint, you're ready to begin developing slides for your speech. In the Online Learning Center for your textbook, you will find step-by-step instructions on how

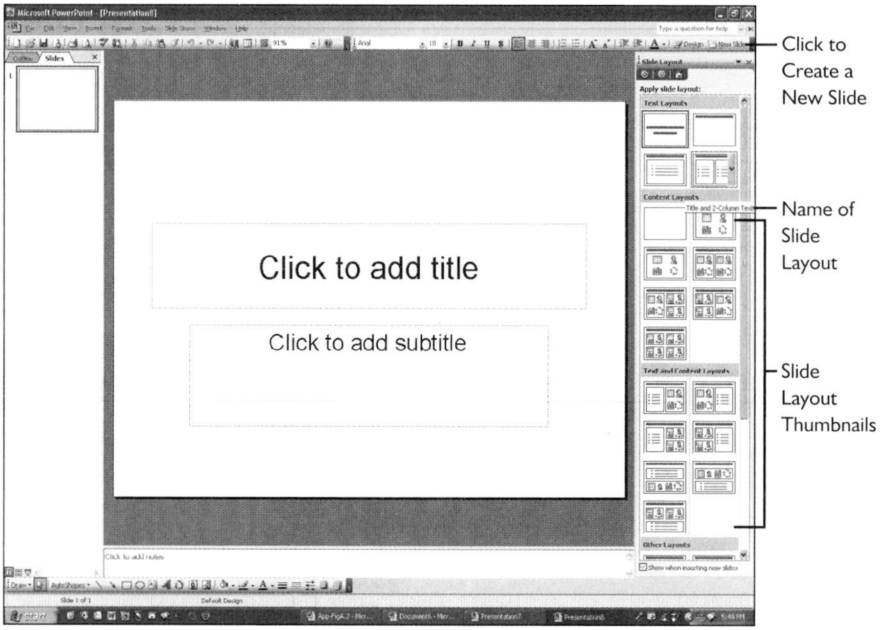

Figure A.3 Slide Layouts

to create slides; how to insert text, images, and sounds onto slides; how to format slides for a crisp, professional look; and how to add special features such as animation and transitions to your slides.

ONLINE LEARNING CENTER

Go to the PowerPoint Tutorials at www.mhhe.com/lucaspowerpoint.

If you have not used PowerPoint before, these instructions will provide the information you need to get started on the right track. If you have used PowerPoint before, keep the instructions in mind as a resource you can turn to if you have questions as you work on your slides. You can access the instructions by going to the Online Learning Center at www.mhhe.com/lucas9 and clicking PowerPoint 2002 or PowerPoint 2003, depending on which version is on your computer.

CD 2: FULL SPEECH

View "The Great Wall of China."

Here we will focus less on technical information than on principles for using PowerPoint effectively in your speeches. As we proceed, we'll illustrate key points with examples from a five-minute informative speech on the Great Wall of China. The full speech is available on CD 2 and is reprinted at the end of this appendix. You may find it helpful to view the speech now, so you will have it in mind as the discussion unfolds. From time to time, we will also refer to brief clips from the speech that demonstrate particular points about how you can use PowerPoint to best advantage.

Elements of PowerPoint Slides

The major elements of PowerPoint slides are text, images, and sounds. They can be used individually or in combination, depending on the specific point you wish to communicate. There are also many kinds of images available to you, ranging from video to still images such as photographs, clip art, and graphs. Let's look at each individually.

Figure A.4
Sample PowerPoint Slide

Text

Most PowerPoint slides contain some kind of text. The text might be no more than a title indicating the subject of the slide, or it might include several lines in the body of the slide. Text can be used by itself, and it can be used in conjunction with photographs, clip art, or other images. For the most part, any text appropriate for a traditional visual aid can be included on a PowerPoint slide.

For example, Figure A.4 shows a slide from the speech on the Great Wall of China. The speaker used this slide in conjunction with his explanation of the first stage of building the Great Wall, during the Qin dynasty. In addition to an image of Qin Shi Huang, the emperor who started construction of the Wall, the slide contains a title plus text identifying Qin Shi Huang and the dates of the Qin dynasty. The slide also includes copyright information for the drawing of Qin Shi Huang.

Photographs

One of the benefits of PowerPoint is the ease with which it allows you to spice up a speech with photographs. If you're speaking on a topic drawn from your personal experience, you can use PowerPoint to display your own photographs. For other topics, you can download photographs from the Web. Here are some of the best online sources for photographs on topics of current and historical interest:

- *Google Image Search* (http://images.google.com). The Web's most comprehensive image resource. Allows you to search for photographs on virtually any topic across thousands of Web sites.
- *Pics4Learning* (www.pics4learning.com). Features thousands of donated images that have no copyright restrictions. Images are divided into categories such as architecture, history, religion, and weather.

- *Yahoo Picture Gallery* (http://images.search.yahoo.com). Comparable to Google Image Search. Some items can be used free of charge; others are subject to copyright restrictions.
- *Free Stock Photos* (www.freestockphotos.com/). Provides links to thousands of photographs, historical and contemporary, that can be used without charge for personal purposes.

Clip Art

Clip art includes pictures and symbols that represent common objects, processes, and ideas. Examples of clip art are a drawing of a microscope to stand for science, or a cartoon of an aircraft circling the globe to symbolize travel.

clip art
Pictures and symbols that represent common objects, processes, and ideas.

Clip art can be humorous and entertaining, but it can also be distracting and inappropriate. If you employ clip art, avoid using it on every slide and use only one piece of clip art on a given slide. Be certain the images you select convey the same emotional tone as your speech, and make sure all the images are drawn in a consistent style.

There are numerous online sources for clip art. Two of the major ones are:

- *Microsoft Design Gallery Live* (http://office.microsoft.com/clipart/). An extensive collection of clip art searchable by category and keyword. Also contains sounds and motions.
- *Barry's Clip Art Server* (www.barrysclipart.com). Contains thousands of pieces of donated clip art that have no copyright restrictions.

Graphs

As we saw in Chapter 13, graphs are excellent for communicating statistical trends and patterns. PowerPoint gives you a number of ways to incorporate graphs into your speeches. One option is to download graphs from the Internet. Web sites for government agencies, newspapers, and magazines are all excellent places to look for graphs on current topics. Another option is to use PowerPoint's graph program to create a graph using data you have gathered.

Figure A.5 (page 357) shows what you will see when you enter the graph program. The datasheet is a separate window. As you replace the labels and numbers on the datasheet with your own labels and numbers, the graph will change accordingly. You can also switch to a different kind of graph, such as a pie graph or bar graph. Whichever kind you use, be sure to follow the general principles for effective graphs discussed in Chapter 13.

Sounds

If you're speaking on a topic such as language development, birdcalls, or the jazz violin, you might want to play a sound clip to illustrate your ideas. PowerPoint offers several methods to add sound to your presentation. You can play an excerpt from a CD, you can use downloaded sounds from the Web, or you can utilize sounds that you have recorded yourself.

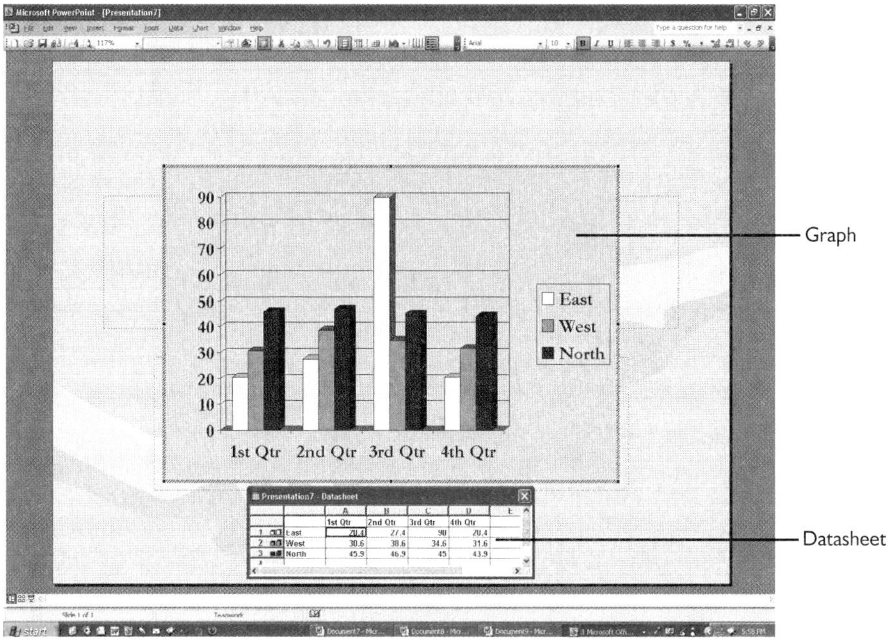

Figure A.5
PowerPoint Graph Program

The most important thing to remember with regard to using sounds of any kind is that they should be absolutely essential for communicating your message. You should never add sounds just for the fun of it. Whatever sounds you include should be limited in length so as to illustrate your points without overwhelming them. Remember, the audience has come to listen to you—not to listen to a series of recordings from other people.

Video

PowerPoint offers a number of options for adding video to a speech. For a presentation based on your own experience, you might be able to draw on your personal video collection. These video recordings can be edited and saved on files which are then available for use on PowerPoint slides. Another option is to download nonstreaming video from the Internet, as long as you are careful to observe copyright restrictions (see pages 365–366).

Video, like sound, should be added to a speech only when it is indispensable to communicating your message. It also needs to be skillfully edited and smoothly integrated with the rest of the speech. Be aware that video files take up large amounts of disk space and are often impractical for presentations run from older computers. If you are planning to include video in your speech, be sure to check it ahead of time with the computer you will use on the day of your speech to make sure the video plays at the correct speed and the sound is properly synchronized with the picture.

Formatting Slides

Once you have the text, images, sounds, and/or videos that you want to include on your slides, the next step is to format the slides to communicate your message as effectively as possible. Although PowerPoint provides a number of advanced formatting features, you can start creating sharp, professional-looking slides right away by following a few basic principles for the use of color, fonts, space, and animation. You should also review the guidelines for preparing visual aids discussed in Chapter 13, pages 338–342.

Color

PowerPoint offers a wide selection of colors for your slides, and you may be tempted to try all of them. But to produce effective visual aids, you need to stick to a limited number of colors and use them consistently. Use one color for background, one color for titles, and one color for other text throughout all your slides. Notice, for example, how the Great Wall of China speech uses a red background for all slides, gold for title text, and white for all other text. This consistency unifies the slides and gives the speech a more professional appearance.

When selecting colors, keep in mind that light text against a dark background provides the best contrast for LCD projection. PowerPoint's Color Schemes feature gives you a dozen preset options for different color combinations (see Figure A.6). Clicking any of the options will transfer it to your slides.

Figure A.6 Color Schemes

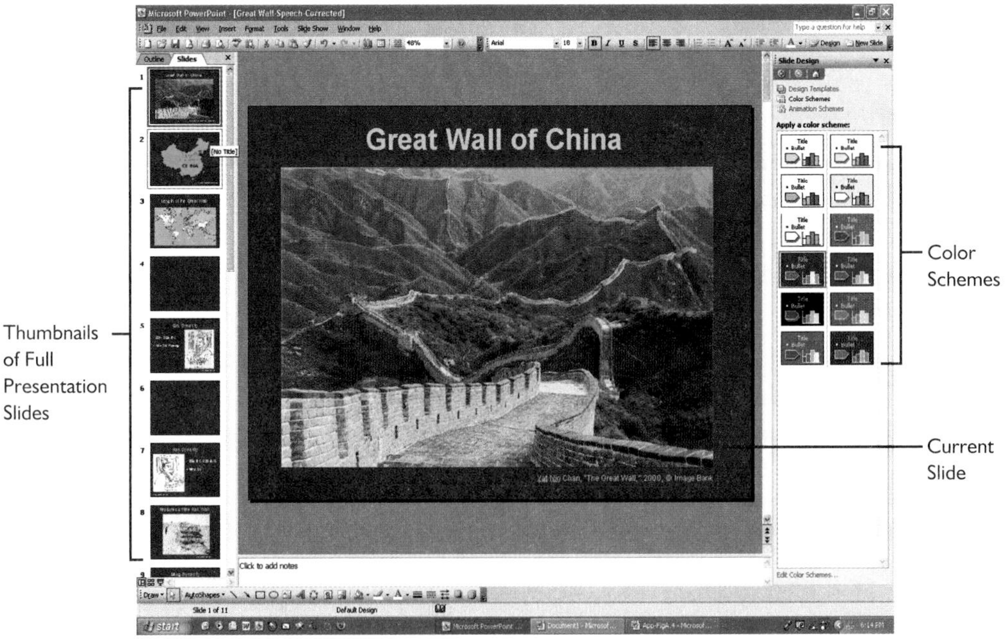

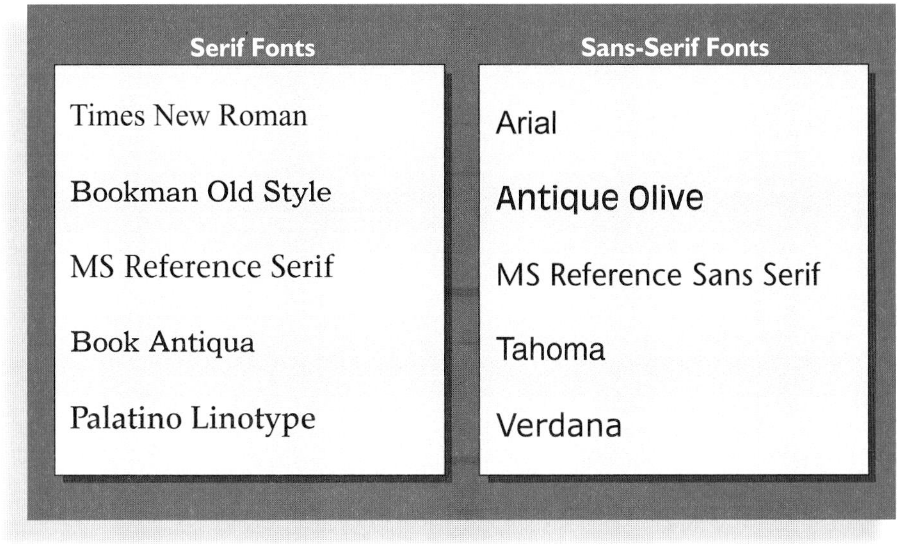

Figure A.7

Fonts

PowerPoint has dozens of fonts to choose from, but they all fall into one or another of two basic categories—serif or sans-serif. Serif fonts have little tails on each letter, like the type you are reading right now. Sans-serif fonts do not have tails, like the type used for the heading Fonts at the start of this section. For examples, see Figure A.7, above.

serif font
A typeface with rounded edges on the letters.

sans-serif font
A typeface with straight edges on the letters.

Serif fonts are easier to read in large patches of text, while sans-serif fonts are better for headings and short bursts of text. Most multimedia experts recommend sans-serif fonts for titles and headings on PowerPoint slides—and there are some who say sans-serif should be used for *all* text in PowerPoint.

The default font for most slides in PowerPoint 2003 is a sans-serif font called Arial. In normal circumstances, there is no reason for you to change from this font. However, if your slides come up with a different font, or if you wish to change the font for some other reason, you can do so fairly easily. When choosing fonts, keep the following guidelines in mind:

- Choose fonts that are clear and easy to read. (For examples, see Chapter 13, pages 340–341.)
- Avoid using ALL CAPS because they are difficult to read.
- Don't use more than two fonts on a single slide—one for the title or major heading and another for subtitles or other text.
- Use the same fonts on all your slides, rather than switching fonts from slide to slide.
- Put titles and major headings in 44- to 36-point type; make subheads and other text 32- to 24-point. The only exception to this rule is copyright credits, which are best in 10-point type.

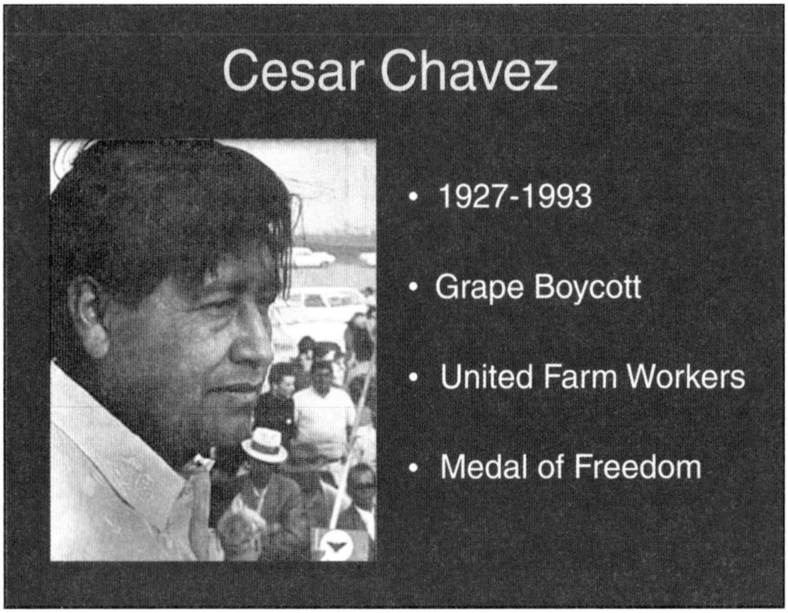

Figure A.8 Effective Visual Balance

Space

One of the biggest mistakes people make when using PowerPoint is putting too much on a single slide. The result is a cluttered, messy slide that detracts from the speaker's message and may well confuse the audience. A general rule for slides that contain only text is to include no more than six or seven lines of type. If you are combining text with images, you may need to limit yourself to fewer lines to keep the text large enough for the audience to read without straining.

Regardless of the elements on your slide, try to achieve a pleasing sense of visual balance when arranging them. Look, for example, at Figure A.8 (above), which shows a slide from a speech about the famous Mexican-American leader Cesar Chavez. Notice how the title is centered at the top of the slide, the photograph fills most of the left side, and the text occupies enough space on the right to compensate for the size of the photograph.

Compare this slide with the one in Figure A.9 on page 361. The second slide contains the same elements as the first, but those elements are not placed effectively. Instead of being centered, the title is located over the photograph, where it takes up two lines rather than one. To compensate, the photograph of Chavez has been reduced in size, so it has less visual impact than the photograph on the first slide. The photograph is also too close to the bottom of the slide, thereby separating it from the title. Finally, the text on the right side is too close to the photograph and is too high on the slide to provide a good sense of visual balance.

If you stick with PowerPoint's default layouts, you should have little trouble creating slides that are visually balanced. Be sure, however, to leave a little extra room at the edges of your slides because what is projected on the viewing screen is sometimes smaller than what you see on your computer.

Figure A.9
Ineffective Visual Balance

Animation

When you read the word "animation," you might think of cartoon characters and Walt Disney movies. In PowerPoint, however, animation refers to the way objects enter or exit a slide. Without animation, all the items on a slide appear at the same time when the slide is displayed. With animation, you can control when words, pictures, and even parts of graphs show up on screen. When used properly, it's a terrific way to spruce up your slides.

animation
The way objects enter or exit a PowerPoint slide.

Recall the speech on the Great Wall of China. For the most part, the speaker avoids special animation effects because they are not necessary to communicate his ideas. However, when explaining the architectural changes made to the Wall during the Ming dynasty, he uses animation to make sure the appropriate text appears on screen just as he begins to discuss each point. By doing so, he focuses the audience's attention and reinforces his ideas at the same time.

CD 1: VIDEO A2.1
View this excerpt from "The Great Wall of China."

When working on your speeches, think about ways you can use animation to help communicate your message. Be wary, however, of animation effects that might distract the attention of listeners. Stick with a limited number of animation effects and use them consistently from slide to slide.

Delivering Your Speech with PowerPoint

Once you have created your slides, it's time to work on the delivery of your speech. As with other aspects of PowerPoint, this requires careful planning. Even the most professional-looking slides will do little good if you can't get the computer and projector to work properly, if the slides can't be seen clearly because of poor lighting, or if you forget to display them at the right moment.

Figure A.10 Slide Sorter View

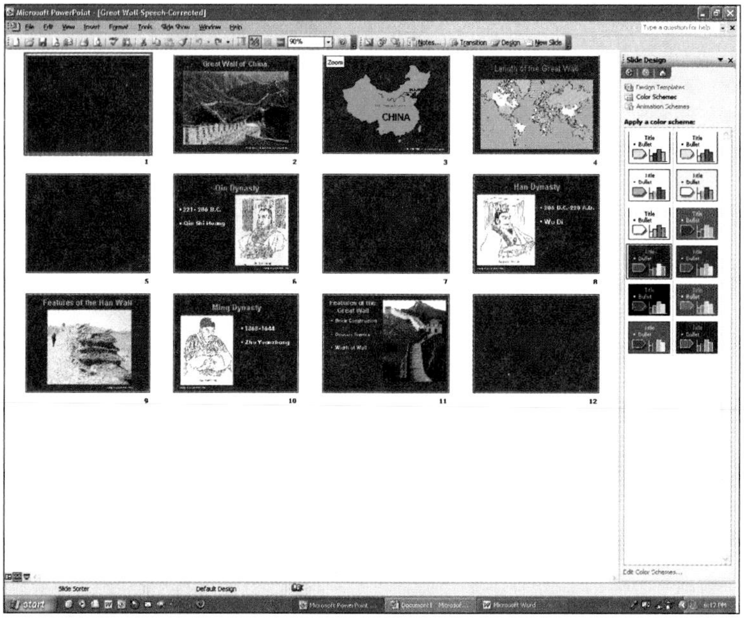

The guidelines presented in Chapter 13 for delivering speeches with other types of visual aids also apply to delivering speeches with PowerPoint. Here we will focus on aspects of delivery that are especially important for speakers who employ PowerPoint.

Recheck Your Slides

Before rehearsing your speech, take time to double-check your slides to see if anything is missing, misplaced, or misspelled. You can review all your slides at a glance in Slide Sorter view (see Figure A.10). It's also a good idea to run through your slides in Slide Show view, which displays the slides as they will appear on screen during your speech. Be sure to save any corrections and changes as you go along.

Know Slide Show Commands

When delivering your speech, you should be able to move effortlessly from slide to slide, as well as among animation effects on individual slides. To do so, you have to know the computer commands for these operations. Figure A.11 (page 363) shows some of the most-used commands.

As you can see, there are multiple options for most commands. If you have not used PowerPoint before, practice with the various options and decide which you want to use. Then stick with them throughout your presentation.

As you gain more experience with PowerPoint, its commands will become second nature. However, just in case you forget something during your speech, you may want to follow the lead of experienced speakers and write the most important commands on a sheet of paper that you can refer to if necessary.

Slide Show Commands

Display slides (enter Slide Show view)	Click View on the menu bar at the top of the screen and select Slide Show from the drop-down menu; or click the podium icon on the left of the tool bar at the bottom of the screen.
Show the next slide	Click the mouse; press Enter; press the right arrow button; or press the "N" key.
Show the previous slide	Press Backspace; press the left arrow button; or press the "P" key.
Show a specific slide	Type the number of the slide and press Enter.
End the show	Press Esc.

Figure A.11

ONLINE LEARNING CENTER

Check the PowerPoint Tutorials at www.mhhe.com/lucaspowerpoint for additional Slide Show commands.

Practice Your Speech with PowerPoint

As we saw in Chapter 13, you should always practice a speech with your visual aids. This is especially important when using PowerPoint. If you don't know the necessary commands, fumble around when operating the equipment, or fail to coordinate your slides with your words, you will quickly lose both your credibility and the attention of listeners.

When you practice your speech using PowerPoint, don't just click the mouse casually or rush quickly over your words. Go through every part of the speech and make sure you know exactly when you want each slide to appear, when you want each to disappear, and what you will say while each is on screen. Mark your speaking notes with cues that will remind you when to display each slide or animation and when to remove it from the screen.

It's usually best to project a slide when you first start discussing the point it illustrates. For a good example, look at the timing of the slides in the speech about the Great Wall of China. The speaker presents each slide at just the right moment and makes sure it is on screen only while he is discussing it. He also times his animation effects to appear just as he is talking about the related point. This kind of precise timing comes from practicing the speech with PowerPoint.

CD 1: VIDEO A2.2

View an excerpt from "The Great Wall of China."

In addition to coordinating your slides with your words, pay attention when you practice to making eye contact with the audience. This is important in any speech, but it is especially challenging when you use PowerPoint because of all the equipment you are operating during the speech. As you rehearse, work with the mouse and keyboard until you can use both without looking down for more than an instant when advancing your slides.

Also concentrate on presenting the speech without looking back at the screen to see what is being projected on it. You can check what is on screen by glancing at the computer each time you advance a slide. There is nothing wrong with looking at the screen now and again as you explain your slides, but remember to address your remarks to the audience and not to the screen. The Great Wall speech provides a good model in this regard.

Given all the things you have to work on when practicing a speech with PowerPoint, you need to allow more time for rehearsal than with other kinds of speeches. No matter how well designed your slides may be, they won't have much impact if you don't present them effectively. So get an early start and give yourself plenty of time to ensure that your delivery is as impressive as your slides.

Display Slides Only While Discussing Them

As with other types of visual aids, you want your PowerPoint slides to be visible only when you are discussing them. You can achieve this goal by adding blank slides as needed between your other slides. Recall, for example, how the speaker in the Great Wall presentation uses blank slides at various parts of the speech. By doing so, he keeps his listeners focused on what he is saying at the moment, rather than having their attention diverted by the previous slide.

Remember that whenever a visual aid is visible, at least part of the audience will be paying attention to it rather than listening to you. Using blank slides is one way to prevent this from happening when you present aids with PowerPoint. (It's also a good idea to add a blank slide at the end of your presentation, so your last content slide will not continue to be exposed after you have finished discussing it.)

Check the Room and Equipment

In ideal circumstances, you will be able to rehearse at least once in the room in which you will present your speech, with the same computer, mouse, and projector you will use on the day of your speech. If this is not possible, try to stop by the room several days beforehand and work with the equipment. If you can't get to the room before the day of the speech, arrive an hour or so ahead of time to familiarize yourself with the equipment and to make sure it's working properly.

There is wide variation among computers and projectors, as well as among rooms equipped with multimedia connections, so even if you have used PowerPoint on previous occasions, you need to check the setup in the room where you will be speaking. Most experienced speakers arrange ahead of time to have a technician present when they arrive, so she or he can take care of any problems.

Think, too, about the location of your equipment. If you're using a portable projector, you will need a table on which to place it, as well as a table or lectern for your computer, mouse, and speaking notes. Make sure you have a place to stand where you don't block the projector and it doesn't shine directly into your eyes. Depending on the setup in your room, you may need to rearrange some seats—or the location of the projector and screen—so everyone will have a clear view of your slides.

Pay attention to the lighting as well. Check whether the projector is bright enough to overpower the room lights and create a sharp image. If it isn't, see if you can dim the lights near the screen while keeping the rest of the room fully lighted. If you are using a limited number of slides, you may be able to dim the lights just during the time you show the slides. If the light switches are far away from where you will be speaking, arrange for someone to assist you with the lighting and make sure to give him or her clear directions.

This may all seem like a lot of fuss and bother, but anyone who has given speeches with PowerPoint will tell you it's absolutely essential.

Develop a Backup Plan

Despite all your preparation and practice, it's possible that technology will fail you. More than one speaker has arrived with PowerPoint in tow only to discover that the computer is acting up, the projector will not work, or the room's power connections are not compatible with the speaker's computer.

What do you do if this happens to you? You can't just cancel the speech. As the old saying has it, "The show must go on." This is why you always need a backup plan—especially for speeches outside the classroom.

One option is to create overhead transparencies that you can use in place of your PowerPoint slides. Given the fact that overhead projectors are available almost everywhere in the world, professional speakers typically carry a set of transparencies to their speeches just in case they run into a problem with PowerPoint.

Even if you have transparencies as a backup to PowerPoint, you should always be prepared for the possibility that you may have to deliver your speech without either PowerPoint or your transparencies. In such a situation, you can usually adapt by making photocopies of your transparencies and giving your speech with handouts—though there may be circumstances in which even that is impossible. The important thing is to think through the potential complications in advance and have a backup plan ready just in case you need it.

Copyright and Fair Use

We have mentioned several times the ease with which photographs, clip art, graphs, charts, and videos can be downloaded from the Internet for use with PowerPoint. It's important, when using such materials, to be aware of and to observe copyright laws. These laws are designed to create a financial incentive for writers, artists, musicians, photographers, and the like to produce original work by limiting the reproduction of that work unless the creator is compensated.

Under copyright law, someone who wishes to use the original work of another person must obtain permission from that person (or whoever owns the material) and often must pay a usage fee. Despite these restrictions, the "fair use" provision of the law permits students and educators to employ portions of copyrighted materials—including images and sounds downloaded from the Web—for educational purposes. Here are basic guidelines for the fair use of electronic materials:[5]

fair use
A provision of copyright law that permits students and teachers to use portions of copyrighted materials for educational purposes.

- You may use portions of copyrighted materials for a multimedia presentation that you create for a specific class. If you include the presentation in an employment portfolio, you may continue to use the copyrighted materials in it.
- You may *not* post copyrighted materials back to the Web without written permission from the copyright owner. In other words, if you download copyrighted photographs for use in your speech, you need written permission from the owner of the photographs to put your PowerPoint presentation on your personal Web page or any other Web site.
- You may use up to three minutes or 10 percent, whichever is less, of a copyrighted film, videotape, or other motion media work without obtaining permission.
- You may use up to 10 percent but no more than 30 seconds of music and lyrics from an individual musical work without obtaining permission.
- You may use an entire photograph or illustration without obtaining permission, but you may use no more than 15 images or 10 percent, whichever is less, of a collection of works.
- You *must* credit your sources and display the copyright symbol—©—when using copyrighted materials in a PowerPoint presentation. For written works, the credit line should include the author, title, and date of publication. For images and sounds, the credit line should include the title of the work (if there is one) and the name of the copyright holder. The usual practice is to type the credit line in 10-point font and to place it immediately under the item for which credit is being given. For an example, see Figure A.4 on page 355.

Keep these guidelines in mind when you search for images and sounds on the Web as well as in books, magazines, and other print sources. Remember to write down credit and copyright information when you download items from the Web; otherwise, you may have to spend extra time searching for it later.

Sample Speech with Commentary

Below is the full text of the informative speech on the Great Wall of China that is available for viewing on CD 2, Video A2.1. As you read the text, notice how it fulfills the criteria for effective speeches discussed elsewhere in the book—sharp focus, clear organization, effective connectives, strong supporting materials, and the like. As you view the speech, pay special attention to the quality of the speaker's PowerPoint slides, to the skill with which he integrates the slides into his presentation, and to the way he maintains eye contact with his audience while discussing his slides.

CD 2: VIDEO A2.1

View "The Great Wall of China."

The Great Wall of China

Commentary	***Speech***
The speaker begins with a quotation to gain attention and interest. He also establishes his credibility by noting that he visited the Great Wall while he was in China.	In China there's a saying, "You won't be considered a great person until you've been to the Great Wall." I visited the wall last year while I was in China. I don't know if it made me a great person, but I do know that the wall is indeed great.
The speaker's first slide is a striking photograph of the Great Wall that shows how it snakes across the tops of the mountains. He then moves to a slide that illustrates the expanse of the wall as it stretches across China. This slide allows people who are not familiar with China's geography to understand where the wall is located. The speaker ends this paragraph by explaining how the Great Wall would stretch from New York City to Berlin, Germany. An animated slide provides visual reinforcement and helps dramatize the extraordinary length of the wall.	As you can see from this photograph, the wall is great in beauty, with its long arms resting on rolling hills and its towers peering across the valleys. The wall stretches across more than half of China, from the sea in the east, past Beijing, to Gansu province in the west. At a total length of 4,000 miles, it is the longest human-made construction in the world. If the Great Wall were transported to the United States and stretched out in a straight line, it would run from New York City completely across the Atlantic Ocean—past Spain, England, and France, all the way to Berlin, Germany.
A clear preview statement specifies the three main points to be covered in the body of the speech. As you watch the speech on CD, notice how the speaker displays a blank slide during this paragraph so as not to distract the audience's attention.	Today I would like to share with you some of the wonders of the Great Wall. I will focus on the three major stages of its construction, moving from the first phase during the Qin Dynasty, to the second phase during the Han Dynasty, and concluding with the third phase during the Ming Dynasty. Let's start more than 2,000 years ago, when the first parts of the wall were built.
The speaker moves into his first main point. As he does so, he projects a slide showing a drawing of Emperor Qin Shi Huang and the dates of the Qin Dynasty. When he finishes this paragraph, he again projects a blank slide so the audience will be focused on his verbal message in the next paragraph.	The beginning of the Great Wall as we know it dates to 221 B.C., when Emperor Qin Shi Huang ordered his top general to lead 300,000 soldiers in rebuilding and connecting separate old walls that had been built by princes of warring states. In just 12 years, Qin had a 3,000-mile wall using primarily wood frames filled with stones and compacted earth.
This paragraph provides interesting details about the building of the wall during the Qin Dynasty. Notice how the speaker identifies	While the wall proved effective in keeping out the tribes who threatened to invade China from the north, it created dissent within China. According to Arthur Waldron's *The Great Wall of China: From History to Myth*, "ditches on the

the source of his quotation about the human cost of the wall's construction.

roadside were filled with corpses of men who had been forced into construction of the Great Wall." Compelled into hard labor and burdened by heavy taxes to finance the project, the people grew unhappy, and a year after Qin's death, the peasants revolted. While the wall stood, the empire collapsed.

A signpost at the start of this paragraph alerts the audience that the speaker is moving into his second main point. After showing a slide with the dates of the Han Dynasty and a drawing of Emperor Wu Di, he projects a photograph to demonstrate how different the Han wall was from the Great Wall as it exists today.

The second major period of construction for the Great Wall occurred during the Han Dynasty, which lasted from 206 B.C. to 220 A.D. Emperor Wu Di ordered expansion of the existing wall to protect land won when his armies defeated the northern tribes. Workers added 300 miles to the existing wall. They built wooden frames, which they filled with willow reeds and a mixture of fine gravel and water. As you can see from this picture of ruins of the Han wall, it was very different in construction and appearance from the Great Wall as it exists today.

As the speaker starts his third main point, he moves immediately from his slide showing the ruins of the Han wall to a slide with a drawing of Emperor Zhu Yuanzhang and the dates of the Ming Dynasty. Because it is parallel in design to the slides used to introduce the first two main points, this slide reinforces the unity and organizational structure of the speech as a whole.

The third major building period of the Great Wall occurred 1,100 years later during the Ming Dynasty. In 1368, during the first year of the Ming Dynasty, Emperor Zhu Yuanzhang ordered more expansion of the wall. Subsequent Ming emperors strengthened and extended the wall until it reached its current length. Builders of the Ming wall made three important architectural advancements which resulted in the distinctive features of the wall as it exists today.

The speaker begins this paragraph by projecting a slide with a photograph that shows the architectural features of the Great Wall. As he discusses each feature, he uses animation to make the appropriate text appear on his slide. This combination of visual and verbal elements, along with the superb timing of the speaker's animation effects, makes this paragraph especially effective and provides an excellent illustration of how to use PowerPoint to maximum advantage.

You can see those features especially well in this photograph. First, rather than using earth and stone, they used kiln-fired bricks to create a stronger wall. Second, they erected more than 3,000 beacon towers to watch the mountain passes for potential invaders. These towers rise from the wall like mighty outposts and are one of the most striking aspects of the wall when you see them in person. Third, the Ming builders made the wall so large that it would be almost impossible to break through. In fact, the wall is so wide that soldiers could ride several horses abreast along the top of the wall.

After signaling that he is moving into his conclusion, the speaker summarizes his main points and ends by reinforcing his central idea. To make sure the audience does not continue to focus on the architectural features of the Great Wall discussed in the previous paragraph, the speaker displays a blank slide that shifts attention back to him during the conclusion.

In conclusion, the Great Wall of China enjoys a rich history. Built over the course of more than 2,500 years during the Qin, Han, and Ming Dynasties, it is a magnificent feat of human engineering. While the wall no longer continues to defend China from invaders, it does continue to play a central role in Chinese culture and international identity. Now that you know a little more about the wall, I hope you have a fuller appreciation of why it's regarded as great, not just in China, but throughout the world.

Key Terms

slide (351)
presentation (351)
clip art (356)
serif font (359)
sans-serif font (359)
animation (361)
fair use (366)

Notes

[1]Joe Downing and Cecile Garmon, "Teaching Students in the Basic Course How to Use Presentation Software," *Communication Education,* 50 (2002), p. 219.

[2]Tad Simons, "Multimedia or Bust," *Presentations* (February 2000), pp. 40–50.

[3]For research on this point, see Richard E. Mayer, Julie Heiser, and Steve Lonn, "Cognitive Constraints on Multimedia Learning: When Presenting More Material Results in Less Understanding," *Journal of Educational Psychology,* 93 (2001), pp. 187–198.

[4]Herbert W. Lovelace, "The Medium Is More Than the Message," *Informationweek.com* (July 16, 2001), p. 74.

[5]Copyright issues are especially complex when it comes to online materials. For more information, check the Copyright and Image Management Web site (www.utsystem.edu/ogc/intellectualproperty/image.htm#elec) and the Copyright Management Center (www.copyright.iupui.edu/quickguide.htm).

CHAPTER FOURTEEN

Speaking to Inform

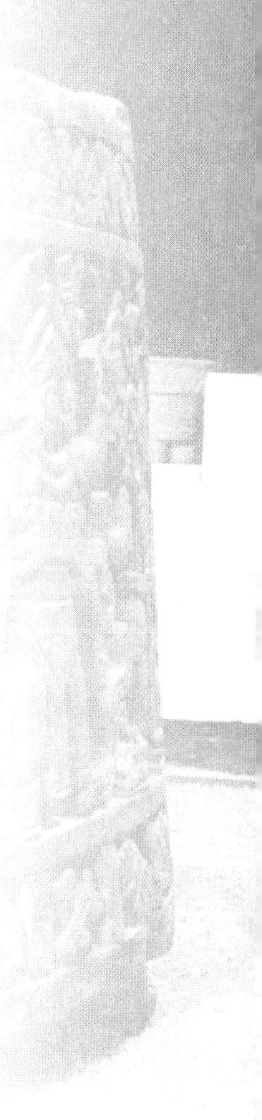

Natalya Petrovich is the advertising manager for a company that sells computer equipment such as routers, network cards, and wireless extensions. She began that particular workday by meeting with her staff to discuss the company's new line of network cards. She pointed out the special features of each piece of equipment, explained what other equipment was compatible with each, and answered questions about them.

Later that morning, Natalya had a long talk with the head of the company's technical division. "Can you show me," she asked, "how to use the new router we're developing? I need to double-check the ad copy my staff has drafted." Natalya then took notes as the head of the technical division went through the uses of the new router. Natalya also asked questions along the way to make sure she understood exactly how the router worked.

In the afternoon, Natalya met with the company's president and sales director to go over the current year's budget for her department, as well as her projections for the new fiscal year. She reviewed advertising campaigns and sales data, assessed the performance of each member of her staff, and then presented her projections of staffing requirements for the next eighteen months. Afterward, the president complimented Natalya for giving such a clear presentation. "Anyone who can communicate that well," the president said, "is going to go a long way in this company."

Natalya doesn't consider herself a "public speaker," but much of her job involves absorbing and communicating information clearly and effectively. Although Natalya is just a single person, her experience is not unusual. In one survey, graduates from five U.S. colleges were asked to rank the speech skills most important to their jobs. They rated informative speaking number one. In another survey, 62 percent of the respondents said they used informative speaking "almost constantly."[1]

Public speaking to inform occurs in a wide range of everyday situations. What kinds of people make informative speeches? The business manager explaining next year's budget. The architect reviewing plans for a new building. The military officer briefing subordinates. The union leader informing members about details of a new contract. The church worker outlining plans for a fund drive. The teacher in a classroom. There are endless situations in which people need to inform others. Competence in this form of communication will prove valuable to you throughout your life.

informative speech
A speech designed to convey knowledge and understanding.

One of your first classroom assignments probably will be to deliver an informative speech in which you will act as a lecturer or teacher. You may describe an object, show how something works, report on an event, explain a concept. Your aim will be to convey knowledge and understanding—not to advocate a cause. Your speech will be judged in light of three general criteria:

Is the information communicated accurately?

Is the information communicated clearly?

Is the information made meaningful and interesting to the audience?

In this chapter, we will look at four types of informative speeches and the basic principles of informative speaking. Along the way, we will apply various general principles discussed in previous chapters.

Types of Informative Speeches: Analysis and Organization

There are many ways to classify informative speeches. Here we focus on the four kinds of informative speeches you are most likely to give in your speech class: (1) speeches about objects, (2) speeches about processes, (3) speeches about events, and (4) speeches about concepts. These are not hard-and-fast categories, but they provide an effective method of analyzing and organizing informative speeches.

Speeches About Objects

As the word is used here, "objects" include anything that is visible, tangible, and stable in form. Objects may have moving parts or be alive; they may include places, structures, animals, even people. Here are examples of subjects for speeches about objects:

object
Anything that is visible, tangible, and stable in form.

Sitting Bull	Mars Rover
Grand Canyon	stock market
the human eye	Elizabeth Cady Stanton
seaweed	digital music players
comic strips	U.S. Army

You will not have time to tell your classmates everything about any of these subjects. Instead, you will choose a specific purpose that focuses on one aspect of your subject. Working from the topics presented above, the following are examples of good specific purpose statements for informative speeches about objects:

To inform my audience about the social functions of comic strips.

To inform my audience about the geological features of the Grand Canyon.

To inform my audience about the role of Elizabeth Cady Stanton in the U.S. women's rights movement.

To inform my audience what to look for when buying a digital music player.

To inform my audience about the commercial uses of seaweed.

Notice how precise these statements are. As we saw in Chapter 4, you should select a specific purpose that is not too broad to achieve in the allotted time. "To inform my audience about Pablo Picasso" is far too general for a classroom speech. "To inform my audience about the major contributions of

Pablo Picasso to modern art" is more exact and is a purpose you could reasonably hope to achieve in a brief talk.

If your specific purpose is to explain the history or evolution of your subject, you will put your speech in *chronological* order. For example:

Specific Purpose: To inform my audience about the major achievements of Frederick Douglass.

Central Idea: Although born in slavery, Frederick Douglass became one of the greatest figures in American history.

Main Points:

I. Douglass spent the first 20 years of his life as a slave in Maryland.
II. After escaping to the North, Douglass became a leader in the abolitionist movement to end slavery.
III. During the Civil War, Douglass helped establish black regiments in the Union Army.
IV. After the war, Douglass was a tireless champion of equal rights for his race.

If your specific purpose is to describe the main features of your subject, you may organize your speech in *spatial* order:

Specific Purpose: To inform my audience about the differences among the five major Hawaiian Islands.

Central Idea: The five major Hawaiian islands run from Kauai in the northwest to Hawaii in the southeast.

Main Points:

I. The northernmost of the major islands, Kauai averages 485 inches of rain a year, making it one of the wettest spots on Earth.
II. Southeast of Kauai is Oahu, home of Honolulu and the most heavily populated of all the islands.
III. Located 26 miles from Oahu, Molokai is known for its friendliness and its large population of native Hawaiians.
IV. Eight miles to the southeast of Oahu lies Maui, famous for its spectacular landscapes, white sandy beaches, and crystal-clear water.
V. The southernmost major island is Hawaii, known as the Big Island, which is twice as large as all the other islands put together.

As often as not, you will find that speeches about objects fall into *topical* order. Here is an example:

Specific Purpose: To inform my audience about the major alternative-fuel cars now being developed.

Central Idea: The major alternative-fuel cars now being developed are powered by electricity, natural gas, methanol, or hydrogen.

Main Points:

I. One kind of alternative-fuel car is powered by electricity.
II. A second kind of alternative-fuel car is powered by natural gas.
III. A third kind of alternative-fuel car is powered by methanol.
IV. A fourth kind of alternative-fuel car is powered by hydrogen.

No matter which of these organizational methods you use—chronological, spatial, or topical—be sure to follow the guidelines discussed in Chapter 8: (1) limit your speech to between two and five main points; (2) keep main points separate; (3) try to use the same pattern of wording for all main points; (4) balance the amount of time devoted to each main point.

Speeches About Processes

A process is a systematic series of actions that leads to a specific result or product. Speeches about processes explain how something is made, how something is done, or how something works. Here are examples of good specific purpose statements for speeches about processes:

process
A systematic series of actions that leads to a specific result or product.

To inform my audience how hurricanes develop.

To inform my audience how to write an effective job resumé.

To inform my audience how to save people from drowning.

To inform my audience how oriental rugs are made.

To inform my audience how to perform Pilates exercises.

As these examples suggest, there are two kinds of informative speeches about processes. One kind explains a process so that listeners will *understand* it better. Your goal in this kind of speech is to have your audience know the steps of the process and how they relate to one another. If your specific purpose is "To inform my audience how underwater robots work," you will explain the basic tasks and mechanisms of underwater robots. You will not instruct your listeners on how they can *operate* an underwater robot.

A second kind of speech explains a process so listeners will be better able to *perform* the process themselves. Your goal in this kind of speech is to have the audience learn a particular skill. Suppose your specific purpose is "To inform my audience how to take pictures like a professional photographer." You will present the basic techniques of professional photography and show your listeners how they can utilize those techniques. You want the audience to be able to *use* the techniques as a result of your speech.

Both kinds of speeches about processes may require visual aids. At the very least, you should prepare a chart outlining the steps or techniques of your process. In some cases you will need to demonstrate the steps or techniques by performing them in front of your audience. One student did sleight-of-hand magic tricks to show the techniques behind them. Another acted out the basic methods of mime. Yet another executed elementary tai chi maneuvers. In each case, the demonstration not only clarified the speaker's process, but captivated the audience as well. (If you are using visual aids of any kind, be sure to review Chapter 13 before your speech.)

When informing about a process, you will usually arrange your speech in *chronological* order, explaining the process step by step from beginning to end. For example:

Specific Purpose: To inform my audience about the major rituals of a traditional Bengali wedding in India.

Central Idea: A traditional Bengali wedding consists of a series of rituals that take place before the wedding, during the wedding ceremony, and after the wedding.

Main Points:

I. Pre-wedding rituals include offering reverence to the ancestors of the bride and groom, giving gifts to the bride and groom, and dressing the bride in traditional fashion.

II. Rituals during the wedding ceremony include an exchange of garlands between the bride and groom, the chanting of mantras, and the giving away of the bride by her uncle.

III. Post-wedding rituals include a celebration at the home of the bride's family, a reception at the home of the groom's family, and the formal exit of the bride and groom to their nuptial quarters.

Sometimes, rather than leading your audience through a process step by step, you will focus on the major principles or techniques involved in performing the process. Then you will organize your speech in *topical* order. Each main point will deal with a separate principle or technique. For example:

Specific Purpose: To inform my audience of the common methods used by stage magicians to perform their tricks.

Central Idea: Stage magicians use two common methods to perform their tricks—mechanical devices and sleight of hand.

Main Points:

I. Many magic tricks rely on mechanical devices that may require little skill by the magician.

II. Other magic tricks depend on the magician's skill in fooling people by sleight-of-hand manipulation.

Concise organization is especially important in speeches about processes. You must make sure each step in the process is clear and easy to follow. If your process has more than four or five steps, group the steps into units so as to limit the number of main points. Otherwise, you will have too many main points for listeners to grasp and recall. For example,

Informative speeches can be organized in many ways. A speech on the growth of modern art would likely be in chronological order, while a speech on the techniques of painting would fall into topical order.

in a speech explaining how to set up a home aquarium, a student presented the following main points:

I. First you must choose the size of your tank.
II. Then you must determine the shape of your tank.
III. You must also decide how much you can afford to pay for a tank.
IV. Once you have the tank, you need a filter system.
V. A heater is also absolutely necessary.
VI. You must also get an air pump.
VII. Once this is done, you need to choose gravel for the tank.
VIII. You will also need plants.
IX. Other decorations will round out the effects of your aquarium.
X. Now you are ready to add the fish.
XI. Freshwater fish are the most common.
XII. Saltwater fish are more expensive and require special care.

Not surprisingly, this was too much for the audience to follow. The speaker should have organized the points something like this:

I. The first step in establishing a home aquarium is choosing a tank.
  A. The size of the tank is important.
  B. The shape of the tank is important.
  C. The cost of the tank is important.
II. The second step in establishing a home aquarium is equipping the tank.
  A. You will need a filter system.
  B. You will need a heater.
  C. You will need an air pump.
  D. You will need gravel.

E. You will need plants.
F. You may also want other decorations.

III. The third step in establishing a home aquarium is adding the fish.
A. Freshwater fish are the most common for home aquariums.
B. Saltwater fish are more expensive and require special care.

As you can see, the subpoints cover the same territory as that originally covered by the twelve main points. But three main points are much easier to understand and remember than twelve.

Speeches About Events

event
Anything that happens or is regarded as happening.

The *Random House Dictionary* defines an event as "anything that happens or is regarded as happening." By this definition, the following are examples of suitable subjects for informative speeches about events:

Holocaust	mountain climbing
civil rights movement	Paralympics
figure skating	job interviews
Cinco de Mayo	tsunamis
attention deficit disorder	Battle of Little Big Horn

As usual, you will need to narrow your focus and pick a specific purpose you can accomplish in a short speech. Here are examples of good specific purpose statements for informative speeches about events:

To inform my audience about the equipment used in mountain climbing.

To inform my audience of the festivities at Mexico's Cinco de Mayo celebration.

To inform my audience about what happened at the Battle of Little Big Horn.

To inform my audience about the techniques of therapeutic massage.

To inform my audience about the experience of working on an archaeological dig.

As you can see, there are many ways to discuss events. If your specific purpose is to recount the history of an event, you will organize your speech in *chronological* order, relating the incidents one after another in the order they occurred. For example:

Specific Purpose: To inform my audience about the history of the Paralympics.

Central Idea: Olympic-style games for athletes with physical disabilities have made great strides since the first competition almost 60 years ago.

Main Points:

I. What would eventually become the Paralympics began in 1948 with a sports competition in Great Britain involving World War II veterans with spinal cord injuries.

THE INTERNET *Connection*

Do you need quick access to facts about your informative speech topic? Log on to the Internet Public Library's Subject Collection (www.ipl.org/div/subject/), which offers links to a wide range of high-quality resources chosen for their accurate and reliable information.

If you are giving an informative speech on a topic with multicultural dimensions, you may find the following Web sites useful:

Yahoo! Regional (http://dir.yahoo.com/Regional/)

WWW Virtual Library: American Indians (www.hanksville.org/NAresources)

Asian American Studies Resources (www.sunysb.edu/library/eresources/www/asian.html)

Latino/Hispanic Resources (www-rcf.usc.edu/~cmmr/Latino.html)

African American Web Connection (www.aawc.com)

ONLINE LEARNING CENTER

You can link to these Web sites at www.mhhe.com/lucas9.

II. In 1952 the event took on an international flavor when athletes from the Netherlands took part.
III. The first official Paralympic Games for international athletes with disabilities took place in Rome in 1960.
IV. In 2001 an agreement was signed allowing for the Paralympic Games to be held alongside both the summer and winter Olympic Games.

Instead of recounting the history of an event, you might take a more analytical approach and explain its causes and/or effects. In such a case, you will organize your speech in *causal* order. Let's say your specific purpose is "To inform my audience why so many lives were lost when a major tsunami hit Southeast Asia in 2004." Working from cause to effect, your outline might look like this:

Specific Purpose: To inform my audience why so many lives were lost when a major tsunami hit Southeast Asia in 2004.

Central Idea: On December 26, 2004, a catastrophic tsunami hit unexpectedly and took the lives of more than 200,000 people caught near the seashore.

Main Points:

I. There were two major causes for the great loss of life when the tsunami struck.
   A. Many resorts and fishing villages were built directly on the beach.
   B. There was no warning system for tsunamis in that part of the world.

II. The effects of these two situations were disastrous.
  A. There was no time for people to escape to higher ground.
  B. Thousands of people who were vacationing, living, or working on the beach were swept away.

There are other ways to deal with an event besides telling what happened or why it happened. Indeed, you can approach an event from almost any angle or combination of angles—features, origins, implications, benefits, future developments, and so forth. In such cases, you will put your speech together in *topical* order. And you should make sure your main points subdivide the subject logically and consistently. For instance:

Specific Purpose: To inform my audience about the four traditional events in women's gymnastics.

Central Idea: The four traditional events in women's gymnastics are floor exercise, vault, balance beam, and uneven parallel bars.

Main Points:

I. The floor exercise combines dancing, acrobatics, and tumbling.
II. The vault features explosive strength and dramatic midair maneuvers.
III. The balance beam requires precise routines and perfect coordination.
IV. The uneven parallel bars demand great strength, flexibility, and agility.

Speeches About Concepts

Concepts include beliefs, theories, ideas, principles, and the like. They are more abstract than objects, processes, or events. The following are some examples of subjects for speeches about concepts:

concept
A belief, theory, idea, notion, principle, or the like.

Confucianism	film theory
philosophies of education	principles of feminism
original-intent doctrine	existentialism
concepts of science	theories of psychology
religious beliefs	international law

Taking a few of these general subjects, here are some specific purpose statements for speeches about concepts:

To inform my audience about the basic principles of Confucianism.

To inform my audience about the doctrine of original intent in constitutional interpretation.

The principles of informative speaking are applicable to a wide range of situations. Knowing those principles will help you whenever you need to convey knowledge and understanding.

To inform my audience about the different philosophies of education in Europe and the United States.

To inform my audience about the concept of patriarchy in feminist thought.

To inform my audience about the major principles of film theory.

Speeches about concepts are usually organized in *topical* order. One common approach is to enumerate the main features or aspects of your concept. For example:

Specific Purpose: To inform my audience about the basic principles of nonviolent resistance.

Central Idea: The basic principles of nonviolent resistance stress using moral means to achieve social change, refusing to inflict violence on one's enemies, and using suffering as a social force.

Main Points:

I. The first major principle of nonviolent resistance is that social change must be achieved by moral means.

II. The second major principle of nonviolent resistance is that one should not inflict violence on one's enemies.

III. The third major principle of nonviolent resistance is that suffering can be a powerful social force.

A more complex approach is to define the concept you are dealing with, identify its major elements, and illustrate it with specific examples. An excellent instance of this came in a student speech about Islam:

Specific Purpose: To inform my audience of the basic principles of Islam.

Central Idea: The beliefs of Islam can be traced to the prophet Muhammad, are written in the Koran, and have produced a number of sects.

Main Points:

I. Islam was founded by the prophet Muhammad in the early 600s.

II. The teachings of Islam are written in the Koran, the holy book of Islam.

III. Today Islam is divided into a number of sects, the largest of which are the Sunnis and the Shiites.

Yet another approach is to explain competing schools of thought about the same subject. For example:

Specific Purpose: To inform my audience of the major arguments for and against homeschooling.

Central Idea: Supporters and opponents of homeschooling both have legitimate arguments.

Main Points:

I. Supporters of homeschooling argue that parents are the best judge of the values and academic subjects their children should be taught.

II. Opponents of homeschooling argue that society requires all children to learn a common set of academic subjects and civic values.

As you can see from these examples, speeches about concepts are often more complex than other kinds of informative speeches. Concepts are abstract and can be very hard to explain to someone who is learning about them for the first time. When explaining concepts, pay special attention to avoiding technical language, to defining terms clearly, and to using examples and comparisons to illustrate the concepts and make them understandable to your listeners.

View an excerpt from "Feng Shui."

Look, for example, at CD 1, Video 14.1, which presents an excerpt from a student speech about the ancient Chinese art of feng shui. Notice how clearly the student defines feng shui and then explains the concept of chi, which is the most important factor in feng shui. If you give an informative speech about a concept, give special thought to how you can make that concept clear and comprehensible to your listeners.

The lines dividing speeches about objects, processes, events, and concepts are not absolute. Some subjects could fit into more than one category, depending on how you develop the speech. You could treat the Declaration of Independence as an object—by explaining its history and its role in the American Revolution. Or you could deal with the meaning of the Declaration, in which case you would be speaking about a concept—an idea bound up with freedom and democracy.

To take another example, a speech about the destruction of ancient Pompeii by the eruption of Mount Vesuvius would probably deal with its subject as an event, but a speech on what causes volcanoes to erupt would most likely treat its subject as a process. The important step is to decide how you will handle your subject—as an object, a process, an event, or a concept. Once you do that, you can develop the speech accordingly.

One final word about organizing your informative speech: Regardless of which method of organization you use, be sure to give your listeners plenty of help in sorting out facts and ideas during the speech. One way is by using enough transitions, internal previews, internal summaries, and signposts (see Chapter 8). Another way is to follow the old maxim: "Tell 'em what you're going to say; say it; then tell 'em what you've said." In other words, preview the main points of your speech in the introduction, and summarize them in the conclusion. This will make your speech not only easier to understand but also easier to remember.

Guidelines for Informative Speaking

All the previous chapters of this book relate to the principles of informative speaking. Choosing a topic and specific purpose, analyzing the audience, gathering materials, choosing supporting details, organizing the speech, using words to communicate meaning, delivering the speech—all of these must be done effectively if your informative speech is to be a success. Here we emphasize five points that will help you avoid the mistakes that plague many informative speakers.

Don't Overestimate What the Audience Knows

In a speech about meteorology, a student said, "If modern methods of weather forecasting had existed in 1900, the Galveston hurricane disaster would never have taken place." Then he was off to other matters, leaving his listeners to puzzle over what the Galveston hurricane was, when it happened, and what kind of destruction it wreaked.

The speaker assumed that the audience already knew these things. But his classmates were not experts on meteorology or on American history. Even those who had heard of the hurricane had only a fuzzy notion of it. Some were not even sure about the location of Galveston. Only the speaker knew that the hurricane, which killed more than 6,000 people when it unexpectedly struck Galveston, Texas, on September 8, 1900, is still the deadliest natural disaster in American history.

As many speakers have discovered, it is easy to overestimate the audience's stock of information. In most informative speeches, your listeners will be only vaguely knowledgeable (at best) about the details of your topic. (Otherwise, there would not be much need for an informative speech!) Therefore, you must lead your listeners step by step, without any shortcuts. You cannot *assume* they will know what you mean. Rather, you must be *sure* to explain everything so thoroughly that they cannot help but understand. As you work on your speech, always consider whether it will be clear to someone who is hearing about the topic for the first time.

Suppose you are talking about Roth IRAs, a type of individual retirement account approved by Congress in 1998. Although some of your classmates might have heard of Roth IRAs, you cannot assume they have a firm grasp of the subject. So you should start by telling them what a Roth IRA is. How will you tell them? Here's one way:

> Introduced in 1998, a Roth IRA is a type of individual retirement account in which annual contributions are made with after-tax dollars but in which earnings and distributions are tax-free once the holder of the account is 59.5 years of age or older.

To someone who knows a lot about economics this is perfectly clear. But someone who does not will probably get lost along the way. The tone of the statement is that of a speaker reviewing information already familiar to the audience—not of a speaker introducing new information.

Here, in contrast, is another explanation of Roth IRAs:

> What is a Roth Individual Retirement Account, or IRA? Let me explain with an example.
>
> Imagine yourself a few years down the road as a recent college graduate. Your job pays a good salary, but you're still concerned with your finances and your future. After all, everyone keeps telling you to start planning for retirement early.
>
> In addition to Social Security, you have a number of retirement-planning options. One is the Roth IRA. Suppose you place $4,000 into a Roth IRA every year. Suppose also that your money grows at an average rate of 8 percent a year.
>
> If you start putting money in at age 25 and withdraw it at age 65, you will have an account worth more than $1.2 million. Moreover, unlike other retirement accounts, you won't have to pay taxes on your $1.2 million, even if you take it out all at once.
>
> So you can see why Roth IRAs are so popular. You win both ways—your money grows tax-free and it is free of taxes when you withdraw it.

This statement is clear and simple. Its tone is that of a teacher unraveling a new subject.

Is it too simple? Will your classmates feel as if you are talking down to them? Almost certainly not. Many students hesitate to speak simply because they are afraid they will sound simpleminded. They think they need big words and complicated sentences to sound intelligent. But nothing could be farther from the truth. The test of a good speaker is to communicate even the most complex ideas clearly and simply. Anyone can go to a book and find a learned-sounding definition of a Roth IRA like the one above. But to say in plain English what a Roth IRA is—that takes hard work and creative thinking.

Also, remember that readers can study a printed passage again and again until they extract its meaning, but listeners don't have that luxury. They must understand what you say in the time it takes you to say it. The more you assume they know about the topic, the greater your chances of being misunderstood.

If you have circulated a questionnaire among your listeners before the speech (see Chapter 5, pages 128–131), you should have a good idea of their

Whether in the classroom or out, effective informative speakers work on communicating their ideas in clear, nontechnical language that relates the topic to their listeners' knowledge and interests.

knowledge about the topic. If not, you will usually do better to aim for the low end of the knowledge spectrum. Some experts recommend preparing a speech as if the audience had never heard of the subject. That may be a bit extreme, but it is one way to make sure you define every special term, clarify every idea, illustrate every concept, and support every conclusion. You cannot go wrong by following the news reporters' code: "Never *over*estimate the information of your audience; never *under*estimate the intelligence of your audience."

Relate the Subject Directly to the Audience

The British dramatist Oscar Wilde arrived at his club after the disastrous opening-night performance of his new play.

"Oscar, how did your play go?" asked a friend.

"Oh," Wilde quipped, "the play was a great success, but the audience was a failure."

Speakers have been known to give much the same answer in saving face after a dismal informative speech. "Oh," they say, "the speech was fine, but the audience just wasn't interested." And they are at least partly right—the audience *wasn't* interested. Then was the speech fine? Not by any objective standard. A speech is measured by its impact on a particular audience. There is no such thing as a fine speech that puts people to sleep. It is the speaker's job to get listeners interested—and to keep them interested.

Informative speakers have one big hurdle to overcome. They must recognize that what is fascinating to them may not be fascinating to everybody. A mathematician, for example, might be truly enthralled by a perfect equation, but most people wouldn't want to hear about it. Once you have chosen a topic that could possibly be interesting to your listeners, you should take special steps to relate it to them. You should tie it in with their interests and concerns.

Start in the introduction. Instead of saying,

> I want to talk with you about chili peppers,

you could say:

> Imagine your mouth burning like wildfire, your eyes squirting out uncontrollable tears, and your face red and sweating profusely. Are you sick? No. You just took a bite of a screaming hot chili pepper. Congratulations. You're partaking in a worldwide tradition that has been spicing up lives and diets for thousands of years.

Get your audience involved right at the beginning. Notice how one student did this in her informative speech about depression. The speaker's classmates all knew something about depression as a medical condition, but the speaker wanted to relate the subject to them on a more personal basis. She began by saying:

CD 1: VIDEO 14.2

View these excerpts from "The Hidden World of Chili Peppers" and "Depression: More Than a Blue Mood."

> You feel exhausted, yet you can't sleep. You have no energy, no hope, and you get no pleasure from your usual activities. You're angry and irritable, and you find that lately you're spending more and more time alone. You feel like you're caught in a trap, and you see no way out.
>
> Have you or someone close to you suffered from these scary feelings? I'd be surprised if you answered no. These are symptoms of depression, and according to the National Institute of Mental Health, about 19 percent of adults, or almost 10 million people, become depressed each year. What's more, symptoms usually begin between ages 15 and 30, making depression a serious concern for college students.

Don't stop with the introduction. Whenever you can, put your listeners into the body of the speech. After all, nothing interests people more than themselves. Don't just rattle off statistics and concepts as if you were reciting a shopping list. Find ways to talk about your topic in terms of your listeners. Bring your material home to them. Get it as close to them as possible.

Here's an example. Let's say you are explaining how people can discover whether they are "secret southpaws"—that is, people who are naturally left-handed but who have grown up preferring the right hand because they were taught to use it as a child. You have plenty of facts and could recite them like this:

> According to *Science* magazine, half of all people who are naturally left-handed assume they are right-handed because that is the hand they use to eat, to write, and to play sports. But how can it be determined whether one is a natural southpaw? According to Abram Blau, author of *The Master Hand,* there are a number of simple tests. For one thing, most natural left-handers can write spontaneously backward or upside down with the left hand. For another, when left-handers clasp their hands in front of themselves, they usually place the left thumb on top. In contrast, when left-handers grab a broom, they normally place their left hand below the right. Finally, when using

the right hand, natural left-handers will draw a circle clockwise, while natural right-handers will draw it counterclockwise. People who give a left-handed response on three or more of these tests may well be secret southpaws.

This is fascinating information, but it is not made fascinating to the audience. Let's try again:

Just because *you* use *your* right hand to eat, to write, and to play sports, *you* may assume that *you're* naturally right-handed. But, says *Science* magazine, half of all people who are naturally left-handed grow up using their right hands.

How can *you* tell if you're a natural lefty? Dr. Abram Blau, author of *The Master Hand*, gives some tests *you* can try.

First, on a sheet of paper see if *you* can write backward or upside down with *your* left hand. If *you* are left-handed, *you* can probably do this spontaneously, without practice or training.

Second, clasp *your* hands together in front of *you*. Whichever thumb *you* place on top is usually *your* dominant hand.

Third, grab hold of a broomstick. Odds are *you'll* place *your* dominant hand on the bottom.

Finally, draw a circle on a piece of paper with *your* right hand. If *you* draw it counterclockwise, *you're* probably a natural right-hander. But if *you* draw it clockwise, *you're* probably a natural lefty.

If *you* test left-handed on three of these tests, there is a good chance *you* are a secret southpaw.

CD 1: VIDEO 14.3

View these excerpts from "Secret Southpaws."

Look at the frequent use of "you" and "your." The facts are the same, but now they are pointed directly at the audience. This is the kind of thing that gets listeners to sit up and pay attention. In addition, research shows that using personal terms such as "you" and "your" in an informative speech significantly increases audience understanding of the speaker's ideas.[2]

Don't Be Too Technical

What does it mean to say that an informative speech is too technical? It may mean the subject matter is too specialized for the audience. Any subject can be popularized—but only up to a point. The important thing for a speaker to know is what can be explained to an ordinary audience and what cannot.

Say your subject is electronic amplifiers. It's no trick to demonstrate how to operate an amplifier (how to turn it on and off, adjust the volume, set the tone and balance controls). It's also relatively easy to explain what an amplifier does (it boosts the sound received from a radio, CD player, or live performance). But to give a full scientific account of how an amplifier works—that is another matter. It cannot be done in any reasonable time unless the audience knows the principles of audio technology. You would be better off not even trying. The material is just too technical to be understood by a general audience.

Even when the subject matter is not technical, the language used to explain it may be. Every activity has its jargon. This is true of golf (bogey, wedge, match play); of chemistry (colloid, glycogen, heavy water); of financial analysis (covered call, reverse bid, toehold acquisition); of ballet (arabesque, jeté, pas de deux). If you are talking to a group of specialists, you can use technical words and be understood. But you must do all you can to avoid technical words when informing a general audience such as your speech class.

jargon
The specialized or technical language of a trade, profession, or similar group.

You may find this hard to do at first. Many people are so addicted to the lingo of their subject that they have trouble escaping it. As you give more speeches, though, you will become increasingly adept at expressing your ideas in everyday, nontechnical language.

Here, for instance, are two statements explaining the process of cryonics, which involves freezing people after death in the hope that medical science will be able to restore them to life in the future. The first is heavily laden with specialized language that would have little impact on ordinary listeners:

> Options for cryonic suspension include freezing the subject's head or complete body. In either case, the process entails complex scientific procedures that, for maximum functionality, must be implemented immediately upon the cessation of biological functioning. Measures must be taken to minimize tissue decomposition so as to ensure that the subject can be successfully resuscitated at some undetermined future period.

The second statement is perfectly understandable. It is from a student speech and shows how technical information can be made clear to the average person:

> Currently, when a person who has signed up to be cryonically suspended dies, a specific procedure, which was outlined in the book *Cryonics: Reaching for Tomorrow,* must be carried out.
>
> First, before death, an individual must decide whether to have his or her entire body frozen or just the head. If the whole body is to be frozen, it must be preserved upon death. Immediately after death—ideally within a matter of minutes—the patient is connected to a heart-lung machine and chemicals such as glucose and heparin are circulated with the oxygenated blood to help minimize the freezing damage. At the same time, the patient's internal temperature is reduced as quickly as possible using cold packs.
>
> If only the head will be frozen, a slightly different procedure must be carried out. The head must be surgically detached from the rest of the body and preserved in a separate container. You may be wondering, "Why would I preserve only my head?" The answer is, with some diseases the body is in a very poor condition. If this is the case and you choose to preserve your head only, you do so with the belief that medical science will be able to create a healthy new body for you in the future.

CD 1: VIDEO 14.4
View this excerpt from "Cryonics."

Much clearer, isn't it? The only specialized words in the whole passage are "glucose," "heparin," and "oxygenated blood," and they do not get in the way. The rest of the language is straightforward, the ideas easy to grasp. This is what you should strive for in your informative speeches.

Avoid Abstractions

"My task," said the novelist Joseph Conrad, "is, before all, to make you see." And make the reader see is just what Conrad did. Witness this passage, in which Conrad describes the aftermath of an explosion aboard a ship:

> The first person I saw was Mahon, with eyes like saucers, his mouth open, and the long white hair standing straight on end round his head like a silver halo. He was just about to go down when the sight of the main deck stirring, heaving up, and changing into splinters before his eyes, petrified him on the top step. I stared at him in unbelief, and he stared at me with a queer kind of shocked curiosity. I did not know that I had no hair, no eyebrows, no eyelashes, that my young mustache was burnt off, that my face was black, one cheek laid open, my nose cut, and my chin bleeding.[3]

A speech is not a novel. Still, too many abstractions are tedious—whether in a novel or in a speech. Many informative speeches would be vastly improved by the novelist's bent for color, specificity, and detail.

One way to avoid abstractions is through *description.* When we think of description, we usually think of external events such as the explosion described by Conrad. But description is also used to communicate internal feelings. Here is how one student tried to convey to his audience the sensations he experienced when he first began sky diving:

description
A statement that depicts a person, event, idea, or the like with clarity and vividness.

> As we wait for the plane to climb to the jump altitude of 12,000 feet, my mind races with a frenzied jumble of thoughts: "Okay, this is the moment you've been waiting for. It's going to be great. Am I really going to jump out of an airplane from 12,000 feet? What if something goes wrong? Can I still back out? Come on now, don't worry. It'll be fine."

Even if we have not been sky diving, we have all had the same kinds of emotions on similar occasions. So what happened next?

> Now it is time to jump. My palms are sweating and my heart is pounding so hard I think it may burst. "Get ready," yells the instructor. As I jump into the blue, I wonder, "What am I doing here?"

Yes—and then what?

> The blast of air resistance blows me backward like a leaf at the mercy of an autumn wind. In about 10 seconds my body levels out and accelerates to a speed of 120 miles an hour. The air supports my body like an invisible flying carpet. There is no sound except for the wind rushing around my face. The earth appears soft and green, rivers look like strips of silver, and in every direction the scenery forms a panoramic landscape. Any fears or doubts I had are gone in the exhilaration of free flight. Every nerve in my body is alive with sensation; yet I am overcome by a peaceful feeling and the sense that I am at one with the sky.

As we listen to the speaker, we are almost up there with him, sharing his thoughts, feeling his heart pound, joining his exhilaration as he floats effortlessly through the sky. The vivid description lends reality to the speech and draws us further in.

Regardless of the situation, informative speakers need to work on relating the topic directly to their audience, on avoiding overly technical language, and on personalizing their ideas.

comparison
A statement of the similarities among two or more people, events, ideas, etc.

Another way to escape abstractions is with *comparisons* that put your subject in concrete, familiar terms. Do you want to convey what would happen if a comet or large asteroid struck the earth? You could say this:

> If a comet or large asteroid struck the earth, the impact would be devastating.

True, but "the impact would be devastating" is vague and abstract. It does not communicate your meaning clearly and concretely. Now suppose you add this:

> To give you an idea how devastating the impact would be, it would be like all the nuclear bombs in the world going off at one spot.

Now you have made the abstract specific and given us a sharp new slant on things.

contrast
A statement of the differences among two or more people, events, ideas, etc.

Like comparison, *contrast* can put an idea into concrete terms. Suppose you want to make the point that a person's chances of winning a state lottery are extremely low. You could say, "The odds, for example, of winning a state lottery are an astronomical 7 million to 1." The word "astronomical" suggests that you consider 7 million to 1 long odds, but long in comparison to what? One speaker offered this contrast:

> The odds of picking the correct six-digit sequence in a typical state lottery are more than 7 million to 1. In contrast, the odds of getting hit by lightning are only 2 million to 1. The chances of being dealt a royal flush in a poker game are 650,000 to 1. The odds of dying in an automobile accident are about 6,000 to 1. In other words, the odds are much stronger that you will get hit by lightning or be killed in a car crash than that you will win the jackpot in a state lottery.

Now an abstract fact has been put into meaningful perspective. See if you can do something similar in your informative speech.

Personalize Your Ideas

personalize
To present one's ideas in human terms that relate in some fashion to the experience of the audience.

Listeners want to be entertained as they are being enlightened.[4] Nothing takes the edge off an informative speech more than an unbroken string of facts and figures. And nothing enlivens a speech more than personal illustrations. Remember, people are interested in people. They react to stories, not statistics. Whenever possible, you should try to *personalize* your ideas and dramatize them in human terms.

Let's say you are talking about autism, the developmental disability marked by impaired communication and interaction skills. You would surely note that the condition affects 1 in every 500 children, occurs four times more frequently in males than in females, and is most prevalent among Caucasian males. You would also note that the symptoms of autism include abnormal introversion, severely limited use of language, repetitive behaviors, avoidance of eye contact, loss of emotional control, and passive responses to affection.

But these are dry facts and figures. If you really want to get your audience involved, you will weave in some examples of children who suffer from autism. One speaker began by telling about Sam, her autistic nephew:

> My nephew Sam was the delight of our family when he was born, the first grandchild of my parents. He cooed and babbled, smiled at his mom and dad, grasped for the playthings around his crib. At family dinners on Sunday, we took turns holding him in our arms, feeding him, and singing him to sleep. He seemed like any normal infant in a secure and loving home.
>
> Then shortly before his second birthday we began to notice unusual behaviors. Sam avoided looking us in the eye, did not seem interested in learning words, played endlessly with the same toy, rocked back and forth in his chair for hours at a time, and was easily frustrated. My sister took him to a specialist, who gave the dreaded diagnosis: Sam was autistic.

During the body of the speech, the speaker mentioned Sam twice more to illustrate different aspects of autism. Then, at the end of the speech, she brought Sam's story to a hopeful conclusion:

> We have seen that autism is a very serious disorder whose causes are not well understood and whose effects on families and the lives of the children themselves can be devastating. But we have also seen that early diagnosis and early intervention can help to modify and even turn around the symptoms of autism.
>
> I am happy to say that Sam has benefited from such intervention. From the time he was two, he has been taught "normal" behavior patterns through aggressive therapy. Now he is able to participate in his class at the local school. He is also more responsive and affectionate at home. Sam continues to be our delight.

CD 1: VIDEO 14.5
View these excerpts from "Autism: Heartbreak and Hope."

It was a powerful ending. By putting a human face on a familiar topic, the speaker took autism out of the realm of statistics and medical jargon and brought it home in personal terms. As one listener said afterward, "Because of your speech, I will never see autism in the same way again."

Sample Speech with Commentary

CD 2: FULL SPEECH

View "Acupuncture: New Uses for an Ancient Remedy."

The following classroom speech provides an excellent example of how to apply the guidelines for informative speaking discussed in this chapter. As you study the speech, notice how the speaker takes what could be a dry, technical topic and makes it interesting. Pay special attention to how crisply the speech is organized, to how the speaker uses well-chosen supporting materials to develop her ideas, and to how she clarifies her ideas with concrete language and personal examples.

Acupuncture: New Uses for an Ancient Remedy

Commentary	*Speech*
The speaker starts with an extended example that captures attention and interest. In this case, the example works particularly well because it is personally related to the speaker and is richly detailed and vividly drawn.	Six months ago, my 78-year-old grandmother was quickly losing her independence. Severe arthritis in both knees hampered her ability to take care of herself. Shopping, getting around the neighborhood, even walking down her front steps was becoming almost impossible. Pain medications helped somewhat, but the side effects created their own problems.
As the speaker continues her opening example, she introduces the subject of her speech by talking about her grandmother's positive experience with acupuncture.	Then her doctor suggested acupuncture. My grandmother was skeptical at first, but she was willing to try just about anything. She did, and the results were miraculous. After six weeks, her pain and stiffness were significantly reduced, she was able to take care of her apartment again, she could get out on her own to go shopping, to visit friends and family, and to do the other things her arthritis had prevented in the past. Acupuncture restored her quality of life and her independence.
Mentioning her own experience with acupuncture helps establish the speaker's credibility.	My grandmother's story is not unique. Performed for well over 2,000 years in China and other parts of Asia, acupuncture is becoming more and more popular in the U.S. and other Western countries for one simple reason—it works. Impressed by my grandmother's experience, I began acupuncture treatments for my migraine headaches, and now my headaches are completely gone.
Here the speaker reinforces her credibility and previews the main points to be discussed in the body of the speech. An explicit preview statement at the end of the introduction is especially important when speaking to inform.	Not surprisingly, I wanted to learn more about this treatment that produced such miraculous results for both my grandmother and myself. Today I will share part of what I have learned by explaining what happens when you receive an acupuncture treatment, how acupuncture works, the kinds of medical conditions that can be treated by acupuncture, and the growing use of acupuncture in combination with Western medical techniques. Let's start by looking at a typical acupuncture treatment.

Now the speaker moves into her first main point. The information in this and the following paragraph answers the audience's questions about what happens during an acupuncture treatment.

Acupuncture is the insertion of needles into the skin to achieve a balanced flow of energy, which in turn restores and preserves health. To prevent any chance of contamination from one person to another, acupuncturists in the U.S. use sterilized needles that are individually packaged and are disposed of after a single use.

Knowing that many people are squeamish about being poked with needles, the speaker makes sure to explain that the needles used in acupuncture are small and essentially painless. Notice that the speaker did not pass the needles around during her speech. As mentioned in Chapter 13, putting visual aids in the hands of the audience during a speech is an almost certain recipe for disaster because listeners will end up paying more attention to the visual aids than to the speaker's words.

I realize that the notion of having needles stuck into you may seem frightening, but the needles are so thin that the process is painless. Acupuncture needles are much smaller than the needles used for drawing blood or getting shots. Here are some needles that I received from my acupuncturist. After my speech I'll pass them around so you can see how incredibly light and small they are. They are so thin—about the thickness of a human hair—that you can hardly tell when they're inserted. And there's usually no sensation other than pain relief once they have been inserted. After being left in for 20 or 30 minutes while you lie in a darkened room, the needles are removed and the treatment is over.

This paragraph begins with a transition into the speaker's second main point. As in the previous paragraph, she relates the topic directly to her audience by speaking in terms of "you."

Now that you know what happens when you're treated by an acupuncturist, you're probably wondering how acupuncture works. The process is explained by Dr. Felix Mann, President of the Medical Acupuncture Society, in his book *Acupuncture: The Ancient Chinese Art of Healing and How It Works Scientifically*. According to traditional Chinese medicine, every life process is based on the flow of vital energy through the body. This energy is known in Chinese as *qi* and flows along channels or pathways called meridians.

As you can see from the video of this speech on CD 2, the speaker uses a visual aid to clarify her explanation of the acupuncture meridians.

The meridians are shown in this visual aid. As you can see, they cover the entire body, running from the top of the head to the bottom of the feet and down both arms. When the free flow of energy through these meridians is blocked, the result is pain, illness, disease, or other physical problems.

The speaker's explanation throughout this main point provides a good example of how to communicate technical information in everyday language. The quotation at the end of the paragraph nicely sums up this section of the speech.

The aim of acupuncture is to restore the open flow of energy through these meridians. This is done by placing needles at specific points on the meridians. Altogether there are more than 1,000 acupuncture points on the meridians. These points have been mapped out over the centuries with scientific precision. In China there is a saying: "There is no pain if there is free flow; if there is pain, there is no free flow."

A signpost of the beginning of this paragraph helps signal that the speaker is moving to her third main point, in which she explains some of the medical conditions that can be treated with acupuncture. As in the rest of the speech, she relies on highly

Although acupuncture is based on a different view of the body from that held by Western doctors, the evidence is clear that it works in treating a wide range of medical conditions. The World Health Organization lists more than 40 conditions that can be effectively treated with acupuncture, including ear, nose, and throat ailments; asthma and other respiratory problems;

credible sources and identifies them clearly. This is crucial if the audience is to accept the accuracy of the speaker's information—especially since she is not an expert on acupuncture.

and nervous system and muscular disorders. A study in the *Annals of Internal Medicine* confirms that acupuncture can relieve low-back pain, while the American Cancer Society reports that acupuncture may even help smokers kick the habit.

People also use acupuncture to build their immune system, to control allergies, and to combat depression and anxiety. Of course, you can't use acupuncture to heal a broken arm. But people in Asia often use acupuncture during surgery instead of Western anesthesia, and it can speed recovery time after surgery.

The speaker's final main point deals with the growing integration of acupuncture with Western medical techniques. In this and the following paragraph, she uses a mix of examples, testimony, and statistics to illustrate her point. All in all, this speech provides an excellent case study in how to use supporting materials to buttress an informative presentation.

In light of all this, it is not surprising that a number of clinics and hospitals are combining acupuncture with Western medicine in an effort to provide patients the benefits of both. For example, Massachusetts General Hospital in Boston, the third oldest hospital in the U.S., has added acupuncture to its wellness center. Positive results have also been seen at the Mattel Children's Hospital at UCLA. Dr. Lonnie Zeltzer, director of the hospital's pediatric pain program, confirms that acupuncture "really does help. Most children accept acupuncture, and in fact, really feel good about it."

As in the rest of her speech, the speaker's quotations are brief and well-chosen. Notice how she identifies the people she is quoting and establishes their credentials before presenting their testimony.

Another example of the integration of acupuncture with Western medicine is the Wasser Pain Management Center at Mount Sinai Hospital in Toronto, Canada. Neurologist Allan Gordon, Director of the Center, says that introducing acupuncture into the hospital "expands the treatment available to chronic pain sufferers" and provides "multiple options for care to our patients." The National Institutes for Health report that more than 8 million Americans have tried acupuncture, and its use throughout the rest of the Western world is growing fast.

The phrase "Today we have learned" signals that the speaker is moving into her conclusion. She then provides a concise summary of the main points developed in the body.

Today we have learned what happens during an acupuncture treatment, how acupuncture works, some of the illnesses that can be treated with acupuncture, and the growing integration of acupuncture with Western approaches to medicine. I hope you now know more about this ancient medical practice and the benefits it can provide.

After reinforcing her central idea about the benefits of acupuncture, the speaker refers back to her grandmother, whom she had discussed in the introduction. This unifies the entire speech and ends it on a personal note.

After years of skepticism about acupuncture, the West is finally beginning to recognize that acupuncture is a highly effective way to improve health and reduce pain and suffering. Just ask my grandmother.

Summary

Speaking to inform occurs in a wide range of everyday situations. Yet it is a difficult task that requires more skill than you might think. Improving your ability to convey knowledge effectively will be most valuable to you throughout your life.

Informative speeches may be grouped into four categories—speeches about objects, speeches about processes, speeches about events, and speeches about concepts. These categories are not absolute, but they are helpful in analyzing and organizing informative speeches.

Objects, as defined here, include places, structures, animals, even people. Speeches about objects usually are organized in chronological, spatial, or topical order. A process is a series of actions that work together to produce a final result. Speeches about processes explain how something is made, how something is done, or how something works. Clear organization is especially important in speeches about processes because listeners must be able to follow each step in the process. The most common types of organization for speeches about processes are chronological and topical.

An event is anything that happens or is regarded as happening. You can approach an event from almost any angle. You might explain its origins, causes, effects, implications, major features, and so on. Usually speeches about events are arranged in chronological, causal, or topical order. Concepts include beliefs, theories, ideas, and principles. Speeches about concepts are often more complex than other kinds of informative speeches, and they typically follow a topical pattern of organization.

No matter what the subject of your informative speech, be careful not to overestimate what your audience knows about it. In most classroom speeches your listeners will be no more than slightly familiar with your topic. Therefore, you cannot assume they will know what you mean. Explain everything so thoroughly they cannot help but understand. Avoid being too technical. Make sure your ideas and your language are fully comprehensible to someone who has no specialized knowledge about the topic.

Equally important, recognize that what is fascinating to you may not be fascinating to everybody. It is your job to make your informative speech interesting and meaningful to your audience. Find ways to talk about the topic in terms of your listeners. Avoid too many abstractions. Use description, comparison, and contrast to make your audience *see* what you are talking about. Finally, try to personalize your ideas. No matter what your subject, you can almost always find a way to dramatize it in human terms.

Key Terms

informative speech (372)
object (373)
process (375)
event (378)
concept (380)
jargon (388)
description (389)
comparison (390)
contrast (390)
personalize (391)

ONLINE LEARNING CENTER

Review these terms by doing the Chapter 14 crossword puzzle at www.mhhe.com/lucas9.

Review Questions

After reading this chapter, you should be able to answer the following questions:

1. What are the four types of informative speeches discussed in the chapter? Give an example of a good specific purpose statement for each type.
2. Why must informative speakers be careful not to overestimate what the audience knows about the topic? What can you do to make sure your ideas don't pass over the heads of your listeners?
3. What should you do as an informative speaker to relate your topic directly to the audience?
4. What two things should you watch out for in making sure your speech is not overly technical?
5. What are three methods you can use to avoid abstractions in your informative speech?
6. What does it mean to say that informative speakers should personalize their ideas?

CD 1: STUDY QUESTIONS

For further review, go to the Study Questions for this chapter.

Exercises for Critical Thinking

1. Below is a list of subjects for informative speeches. Your task is twofold: (a) Select four of the topics and prepare a specific purpose statement for an informative speech about each of the four. Make sure your four specific purpose statements include at least one that deals with its topic as an object, one that deals with its topic as a process, one that deals with its topic as an event, and one that deals with its topic as a concept. (b) Explain what method of organization you would most likely use in structuring a speech about each of your specific purpose statements.

hobbies	sports
animals	music
science	cultural customs
education	technology
media	health

2. Analyze "The Hidden World of Chili Peppers" in the appendix of sample speeches that follows Chapter 18. Identify the specific purpose, central idea, main points, and method of organization. Evaluate the speech in light of the guidelines for informative speaking discussed in this chapter.

Applying the POWER of PUBLIC SPEAKING

As the manager for a local chain of coffeehouses, you have been asked to speak to a gourmet group about how to make genuine Italian cappuccino. As you write down ideas for your speech, you find that you have the following main points:

I. First you must make the espresso.
II. Grind the coffee beans so they are fine but not too fine.
III. Place the ground coffee in the filter holder of the espresso machine.
IV. Tamp the coffee once lightly to level the grind in the filter holder.
V. Lock the filter holder onto the brew head of the espresso machine.
VI. Activate the on switch to extract the espresso.
VII. In addition to making the espresso, you must prepare frothed milk for cappuccino.
VIII. Fill a steaming pitcher 1/3 full of very cold milk.
IX. Place the steam vent of the espresso machine just below the surface of the milk in the pitcher.
X. Fully open the steam vent.
XI. Keeping the tip of the steam vent just below the surface of the milk, move the pitcher in a circular motion.
XII. Be careful not to overheat or scald the milk, which will ruin the froth.
XIII. Once you have the desired amount and consistency of froth, turn the steam vent off and remove it from the pitcher.
XIV. Now you are ready to combine the espresso and frothed milk.
XV. The normal proportions for cappuccino are 1/3 espresso to 2/3 frothed milk.
XVI. Some people prefer to pour the espresso into the frothed milk in a cappuccino cup.
XVII. Other people prefer to pour or spoon the frothed milk over the espresso.

Having taken a speech class in college, you know this is too many main points for an audience to keep track of. As you look over your list again, however, you realize that it can easily be reorganized into three main points, each with several subpoints. What are those main points and subpoints?

Notes

[1]John R. Johnson and Nancy Szczupakiewicz, "The Public Speaking Course: Is It Preparing Students with Work-Related Public Speaking Skills?" *Communication Education,* 36 (1987), pp. 131–137; Andrew D. Wolvin and Diana Corley, "The Technical Speech Communication Course; A View from the Field," *Association for Communication Administration Bulletin,* 49 (1984), pp. 83–91.

[2]Richard E. Mayer, Sherry Fennell, Lindsay Farmer, and Julie Campbell, "A Personalization Effect in Multimedia Learning: Students Learn Better When Words Are in Conversational Style Rather Than Formal Style," *Journal of Educational Psychology*, 96 (2004), pp. 389–395.

[3]Joseph Conrad, "Youth: A Narrative," in Samuel Hynes (ed.), *Collected Stories of Joseph Conrad* (Hopewell, NJ: Ecco Press, 1991), p. 166.

[4]James Humes, *Roles Speakers Play* (New York: Harper and Row, 1976), p. 25.

CHAPTER FIFTEEN

Speaking to Persuade

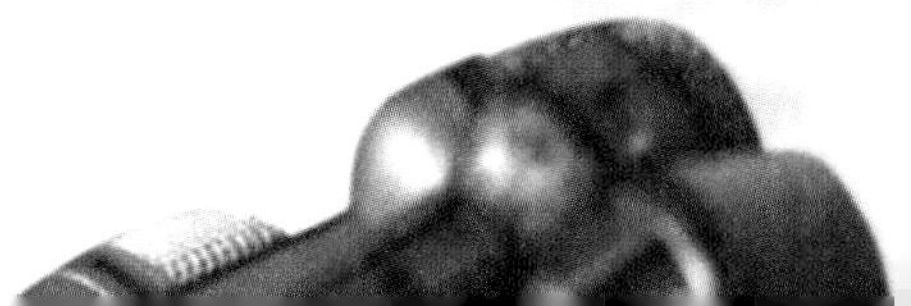

Ramon Trujillo started that particular school day by stopping at the library to return an overdue book. "Look," he explained to the librarian, "I know this book was due last week, but I was sick with the flu and couldn't even get out of bed. Do I still have to pay the fine? I can get you a note from the doctor if you need one." The librarian hemmed and hawed. Then he said, "Okay. You don't have a record of any other fines. Just this once."

With a sigh of relief, Ramon went on to his morning classes. At noon he was dashing across campus when a friend stopped him. "How about some lunch?" she asked. "I really can't," replied Ramon. "I have to stand at the table and get signatures on the antidiscrimination petition. I'll see you later, though."

During the afternoon, Ramon went to his job at a computer sales company. He arrived just in time for the weekly staff meeting, where he presented his ideas on how to increase customer satisfaction. "One thing I've noticed," he said, "is that most people don't realize they only have seven days to return unopened merchandise for a full refund. Most stores have a 14-day return policy, and I know we've lost some customers because ours is shorter. Changing it might be inconvenient at first, but it will definitely help business in the long run." After listening to Ramon, the sales manager said, "I've always thought seven days was plenty of time, but you've convinced me that we ought to change. Let's give it a try."

If you asked Ramon how he spent his day, he might say, "I returned a book, I went to class, I worked the antidiscrimination table, I had a staff meeting at my job." In fact, he spent a large part of his day *persuading*—persuading people to do things they were reluctant to do or that had not occurred to them.

The Importance of Persuasion

persuasion
The process of creating, reinforcing, or changing people's beliefs or actions.

Most of us do a certain amount of persuading every day, although we may not realize it or call it that. Persuasion is the process of creating, reinforcing, or changing people's beliefs or actions.[1] The ability to speak (and write) persuasively will benefit you in every part of your life, from personal relations to community activities to career aspirations. In a recent study, economists added up the number of people—lawyers, sales representatives, public relations specialists, counselors, administrators, and others—whose jobs depend largely on persuading people to adopt their point of view. The economists concluded that persuasion accounts for 26 percent of the U.S. gross domestic product![2]

Understanding the principles of persuasion is also vital to being an informed citizen and consumer. By age 20, the average American has been exposed to 1 million television commercials—an average of 150 every day.[3] Politicians and advertisers, salespeople and interest groups, fund-raisers and community activists—all vie for your attention, votes, money, time, and support. The more you know about persuasion, the more effective you can be in using your powers of critical thinking to assess the barrage of persuasive messages you are exposed to every day.

Although persuasion has been studied for more than 2,000 years, it is still the subject of lively debate among scholars. There are a number of scientific models of the persuasive process and a wide range of respected theories about how persuasion works.[4] In this chapter and the next, we will explore the principles of persuasion as they apply to public speaking.

When you speak to persuade, you act as an advocate. Your job is to get listeners to agree with you and, perhaps, to act on that belief. Your goal may be to defend an idea, to refute an opponent, to sell a program, or to inspire people to action. Because persuasive speakers must communicate information clearly and concisely, you will need all the skills you used in speaking to inform. But you will also need new skills—skills that take you from giving information to affecting your listeners' attitudes, beliefs, or actions. If you work at mastering these skills, you will reap the benefits not just in public speaking, but in many other aspects of your life.

Ethics and Persuasion

As we saw in Chapter 2, questions of ethics come into play whenever a speaker addresses an audience. No matter what the speaking situation, you need to make sure your goals are ethically sound and that you use ethical methods to communicate your ideas. Meeting these obligations can be especially challenging when you speak to persuade. Would you be willing to shade the truth "just a bit" if it would guarantee a successful speech? How about juggling statistics, doctoring quotations, passing off opinions as facts, or pandering to prejudice and stereotypes?

Unfortunately, there is no shortage of speakers—and other persuaders—who are willing to take ethical shortcuts to achieve their objectives. Yet, as Martin Luther King stated years ago, it is not possible to bring about a truly beneficial result by using unethical methods. Maintaining the bond of trust with listeners is also vital to a speaker's credibility. As in other kinds of public speaking, the ideal of effective persuasion is the good person speaking well.

When you work on your persuasive speech, keep in mind the guidelines for ethical speaking discussed in Chapter 2 and do your best to follow them every step of the way. Make sure your goals are ethically sound and that you can defend them if they are questioned or challenged. Study the topic thoroughly so you won't mislead your audience through shoddy research or muddled thinking. Learn about all sides of an issue, seek out competing viewpoints, and get your facts right.

But knowing the facts is not enough. You also need to be honest in what you say. There is no place in ethical speechmaking for deliberately false or deceptive statements. Also be on guard against more subtle forms of dishonesty such as quoting out of context, portraying a few details as the whole story, and misrepresenting the sources of facts and figures. Take care to present statistics, testimony, and other kinds of evidence fairly and accurately.

Keep in mind as well the power of language and use it responsibly. Show respect for the rights of free speech and expression, and stay away from name-calling and other forms of abusive language. Finally, check the section of Chapter 16 that discusses the role of emotional appeal in persuasive speaking (pages 455–460). If you engage in emotional appeal during your speech, make sure it's appropriate to the topic and that you build your speech on a firm base of facts and logic before appealing to your audience's emotions. In this regard, as in others, aim at the highest standards and construct your speech so it will be both convincing *and* ethically sound.[5]

The Psychology of Persuasion

As with other kinds of public speaking, you will be most effective in persuasion if you approach it systematically. The first step is to understand that persuasion is a psychological process. It occurs in a situation where two or more points of view exist. The speaker supports Social Security reform, but many listeners do not. The speaker considers doctor-assisted suicide immoral, but some in the audience think it is justified in certain circumstances. The speaker wants everyone in the audience to sign up immediately to learn CPR, but most listeners are inclined to procrastinate and will do it "someday." The different points of view may be completely opposed, or they may simply be different in degree. Whichever the case, there must be a disagreement, or else there would be no need for persuasion.

The Challenge of Persuasive Speaking

Of all the kinds of public speaking, persuasion is the most complex and the most challenging. Your objective is more ambitious than in speaking to inform, and audience analysis and adaptation become much more demanding. In some persuasive speeches you will deal with controversial topics that touch on your listeners' most basic attitudes, values, and beliefs. This will increase your listeners' resistance to persuasion and make your task that much more difficult.

It is much easier, for example, to explain the history of capital punishment than to persuade an audience either that capital punishment should be abolished or that it should be reinstituted in every state. In the persuasive speech you must contend not only with your audience's knowledge of capital punishment but also with their attitudes toward crime and justice, their beliefs about whether capital punishment deters people from committing violent crimes, and their values about the taking of human life. Lines of argument that work with one part of the audience may fail with—or even upset—another part. What seems perfectly logical to some listeners may seem wildly irrational to others. No matter how expert you are on the topic, no matter how skillfully you prepare the speech, no matter how captivating your delivery—some listeners will not agree with you.

This does not mean persuasion is impossible. It does mean you should enter a persuasive speaking situation with a realistic sense of what you can accomplish. You can't expect a group of die-hard Democrats to become Republicans or a steak lover to turn vegetarian as a result of one speech.

In every persuasive speech, you will face some listeners who are strongly in favor of your position, some who are neutral, and some who are adamantly opposed. If listeners are neutral or only moderately committed one way or another, you can realistically hope your speech will move at least some of them toward your side. If listeners are strongly opposed to your viewpoint, you can consider your speech a success if it leads even a few to reexamine their views.

When thinking about the range of persuasive responses, you may find it helpful to visualize listeners on a scale such as that shown in Figure 15.1

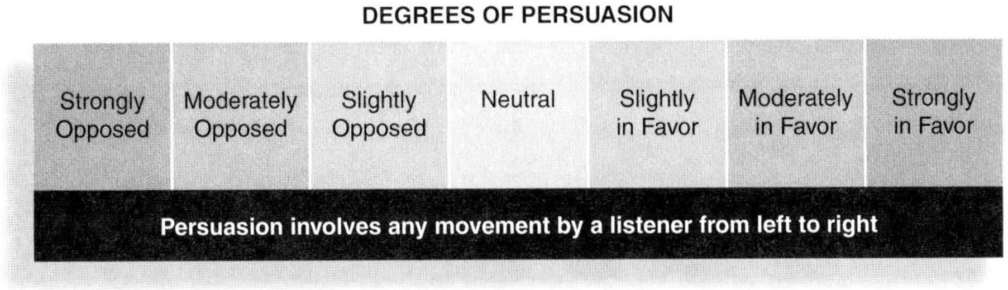

Figure 15.1

(above). Persuasion involves any movement by a listener from left to right on the scale, no matter where the listener begins and no matter how great or small the movement.[6]

How successful you are in any particular persuasive speech will depend above all on how well you tailor your message to the values, attitudes, and beliefs of your audience. Persuasion is a strategic activity. Just as a businesswoman or a military commander plots a strategy to gain a big sale or to be victorious in battle, so a persuasive speaker must have a strategy to win the audience to her or his side.

In Chapter 5 we considered the general principles of audience analysis and adaptation. Here we need to emphasize two additional principles that are crucial to the psychology of persuasion. The first deals with how listeners process and respond to persuasive messages. The second pertains to the target audience for persuasive speeches.

How Listeners Process Persuasive Messages

We often think of persuasion as something a speaker does *to* an audience. In fact, as a great deal of research shows, persuasion is something a speaker does *with* an audience. Although audiences in the United States seldom interrupt a speaker while she or he is talking, they do not just sit passively and soak in everything the speaker has to say.

Instead, they often engage in a mental give-and-take with the speaker. While they listen, they actively assess the speaker's credibility, delivery, supporting materials, language, reasoning, and emotional appeals. They may respond positively at one point, negatively at another. At times they may argue, inside their own minds, with the speaker. This mental give-and-take is especially vigorous when listeners are highly involved with the topic of the speech and believe it has a direct bearing on their lives.[7]

In a sense, the psychological interaction between a speaker and audience during a persuasive speech is similar to what happens vocally during a conversation—as in this example:

Jordan: The federal government really needs to clamp down on hate speech. Publications and Web sites that demonize gays and lesbians are inciting violence, sometimes even murder.

Keisha: I agree that violence against gays and lesbians is wrong, but I'm not sure censorship is the right approach. There's no proof these writings actually cause violence. Besides, doesn't the First Amendment guarantee the right to free speech, even for people who support detestable causes?

No matter what the situation, a persuasive speech will be more effective if the speaker has a clear goal, delivers the message sincerely, and adapts it to the target audience.

Jordan: Free speech is important, but people have a right to live without being persecuted. Doesn't our government have a responsibility to do what it can to keep people safe from discrimination?

Keisha: We can't compromise on free speech. It's a very dangerous idea to let someone in government decide what's acceptable speech and what's not. Once we ban hate speech, we might start banning other forms of expression, too.

Jordan: Not necessarily. We already outlaw some kinds of speech because they are dangerous to the community—such as threatening the life of the President or shouting "Fire" in a crowded building. Why is banning hate speech any different?

Much the same kind of interaction might occur during a persuasive speech, except that the listener—in this case, Keisha—would respond to herself rather than out loud.

mental dialogue with the audience
The mental give-and-take between speaker and listener during a persuasive speech.

What does this mean to you as a speaker? It means you must think of your persuasive speech as a kind of *mental dialogue* with your audience. Most important, you must anticipate possible objections the audience will raise to your point of view and then answer those objections in your speech. You cannot convert skeptical listeners unless you deal directly with the reasons for their skepticism.

As you prepare your persuasive speech, put yourself in the place of your audience and imagine how they will respond. For this to work, you must be as tough on your speech as your audience will be. Every place they will raise a question, answer it. Every place they will have a criticism, deal with it. Every place they will see a hole in your argument, fill it. Leave nothing to chance.[8]

The Target Audience

Unfortunately, no matter how carefully you plot your speech, you will seldom be able to persuade all your listeners. Some will be so opposed to your views that you have absolutely no chance of changing their minds. Others will already agree with you, so there is no need to persuade them. Like most audiences, yours will probably contain some listeners who are hostile to your position, some who favor it, some who are undecided, and some who just don't care. You would like to make your speech equally appealing to everyone, but this is rarely possible. Most often you will have a particular *part* of the whole audience that you want to reach with your speech. That part is called the *target audience.*

target audience
The portion of the whole audience that the speaker most wants to persuade.

Concentrating on a target audience does not mean you should ignore or insult the rest of your listeners. You must always keep in mind the ideas and feelings of your entire audience. But no matter how noble your intentions or how hard you try, you can't persuade all the people all the time. It only makes sense, then, to decide which portion of the audience you *most* want to reach.

Advertising gives us an effective model. Successful commercials are aimed at particular segments of the market, and their appeals are picked to fit the target audience. Mutual funds are now directing many of their advertisements at women. Why? Because more and more women are investing in the stock market. Beer commercials, on the other hand, are directed at men because they drink the most beer. Soft-drink commercials? They are meant to hook young people, so they feature teenagers, play their kind of music, and echo their values.

For your classroom speeches, you don't have the sophisticated research capability of a large advertising agency. But as we saw in Chapter 5, you can use observation, interviews, and questionnaires to find out where your classmates stand on your speech topic. This is your equivalent of market research. From it you can identify your target audience and the issues you will have to discuss to be convincing. Once you know where your target audience stands, you can tailor your speech to fit their values and concerns—aim at the target, so to speak.

Here, for example, is how one student, Amy Shapiro, determined her target audience for a persuasive speech urging her classmates to pass on the gift of life by signing organ donor cards.

There are 22 students in my audience. My audience-analysis questionnaires show that 3 are opposed to donating their organs under any circumstances. I can't persuade them no matter what I say. My questionnaires also show that 4 have already signed organ donor cards. I don't need to persuade them. The other 15 students could be persuaded if they knew more about the need for organ donors and about how the process works. They are my taget audience.

Not only did Amy pinpoint her target audience, she also knew from her audience-analysis questionnaire the issues she would have to discuss to be convincing:

The members of my target audience break down this way: 7 give "fear of being pronounced dead prematurely" as their main reason for not signing organ cards; 5 are concerned about their body being "cut up or disfigured"; and 3 cite religious reasons for their opposition. The questionnaires also show that 8 of the 15 don't fully understand the need for organ donors.

With all this information, Amy was able to put together a first-rate speech that focused specifically on her classmates' attitudes and beliefs about signing organ donor cards. In the speech, she showed the need for organ donations by explaining that there are thousands of people whose only hope for life is to receive a heart, liver, or kidney transplant. She also took care to answer her classmates' fears and objections. She showed that there are strict safeguards to prevent doctors from pulling the plug prematurely to make a heart or liver available for transplant surgery, that donated organs are removed as carefully as if the doctor were operating on a live patient, and that almost all religious leaders approve of organ donation as a way to help save lives. As a result, she was able to convince several of her classmates to sign organ donor cards.

In the next chapter, we'll discuss the methods you can use to hit the target in your persuasive speeches. In the rest of this chapter, we focus on the three major kinds of persuasive speeches and how to organize them most effectively. We will look first at speeches on questions of fact, then at speeches on questions of value, and finally at speeches on questions of policy.

Persuasive Speeches on Questions of Fact

What Are Questions of Fact?

What college basketball team has won the most games since 1990? Who was the first African American to sit on the U.S. Supreme Court? How far is it from New York to Baghdad? These questions of fact can be answered absolutely. You can look up the answers in a reference book, and no reasonable person would dispute them. The answers are either right or wrong.

question of fact
A question about the truth or falsity of an assertion.

But many questions of fact cannot be answered absolutely. There is a true answer, but we don't have enough information to know what it is. Some questions like this involve prediction: Will the economy be better or worse next year? Who will win the Super Bowl this season? Will another major earthquake strike California before the year 2010?

Other questions deal with issues on which the facts are murky or inconclusive. What will happen next in the Middle East? Is sexual orientation genetically determined? Are daily megadoses of vitamins beneficial to human health? Did William Shakespeare really write the plays attributed to him? No one knows the final answers to these questions, but that doesn't stop people from speculating about them or from trying to convince other people that they have the best possible answers.

Analyzing Questions of Fact

In some ways, a persuasive speech on a question of fact is similar to an informative speech. But the two kinds of speeches take place in different kinds of situations and for different purposes. The situation for an informative speech is *nonpartisan*. The speaker acts as a lecturer or a teacher. The aim is to give information as impartially as possible, not to argue for a particular point of view. On the other hand, the situation for a persuasive speech on a question of fact is *partisan*. The speaker acts as an advocate. His or her aim is not to be impartial but to present one view of the facts as persuasively as possible. The speaker may mention competing views of the facts, but only to refute them.

For example, consider the assassination of John F. Kennedy. After more than 40 years, there is still much public debate about what really happened in Dallas on November 22, 1963. Did Lee Harvey Oswald act alone, or was he part of a conspiracy? How many shots were fired at President Kennedy and from what locations? If there was a conspiracy, who was involved in it? The informative speaker would merely recite the known facts on both sides of these questions without drawing a conclusion about which side is correct. The persuasive speaker, however, would draw a conclusion from the known facts and try to convert listeners to his or her point of view.

If there were no possibility of dispute on questions of fact, there would be no need for courtroom trials. In a criminal trial there is usually at least one known fact—a crime has been committed. But did the defendant commit the crime? And if so, for what reason? The prosecuting attorney tries to persuade the jury that the defendant is guilty. The defense attorney tries to persuade the jury that the defendant is innocent. It is up to the jury to decide which view of the facts is more persuasive.[9]

Organizing Speeches on Questions of Fact

Persuasive speeches on questions of fact are usually organized *topically*. Suppose, for example, you want to convince your classmates that a major earthquake of 9.0 or above on the Richter scale will hit California within

Many persuasive speeches revolve around questions of fact. Here NASA administrator Sean O'Keefe presents his views on the feasibility of plans for an eventual U.S. mission to Mars.

the next ten years. Each main point in your speech will present a *reason* why someone should agree with you:

Specific Purpose: To persuade my audience that an earthquake of 9.0 or above on the Richter scale will hit California in the next ten years.

Central Idea: There are three good reasons to believe that an earthquake of 9.0 or above on the Richter scale will hit California in the next ten years.

Main Points:

I. California is long overdue for a major earthquake.
II. Many geological signs indicate that a major earthquake may happen soon.
III. Experts agree that an earthquake of 9.0 or above could strike California any day.

To take another example, suppose you are trying to persuade your classmates that the plays attributed to William Shakespeare were not actually written by him. Your specific purpose, central idea, and main points might be:

Specific Purpose: To persuade my audience that William Shakespeare did not write the plays attributed to him.

Central Idea: There is considerable evidence that the plays attributed to William Shakespeare were actually written by Francis Bacon or Edward de Vere.

Main Points:

I. Biographical and textual evidence suggest that William Shakespeare did not write the plays attributed to him.
II. Historical evidence indicates that Shakespeare's plays were probably written by either Sir Francis Bacon or Edward de Vere, 17th Earl of Oxford.

Occasionally you might arrange a persuasive speech on a question of fact *spatially.* For example:

Specific Purpose: To persuade my audience that poaching of wild animals is a serious international problem.

Central Idea: Poaching is threatening the survival of animal species throughout the world.

Main Points:

I. In Africa, poaching has claimed thousands of leopards, cheetahs, rhinoceroses, and elephants.
II. In Asia, poaching has all but eliminated Bengal tigers, snow leopards, and musk deer.

III. In South America, poaching has driven jaguars and swamp deer to the brink of extinction.
IV. In North America, poaching has reduced the number of bald eagles, grizzly bears, timber wolves, and giant otters.

Notice that in all these examples the speaker's purpose is limited to persuading the audience to accept a particular view of the facts. Sometimes, however, the dispute that gives rise to a persuasive speech will go beyond a question of fact and will turn on a question of value.

Persuasive Speeches on Questions of Value

What Are Questions of Value?

What is the best movie of all time? Is cloning morally justifiable? What are the ethical responsibilities of journalists? Such questions not only involve matters of fact, but they also demand *value judgments*—judgments based on a person's beliefs about what is right or wrong, good or bad, moral or immoral, proper or improper, fair or unfair.

Take the issue of cloning. It can be discussed at a purely factual level by asking such questions as "What are the scientific methods of cloning?" Or "What are the differences between cloning and genetic engineering?" Or "What are the laws about cloning in different countries?" These are factual questions. The answers you reach are independent of your belief about the morality of cloning.

question of value
A question about the worth, rightness, morality, and so forth of an idea or action.

But suppose you ask, "Is it morally justifiable to clone human beings?" Or "Is it ethically acceptable to clone human cells in an effort to cure diseases such as AIDS and cancer?" Now you are dealing with questions of value. How you answer will depend not only on your factual knowledge about cloning, but also on your moral values.

Analyzing Questions of Value

Contrary to what many people think, questions of value are not simply matters of personal opinion or whim. If you say, "I enjoy bicycle riding," you do not have to give a reason why you enjoy it. You are making a statement about your personal taste—not about the value of biking as a sport or a form of transportation. Even if bicycle riding were the most unpleasant activity ever invented, it could still be one of your favorites.

On the other hand, if you say, "Bicycle riding is the ideal form of land transportation," you are no longer making a statement about your personal enjoyment of biking. Now you are making a statement about a question of value. Whether bicycling is the ideal form of land transportation does not depend on your own likes and dislikes. To defend the statement, you cannot say, "Bicycle riding is the ideal form of land transportation because I like it."

Instead, you must *justify* your claim. The first step is to define what you mean by an "ideal form of land transportation." Do you mean a mode of transportation that gets people where they want to go as fast as possible? That is relatively inexpensive? That is fun? Nonpolluting? Beneficial for the user? In other words, you must establish your *standards* for an "ideal form of land transportation." Then you can show how bicycle riding measures up against those standards.

Whenever you give a speech on a question of value, be sure to give special thought to the standards for your value judgment.

Organizing Speeches on Questions of Value

Persuasive speeches on questions of value are almost always organized *topically*. The most common approach is to devote your first main point to establishing the standards for your value judgment and your second main point to applying those standards to the subject of your speech.

Think back for a moment to the speech about bicycle riding as the ideal form of land transportation. If you organized this speech in topical order, your first main point would identify the standards for an ideal form of land transportation. Your second main point would show how biking measures up against those standards. Here is how your specific purpose, central idea, and main points might look:

Specific Purpose: To persuade my audience that bicycle riding is the ideal form of land transportation.

Central Idea: Bicycle riding is the ideal form of land transportation because it is faster than walking or running, does not exploit animals or people, is nonpolluting, and promotes the health of the rider.

Main Points:

I. An ideal form of land transportation should meet four major standards.
   - A. It should be faster than running or walking.
   - B. It should not exploit animals or people.
   - C. It should be nonpolluting.
   - D. It should be beneficial for the person who uses it.

II. Bicycle riding meets all these standards for an ideal form of land transportation.
   - A. Bicycle riding is faster than walking or running.
   - B. Bicycle riding does not exploit the labor of animals or of other people.
   - C. Bicycle riding is not a source of air, land, water, or noise pollution.
   - D. Bicycle riding is extremely beneficial for the health of the rider.

When you speak on a question of value, you do not always have to devote your first main point to setting forth the standards for your value judgment and the second to applying those standards to the topic of the speech. But you must make sure to justify your judgment against *some* identifiable standards. In the following example, notice how the speaker devotes her first main point to judging capital punishment against moral standards and her second main point to judging it against legal standards:

Specific Purpose: To persuade my audience that capital punishment is morally and legally wrong.

Central Idea: Capital punishment violates both the Bible and the U.S. Constitution.

Main Points:

I. Capital punishment violates the biblical commandment "Thou shalt not kill."

II. Capital punishment violates the constitutional ban on "cruel and unusual punishment."

As you can see, speeches on questions of value may have strong implications for our actions. A person who is persuaded that capital punishment is morally and legally wrong is more likely to support legislation abolishing the death penalty. But speeches on questions of value do not argue directly for or against particular courses of action. They do not urge listeners to *do* anything. Once you go beyond arguing right or wrong to arguing that something should or should not be done, you move from a question of value to a question of policy.

Persuasive Speeches on Questions of Policy

What Are Questions of Policy?

Questions of policy arise daily in almost everything we do. At home we debate what to do during spring vacation, whether to buy a high-definition TV, which movie to see on the weekend. At work we discuss whether to go on strike, what strategy to use in selling a product, how to improve communication between management and employees. As citizens we ponder whether to vote for or against a political candidate, what to do about airport security, how to maintain economic growth and protect the environment.

question of policy
A question about whether a specific course of action should or should not be taken.

All these are questions of policy because they deal with specific courses of action. Questions of policy inevitably involve questions of fact. (How can we decide whether to vote for a candidate unless we know the facts of her or his stand on the issues?) They may also involve questions of value. (The policy you favor on abortion will be affected by whether you think abortion is moral or immoral.) But questions of policy *always* go beyond questions of fact or value to decide whether something should or should not be done.

When put formally, questions of policy usually include the word "should," as in these examples:

What measures should be taken to protect the United States against terrorist attacks?

Should same-sex marriages be legalized?

What steps should be taken to ensure that all people in the United States receive adequate health care?

How should colleges and universities deal with students who are caught cheating?

Should there be restrictions on the use of stun guns by law-enforcement personnel?

Types of Speeches on Questions of Policy

When you speak on a question of policy, your goal may be either to gain passive agreement or to motivate immediate action from your listeners. Deciding which goal you want to achieve is crucial, for it will affect almost every aspect of your speech.

Speeches to Gain Passive Agreement

speech to gain passive agreement
A persuasive speech in which the speaker's goal is to convince the audience that a given policy is desirable without encouraging the audience to take action in support of the policy.

If your goal is passive agreement, you will try to get your audience to agree with you that a certain policy is desirable, but you will not necessarily encourage the audience to do anything to enact the policy. For example, suppose you want to persuade people that the United States should abolish the electoral college and elect the President by direct popular vote. If you seek passive agreement, you will try to get your audience to concur that the President should be chosen directly by the people rather than by the electoral college. But you will not urge the audience to take any action right now to help change presidential election procedures.

Here are some specific purpose statements for policy speeches that seek passive agreement:

To persuade my audience that there should be stricter safety standards on amusement-park rides.

To persuade my audience that the age for full driving privileges should be raised to 18.

To persuade my audience that the federal government should require seat belts on all school buses in the United States.

To persuade my audience that school districts should not allow soft-drink companies to stock their products in school vending machines.

To persuade my audience that all sports teams should be required to change names and mascots that are demeaning to Native Americans.

In each of these cases, the speaker's aim is to affect the thinking of listeners—to convince them that the speaker's policy is necessary and practical. The speaker is not trying to get listeners to take action in support of the policy.

Speeches to Gain Immediate Action

speech to gain immediate action
A persuasive speech in which the speaker's goal is to convince the audience to take action in support of a given policy.

When your goal is immediate action, you want to do more than get your listeners to nod their heads in agreement. You want to motivate them to action. Beyond convincing them that your cause is sound, you will try to rouse them to take action right away—to sign a petition for abolishing the electoral college, to campaign for lower tuition, to purchase organic foods, to contribute to a fund drive, to vote for a political candidate, and so forth.

Persuasive speeches on questions of policy are given whenever people debate specific courses of action. Such speeches can seek either passive agreement or immediate action.

Here are some examples of specific purpose statements for policy speeches that seek immediate action:

To persuade my audience to give blood through the Red Cross.

To persuade my audience to vote in the next presidential election.

To persuade my audience to sign a petition against reducing student loans.

To persuade my audience to start a regular exercise program.

To persuade my audience to donate time to become literacy tutors.

Some experts say you should seek action from your audience whenever possible. Although it is much easier to evoke passive agreement than to elicit action, the listener is not making much of a commitment by thinking, "Sure, I agree with you." Within a day or two that same listener may forget entirely about your speech—and about her or his agreement with it.

Action, however, reinforces belief. A great deal of research shows that if you can persuade a listener to take some kind of action—even if it is no more than signing a petition, putting a bumper sticker on a car, or attending a meeting—you have gained a more serious commitment. Once a listener acts on behalf of a speaker's position, no matter if the action is minor, she or he is more likely to remain committed to the speaker's position and to take future action in support of it.[10]

When you call for action in a persuasive speech, you should make your recommendations as specific as possible. Don't just urge listeners to "do something." Tell them exactly what to do and how to do it. For an excellent

CD 1: VIDEO 15.1
View this section of "Making a Difference Through the Special Olympics."

example, look at CD 1, Video 15.1. The speaker's aim was to convince her classmates to donate time to the Special Olympics. After talking about the mission of Special Olympics, the need for volunteers, and the rewarding feelings experienced by volunteers, she explained how students can get involved for whatever amount of time they are able to commit at the moment. She also brought along brochures with additional information to pass out after her speech. When you construct your persuasive speech, remember that the more specific your instructions, the more likely your call to action will succeed.[11]

Analyzing Questions of Policy

Regardless of whether your aim is to elicit passive agreement or to gain immediate action, you will face three basic issues whenever you discuss a question of policy—need, plan, and practicality.

need
The first basic issue in analyzing a question of policy: Is there a serious problem or need that requires a change from current policy?

Need

There is no point in arguing for a policy unless you can show a need for it:

> Is there a need for more student parking on campus?
>
> Is there a need for the school district to charge special fees for students who participate in extracurricular activities?
>
> Is there a need for a national ID card in the United States?

Your first step is to convince listeners that there is a problem with things as they are. No doubt you have heard the old saying "If it ain't broke, don't fix it." People are not inclined to adopt a new policy unless they are convinced the old one is not working. This is why the *burden of proof* always rests with the speaker who advocates change. If you are speaking in favor of a new policy, you must prove to your listeners' satisfaction that there is a serious problem with existing policy, that the problem will only get worse with time, and that action must be taken now to solve the problem. (Of course, you may be defending present policy, in which case you will argue that there is *no* need to change—that things are already working as well as can be expected.)

burden of proof
The obligation facing a persuasive speaker to prove that a change from current policy is necessary.

Plan

The second basic issue of policy speeches is plan. Once you have shown that a problem exists, you must explain your plan for solving it.

plan
The second basic issue in analyzing a question of policy: If there is a problem with current policy, does the speaker have a plan to solve the problem?

> What can we do to get more student parking on campus?
>
> What specific fees should be charged for participation in extracurricular activities? Should the fees be required for all extracurricular activities or just for some activities?
>
> What information should be included on a national ID card? Who will be responsible for collecting the information and creating the cards?

Answering such questions is especially important if you call for a new policy. It's easy to complain about problems; the real challenge is to develop solutions.

In most classroom speeches, you will not have time to describe your plan in detail, but you should at least identify its major features. For example, if you advocate health care reform in the United States, you might follow the lead of some proponents and call for a program similar to that in Canada. When explaining your plan, you would state that Canada provides universal coverage for all medically necessary hospital visits and physician services. You might also note how Canada's system is funded and administered, the quality of health care it provides, and any major modifications that would be needed to make it work in the United States. But whatever your plan, be sure to explain any aspects of it that might seriously affect your audience's willingness to accept it.

Practicality

The third basic issue of policy speeches is practicality. Once you have presented a plan, you must show that it will work. Will it solve the problem? Or will it create new and more serious problems?

practicality
The third basic issue in analyzing a question of policy: Will the speaker's plan solve the problem? Will it create new and more serious problems?

> Building a multilevel parking garage on campus would provide more student parking, but the cost would require a sharp increase in tuition.
>
> Charging special fees for extracurricular activities would ease the school district's financial burden, but it would increase the burden on families and might prevent many students from participating in extracurricular activities.
>
> A national ID card might be an easy way for people to verify their identity for security purposes, but it could also infringe on civil liberties and give the government too much personal information about indviduals.

These are significant concerns. Whenever you advocate a new policy, you must be prepared to show that it is workable. No matter how serious a problem may be, listeners usually want some assurance that a speaker's plan will actually solve the problem.[12] One way to provide this assurance is to show that a plan similar to yours has been successfully implemented elsewhere. For example, CD 1, Video 15.2 shows an excerpt from a student speech calling for mandatory foreign-language instruction in elementary schools. As you view the clip, notice how the speaker clearly presents her plan and then points to the effectiveness of similar plans in other states and countries.

CD 1: VIDEO 15.2
View the discussion of practicality in "Multicultural, Multilingual."

If you oppose a shift in policy, one of your major arguments will be that the change is impractical—that it will create more problems than it can solve. Many parents and educators, for instance, say that imposing standardized national tests for high-school graduation will destroy the autonomy of local school districts and result in federal control of classrooms in every part of the nation. Other opponents say that such tests will discriminate against late bloomers, racial and ethnic minorities, and other children with special needs. If listeners accept these arguments, they will probably decide that a policy requiring standardized national tests for high-school graduation should not be adopted.

How much of your speech should you devote to need, to plan, and to practicality? The answer depends on your topic and your audience. If your audience is not aware of the health and environmental problems caused by the use of antibacterial chemicals in household products, you will have to give much of your time to need before covering plan and practicality. On the other hand, if your listeners already know about the problems caused by antibacterial household products, you can quickly remind them of need and then devote most of your speech to plan and practicality.

Or suppose you advocate increasing the tax on cigarettes to $3.00 a pack in order to reduce smoking among teenagers. Most people agree that teen smoking is a serious health problem, but many would question whether increasing the price of cigarettes will do much to solve the problem. Therefore, you should devote a fair part of your speech to practicality—to showing that in countries which have drastically raised their cigarette taxes, the smoking rate among teenagers has dropped by as much as 60 percent.

Organizing Speeches on Questions of Policy

Effective organization is crucial when you seek to persuade listeners on a question of policy. Although any of the basic patterns of organization explained in Chapter 8 can be used when discussing a question of policy, four special patterns are especially useful for policy speeches. They are problem-solution order, problem-cause-solution order, comparative advantages order, and Monroe's motivated sequence.

Problem-Solution Order

If you advocate a change in policy, your main points often will fall naturally into problem-solution order. In the first main point you demonstrate the need for a new policy by showing the extent and seriousness of the problem. In the second main point you explain your plan for solving the problem and show its practicality, for example:

problem-solution order
A method of organizing persuasive speeches in which the first main point deals with the existence of a problem and the second main point presents a solution to the problem.

Specific Purpose: To persuade my audience that the use of antibacterial chemicals in household products is creating health and environmental problems.

Central Idea: The use of antibacterial chemicals in household products is a serious problem that requires action by government and consumers alike.

Main Points:

I. The use of antibacterial chemicals in household products is a serious problem.
   A. Rather than making us more healthy, antibacterial chemicals in household products are contributing to long-term health problems.
   B. The antibacterial chemicals in household products are also creating environmental problems because they eventually end up in the U.S. water supply.

II. Solving these problems requires a combination of government and consumer action.

Regardless of how you organize your persuasive speech, you will need strong supporting materials. The better your research, the more convincing your arguments are likely to be.

A. The Food and Drug Administration should institute regulations controlling the use of antibacterial chemicals in household products.
B. Consumers should avoid purchasing household products that contain antibacterial chemicals.

CD 1: VIDEO 15.3

View an excerpt from "Bursting the Antibacterial Bubble."

You can use the problem-solution format just as easily to organize a speech opposing a change in policy. In such a speech your job is to defend the current system and to attack your opponents' proposed policy. Thus in the first main point you might argue that there is *not* a need for change. In the second main point you might show that even if there were a serious problem, the suggested new policy would *not* solve it and would create serious problems of its own. For example:

Specific Purpose: To persuade my audience that the city council should not pass legislation merging the police and fire departments.

Central Idea: Merging the police and fire departments is neither necessary nor practical.

Main Points:

I. Merging the police and fire departments is not necessary.
   A. Under the current system, the police department has developed a reputation for excellence that has made it a model for departments in other cities,
   B. The fire department is equally well-respected for doing its job quickly and efficiently.

II. Besides being unnecessary, merging the police and fire departments is highly impractical.
   A. Rather than saving the city money, merging the departments would increase costs over the long run.
   B. Merging the departments would harm morale and reduce the high level of performance we have come to expect from our police force and firefighters.

Problem-Cause-Solution Order

problem-cause-solution order
A method of organizing persuasive speeches in which the first main point identifies a problem, the second main point analyzes the causes of the problem, and the third main point presents a solution to the problem.

For a variation on problem-solution order, you might arrange your speech in problem-cause-solution order. This produces a speech with three main points—the first identifying a problem, the second analyzing the causes of the problem, and the third presenting a solution to the problem. For example:

Specific Purpose: To persuade my audience that the age for full motor-vehicle driving privileges should be raised to 18.

Central Idea: The number of accidents and deaths involving teenage drivers is a serious problem that can be controlled by raising the age for full driving privileges to 18.

Main Points:

I. The number of accidents and deaths involving teenage drivers is a serious national problem.
   A. Each year more than 8,000 people are killed in accidents involving teenage drivers.
   B. The risks of being involved in a fatal accident are highest for 16- and 17-year-old drivers.

II. There are four main causes of the problem.
   A. Younger drivers haven't had enough experience to develop their driving skills.
   B. Younger drivers are more prone to risk-taking and dangerous driving behaviors.
   C. Younger drivers are more likely to have accidents when driving after dark.
   D. Younger drivers are easily distracted by the presence of other teenagers in the car.

III. We can help solve these problems by raising the age for full driving privileges.
   A. Although 16- and 17-year-olds should have limited driving privileges, they should not receive an unrestricted license until age 18.
   B. This will allow younger drivers time to gain maturity and experience before receiving unlimited driving privileges.

CD 1: VIDEO 15.4
View an excerpt from "Putting the Brakes on Teenage Driving."

Some teachers prefer this method of organization because it requires a speaker to identify the causes of the problem. This in turn makes it easier to check whether the proposed solution will get at the causes of the problem.

Comparative Advantages Order

When your audience already agrees that a problem exists, you can devote your speech to comparing the advantages and disadvantages of competing solutions. In such a situation, you might put your speech in comparative advantages order. Rather than dwelling on the problem, you would devote each main point to explaining why your solution is preferable to other proposed solutions.

comparative advantages order
A method of organizing persuasive speeches in which each main point explains why a speaker's solution to a problem is preferable to other proposed solutions.

Suppose you want to convince your audience that the U.S. space program should shift its emphasis from highly glamorous staffed flights such as the space shuttle to unstaffed scientific missions that gather information about other planets and the nature of the solar system. Using comparative advantages order, you would compare unstaffed scientific missions with staffed space flights and show why the former is a better choice. Your specific purpose, central idea, and main points might look like this:

Specific Purpose: To persuade my audience that the U.S. space program should put greater priority on unstaffed scientific missions that gather information about the planets and the solar system.

Central Idea: Unstaffed scientific missions are less costly and more beneficial than staffed space flights.

Main Points:

I. Unstaffed scientific missions are less costly than staffed space flights.

II. Unstaffed scientific missions provide more practical benefits than staffed space flights.

Monroe's Motivated Sequence

Developed in the 1930s by Alan Monroe, a professor of speech at Purdue University, the motivated sequence is tailor-made for policy speeches that seek immediate action. The sequence has five steps that follow the psychology of persuasion:[13]

Monroe's motivated sequence
A method of organizing persuasive speeches that seek immediate action. The five steps of the motivated sequence are attention, need, satisfaction, visualization, and action.

1. *Attention.* First you gain the attention of your audience. You do this in the introduction by using one or more of the methods described in Chapter 9: relating to the audience, showing the importance of the topic, making a startling statement, arousing curiosity or suspense, posing a question, telling a dramatic story, or using visual aids.

2. *Need.* Having captured the interest of your audience, you next make them feel a need for change. You show there is a serious problem with the existing situation. It is important to state the need clearly and to illustrate it with strong supporting materials—statistics, examples, and testimony—that relate directly to the audience's values or vital interests. By the end of this step, listeners should be so concerned about the problem that they are psychologically primed to hear your solution.

3. *Satisfaction.* Having aroused a sense of need, you satisfy it by providing a solution to the problem. You present your plan and show how it will work. Be sure to offer enough details about the plan to give listeners a clear understanding of it.

4. *Visualization.* Having given your plan, you intensify desire for it by visualizing its benefits. The key to this step is using vivid imagery to show your listeners how *they* will profit from your policy. Make them *see* how much better conditions will be once your plan is adopted.

5. *Action.* Once the audience is convinced your policy is beneficial, you are ready to call for action. Say exactly what you want the audience to do—and how to do it. Give them the address to write. Tell them where they should go to join the Young Republicans. Show them how to sign up for counseling. Then conclude with a final stirring appeal that reinforces their commitment to act.

Many students prefer the motivated sequence because it is more detailed than problem-solution order. It follows the process of human thinking and leads the listener step by step to the desired action. One indication of its effectiveness is that it is widely used by people who make their living by persuasion—especially advertisers. The next time you watch television, pay close attention to the commercials. You will find that many of them follow the motivated sequence, as in this example:

Attention:	It's a sunny spring day. Flowers are in bloom and the wind is blowing. The camera focuses on two women, both in their late twenties or early thirties, jogging through a city park. Suddenly one of the women stops, bends over, and rests her hands on her hips. Her eyes are watering and she is breathing heavily. A tightly framed close-up heightens the sense that something is wrong.
Need:	"Are you all right?" asks her friend. "It's my allergies," the woman replies. "Every spring it's the same thing. I feel great and then my hay fever ruins everything. You'd better go on without me."
Satisfaction:	"I used to have the same problem," says the woman's friend. "Then I tried AllArrest. It knocked out my hay fever completely. Now I can do everything I want in the spring. You should try it." The announcer, in voice-over, tells us: "AllArrest provides the most effective hay fever relief available—and without causing drowsiness."
Visualization:	We see the same two women jogging a week or so later. Both are running briskly and breathing easily. "That AllArrest really does work," says the woman who had to stop running in the opening scene. "I feel like a new person since I started taking it. Thanks to AllArrest, I can enjoy spring again!"
Action:	The audience is urged to use AllArrest whenever they suffer from hay fever or other allergies.

Try using the motivated sequence when you want to spur listeners to action. You should find it easy and effective, as did one student who used it in a speech urging classmates to work for passage of a local tenants' rights bill. Here are the highlights of his speech.

THE INTERNET *Connection*

As a persuasive speaker, you must understand both sides of an issue so you can answer the objections of listeners who do not support your point of view. You can use the Internet to help by visiting the Web sites of organizations that take opposing views. For example, if your topic is stem cell research, visit both the Stem Cell Research Foundation (www.stemcellresearchfoundation.org) and Do No Harm: The Coalition of Americans for Research Ethics (www.stemcellresearch.org/). Or, if you are speaking on gun control, access the National Rifle Association (www.nra.org) and the Coalition to Stop Gun Violence (www.csgv.org/).

If you want your listeners to take action by writing their U.S. Senator or Representative, encourage them to use e-mail. For a list of Senate e-mail addresses, see Contacting the Senate (www.senate.gov/contacting/index.cfm). For assistance in contacting members of the House, log on to www.house.gov/writerep/.

ONLINE LEARNING CENTER

You can link to these Web sites at www.mhhe.com/lucas9.

Attention: Have you ever had cockroaches running through the cupboards in your apartment? Have you sweltered in the heat because the air conditioning didn't work? Or shivered in the cold because the furnace was broken? Or waited months for the security deposit you never got back even though you left your apartment as clean as when you moved in?

Need: Throughout this city students and other apartment tenants are being victimized by unresponsive and unethical landlords. Just last year more than 200 complaints were filed with the city housing department, but no action has been taken against the landlords.

Satisfaction: These problems could be solved by passing a strong tenants' rights bill that defines the rights of tenants, specifies the obligations of landlords, and imposes strict penalties for violators.

Visualization: Such bills have worked in a number of college communities across the nation. If one were passed here, you would no longer have to worry about substandard sanitary or safety conditions in your apartment. Your landlord could not violate the terms of your lease or steal your security deposit.

Action: A tenants' rights bill has been proposed to the city council. You can help get it passed by signing the petition I will pass around after my speech. I also urge you to help by circulating petitions among your friends and by turning out to support the bill when it is debated in the city council next week. If we all work together, we can get this bill through the council.

Because it follows the process of human thinking, Monroe's motivated sequence is especially useful for persuasive speakers who seek immediate action from their listeners.

Monroe's motivated sequence is entirely compatible with the standard method of outlining discussed in Chapter 10. The following outline shows how one speaker incorporated the sequence into a speech urging her classmates to help children around the globe by contributing to an organization called Compassion International. In its full form, the outline included supporting materials for all the points in the speech.

Specific Purpose: To persuade my audience to help children worldwide by contributing to Compassion International.

Central Idea: Contributing to an organization such as Compassion International can help break the cycle of poverty that affects millions of children.

Introduction

Attention:

I. For every morning that you wake up and eat breakfast, millions of children begin their daily struggle with chronic hunger and poverty.

II. By sponsoring a child for two years through an organization called Compassion International, I have seen the difference it can make in a child's life.

III. Today, I would like to encourage all of you to become involved with Compassion International.

Body

Need:

I. Millions of children in developing countries suffer from poverty, hunger, and lack of education.

A. Poverty destroys the quality of life for children in developing countries from Asia to South America.
B. Hunger takes the lives of almost 20,000 children under the age of five each day.
C. Lack of education helps perpetuate the vicious cycle of hunger and poverty.

Satisfaction: II. Groups such as Compassion International can help break this cycle.
A. Compassion International provides food, clothing, education, shelter, and health care for children across the globe.
B. You can sponsor a child for just $28 a month.
C. For two years I have been sponsoring a little boy in Ecuador named José Francisco.

CD 1: VIDEO 15.5

View an excerpt from "To Save a Child."

Visualization: III. Compassion International has an impressive record as a truly effective charity.
A. According to the Better Business Bureau, 78 percent of donated funds go directly to the children.
B. Internal and external audits ensure that all funds are properly received, tracked, and managed for each child.
C. *Smart Money* magazine ranks Compassion International as one of the top 10 charities in the United States.

Conclusion

Action: I. So I encourage each of you to sponsor a child through Compassion International.
II. As Compassion International states, "while we cannot individually change the world, we can change the world for one child."

Try using the motivated sequence when you seek immediate action from your listeners. Over the years it has worked for countless speakers—and it can work for you as well.

Sample Speech with Commentary

The following persuasive speech deals with a question of policy and provides an excellent example of problem-cause-solution structure. As you read the speech, notice how the speaker deals with the issues of need, plan, and practicality. Notice also how she uses strong, well-chosen supporting materials to back up her point of view on what she knew would be an unpopular issue among her classmates. Finally, observe how clear and uncluttered the speech is. There are few wasted words and the ideas progress cleanly and crisply.

CD 2: FULL SPEECH

View "Putting the Brakes on Teenage Driving."

Putting the Brakes on Teenage Driving

Commentary	*Speech*
The speaker begins with a vivid, richly detailed story that gains attention and draws the audience into the speech.	On a chilly November night two years ago, a Ford Explorer was charging down a California highway. The 16-year-old driver and three of his friends were returning from a concert in Los Angeles. These young people were good students, gifted athletes, talented artists and musicians. And none were drunk or impaired by drugs.
As the speaker completes her opening story, she reveals that one of the students injured in the accident was her nephew. This personal involvement helps establish her credibility and goodwill, both of which are vital when one is speaking on a controversial subject.	They were, however, driving too fast, and the driver lost control of the car. The car went into a ditch and hit a tree. The driver and one passenger were killed. The other two passengers escaped with severe injuries. One of these passengers was my nephew. Today he is finishing high school in a wheelchair, a wheelchair he will occupy for the rest of his life.
The speaker strengthens her credibility and reveals the central idea of her speech.	Unfortunately, tragic auto accidents involving teenage drivers are much too common in all parts of the United States. After researching the subject for my speech, I have come to the same conclusion as the experts—that the best way to prevent such accidents is to raise the age for full driving privileges to 18 or older.
The speaker uses her audience-analysis survey both to acknowledge her classmates' opposition to raising the driving age and to stress their recognition that there are reasons to consider instituting such a policy. After asking them to listen with an open mind, she previews the main points she will discuss in the body of the speech.	I know from my audience-analysis questionnaire that most of you oppose such a plan. But I also know from my questionnaires that most of you recognize that 16- and 17-year-old drivers are less skilled and less responsible than older drivers. So I ask you to listen with an open mind while we discuss some of the problems associated with teenage driving, the major causes of the problems, and a plan that will go a long way toward solving the problems.
This speech is organized in problem-cause-solution order. Here the speaker starts the body by identifying the problem—the large number of accidents, deaths, and injuries involving teenage drivers. She supports her claim with statistics from the National Highway Traffic Safety Administration. As you can see from the video of the speech on CD 2, she uses PowerPoint to present her statistics and to heighten their impact as she moves from figure to figure. She then relates the statistics directly to her audience by comparing the annual number of deaths in accidents involving teenage drivers to the number of students at the speaker's school.	No matter how one looks at the evidence, it all leads to one fact: There are too many motor vehicle accidents, deaths, and injuries involving teenage drivers. According to the National Highway Traffic Safety Administration, while teenagers make up 7 percent of the nation's licensed drivers, they represent 14 percent of all motor vehicle fatalities. The NHTSA reports that last year 3,657 drivers age 16 to 20 were killed in automobile accidents. In addition to killing the drivers, these same accidents took the lives of 2,384 teenage passengers. But these accidents didn't affect teenagers alone. They also took the lives of 2,625 people aged 21 or older. So the total number of people killed last year in automobile accidents involving teenage drivers was 8,666—almost exactly the number of full-time students at this campus.

As in the previous paragraph, the statistics in this paragraph come from credible, clearly identified sources. Although most listeners did not favor the speaker's position at the start of her speech, the strength of her evidence eventually led some to concede that her position needed to be taken seriously.

Evidence also shows that the younger the driver, the greater the risk. According to the Insurance Institute for Highway Safety, 16-year-olds have "the highest percentage of crashes involving speeding, the highest percentage of single-vehicle crashes, and the highest percentage of crashes involving driver error." Moreover, as *USA Today* reports, 16-year-olds are three times more likely to be involved in fatal crashes than are older drivers.

A transition moves the speaker into her second main point, in which she explores four major causes of the problem. As she proceeds, notice how she uses a signpost to introduce each cause.

Now that we've seen the extent of the problem, we can explore its causes. One of the causes is inexperience. New drivers just haven't had enough time on the road to develop their driving skills. But inexperience is far from the only cause of the problem. After all, there will always be inexperienced drivers—even if the driving age is raised to 21 or even to 25.

The evidence in this paragraph connects the tendency of younger drivers to take dangerous risks with the state of brain development among 16-year-olds. In addition to coming from highly respected sources, the evidence provides a scientific foundation for what the speaker's audience knew from their own experience about the propensity for risk-taking among teenagers.

A second cause is revealed by brain research. Findings from the National Institute of Mental Health show that the brain of an average 16-year-old has not developed to the point where he or she is able to effectively judge the risk of a given situation. Dr. Jay Giedd, who led the research team that conducted the study, states: "When a smart, talented, and very mature teen does something that a parent might call 'stupid,' it's this underdeveloped part of the brain that has most likely failed." Steven Lowenstein, a medical professor at the University of Colorado, has just finished a five-year study comparing the traffic records of 16-year-old drivers to drivers aged 25 to 49. His conclusion? "Deliberate risk-taking and dangerous and aggressive driving behaviors predominated" among the 16-year-olds.

Now the speaker discusses the third cause of the problem—night driving. Knowing that night driving is more dangerous for all age groups, she takes care to note that it is particularly perilous for teenagers because of their risk-taking and their inexperience behind the wheel.

A third cause of motor vehicle fatalities among teenage drivers is night driving. According to *The Washington Post*, when 16-year-olds get behind the wheel of a car after dark, the likelihood of having an accident increases several times over. Of course, nighttime driving is less safe for everyone, but it becomes particularly dangerous when combined with a young driver's inexperience and reduced ability to gauge risk.

This paragraph is especially effective. If you watch the speech on CD 2, you can see how the speaker uses her voice, gestures, and facial expressions to enhance the impact of her ideas, to establish a strong bond with the audience, and to pull them deeper into the speech.

Finally, there is the presence of teenage passengers in the car. We all know what it's like to drive with our friends—the stereo is up loud, cell phones are ringing, everybody's laughing and having a good time. The problem is that all these factors create distractions, distractions that too often result in accidents, injury, and death. Allan Williams, chief scientist at the Insurance Institute for Highway Safety, reports that one teenage passenger doubles the risk of a fatal crash. With two or more passengers, the risk is five times greater. Remember my nephew's accident I mentioned at the start of my speech? There were three passengers in the car.

A transition signals that the speaker is moving into her third main point. As in her second main point, she uses a signpost to introduce each of the subpoints.

So the extent of the problem is clear. So, too, are its causes. What steps can we take to help bring about a solution? First, we need a national policy that no one can receive a learner's permit until age 16, and no one can receive full driving privileges until age 18. This will allow 16-year-olds time to gain driving experience before having an unrestricted license and to reach a stage of brain development where they are better able to handle the risk and responsibility of driving.

As this section of the speech proceeds, notice how the speaker's plan addresses all four causes of the problem discussed in main point two—inexperience, brain development, night driving, and the number of teenage passengers in a car.

Second, we need to restrict nighttime driving so as to keep younger drivers off the road when conditions are riskiest. Some states have tried to address this problem by banning teenagers from driving after midnight or 1 A.M., but as the Insurance Institute for Highway Safety reports, these laws don't go far enough. According to the Institute, we need a 9:00 P.M. or 10:00 P.M. limit until drivers reach the age of 18.

Because the speaker is not an authority on highway safety, she uses expert testimony throughout her third main point to prove that her plan will help reduce teenage driving fatalities. Notice how much less effective the speech would be if the speaker had merely stated the steps of her plan without providing evidence of its effectiveness.

Third, we need to restrict the number of teenage passengers in cars driven by younger drivers. In fact, says Kevin Quinlan from the National Transportation Safety Board, "passenger restriction is the first and foremost measure you can take" to reduce teenage driving fatalities. According to Quinlan, the optimal policy would be to bar drivers age 17 or younger from having any passengers in the car unless the riders are adults or family members. Drivers from the age of 17 to 18 should not be allowed to carry more than one teenage passenger.

Here the speaker deals with the objection that her plan would be harsh and inconvenient. The quotation from a father who lost his teenage son in a car accident puts the harshness issue in perspective and forces listeners to think about the trade-off between saving lives and instituting tougher driving-age requirements.

Now I know all of this might sound harsh and perhaps inconvenient, but the evidence is clear that it would save a significant number of lives. "If you want to discuss harsh," said one father whose 17-year-old son died in an accident three years ago, "I can talk to you about harsh. It's being awakened at 2:30 in the morning by the State Patrol telling you that your son has just been killed."

The conclusion builds on the emotional appeal generated by the quotation at the end of the previous paragraph. The final sentence, in which the speaker notes that her nephew would gladly accept the inconvenience caused by her policy for the chance to walk again, is compelling and ends the speech on a dramatic note.

Everyone in this room has lived to college age. But this year alone, thousands of teenage drivers will not live that long. And they won't live that long due to factors that we can prevent. There's no way to solve all the problems we encounter on the road, but we can do something to help save the lives of younger drivers and make the road safer for all of us. As I said earlier, this might sound harsh or inconvenient, but I know my nephew would gladly trade both for the chance to walk again.

Summary

Persuasion is the process of creating, reinforcing, or changing people's beliefs or actions. When you speak to persuade, you act as an advocate. Your job is to sell a program, to defend an idea, to refute an opponent, or to inspire people to action. The ability to speak persuasively will benefit you in every part of your life, from personal relations to community activities to career aspirations.

How successful you are in any particular persuasive speech will depend above all on how well you tailor your message to the values, attitudes, and beliefs of your audience. Careful listeners do not sit passively and soak in everything a speaker has to say. While they listen, they actively assess the speaker's credibility, supporting materials, language, reasoning, and emotional appeals.

You should think of your speech as a kind of mental dialogue with your audience. Most important, you need to identify your target audience, anticipate the possible objections they will raise to your point of view, and answer those objections in your speech. You cannot convert skeptical listeners unless you deal directly with the reasons for their skepticism.

Persuasive speeches may center on questions of fact, questions of value, or questions of policy. Some questions of fact can be answered absolutely. Others cannot—either because the facts are murky or because there is not enough information available to us. When giving a persuasive speech about a question of fact, your role is akin to that of a lawyer in a courtroom trial. You will try to get your listeners to accept your view of the facts.

Questions of value go beyond the immediate facts to involve a person's beliefs about what is right or wrong, good or bad, moral or immoral, ethical or unethical. When speaking about a question of value, you must justify your opinion by establishing standards for your value judgment. Although questions of value often have strong implications for our actions, speeches on questions of value do not argue directly for or against particular courses of action.

Once you go beyond arguing right or wrong to urging that something should or should not be done, you move to a question of policy. When you speak on a question of policy, your goal may be to evoke passive agreement or to spark immediate action. In either case, you will face three basic issues—need, plan, and practicality. How much of your speech you devote to each issue will depend on your topic and your audience.

There are several options for organizing speeches on questions of policy. If you advocate a change in policy, your main points will often fall naturally into problem-solution order or into problem-cause-solution order. If your audience already agrees that a problem exists, you may be able to use comparative advantages order. Whenever you seek immediate action from listeners, you should consider a more specialized organizational pattern known as Monroe's motivated sequence, whose five steps are based on the psychology of persuasion.

Regardless of your speech topic or method of organization, you need to make sure your goals are ethically sound and that you use ethical methods to persuade your audience. In this regard, as in others, you should aim at the highest standards and construct your speech so it will be ethical as well as convincing.

Key Terms

ONLINE LEARNING CENTER

Review these terms by doing the Chapter 15 crossword puzzle at www.mhhe.com/lucas9.

persuasion (400)
mental dialogue with the audience (404)
target audience (405)
question of fact (406)
question of value (409)
question of policy (411)
speech to gain passive agreement (412)
speech to gain immediate action (412)
need (414)
burden of proof (414)
plan (414)
practicality (415)
problem-solution order (416)
problem-cause-solution order (418)
comparative advantages order (419)
Monroe's motivated sequence (419)

Review Questions

CD 1: STUDY QUESTIONS

For further review, go to the Study Questions for this chapter

After reading this chapter, you should be able to answer the following questions:

1. What is the difference between an informative speech and a persuasive speech? Why is speaking to persuade more challenging than speaking to inform?
2. What does it mean to say that audiences engage in a mental dialogue with the speaker as they listen to a speech? What implications does this mental give-and-take hold for effective persuasive speaking?
3. What is the target audience for a persuasive speech?
4. What are questions of fact? How does a persuasive speech on a question of fact differ from an informative speech? Give an example of a specific purpose statement for a persuasive speech on a question of fact.
5. What are questions of value? Give an example of a specific purpose statement for a persuasive speech on a question of value.
6. What are questions of policy? Give an example of a specific purpose statement for a persuasive speech on a question of policy.
7. Explain the difference between passive agreement and immediate action as goals for persuasive speeches on questions of policy.
8. What are the three basic issues you must deal with when discussing a question of policy? What will determine the amount of attention you give to each of these issues in any particular speech?
9. What four methods of organization are used most often in persuasive speeches on questions of policy?
10. What are the five steps of Monroe's motivated sequence? Why is the motivated sequence especially useful in speeches that seek immediate action from listeners?

Exercises for Critical Thinking

1. Look back at the story of Ramon Trujillo at the beginning of this chapter (page 400). Like Ramon, most people do a certain amount of persuading every day in normal conversation. Keep a journal of your communication activities for an entire day, making special note of all instances in which you tried to persuade someone else to your point of view. Choose one of those instances and prepare a brief analysis of it.

   In your analysis, answer the following questions: (1) Who was the audience for your persuasive effort? (2) What were the "specific purpose" and the "central idea" of your persuasive message? (3) Did you rehearse your persuasive message ahead of time, or did it arise spontaneously from the situation? (4) Were you successful in achieving your specific purpose? (5) If you faced the same situation again, what strategic changes would you make in your persuasive effort?

2. Below are four specific purposes for persuasive speeches. In each case explain whether the speech associated with it concerns a question of fact, a question of value, or a question of policy. Then rewrite the specific purpose statement to make it appropriate for a speech about one of the other two kinds of questions. For instance, if the original purpose statement is about a question of policy, write a new specific purpose statement that deals with the same topic as either a question of fact or a question of value.

   Example

   Original statement: To persuade my audience that it is unfair for judges to favor natural parents over adoptive parents in child custody disputes. (question of value)

   Rewritten statement: To persuade my audience that the courts should establish clear guidelines for settling disputes between adoptive parents and natural parents in child custody cases. (question of policy)

   a. To persuade my audience to donate time as a community volunteer.
   b. To persuade my audience that violence on television is a major cause of violent behavior in society.
   c. To persuade my audience that a national sales tax should be adopted to help pay off the national debt.
   d. To persuade my audience that it is unethical for businesses to use genetic testing in screening potential employees.

3. Choose a topic for a persuasive speech on a question of policy. Create two specific purpose statements about that topic—one for a speech to gain passive agreement, another for a speech to motivate immediate action. Once you have the specific purpose statements, explain how the speech seeking immediate action would differ in structure and persuasive appeals from the speech seeking passive agreement. Be specific.

4. Analyze the sample speech with commentary at the end of this chapter ("Putting the Brakes on Teenage Driving," pages 424–426). Pay special attention to how the speaker supports her ideas as she moves through

the problem, cause, and solution sections. Does the present a convincing case that a serious problem exists? What does she identify as the major causes of the problem? Does her plan address all of those causes?

5. Select a television commercial that is organized according to Monroe's motivated sequence. Prepare a brief analysis in which you (a) identify the target audience for the commercial and (b) describe each step in the motivated sequence as it appears in the commercial.
6. Analyze "The Ultimate Gift," in the appendix of sample speeches that follows Chapter 18 (pp. A15–A17). Because this speech is organized in Monroe's motivated sequence, pay special attention to how the speaker develops each step in the sequence—attention, need, satisfaction, visualization, action. Identify where each step of the sequence occurs in the speech and explain how the persuasive appeal of the speech builds from step to step.

Applying the POWER of PUBLIC SPEAKING

As a local union leader, it is your job to present a contract offer made by management to your striking membership. Though the proposed offer falls short of meeting all your union's demands, you believe it is a good offer, and in your speech, you will recommend that the union members vote to accept it.

The contract issues have been hotly debated, so you have an idea how some of your 42 members will cast their ballots. One issue is that management has guaranteed to maintain full benefits for current workers but wants to reduce benefits for new workers. Though the proposed offer limits these reductions, you know of 12 members who will vote against any proposal that limits the benefits of future workers. Already with you, however, are the 8 members who voted not to strike at all and who will vote to accept any reasonable offer. Among the undecided voters are those who think that since the strike is only in its second week, a better contract may be offered if this proposal is rejected.

Who is the target audience for your speech? How will you persuade them to vote yes on the contract offer? Which of the following methods of organization will you use for your speech, and why: problem-solution, comparative advantages, Monroe's motivated sequence?

Notes

[1]There are many competing definitions of persuasion. Mine is drawn from Gerald R. Miller, "On Being Persuaded: Some Basic Distinctions," in James Price Dillard and Michael Pfau (eds.), *The Persuasion Handbook: Developments in Theory and Practice* (Thousand Oaks, CA: Sage, 2002), pp. 3–16.

[2]Amanda Bennett, "Economics + Meeting = A Zillion Causes and Effects," *The Wall Street Journal*, January 10, 1995, p. B1.

[3]Herbert W. Simons, *Persuasion in Society* (Thousand Oaks, CA: Sage, 2001), p. 12.

[4]For a comprehensive review of the major theories of persuasion, see Richard M. Perloff, *The Dynamics of Persuasion: Communication and Attitudes in the 21st Century*, 2nd ed. (Mahwah, NJ: Erlbaum, 2003).

[5]See Richard L. Johannesen, *Ethics in Human Communication*, 5th ed. (Prospect Heights, IL; Waveland Press, 2002), for a full look at communication ethics.

[6]Adapted from Simons, *Persuasion in Society*, p. 30.

[7]This view of the interaction between speaker and listener reflects cognitive processing models of persuasion in general and the Elaboration Likelihood Model in particular. For a concise explanation of the latter, see Em Griffin, *A First Look at Communication Theory*, 6th ed. (New York: McGraw-Hill, 2006), pp. 216–227.

[8]There is a great deal of research confirming the need for persuasive speakers to answer potential objections to their arguments. For a recent study, see Chasu An and Michael Pfau, "The Efficacy of Inoculation in Televised Political Debates," *Journal of Communication*, 54 (2004), pp. 421–436.

[9]For a superb look at the research on courtroom persuasion, see John C. Reinard, "Persuasion in the Legal Setting," in Dillard and Pfau, *Persuasion Handbook*, pp. 543–602.

[10]Robert B. Cialdini, *Influence: Science and Practice*, 4th ed. (Boston: Allyn and Bacon, 2001), pp. 65–68.

[11]Daniel J. O'Keefe, *Persuasion: Theory and Research*, 2nd ed. (Thousand Oaks, CA: Sage, 2002), pp. 218–219.

[12]See, for example, Rajiv N. Rimal and Kevin Real, "Perceived Risk and Efficacy Beliefs as Motivators of Change: Use of the Risk Perception Attitude (RPA) Framework to Understand Health Behaviors," *Human Communication Research*, 29 (2003), pp. 370–399.

[13]Raymie E. McKerrow, Bruce E. Gronbeck, Douglas Ehninger, and Alan H. Monroe, *Principles and Types of Speech Communication*, 15th ed. (New York: Longman, 2003).

CHAPTER SEVENTEEN

Speaking on Special Occasions

Special occasions are the punctuation marks of day-to-day life, the high points that stand out above ordinary routine. Christenings, weddings, funerals, graduations, award ceremonies, inaugurals, retirement dinners—all these are occasions, and they are very special to the people who take part in them. Nearly always they are occasions for speechmaking. A close friend proposes a toast to the bride and groom; the sales manager presents an award to the sales representative of the year; the president delivers an inaugural address; the basketball coach gives a speech honoring the team's most valuable player; a family member delivers a moving eulogy to the deceased. These speeches help give the occasion its "specialness." They are part of the ceremonial aura that marks the event.

Speeches for special occasions are different from the speeches we have considered so far in this book. They may convey information, but that is not their primary purpose. Neither is their primary purpose to persuade. Rather, they aim to fit the special needs of a special occasion. In this chapter we look at the most common special occasions and the kinds of speeches appropriate for each.

Speeches of Introduction

"Distinguished guests, the President of the United States." If you are ever in a situation in which you have to introduce the President, you will need no more than the eight words that begin this paragraph. The President is so well known that any further remarks would be inappropriate and almost foolish.

speech of introduction
A speech that introduces the main speaker to the audience.

Most of the time, however, a speech of introduction will be neither this brief nor this ritualized. If you are introducing another speaker, you will need to accomplish three purposes in your introduction:

Build enthusiasm for the upcoming speaker.

Build enthusiasm for the speaker's topic.

Establish a welcoming climate that will boost the speaker's credibility.

A good speech of introduction can be a delight to hear and can do much to ease the task of the main speaker. Usually you will say something about the speaker and about the topic—in that order. Following are some guidelines for speeches of introduction.

Be Brief

During World War I, Lord Balfour, Great Britain's foreign secretary, was to be the main speaker at a rally in the United States. But the speaker introducing Lord Balfour gave a 45-minute oration on the causes of the war. Then, almost as an afterthought, he said, "Now Lord Balfour will give his address." Lord Balfour rose and said, "I'm supposed to give my address in the brief time remaining. Here it is: 10 Carleton Gardens, London, England."[1]

Every speaker—and audience—who has ever sat through a long-winded introduction knows how dreary it can be. The purpose of a speech of introduction is to focus attention on the main speaker, not on the person making the introduction. Under normal circumstances, a speech of introduction will be no more than two to three minutes long, and it may be shorter if the speaker is already well known to the audience.

Make Sure Your Remarks Are Completely Accurate

Many an introducer has embarrassed himself or herself, as well as the main speaker, by garbling basic facts about the speaker. Always check with the speaker ahead of time to make sure your introduction is accurate in every respect.

Above all, get the speaker's name right. This may seem obvious, but it needs repeating. Remember that nothing is more important than a person's name. If the speaker's name is at all difficult—especially if it involves a foreign pronunciation—practice saying it well in advance. However, don't practice so much that you frighten yourself about getting it wrong. This was the plight of an announcer whose gaffe is now a classic: "Ladies and gentlemen, the President of the United States—Hoobert Heever!"

Adapt Your Remarks to the Occasion

In preparing your introduction, you may be constrained by the nature of the occasion. Formal occasions require formal speeches of introduction. If you were presenting a guest speaker at an informal business meeting, you might be much more casual than if you were presenting the same speaker to the same audience at a formal banquet.

Adapt Your Remarks to the Main Speaker

No matter how well it is received by the audience, a speech of introduction that leaves the main speaker feeling uncomfortable has failed in part of its purpose. How can you make a main speaker uncomfortable? One way is to overpraise the person—especially for his or her speaking skills. Never say, "Our speaker will keep you on the edge of your seat from beginning to end!" This is like prefacing a joke with the line, "Here is the funniest joke you've ever heard." You create a set of expectations that are almost impossible to fulfill.

Another way to create discomfort is by revealing embarrassing details of the speaker's personal life or by making remarks that are in poor taste from the speaker's point of view. An introducer may think this line is funny: "Why, I've known Anita Fratello since she was 10 years old and so fat that everybody in the class called her Blimpo!" To the speaker, however, the statement will probably not be a bit funny and may be painful.

Adapt Your Remarks to the Audience

Just as you adapt other speeches to particular audiences, so you need to adapt a speech of introduction to the audience you are facing. Your aim is to make *this* audience want to hear *this* speaker on *this* subject. If the speaker is not well known to the audience, you will need to establish her or his credibility by recounting some of the speaker's main achievements and explaining why she or he is qualified to speak on the topic at hand. But if the speaker is already personally known to the audience, it would be absurd to act as if the audience had never heard of the person.

Speeches for special occasions are part of the ceremonial aura that helps make certain events special—as in this address by Isabella Rossellini at a UNICEF dedication in New York City.

Also, you will want to tell each audience what *it* wants to hear—to give the kind of information that is interesting and accessible to the members of that audience. If you were introducing the same speaker to two different groups, some of the information in the speeches of introduction might be the same, but it would be slanted differently. Suppose, for example, J. K. Rowling, author of the Harry Potter series, is going to address two groups—an audience of elementary school children and an audience of educators at the annual meeting of the International Reading Association. The introduction to the schoolchildren might go something like this:

> Children, we have a very important guest today. You know her by the character she has created—Harry Potter. What you don't know is all the hard work that goes into writing the books that we all love to read. Today she is going to tell us how she came up with the idea of Harry Potter and his friends and how she goes about writing her books. Let's give a big round of applause to J. K. Rowling.

But the introduction to the International Reading Association would be along these lines:

> Ladies and gentlemen, it is my privilege to introduce to you today the world's best-selling author. We are all well acquainted with her Harry Potter series that has captured the imagination of children—and more than a few adults—around the globe.
>
> Many of us know the remarkable story of her writing life: The inspiration for Harry Potter came on a train ride from Manchester to London in 1990. Over the next few years, she compiled notes as the story took shape in her mind. The bulk of the writing took place when she was a single mother on public assistance in Edinburgh. She was teaching French to teenagers in the mid-1990s when she heard that the first Harry Potter book had been accepted for publication. The rest is literary history.

She will be telling us this afternoon more about what inspired her fascinating story of wizardry, where she gets her ideas, and what kinds of books she wants to write after Harry has safely—we hope—graduated from Hogwarts. Please give a warm welcome to J. K. Rowling.

Try to Create a Sense of Anticipation and Drama

You may have noticed one detail shared by the two speeches introducing J. K. Rowling: In both cases the speaker's name was saved for last. This is a convention in speeches of introduction. While there may occasionally be a good reason to break the convention, usually you will avoid mentioning the speaker's name until the final moment—even when the audience knows exactly whom you are discussing. By doing this you build a sense of drama, and the speaker's name comes as the climax of your introduction.

Often you will find yourself in the situation of introducing someone who is fairly well known to the audience—a classmate, a colleague at a business meeting, a neighbor in a community group. Then you should try to be creative and cast the speaker in a new light. Try to increase the audience's eagerness to hear the speaker. Talk to the speaker beforehand and see if you can learn some interesting facts that are not generally known—especially facts that relate to the speaker's topic.

Above all, if you expect to be creative and dramatic, be sure to practice your speech of introduction thoroughly. You should be able to deliver it extemporaneously, with sincerity and enthusiasm.

Speeches of Presentation

Speeches of presentation are given when someone is receiving publicly a gift, an award, or some other form of public recognition. Usually such speeches are relatively brief. They may be no more than a mere announcement ("And the winner is . . . ") or be up to four or five minutes in length.

As with other kinds of speeches, speeches of presentation need to be adapted to the audience and to the occasion. The main theme of a speech of presentation is to acknowledge the achievements of the recipient. You need to tell the audience why the recipient is receiving the award. Point out her or his contributions, achievements, and so forth. Do not deal with everything the person has ever done. Focus on achievements related to the award, and discuss these achievements in a way that will make them meaningful to the audience.

speech of presentation
A speech that presents someone a gift, an award, or some other form of public recognition.

Depending on the audience and the occasion, you may also need to discuss two other matters in a speech of presentation. First, if the audience is not familiar with the award and why it is being given, you should explain briefly—or at least allude to—the purpose of the award. Second, if the award was won in a public competition and the audience knows who the losers are, you might take a moment to praise the losers as well.

Below is a sample speech of presentation. It was delivered by President Bill Clinton in presenting the Congressional Gold Medal to former

South African President Nelson Mandela at a ceremony in the Rotunda of the United States Capitol in Washington, D.C. Because the Congressional Gold Medal is a special honor bestowed by the U.S. Congress, there are no public competitors for the award. Thus Clinton did not need to say anything about the "losers." His speech focused on Mandela's battle against apartheid and his efforts to promote reconciliation among the people of South Africa.

Presenting the Congressional Gold Medal

Bill Clinton

To my friend, President Mandela, Americans as one today, across all the lines that divide us, pay tribute to your struggle, to your achievement, and to the inspiration you have given us to do better. Today we offer a man who has received the Nobel Prize the highest honor within the gift of this country. . . .

Those of us who share his vision and lift him up in honor today owe it to him to build a permanent partnership between Americans and Africans—for the education of our children, for the solution of our problems, for the resolution of our differences, for the elevation of what is best about us all. . . .

In forgiving those who imprisoned him, he reminded us of the most fundamental lesson of all—that in the end apartheid was a defeat of the heart, the mind, the spirit. It was not just a structure outside and jail houses within which people were kept; it was a division of the mind and soul against itself. We owe it to Nelson Mandela not simply to give him this award, but to live by the lesson he taught us and to tear down every last vestige of apartheid in our own hearts—everything that divides us, one from another.

For those of us who have been privileged to know this remarkable man, no medal, no award, no fortune, nothing we could give him could possibly compare to the gift he has given to us and to the world. The only gift that is true recompense is to continue his mission and to live by the power of his profound and wonderful example.

Now, as prescribed by the law, it is my privilege to present the Congressional Gold Medal to President Nelson Mandela.

Speeches of Acceptance

The purpose of an acceptance speech is to give thanks for a gift or an award. When giving such a speech, you should thank the people who are bestowing the award, and you should recognize the people who helped you gain it.

acceptance speech
A speech that gives thanks for a gift, an award, or some other form of public recognition.

The acceptance speech that follows is the companion piece to the speech of presentation by Bill Clinton. It was delivered by Nelson Mandela in accepting the Congressional Gold Medal Award, and it exemplifies the major traits of a good acceptance speech—brevity, humility, and graciousness.[2]

Accepting the Congressional Gold Medal

Nelson Mandela

Thank you. President Clinton, Mr. Speaker, distinguished members of the Senate and the House, ladies and gentlemen . . .

It has been my great privilege to serve a people whose bondage to an inhuman system evoked the solidarity of all those who love freedom and justice, a people whose triumph over the divisions of racist doctrine has given new life to humanity's hope for a world without hatred and discrimination. I am conscious that in bestowing the Congressional Gold Medal upon me you are evoking these bonds between our nations and paying tribute to the whole South African nation for its achievements in realizing our shared ideals.

It is in that spirit that I humbly accept the award, aware at the same time of the great honor you do me by using me as the vehicle of a unique distinction conferred by this hallowed institution of American democracy. As one who has dedicated his life to the pursuit of unity, I am moved by the consensus in your nation's regard for the achievements of my people. And I feel a great pride in the fact that with a few citizens of other countries who have received this high honor, the name of an African is now added. . . .

The award with which you honor me today is an expression of the common humanity that binds us, one person to another, nation to nation, and people of the north to people of the south. I receive it with pride as a symbol of partnership for peace, prosperity, and equity as we enter the new millennium. I thank you.

CD 1: VIDEO 17.1

View an excerpt from Nelson Mandela's acceptance speech.

Commemorative Speeches

Commemorative speeches are speeches of praise or celebration. Eulogies, Fourth of July speeches, testimonial addresses, and dedications are examples of commemorative speeches. Your aim in such speeches is to pay tribute to a person, a group of people, an institution, or an idea.

As in an informative speech, you probably will have to give the audience information about your subject. After all, the audience must know *why* your subject is praiseworthy. They will need to know something about the history of the institution or the life of the person being praised. As in other speeches, you may draw on examples, testimony, even statistics to illustrate the achievements of your subject.

Your fundamental purpose in a commemorative speech, however, is not just to inform your listeners but to *inspire* them—to arouse and heighten their appreciation of or admiration for the person, institution, or idea you are praising. If you are paying tribute to a person, for example, you should not compose a biography that simply recounts the details of the person's life. Rather, you should create a speech that goes beyond biography—that penetrates to the *essence* of your subject and generates in your audience a deep sense of respect.

commemorative speech
A speech that pays tribute to a person, a group of people, an institution, or an idea.

When speaking to commemorate, you do not exhort like the advocate or explain like the lecturer. You want to express feelings, to stir sentiments—joy and hope when a new building is dedicated or a new President is inaugurated; anticipation and good wishes at a commencement celebration;

The primary traits of a good acceptance speech are brevity, humility, and graciousness. Here the late Arthur Miller accepts the National Book Foundation's Medal for Distinguished Contribution to American Letters.

lament and consolation at a funeral or memorial service; admiration and respect at a testimonial dinner. In some ways, a commemorative speech is like an impressionist painting—"a picture with warm colors and texture capturing a mood or a moment."[3]

But while the painter works with brush and colors, the commemorative speaker works with language. Of all the kinds of speeches, perhaps none depends more on the creative and subtle use of language than does the speech to commemorate. Some of the most memorable speeches in history, including Abraham Lincoln's Gettysburg Address, have been commemorative. We remember such speeches—we continue to find them meaningful and inspiring—largely because of their eloquent use of language.

CD I: VIDEO 17.2

View the ending of Ronald Reagan's eulogy to the *Challenger* astronauts.

One of the most effective commemorative speakers in our recent history was President Ronald Reagan. After the explosion of the space shuttle *Challenger* in 1986, Reagan delivered a nationally televised eulogy to the astronauts killed in the blast. Below are two versions of Reagan's closing lines. The first is what he *might* have said, stripping the text of its warm emotional content and poignant language:

> Like Francis Drake, the great explorer of the oceans, the *Challenger* astronauts gave their lives for a cause to which they were fully dedicated. We are honored by them, and we will not forget them. We will always remember seeing them for the last time this morning as they prepared for their flight.

Here is what Reagan *actually* said:

> There's a coincidence today. On this day 390 years ago, the great explorer Francis Drake died aboard ship off the coast of Panama. In his lifetime the great frontiers were

the oceans, and an historian later said, "He lived by the sea, died on it, was buried in it." Well, today we can say of the *Challenger* crew: Their dedication was, like Drake's, complete.

The crew of the space shuttle *Challenger* honored us by the manner in which they lived their lives. We will never forget them, nor the last time we saw them, this morning, as they prepared for their journey and waved goodbye and "slipped the surly bonds of earth" to "touch the face of God."

The final words—"'slipped the surly bonds of earth' to 'touch the face of God'"—are especially effective. Drawn from a sonnet called "High Flight" that many pilots keep with them, they ennoble the deaths of the astronauts and end the speech on an eloquent, moving, and poetic note.

When speaking to commemorate, you will deal for the most part with intangibles. Your success will depend on your ability to put into language the thoughts and emotions appropriate to the occasion. It is easy—too easy—to fall back on clichés and trite sentiments. Your challenge will be to use language imaginatively in order to invest the occasion with dignity, meaning, and honest emotion.

In doing so, you may want to utilize the special resources of language discussed in Chapter 11 to enhance the imagery and rhythm of your prose. Metaphor, simile, parallelism, repetition, antithesis, alliteration—all are appropriate for commemorative speeches. Some highly acclaimed commemorative speeches—including Martin Luther King's "I Have a Dream" and John Kennedy's inaugural address—are distinguished by their creative use of such devices.

Confronted with the evocative speeches of a Kennedy or a King, you may decide that the speech of commemoration is far beyond your abilities. But other students have delivered excellent commemorative speeches—not immortal, perhaps, but nonetheless dignified and moving.

Look, for example, at "My Crazy Aunt Sue" in the appendix of sample speeches that follows Chapter 18 (pages A17–A18). The speaker's aim was to pay tribute to her aunt, who for years had battled heroically against the debilitating disease of rheumatoid arthritis. Although the speaker provides basic information about aunt Sue and her physical condition, the speech is not a biography. It does not seek to recount all the details of aunt Sue's life. Instead, it focuses on her courage, her sense of humor, and her refusal to complain about her fate. The speaker provides enough details to let us see why aunt Sue is so commendable, but not so many as to slow the pace of the speech.

The speaker also uses vivid language, repetition, and parallel structure to give the speech the kind of formal tone appropriate for a commemorative speech. You can see this even in the opening lines, which set the tone for the rest of the speech:

The strongest person I know cannot peel a potato. The strongest person I know has trouble putting on her makeup. The strongest person I know needs a special key holder to turn the key in her car's ignition.

In addition to arousing curiosity about the subject of the speech, these lines have a simple elegance that comes partly from the repetition of "The strongest person I know" at the start of each sentence. Consider, in contrast, how much less effective the opening would have been if the speaker had said:

> My aunt Sue can't peel a potato, has trouble putting on her makeup, and needs a special key holder to turn the key in her car's ignition.

CD 2: FULL SPEECH

View "My Crazy Aunt Sue."

These lines convey the same information, but not with the same effect. When you construct your commemorative speech, think how you can phrase your ideas to give them special meaning and impact.

For another example, consider the student commemorative speech that is printed below. The subject is the 54th Regiment of the Massachusetts Volunteer Infantry. The first black regiment to fight in the Civil War, the Massachusetts 54th had a distinguished record of bravery and was later immortalized in the movie *Glory.* As you read the speech, notice how effectively the speaker uses the resources of language to give his ideas artistic unity and emotional power.

The Massachusetts 54th

Staring at a once beautiful valley now filled with bodies that serve only as a reminder of the morning's gruesome events, a lonely grave digger thinks to himself. Unable to fight in the Civil War because he is black, he can only bury the soldiers that fight and die for his freedom, wondering when he will get his chance to fight.

In the movie *Glory,* this grave digger is played by Morgan Freeman, and he is given his chance to fight as a member of the 54th Regiment of the Massachusetts Volunteer Infantry. The Massachusetts 54th was the first black regiment of the Civil War. Led by Colonel Robert Gould Shaw, the 54th showed remarkable bravery, patriotism, and sacrifice.

Even though the North was opposed to slavery, many Northerners held on to anti-black attitudes. Because of these attitudes, the Massachusetts 54th was given dangerous assignments and equipped with substandard, or even broken, equipment. Wearing shoes no better than wrapped cloth, tattered uniforms that did little or nothing to ward off the cold, and using guns that would misfire every other shot, the 54th still proved to be one of the bravest regiments in the Civil War.

On top of their bravery, the members of the Massachusetts 54th exhibited the highest levels of patriotism. Despite the racism and other struggles they faced, they were proud to wear their uniforms and to carry the Union flag into battle. Their patriotism can best be seen when one observes the number of deserters from this regiment—none. Despite the thousands of desertions suffered by many other regiments on the Northern side, not a single soldier deserted from the Massachusetts 54th.

I have spoken so far of bravery and of patriotism, but it is the sacrifice of the 54th that has etched them into the pages of history. That sacrifice occurred during the assault on Fort Wagner in 1863. This heavily guarded Confederate fort lay on the beaches of South Carolina, nearly unapproachable. A frontal assault was needed to weaken the fort enough to allow for a full-scale attack. It was a suicidal mission, but the 54th volunteered for it.

They were the first regiment to storm Fort Wagner, and so would suffer the highest casualties. Rushing forward, they reached the fort well before any reinforcements that were supposed to back them up. Believing the reinforcements to be close behind, the 54th attacked Fort Wagner and found nothing but the enemy. When the charge was over, more than 250 soldiers from the regiment had been killed, wounded, or captured.

To join an army that didn't believe in you. To fight with an army who didn't like you. To die for an army that didn't respect you. This was the Massachusetts 54th. Today they lay where they died, on the beaches of South Carolina. Colonel Shaw and his men were piled together in a mass grave, which has since been covered by the shifting tides of the Atlantic. A small statue stands in Boston—a reminder of their sacrifice.

Bravery, patriotism, and sacrifice. These are qualities of the Massachusetts 54th. With the help of their efforts, along with all the other black regiments that followed them, slavery did eventually come to an end.

In the movie *Glory,* Morgan Freeman talks of his chance to fight for the freedom of his own people. The 54th grasped this chance, they fought for it, and they eventually died for it. In the words of Union General Truman Seymour, "On every inch of the sands in front of Fort Wagner will be forever traced in undying glory the story of the determination and courage of the Massachusetts 54th."

CD 2: FULL SPEECH

View "The Massachusetts 54th."

After-Dinner Speeches

After-dinner speeches may be harder to define than any other kind of speech. While the custom of saying a few words of tribute or celebration after a meal is as old as civilization itself, after-dinner speeches as a formal type of speech developed in England during the early 1800s. At that time, they were delivered, literally, after dinner. Today, because of the popularity of lunch meetings for various civic and business groups, you are as likely to hear an "after-dinner" speech during the noon hour as during the evening.

After-dinner speeches are best thought of as a kind of speech to entertain. Whether presented after breakfast, lunch, or dinner—in a formal dining room or at an outdoor barbecue—they usually have a lighter tone than a speech to inform or to persuade. This difference in tone will obviously have some impact on your choice of topic. AIDS, child abuse, terrorism, drunk driving, gun violence—all are important, but audiences do not expect to hear about such weighty matters in the relaxed atmosphere of the typical after-dinner speech. For the most part, though, any topic suitable for an informative or persuasive speech can be appropriate for an after-dinner speech, as long as you approach it in a lighthearted manner.

after-dinner speech
A speech to entertain that makes a thoughtful point about its subject in a lighthearted manner.

Suppose your subject is nutrition. If you were giving an informative speech on this topic, your specific purpose might be "To inform my audience of the four basic nutrients in the human diet." If you were presenting a persuasive speech, your specific purpose might be "To persuade my audience that they should reduce their consumption of red meat in favor of more fish, vegetables, and grains." But if you were giving an after-dinner speech on the topic of nutrition, your specific purpose might be "To entertain my audience by showing them the ridiculous extremes some people go to in following special diets."

As this example suggests, after-dinner speeches should not be technical or argumentative. They may contain information that is new to the audience, and they may even have a persuasive impact, but their supporting materials

THE INTERNET *Connection*

As discussed in this chapter, Ronald Reagan's eulogy to the *Challenger* astronauts is one of the most effective commemorative speeches in U.S. history and was judged the eighth best speech of the 20th century. You can read the entire text of Reagan's address, along with the rest of the top 100, at www.mhhe.com/lucastop100.

Presidential inaugural addresses are a major kind of special-occasion speech. You can access these historical documents at either Bartleby's Inaugural Addresses of the Presidents (www.bartleby.com/124/) or the Yale Law School's Avalon Project (www.yale.edu/lawweb/avalon/presiden/inaug/inaug.htm).

ONLINE LEARNING CENTER

You can link to these Web sites at www.mhhe.com/lucas9.

should be chosen primarily for their entertainment value. Audiences for after-dinner speeches are seldom in a mood to follow a close train of reasoning or a complicated set of statistics. They are looking for a good-natured speech that stimulates the imagination by approaching the topic in a novel way, treating it lightly, even whimsically.

This is not to say that after-dinner speeches should be rambling or totally frivolous. Like all other speeches, they require careful preparation and organization. They should have a central theme, and they should strive to make a thoughtful point about that theme—whether it is an aspect of human nature (such as vanity or the desire for immortality), of college life (such as final exams or finding a decent apartment), of work (such as putting up with the boss or dealing with weird customers), of travel (such as poor service by the airlines or dealing with unusual customs abroad), of family life (such as the perils of summer vacations or the experience of being a parent for the first time), or even of current events (such as how we choose presidential candidates or jitters over the stock market).

As you might imagine, humor can be an important part of after-dinner speeches. Some of America's finest after-dinner speakers have been humorists such as Mark Twain and Dave Barry, but you don't need to be a stand-up comic to be a successful after-dinner speaker. The purpose of humor in an after-dinner speech is more to provoke smiles or chuckles than to convulse the audience with a series of one-liners. Nor is humor used merely to make the audience laugh. In the best speeches, humor grows naturally out of the speech materials and helps the speaker make his or her point by providing special insight into the topic.

Tickling an audience's funnybone, however, can be difficult even for accomplished public speakers. If you don't feel confident working for a laugh, don't worry. Humor can contribute to a successful after-dinner speech, but it is not essential. Indeed, the best approach is usually not to work specifically for laughs. If you deal with the topic creatively, select supporting materials that are interesting in their own right, and use the resources of language to create sharp imagery, vivid descriptions, colorful details, and clever phrasing, you should do just fine.

All these traits can be seen in the following after-dinner speech, which was delivered in a public speaking class at the University of Wisconsin.

The Horror of It All

They never did find his head or hands. I crouched in the corner, peering through my fingers as he moaned and wailed in an endless search for his missing appendages. I was terrified—but not as terrified as poor Bette Davis. They put her in the nuthouse. I simply turned on the light and ran to the safety of my father's lap. As I perched, shuddering, he said the phrase I was to hear over and over through the coming years, "It's okay, it's only a movie." It did not end for me there, however. The movie *Hush, Hush, Sweet Charlotte* was just the beginning of my love/hate relationship with horror movies.

My scaredy-cat tendencies actually began at a very early age. As a young child, I insisted the hall light be kept on when I went to bed—no measly night-light would do for a hard-core chicken. My parents would come upstairs after the news and tell each other to "turn off the l-i-g-h-t." I could be heard miles away screaming, "NO! I know what that spells!" After *The Ghost and Mr. Chicken* with Don Knotts, my bedtime ritual went something like this—look under the bed, look in the closet, turn off the light, and leap into the sack. As time passed, however, this childish nonsense began to subside. I was growing up.

But then it happened. Theater owners offered up *The Exorcist,* a temptation I could not resist. That delicious, horrible feeling of being terrified was renewed. I was hooked. I stayed pretty sane, though, until I read the book, at which time I discovered I was possessed by the Devil. I had six of the ten symptoms, including headaches, nausea, and loss of sleep. It may not have been Satan himself, but there was definitely a demon lurking somewhere.

Over the next several years, the movie industry fed my passion for terror—and my paranoia. The movie *Halloween* ended any possibility of parking on a deserted road after a date. I was not going to fog up the windows making myself a sitting duck for any escaped mental patient. The *Friday the 13th* series put a stop to any thought of camping overnight in the wilderness, while *Night of the Living Dead* put a dent in my car. I was in such a panic to get out of the dark parking lot after viewing this old classic that I slammed into a pole, causing $300 damage to my trusty Chevy.

My fright-flick fanaticism was taking a toll on my everyday life. I began to notice that guys who took me to these movies didn't often ask me out again—apparently my squirming and screaming in the theater embarrassed them a bit. Some people just don't know how to really get into a movie. I no longer took babysitting jobs because I was afraid to be alone in a strange house. I wouldn't do laundry at night because that meant I had to go down to the basement.

My fears weren't even limited to being alone. One Friday night I was home watching HBO with my Mom. Let me explain that our house is situated in the dead center of a very isolated woods. As a kid I remember thinking it would be an ideal place for escaped convicts to hide out and hold hostages. Anyway, there we were, munching away on junk food, when suddenly the lights went out. Keep in mind that this was a calm summer evening—no rain, no lightning, not even any wind. There was only one explanation—we had a madman in the basement.

In my alarm I turned to the woman who had protected me all my life. My Mom looked at me and said the only thing she could say, "Grab the potato chips." Chips and keys in tow, we bolted for the car. But this was not to be the end of our ordeal—no electricity, no electric garage door opener. I looked at my Mom and said the only thing I could say, "Ram it!" Bravely, Mom kept her head. She crept out of the security of the locked car to manually open the garage door and drive us, in our pajamas, to safety. It was then that I knew I was out of control. It was then that I decided to go cold turkey—no more horror films.

It's been two years now, and I can finally look back at these escapades and laugh. It's been two years now, and I pride myself on the fact that I live alone. The only thing that keeps me awake nights these days is writing speeches. I'm not going to end up in the nuthouse like Bette Davis. But I'm not going to get too overconfident, either. Remember all those unsuspecting kids in *Halloween?* They were just out having a good time when, WHAM—and the rest is history.

Summary

Special occasions include weddings, funerals, dedications, award ceremonies, retirement dinners, and the like. Nearly always they are occasions for speechmaking. In this chapter we have considered speeches of introduction, speeches of presentation, speeches of acceptance, commemorative speeches, and after-dinner speeches.

When you make a speech of introduction, your job is to build enthusiasm for the main speaker and to establish a welcoming climate that will boost his or her credibility and confidence. Keep your remarks brief, make sure they are completely accurate, and adapt them to the audience, the occasion, and the main speaker.

Speeches of presentation are given when someone is receiving publicly a gift or an award. The main theme of such a speech is to acknowledge the achievements of the recipient. The purpose of an acceptance speech is to give thanks for a gift or an award. When delivering such a speech, you should thank the people who are bestowing the award and recognize the contributions of people who helped you gain it. Be brief, humble, and gracious.

Commemorative speeches are speeches of praise or celebration. Your aim in such a speech is to pay tribute to a person, a group of people, an institution, or an idea. When making a commemorative speech you want to inspire your audience—to arouse and heighten their appreciation of and admiration for the subject. Your success will depend largely on how well you put into language the thoughts and feelings appropriate to the occasion.

After-dinner speeches are best thought of as a kind of speech to entertain, and they usually have a lighter tone than informative or persuasive speeches. Neither technical nor argumentative, they seek to stimulate the imagination by approaching the topic in a novel or unexpected way. Although humor can be an important part of after-dinner speeches, it is not essential. If you do use humor, it should grow naturally out of the speech materials and provide insight into the topic.

Key Terms

ONLINE LEARNING CENTER

Review these terms by doing the Chapter 17 crossword puzzle at www.mhhe.com/lucas9.

speech of introduction (470)
speech of presentation (473)
acceptance speech (474)
commemorative speech (475)
after-dinner speech (479)

Review Questions

After reading this chapter, you should be able to answer the following questions:

1. What are the three purposes of a speech of introduction? What guidelines should you follow in preparing such a speech?
2. What is the main theme of a speech of presentation? Depending on the audience and occasion, what two other themes might you include in such a speech?
3. What are the three major traits of a good acceptance speech?
4. What is the fundamental purpose of a commemorative speech? Why does a successful commemorative speech depend so much on the creative and subtle use of language?
5. What is the primary difference between an after-dinner speech and a speech to inform or to persuade? What is the role of humor in after-dinner speaking?

CD 1: STUDY QUESTIONS

For further review, go to the Study Questions for this chapter.

Exercises for Critical Thinking

1. Attend a speech on campus. Pay special attention to the speech introducing the main speaker. How well does it fit the guidelines discussed in this chapter?
2. Observe several speeches of presentation and acceptance—at a campus awards ceremony or on a television program such as the Academy Awards, Grammy Awards, Emmy Awards, or Tony Awards. Which speeches do you find most effective? Least effective? Why?
3. Analyze "The Massachusetts 54th" (pages 478–479) in light of the criteria for commemorative speaking presented in this chapter.
4. Analyze "The Horror of It All" (pages 481–482) in light of the criteria for after-dinner speaking discussed in this chapter.

Notes

[1]James C. Humes, *Roles Speakers Play* (New York: Harper and Row, 1976), p. 8.

[2]For both speeches, see "Remarks by President Clinton and President Nelson Mandela at Presentation of the Congressional Gold Medal to President Nelson Mandela," September 23, 1998. <*http://clinton4.nara.gov/WH/New/html/19980923-977.html*> January 28, 2003.

[3]Humes, *Roles Speakers Play,* pp. 33–34, 36.

CHAPTER EIGHTEEN

Speaking in Small Groups

What Is a Small Group?

Leadership in Small Groups

Kinds of Leadership

Functions of Leadership

Responsibilities in a Small Group

Commit Yourself to the Goals of Your Group

Fulfill Individual Assignments

Avoid Interpersonal Conflicts

Encourage Full Participation

Keep the Discussion on Track

The Reflective-Thinking Method

Define the Problem

Analyze the Problem

Establish Criteria for Solutions

Generate Potential Solutions

Select the Best Solution

Presenting the Recommendations of the Group

Oral Report

Symposium

Panel Discussion

The publisher of a national sports magazine asked Mike Lee, the new head of the human resources department, to organize an October retreat for the magazine's editorial staff. Mike went to work on setting a date, finding a place to stay, and creating an agenda for the retreat.

Mike was very pleased with his plan. He thought he had taken everyone's needs into account. But when he explained his plan at the magazine's next staff meeting, no one seemed happy.

"The date you set for the retreat is over Halloween," said the editorial manager. "I know you don't have children, but no one with kids is going to want to be away at that time."

The administrative assistant responded next. "Do you realize," she said, "that the hotel you booked is the same one we used for a retreat five years ago? It was a disaster! The food was awful, the meeting rooms were uncomfortable, and the tech support was nonexistent."

Next a member of the magazine's junior editorial staff said, "I see that all the sessions involve members of the senior editorial staff. Did you mean to exclude all the younger editors? Don't you think we're important to the magazine?"

Finally, the managing editor said, "I wish you had checked with me at some point. I could have warned you about the hotel, the conflict with Halloween, and the need to include junior staff."

What went wrong? Mike did not have enough time or resources on his own to create a successful retreat. If a group, instead of a single person, had been assigned to plan the retreat, the problems might have been averted. One person could have taken charge of looking into the best dates, another of finding accommodations, a third of coordinating with other staff members about who should be included in the retreat, and so forth. The plan would have taken *all* factors into account.

Of course, you may have heard the old saying that "a camel is a horse designed by a committee." If you have ever been part of a group that seemed to get nothing done, you may be inclined to say, "Oh, let one person decide and get it over with." The problem in such cases, however, is not that there is a group, but that the group is not functioning properly. A great deal of research shows that if members of a group work well together, they can almost always resolve a problem better than a single person.[1]

This chapter deals with speaking in a particular kind of group—the problem-solving small group.

What Is a Small Group?

dyad
A group of two people.

As its name implies, a small group has a limited number of members. The minimum number is three. (A group of two persons is called a *dyad,* and it operates quite differently from a group of three or more.) There is some difference of opinion about the maximum number of people who constitute a small group. Most experts set the maximum number at seven or eight; some go as high as twelve.[2] The important point is that the group must be small enough to allow free discussion among all members. In small-group communication, all participants are potentially speakers *and* listeners. A manageable number of people permits everyone to shift easily between speaking and listening.

Members of a small group assemble for a specific purpose. They are not just a band of three to twelve people who happen to end up in the same room. Several shoppers milling around the clothing section of a department store are not a small group, even if they speak to one another or comment about high prices and poor service. But if those same shoppers decided to meet together and prepare a formal complaint to the store manager about high prices and poor service, they would then constitute a small group. They would have assembled for a specific purpose.

small group
A collection of three to twelve people who assemble for a specific purpose.

A *problem-solving small group* is formed to solve a particular problem. Such groups exist in every area of life. Business groups consider ways of increasing sales. Church groups discuss how to raise funds and provide for the needy. Groups of parents work on improving day care facilities. The President's cabinet debates a foreign policy move. A ski club evaluates proposals for the next outing. You will almost surely be a member of many problem-solving small groups during your life.

problem-solving small group
A small group formed to solve a particular problem.

Although speaking in a small group is not the same as public speaking, it involves many similar skills. Members of a small group influence one another through communication. At times they inform their fellow members. At other times they seek to persuade them. As a participant in a small group, you might influence your colleagues by giving them important information, by encouraging them to speak, by convincing them to change their minds, by leading them into a new channel of communication, even by getting them to end a meeting of the group. All other members of the group have the same opportunity to influence you through effective communication.[3]

Leadership in Small Groups

We have said that small groups often make better decisions than do individuals. But the word "often" should be stressed here. To make sound decisions, groups need effective leadership.

Kinds of Leadership

Sometimes there is *no specific leader.* In such a situation, members of effective groups tend to have equal influence. When a need for leadership arises, any of the members can—and one probably will—provide the necessary leadership. A typical instance might be a class project, in which you and several classmates are working together. From time to time each of you will help the group move toward its goal by suggesting when and where to meet, by outlining the strengths and weaknesses of a certain viewpoint, by resolving disagreements among other members, and so forth.

leadership
The ability to influence group members so as to help achieve the goals of the group.

In some circumstances a group may have an *implied leader.* For example, if a business meeting includes one vice president and several subordinates, the vice president becomes the implied leader. The same is true if one member

implied leader
A group member to whom other members defer because of her or his rank, expertise, or other quality.

of the group is a specialist in the topic at hand and the others are not. Members will likely defer to the person with the highest rank or greatest expertise, and that person will become the group's implied leader.

emergent leader
A group member who emerges as a leader during the group's deliberations.

Even when a group starts out leaderless, there may be an *emergent leader.* This is a person who, by ability or by force of personality, or just by talking the most, takes a leadership role. The emergence of a leader may or may not be desirable. If the group is stalemated or has dissolved into bickering or making jokes, an emergent leader can put the group back on track. There is a danger, however, that the emergent leader may be not the most effective leader but merely the most assertive personality. Ideally, each member of the group should be prepared to assume a leadership role when necessary.

designated leader
A person who is elected or appointed as leader when the group is formed.

Finally, there may be a *designated leader*—a person elected or appointed as leader when the group is formed. A group that meets for only one session should almost always have a designated leader who takes care of the procedural tasks and serves as spokesperson for the group. Likewise, a formal committee will usually have a designated chairperson. The chair can perform leadership functions or delegate them, but he or she remains in charge of the group.[4]

A group may or may not need a specific leader, but it always needs leader*ship*. When all members of the group are skilled communicators, they can take turns at providing leadership even if the group has a designated or implied leader. As you develop group communication skills, you should be prepared to assume a leadership role whenever necessary.[5]

Functions of Leadership

An effective leader helps the group reach its goals by fulfilling three overlapping sets of needs—procedural needs, task needs, and maintenance needs.

Procedural Needs

procedural needs
Routine "housekeeping" actions necessary for the efficient conduct of business in a small group.

Procedural needs can be thought of as the "housekeeping" requirements of the group. They include:

- Deciding when and where the group will meet.
- Reserving the room, checking the number of chairs, making sure the heat or air conditioning is turned on.
- Setting the agenda of each meeting.
- Starting the meeting.
- Taking notes during the meeting.
- Preparing and distributing any written handouts needed for the meeting.
- Summarizing the group's progress at the end of the meeting.

If there is a designated leader, she or he can attend to these needs or assign one or more group members to do so. Otherwise, members of the group must devise ways to split the procedural responsibilities.

Small groups require effective leadership to accomplish their goals. Some groups have a designated leader, while others have an implied leader or an emergent leader.

Task Needs

Task needs go beyond procedural needs and are substantive actions necessary to help the group complete the particular task it is working on. They include:

task needs
Substantive actions necessary to help a small group complete its assigned task.

Analyzing the issues facing the group.

Distributing the workload among the members.

Collecting information.

Soliciting the views of other members.

Keeping the group from going off on a tangent.

Playing devil's advocate for unpopular ideas.

Formulating criteria for judging the most effective solution.

Helping the group reach consensus on its final recommendations.

Most members will help the group satisfy its task needs. Leadership becomes necessary when some task needs are not being fulfilled adequately, as in this example:

A group of students had undertaken to solve the parking problems on their campus. The group had held several meetings, and most of its task needs had been met. Members had done a good job polling students for their opinions, discussing alternative solutions with the administration, and considering the relative merits of each solution. However, one member of the group, Pilar, noticed that two items had not been given enough attention: No one had investigated potential sources of money for new parking facilities, and no one had studied the environmental impact of constructing additional parking spaces. Therefore, Pilar briefly took a leadership role to perform a task need for the group. She pointed out that these two areas had been neglected and recommended that the group explore them further.

The effective leader—whether permanent or temporary—has a realistic notion of the group's task needs and of how to meet them.

Maintenance Needs

maintenance needs Communicative actions necessary to maintain interpersonal relations in a small group.

Maintenance needs involve interpersonal relations in the group. They include such factors as:

How well members get along with one another.

How willing members are to contribute to the group.

Whether members are supportive of one another.

Whether members feel satisfied with the group's accomplishments.

Whether members feel good about their roles in the group.

If interpersonal problems dominate discussion, the group will have a difficult time working together and reaching a decision. This is one of the more important areas calling for effective leadership. A leader can do much to create and sustain supportive communication in the group. By helping group members handle conflict, by working out differences of opinion, by reducing interpersonal tension, by encouraging participation from all members, by being alert to personal feelings, and by promoting solidarity within the group, a leader can make a tremendous contribution toward helping the group achieve its goals.[6]

Responsibilities in a Small Group

Every member of a small group must assume certain responsibilities, which can be divided into five major categories: (1) commit yourself to the goals of your group; (2) fulfill individual assignments; (3) avoid interpersonal conflicts; (4) encourage full participation; (5) keep the discussion on track. Some of these responsibilities involve leadership roles, but all five are so important that each participant should take them as personal obligations, regardless of the group's leadership. Let us look more closely at each of these responsibilities.

Commit Yourself to the Goals of Your Group

For a group to succeed, members must align their personal goals with the group's goal. This sounds obvious, but it is not always easy. When you are working with other students on a class project, the group goal—and most likely the goal of each member—is to get a good grade, which should ensure a positive attitude toward the group. There is a strong incentive for members to cooperate and commit themselves to completing the task.

Problems arise when one or more members have personal goals that conflict with the group's goal. Here is the kind of situation that can occur:

Sherri Baines is a member of the committee to buy new equipment for the local newspaper's employee cafeteria. Because the budget is very tight, the committee's goal is to get the best equipment for the lowest price. But unknown to the other members of the group, Sherri's son-in-law is a salesman for a distributor of high-priced kitchen appliances. Privately, Sherri has reasoned that if she can sway the committee toward that company, her son-in-law will get a large commission. Sherri does not mention this fact to the group. Instead, she argues that *quality*—not price—should be the determining factor in the purchase. The group process breaks down because Sherri will not surrender her private goal.

This is an extreme example, but there can be more subtle kinds of private goals, as in the following case:

Carlos and Rachel are part of a group, and Carlos would like to be on closer terms with Rachel. In order to impress her, he may agree with everything she says, regardless of whether he really shares her views. Consequently, Carlos's expressed views are not his actual views. In short, Carlos has a *hidden agenda* in the group meeting. The group's agenda is to solve the problem, but Carlos's agenda is to get a date with Rachel.

Group members may have all sorts of hidden agendas. One may be experiencing personal problems—lowered grades, a breakup with a friend, trouble at home, or just a bad day. Another may have a commitment to a different group whose goals conflict with those of the present group. A third may want to take charge of the group for reasons of personal power, regardless of the group's task.

hidden agenda
A set of unstated individual goals that may conflict with the goals of the group as a whole.

Remember that what one member of a group does affects all the other members. You should not try to advance your own interests or boost your own ego at the expense of the group and its goals. Beware of hidden agendas—whether yours or someone else's—and participate with a positive spirit. If a group is to work effectively, all members must commit themselves to the goals of the group and cooperate to achieve them.

Fulfill Individual Assignments

As mentioned earlier, one of the advantages of the group process is that it divides the workload among several people. Work assignments might involve gathering information, making arrangements for a meeting, researching a particular aspect of the group's topic, taking notes at a meeting, and so forth. Unless every member fulfills his or her assignments, the group's entire project may fail—as in the following example:

Several years ago, one student group decided that as a class project they would bring Easter baskets to the patients in the children's ward of a local hospital. After the project had been approved, assignments were given out. Navid would coordinate with the hospital authorities. Corrine would handle fund-raising for the needed supplies. Jesse would supervise the egg-decorating team. Liu would be responsible for buying baskets and chocolate bunnies. Justin would arrange for transportation to the hospital.

Everybody completed their assignments except Justin, who was busy writing a term paper. He asked a friend to pick up a bus schedule and assumed everything would be fine. On Easter morning the group assembled at the bus stop, loaded down with baskets for the children. And they waited and waited. After an hour Justin called the bus company, only to discover that the buses did not run on holidays. By the time Justin had made other arrangements to get to the hospital, visiting hours were over, and the group could not get in.

No matter what other assignments they may have, *all* members of a group have one very critical assignment—listening. If you tune out the person who is speaking, or if you concentrate entirely on what *you* plan to say next, the group is not going to make much progress.

Effective listening is vital to small-group communication. First, it helps you understand what is happening in the group. And unlike a public speaking situation, you can stop the speaker and ask for clarification on any point about which you are confused. Second, listening helps you evaluate the merits of the speaker's position in relation to your own. Third, listening provides support for the speaker and helps establish a positive climate for discussion. In group discussion, as in other kinds of situations, listening is crucial to effective communication.[7]

Avoid Interpersonal Conflicts

If groups were made up of robots, there would be no problem with interpersonal conflicts. But groups are made up of people—people with likes and dislikes and animosities and prejudices and very different personalities. It is vital to the group process that disagreements be kept on a task level, rather than on a personal level.

Suppose you disagree with another member's idea. Disagreement on the personal level could sound like this: "That's the most stupid idea I ever heard of! Do you realize how much money it would cost to do that?" But on the task level, disagreement is aimed at the *idea,* not the person: "Potentially that's a very good solution, but I'm not sure we have enough money to accomplish it."

When disagreements are allowed to become personal, some members may start to see the group as a kind of debating society. Rather than focusing on the task, they may spend their time getting even with other participants, defending themselves, trying to score points, and jumping on people's ideas. Other members—especially those who are shy or soft-spoken—may recoil from the verbal combat and withdraw from active participation in the group's deliberations.

No matter what the group, personal antagonism leaves a bad taste in everyone's mouth and harms the performance of the group. It's essential that someone take a leadership role and bring the discussion back to the relevant issues. Let's say you are part of a committee charged with setting up a

THE INTERNET *Connection*

Interested in learning more about leadership? Log on to the Center for Creative Leadership's research site at www.ccl.org/research/. The center works with individuals and groups around the world to help organizations of all kinds improve their managerial and leadership skills.

The University of North Texas Center for the Study of Work Teams deals with a wide range of topics relevant to small-group communication. You can access the center's Web site at www.workteams.unt.edu/.

ONLINE LEARNING CENTER

You can link to these Web sites at www.mhhe.com/lucas9.

speakers' series on your campus. The discussion might go like this:

Angela: We definitely should have Representative Hightower speak on campus. He has been very active in protecting the environment.

Minh: That bleeding heart liberal? All he cares about are rabbits and trees. He could care less about economic development. No way he's going to speak here.

Angela: Oh, so you're willing to destroy our national forests and wilderness areas just to get a few more barrels of oil?

Minh: It's people like you that have made us dependent on foreign sources of oil—which threatens our prosperity and national security by making us vulnerable to economic blackmail from abroad.

Leader: Just a minute. This might make a good subject for our speakers' series. We can ask both Representative Hightower and a spokesperson for one of the oil companies to debate each other.

None of this is to say that members of a group should never disagree. In fact, a serious problem occurs when members get along so well and are so concerned about maintaining the harmony of the group that they will not disagree with one another about anything. Whenever one member makes a suggestion, everybody else thinks it's a wonderful idea. When this happens, the group misses the benefit of having a group in the first place. There is no chance to reach the best decision by exploring an array of perspectives, opinions, and information. A group that is concerned above all with dodging disagreement will not be any more effective than one that dissolves into personal quarreling.

The point, then, is not that groups should avoid conflict but that they should keep it at the task level and not allow it to degenerate into personal feuding. There is usually little achievement—and even less feeling of satisfaction—when a group is consumed by personal bickering and antagonism.

Encourage Full Participation

If a group is to work effectively, all members must contribute fully and share their ideas with one another. Every member of a group should take responsibility for encouraging other members to participate. You can do this, first of all, by listening attentively. Listening provides support for the speaker. After all, how would you like to speak in a group where everybody else appears bored or distracted?

If there are one or two quiet members in the group, you can draw them into the discussion by asking their opinions and showing your interest in their ideas and information. For instance, you can say something like, "We haven't heard from Jason in a while, and he has some personal experience in this matter. Jason, can you tell the others what you told me about this plan?"

Another way to encourage participation is to help build a supportive environment. When a member speaks, you can say, "That's an interesting idea." Or "I never knew that; can you tell us more about it?" Conversely, try to avoid negative comments that will squelch a speaker before she or he has finished—comments like "Oh, no, that never works" or "What a dumb idea." Supportive comments create goodwill among group members and make everyone feel free to discuss their ideas without ridicule or embarrassment.

If you are shy or afraid your ideas will be taken too critically, you may be unwilling to participate at first. To overcome your diffidence, try to remember that your contribution is necessary to the group. This is why you are there. At the very least, you can help provide a supportive environment for discussion by listening, reacting, and encouraging the free exchange of ideas.

Keep the Discussion on Track

In some groups the discussion proceeds like a stream-of-consciousness exercise. Here is a hypothetical example in which a town planning board is considering installing a new traffic light at a busy intersection:

Sharif: You know, we're going to have trouble getting cars to come to a full stop even if we do put in a traffic light.

Diana: Tell me about it! I came through there yesterday and hit my brakes, and the car just kept going. Maybe I need the brakes adjusted, though.

Mike: Get ready to pay through the nose. I had a brake job on my car last week, and it was nearly twice as much as last time.

Rico: That's nothing. Have you looked at lawnmowers lately? And if you think lawnmowers are high . . .

Jill: Who mows lawns? I had my yard planted with ground cover and put gravel over the rest. It's . . .

Leader: Excuse me, folks, but weren't we talking about the *traffic light?*

Every member has a responsibility to keep the discussion on track and to intervene if the group wanders too far afield. There is nothing wrong with a little casual conversation to break the tension or provide a brief respite from work, but it shouldn't be allowed to get out of hand. When working

In effective small groups, all members participate fully and interact with each other. They also feel that their contributions are respected and valued by the full group.

in a problem-solving group, make sure the group's ultimate goal is always in the forefront. Do your best to see that discussion proceeds in an orderly fashion from one point to the next and that the group does not get bogged down in side issues.

On the other hand, you need to guard against the tendency to progress to a solution too quickly, without thoroughly exploring the problem. This concern can be especially serious when members of a group are tired or discouraged. If you feel your group is taking the easy way out and jumping at an easy solution, try to make the other members aware of your concern. By suggesting that they talk about the problem in more detail, you may bring out vital information or ideas. One group learned the perils of making a snap decision:

> The board of the town library met to discuss ways to get more children to visit the library during the upcoming spring vacation. Near the beginning of the meeting one member suggested sponsoring a parade through town in which children would march to the library dressed as their favorite book character. After a joke about all the Harry Potter clones who would show up, the board members agreed that it was a terrific idea. They wrapped up their session early, congratulating themselves on having reached a solution so easily.
>
> But what looked at first like a great idea proved to have a crucial drawback. Any parades in the town had to be approved by the town council and cleared with the police department. There was not enough time before spring vacation to apply for these permissions and get them approved. The quick solution proved to be no solution at all.

Fortunately, there are systematic ways to keep the discussion on track and to avoid hasty group decisions. Research shows that if your group follows a tested method of decision making, it will have a much better chance of reaching a satisfactory decision.[8] We turn, therefore, to the most common decision-making technique for small groups—the reflective-thinking method.

The Reflective-Thinking Method

reflective-thinking method
A five-step method for directing discussion in a problem-solving small group.

The reflective-thinking method is derived from the writings of the American philosopher John Dewey. It offers a logical, step-by-step process for discussion in problem-solving groups. The method consists of five steps: (1) defining the problem; (2) analyzing the problem; (3) establishing criteria for solving the problem; (4) generating potential solutions; (5) selecting the best solution. By following these steps, your group will make its work much easier.

Let's take a closer look at the reflective-thinking method. As we do, we'll illustrate each step by following a single group through the entire process.

Define the Problem

Before a problem-solving group can make progress, it must know exactly what problem it is trying to solve. Defining the problem may seem easy, but it is not always so. In a sense, defining the problem for group discussion is akin to settling on a specific purpose for a speech. Unless it is done properly, everything that follows will suffer.

question of policy
A question about whether a specific course of action should or should not be taken.

The best way to define the problem is to phrase it as a question of policy. We discussed questions of policy in Chapter 15 (see pages 411–416). Here it is enough to note that questions of policy inquire about the necessity and/or practicality of specific courses of action. Questions of policy typically include the word "should." For example:

> What measures should our school take to improve relations among different ethnic groups on campus?
>
> What steps should the federal government take to protect civil liberties without harming the war on terrorism?
>
> What policy should the United States adopt with respect to the exploitation of child labor in other countries around the world?

When phrasing the question for discussion, your group should follow several guidelines. First, make sure the question is as clear and specific as possible. For example:

Ineffective: What should be done about fraudulent charities?

More Effective: What should the federal government do to control the activities of fraudulent charities?

Second, phrase the question to allow for a wide variety of answers. Be especially wary of questions that can be answered with a simple yes or no. For example:

Ineffective: Should the city build a new elementary school?

More Effective: What steps should the city take to deal with increasing enrollment in the elementary schools?

Third, avoid biased or slanted questions. For example:

Ineffective: How can we keep the campus bookstore from ripping off students?

More Effective: What changes, if any, should be made in the pricing policies of the campus bookstore?

Fourth, make sure you pose a single question. For example:

Ineffective: What revisions should the college consider in its admissions requirements and in its graduation requirements?

More Effective: What revisions should the college consider in its admissions requirements?

More Effective: What revisions should the college consider in its graduation requirements?

To clarify this first step of the reflective-thinking method, let's see how our model problem-solving group defined the problem:

As a class project, the group set out to discuss the problem of rising costs for attending college. Following the reflective-thinking method, they began by defining the problem. After several false starts they phrased the problem this way: "What steps should our school take to reduce student costs for attending college?"

Analyze the Problem

After the problem has been defined, the group begins to analyze it. Too often, groups (like individuals) start mapping out solutions before they have a firm grasp of what is wrong. This is like a doctor prescribing treatment before fully diagnosing the patient's ailment. If your group investigates the problem as thoroughly as possible, you will be in a much better position to devise a workable solution.

In analyzing the problem, pay particular attention to two questions. First, how severe is the problem? Investigate the scope of the problem. Determine how many people it affects. Assess what might happen if the problem is not resolved. Second, what are the causes of the problem? Check into the history of the problem. Learn what factors contributed to it. Ascertain its major causes.

As you might imagine, analyzing the problem requires research. Effective group decisions depend on having the best information available. You can get this information in the same way you gather materials for a speech. Sometimes you can rely on your own knowledge and experience. More often, you need to get information from other sources—by looking on the Internet, by interviewing someone with expertise on the topic, or by working in the library (see Chapter 6). When meeting with your group, make sure you have done the research assigned to you so you can offer complete and unbiased information.

Let's return now to our sample group and see how it analyzed the problem of rapidly escalating student costs for attending college:

The group talked first about the severity of the problem. Tuition had risen dramatically, as had outlays for books and incidentals. One member found statistics showing that the cost of attending college had more than doubled in the past 10 years and was continuing to increase at twice the inflation rate. Another provided evidence that average annual costs were now close to \$15,000 for students at in-state public colleges and universities, and roughly \$30,000 for students at private schools.

To determine the causes of the problem, the group researched articles in the library about the rise in student costs for attending college across the nation. They also interviewed an economics professor and the head of the student aid program on campus. After studying the matter thoroughly, the group identified several major causes, including administrative costs, faculty salaries, the price of textbooks, and increased living expenses.

Establish Criteria for Solutions

criteria
Standards on which a judgment or decision can be based.

If you planned to buy a car, how would you proceed? You would probably not just walk into a dealer's showroom and buy whatever appealed to you on the spur of the moment. You would most likely decide ahead of time what kind of car you wanted, what options it should have, and how much money you could afford to spend. That is, you would establish *criteria* to guide you in deciding exactly which car to buy.

You should do much the same thing in group discussion. Once your group has analyzed the problem, you should not jump immediately to proposing solutions. Instead, you should take time to establish criteria—standards—for responsible solutions. You should work out (and write down) exactly what your solutions must achieve and any factors that might limit your choice of solutions. If, for example, a committee is authorized to spend a maximum of \$1,000 on a club's annual banquet, one of the criteria for the committee's decision will be that the banquet cost no more than \$1,000.

A common failing of problem-solving groups is that they start to discuss solutions before agreeing on criteria for the solutions. When this happens, a group runs into trouble. Some people will propose solutions based on one set of criteria, while others will propose solutions based on different criteria. You can avoid such conflicts by making sure the group sets up criteria before proposing solutions.

To give a better idea of how this stage of the reflective-thinking method works, let's look at the cost-cutting group we have been following:

After some discussion, the group established these criteria for possible solutions: (1) The solution should significantly reduce students' costs. (2) The solution should come into force at the start of the next school year. (3) The solution should not hurt the prestige of the college. (4) The cost of the solution should be minimal and should be paid by the administration. (5) The human resources needed to implement the solution should come from administrative personnel already working on the school's staff. (6) The solution should involve only actions controlled by the college—not matters controlled by outside individuals or agencies.

Generate Potential Solutions

Once your group has the criteria firmly in mind, you are ready to discuss solutions. Your goal at this stage is to come up with the widest possible range of potential solutions—not to judge the solutions. That comes later. At this stage you are only suggesting possibilities. One member of the group should be responsible for writing down all the solutions proposed at this time.

brainstorming
A method of generating ideas by free association of words and thoughts.

Many groups find the technique of *brainstorming* helpful in this stage. Brainstorming allows a group to generate a variety of solutions without prematurely evaluating them. In Chapter 4 we discussed how brainstorming can work for an individual in choosing a speech topic. Here brainstorming is expanded to the whole group.

The best approach is to begin by having each member of the group list all the possible solutions he or she can think of. One member of the group should then consolidate the individual lists into a single master list. The group should discuss the master list to make sure potential solutions have not been overlooked. At this stage, members often "piggyback" new ideas onto ideas on the master list. For example, if one suggestion is "Establish food co-ops," a group member might say, "Yes, and we could establish clothing co-ops, too." One member should be responsible for writing down these new ideas and adding them to the master list. The brainstorming process continues until the group cannot think of any more solutions.

Brainstorming in this fashion has two advantages. First, it encourages creativity. There is a great deal of research to show that beginning with written lists usually produces more and higher-quality ideas than when a group tries to generate potential solutions by oral discussion.[9] Second, this method of brainstorming encourages equal participation. Having each member create his or her own list of potential solutions makes it less likely that one or two members will dominate the process or that anyone will hold back ideas for fear of being hooted down.

Let's see how our cost-cutting group handled this stage:

By brainstorming, the group came up with the following possible solutions: (1) reduce the number of required books for each course; (2) cut some of the "fat" from the administrative staff; (3) make all professors teach more courses; (4) approach landlords about stabilizing rent and utility costs; (5) establish food and clothing co-ops; (6) increase financial aid; (7) decrease the amount of money available for faculty research; (8) boycott businesses around the campus where price markups are highest; (9) increase out-of-state tuition; (10) decrease dormitory expenses; (11) organize fund-raising programs with the student government, (12) redirect some money from construction of new buildings to student aid. This was a good yield from a brainstorming session—twelve solid suggestions.

Working in a small group requires many of the skills involved in public speaking. Formal presentations may occur during a group's deliberations or when the group presents its report.

Select the Best Solution

After all potential solutions have been listed, it is time to evaluate them and choose the best solution or solutions. The best way to proceed is to take a particular solution, discuss it with regard to the criteria established earlier in the group's deliberations, then move on to the next solution, and so on. This orderly process ensures that all potential solutions receive equal consideration.

consensus
A group decision that is acceptable to all members of the group.

As each potential solution is discussed, the group should make every effort to reach *consensus.* A consensus decision is one that all members accept, even though the decision may not be ideal in the eyes of every member. In other words, consensus may range from full approval of a decision to "Well, I can live with it." Because it usually results in superior decisions as well as in a high degree of unity within the group, consensus is the ideal of group decision making. It comes about when members have been so cooperative that they reach a common decision through reasoning, honest exchange of ideas, and full examination of the issues.[10]

Like most ideals, consensus can be difficult to achieve. If there are different viewpoints, members of the group will often try to find the easiest way to resolve the differences. Sometimes a member will call for a vote, which is very agreeable to those holding a majority opinion (since they will win) but not so pleasant for those in the minority. Resorting to a vote does resolve the immediate conflict, but it may not result in the best solution. Moreover, it weakens unity in the group by fostering factions and perhaps by creating bitterness among the members who lose on the vote. A group should vote only when it has failed in every other attempt to find a solution agreeable to all members.

REFLECTIVE-THINKING METHOD CHECKLIST

yes	no	
☐	☐	1. Did the group clearly define the problem for discussion?
☐	☐	2. Did the group phrase the question for discussion as a question of policy?
☐	☐	3. Did the group phrase the question for discussion as clearly as possible?
☐	☐	4. Did the group phrase the question for discussion so as to allow for a wide variety of answers?
☐	☐	5. Did the group phrase the question for discussion in an unbiased manner?
☐	☐	6. Did the group phrase the question for discussion as a single question?
☐	☐	7. Did the group analyze the problem thoroughly before attempting to map out solutions?
☐	☐	8. Did the group establish criteria for an ideal solution to the problem before discussing specific solutions?
☐	☐	9. Did the group brainstorm to generate a wide range of potential solutions to the problem?
☐	☐	10. Did the group evaluate each potential solution in light of the criteria for an ideal solution?
☐	☐	11. Did the group make a determined effort to reach consensus with regard to the best solution?
☐	☐	12. Did the group achieve consensus?

CD 1: SPEECH CHECKLIST

You can print a copy of this checklist from the CD-ROM.

What kind of final decision did our model cost-cutting group reach? Let's see:

The cost-cutting group had 12 possible solutions to evaluate. Three were rejected because they violated the group's criterion that an acceptable solution must involve only actions controlled directly by the college. Redirecting building money to student aid could be done only by the state legislature. Approaching landlords about stabilizing rent and boycotting campus businesses were also outside the jurisdiction of college administrators.

Three more solutions were rejected because they were economically impractical. Increasing financial aid would hurt many students because the funds would have to come from student fees. Raising out-of-state tuition would drive away 10 percent of the college's out-of-state students. And decreasing dorm costs would make it impossible to provide minimally acceptable services.

The proposal to reduce funds for faculty research was also rejected since most research money comes from government, corporations, and foundations. Besides, research was recognized as a primary means of maintaining the college's prestige. Finally, the suggestion to reduce administrative "fat" was rejected as too costly because a group would have to be established to audit all administrative duties.

After refining the suggestions, the group finally reached consensus on a solution that included the following provisions: (1) A student should not have to spend more than $100 on required books for any single course. (2) The university should authorize the student government to organize food, book, and clothing co-ops. (3) The student government should conduct five fund-raising projects each academic year. (4) Each professor should teach one more class a year.

Once consensus has been reached on a solution or solutions to the problem, the group is ready to present its findings.[11]

Presenting the Recommendations of the Group

The work of a problem-solving group does not end with the last stage of the reflective-thinking process. Once a group has agreed on its recommendations, it usually needs to present them to somebody. A business group might report to the president of the company or to the board of directors. A special committee of the city council reports to the full council. A presidential commission reports to the President and to the nation at large. A classroom group reports to the instructor and to the rest of the class. The purpose of such reports is to present the group's recommendations clearly and convincingly.

Sometimes a group will prepare a formal written report. Often, however, the written report is supplemented with—or replaced by—an oral report, a symposium, or a panel discussion.

Oral Report

oral report
A speech presenting the findings, conclusions, decisions, etc. of a small group.

An oral report is much the same in content as a written report. If the group has a designated leader, she or he will probably deliver the report. Otherwise, the group will have to select one person for the job.

If you are picked to present your group's report, you should approach it as you would any other speech. Your task is to explain the purpose, procedures, and recommendations of your group. As with any speech, your report should have three main sections. The introduction will state the purpose of the report and preview its main points. The body will spell out the problem addressed by your group, the criteria set for a solution, and the solution being recommended. The conclusion will summarize the main points and, in some cases, urge that the group's recommendations be adopted.

As with any other speech, you should adapt your report to the audience. Use supporting materials to clarify and strengthen your ideas, and consider whether using visual aids will enhance your message. Make sure your language is accurate, clear, vivid, and appropriate. Rehearse the report so you can deliver it fluently and decisively. Afterward, you—and possibly other members of the group—may be called on to answer questions from the audience. (Review the section on answering questions in Chapter 12, pages 318–322.)

Symposium

A symposium consists of a moderator and several speakers seated together in front of an audience. If the group presenting the symposium has a designated leader, he or she will typically be the moderator. The moderator's job is to introduce the topic and the speakers. Each speaker in turn delivers a prepared speech on a different aspect of the topic. After the speeches, there may be a question-and-answer session with the audience.

symposium
A public presentation in which several people present prepared speeches on different aspects of the same topic.

The symposium is often used for group reports in speech classes. One way to organize it is to have each member of the group present a brief talk sketching the group's work and decisions during one stage of the reflective-thinking process. Another way is to have each speaker deal with a major issue relating to the discussion topic. A group dealing with capital punishment, for example, might have one speaker present the group's conclusion on the issue of whether capital punishment is an effective deterrent to crime, another speaker present the group's position on the morality of capital punishment, and so forth.

No matter what kind of symposium your group presents, all the speeches should be carefully planned. They should also be coordinated with one another to make sure the symposium reports on all important aspects of the group's project.

Panel Discussion

A panel discussion is essentially a conversation in front of an audience. The panel should have a moderator, who introduces the topic and the panelists. Once the discussion is under way, the moderator may interject questions and comments as needed to focus the discussion. The panelists speak briefly, informally, and impromptu. They talk to each other, but loudly enough for the audience to be able to hear. As with a symposium, a panel discussion may be followed by a question-and-answer session with the audience.

panel discussion
A structured conversation on a given topic among several people in front of an audience.

Because of its spontaneity, a panel discussion can be exciting for participants and audience alike. But, unfortunately, that spontaneity inhibits systematic presentation of a group's recommendations. Thus the panel discussion is seldom used by problem-solving groups, although it can work well for information-gathering groups.

If you are a participant in a panel discussion, beware of the common fallacy that no serious preparation is required. Although you will speak impromptu, you need to study the topic ahead of time, analyze the major issues, and map out the points you want to be sure to make during the discussion. An effective panel discussion also requires planning by the moderator and panelists to decide what issues will be discussed and in what order. Finally, all panelists must be willing to share talking time. One purpose of a panel is to have all participants voice their ideas, not to have one or two members monopolize the discussion.

Whatever method your group uses to present its findings, you can benefit from the public speaking guidelines given throughout this book. The techniques of effective speech need refinement for different situations, but the principles remain the same whether you are one person addressing an audience, part of a small group of people working to solve a problem, or a participant in a symposium or a panel discussion.

Summary

A small group consists of three to twelve people assembled for a specific purpose. A problem-solving small group, as its name implies, is formed to solve a particular problem. When such a group has effective leadership, it usually makes better decisions than do individuals by themselves. Most groups have a designated leader, an implied leader, or an emergent leader. Some groups have no specific leader, in which case all members of the group must assume leadership responsibilities. An effective leader helps a group reach its goals by fulfilling procedural needs, task needs, and maintenance needs. As you develop your skills in group communication, you should be prepared to assume a leadership role whenever necessary.

Apart from leadership, all members of a group have five basic responsibilities. You should commit yourself to the goals of your group, fulfill your individual assignments, avoid interpersonal conflict within the group, encourage full participation by all members, and help keep the group on track. Meeting these responsibilities is vital if your group is to be successful.

Your group will also be more successful if it follows the reflective-thinking method, which offers a logical, step-by-step process for decision making in problem-solving groups. The method consists of five steps: (1) defining the problem as clearly and specifically as possible; (2) analyzing the problem to determine its severity and causes; (3) establishing criteria to guide the group in evaluating solutions; (4) generating a wide range of potential solutions; (5) selecting the best solution or solutions.

Once your group has agreed on its recommendations, it usually has to present them to somebody. Sometimes this presentation will be in the form of a written report. Often, however, it will be an oral presentation—a report by one member of the group, a symposium, or a panel discussion. Whichever kind of oral presentation your group gives will call for the skills of effective speechmaking explained throughout this book.

Key Terms

ONLINE LEARNING CENTER

Review these terms by doing the Chapter 18 crossword puzzle at www.mhhe.com/lucas9.

dyad (486)
small group (487)
problem-solving small group (487)
leadership (487)
implied leader (487)
emergent leader (488)
designated leader (488)
procedural needs (488)
task needs (489)
maintenance needs (490)
hidden agenda (491)
reflective-thinking method (496)
question of policy (496)
criteria (498)

brainstorming (499)
consensus (500)
oral report (502)
symposium (503)
panel discussion (503)

Review Questions

After reading this chapter, you should be able to answer the following questions:

1. What is a small group? What is a problem-solving small group?
2. What are the four kinds of leadership that may occur in a small group? Explain the three kinds of needs fulfilled by leadership in a small group.
3. What are the five major responsibilities of every participant in a small group?
4. What are the stages of the reflective-thinking method? Explain the major tasks of a group at each stage.
5. What are the three methods for presenting orally the recommendations of a problem-solving group?

CD 1: STUDY QUESTIONS

For further review, go to the Study Questions for this chapter.

Exercises for Critical Thinking

1. Identify the flaw (or flaws) in each of the following questions for a problem-solving group discussion. Rewrite each question so it conforms with the criteria discussed in the chapter for effective discussion questions.
    a. Should all students be required to take two years of a foreign language to graduate from college?
    b. What should be done to prevent the utterly ridiculous shortage of computers for students at this school?
    c. What should be done about child abuse?
    d. What should our state government do to control taxes and to combat drunk driving?
    e. Should the federal government institute a system of standardized national tests for all schoolchildren?
2. If possible, arrange to observe a problem-solving small group in action. You might attend a meeting of your city council, the school board, the zoning commission, a local business, a church committee. To what extent does the discussion measure up to the criteria of effective discussion presented in this chapter? What kind of leadership does the group have, and how well does the leader (or leaders) fulfill the group's procedural needs, task needs, and maintenance needs? How do the other members meet their responsibilities? What aspects of the meeting are handled most effectively? Which are handled least effectively?
3. Identify a relatively important decision you have made in the last year or two. Try to reconstruct how you reached that decision. Now suppose you

could remake the decision following the reflective-thinking method. Map out exactly what you would do at each stage of the method. Do you still reach the same decision? If not, do you believe the reflective-thinking method would have led you to a better decision in the first place?

4. Attend a symposium or panel discussion on campus. Prepare a brief analysis of the proceedings. First, study the role of the moderator. How does she or he introduce the topic and participants? What role does the moderator play thereafter? Does she or he help guide and focus the panel discussion? Does she or he summarize and conclude the proceedings at the end?

   Second, observe the participants. Are the speeches in the symposium well prepared and presented? Which speaker (or speakers) do you find most effective? Least effective? Why? Do participants in the panel discussion share talking time? Does their discussion appear well planned to cover major aspects of the topic? Which panelist (or panelists) do you find most effective? Least effective? Why?

Notes

[1]See, for example, Andrea B. Hollingshead and David P. Brandon, "Potential Benefits of Communication in Transactive Memory Systems," *Human Communication Research,* 29 (2003), pp. 607–615.

[2]For a summary of research on the question of group size, see Gloria J. Galanes, Katherine Adams, and John K. Brilhart, *Effective Group Discussion: Theory and Practice*, 11th ed. (New York: McGraw-Hill, 2004), pp. 145–146.

[3]For a review of scholarship in this area, see Charlan Jeanne Nemeth and Jack A. Goncalo, "Influence and Persuasion in Small Groups," in Timothy C. Brock and Melanie C. Green (eds.), *Persuasion: Psychological Insights and Perspectives,* 2nd ed. (Thousand Oaks, CA: Sage, 2005), pp. 171–194.

[4]For an excellent discussion of the responsibilities of designated group leaders, see Galanes, Adams, and Brilhart, *Effective Group Discussion,* pp. 257–288.

[5]Dennis S. Gouran, "Leadership As the Art of Counteractive Influence in Decision-Making and Problem-Solving Groups," in Randy Y. Hirokawa, Robert S. Cathcart, Larry A. Samovar, and Linda D. Henman (eds.), *Small Group Communication: Theory and Practice,* 8th ed. (Los Angeles, CA: Roxbury, 2003), pp. 172–198.

[6]See, for example, Andrew J. Flanagin, Hee Sun Park, and David R. Seibold, "Group Performance and Collaborative Technology: A Longitudinal and Multilevel Analysis of Information Quality, Contribution Equity, and Members' Satisfaction in Computer-Mediated Groups," *Communication Monographs,* 71 (2004), pp. 352–372.

[7]Larry L. Barker, Kathy J. Wahlers, and Kittie W. Watson, *Groups in Process: An Introduction to Small Group Communication,* 6th ed. (Boston: Allyn and Bacon, 2001), pp. 83–114.

[8]Charles Pavitt and Kelly K. Johnson, "Scheidel and Crowell Revisited: A Descriptive Study of Group Proposal Sequencing," *Communication Monographs,* 69 (2002), pp. 19–32.

[9]For a recent study on this subject, see Michele H. Jackson and Marshall Scott Poole, "Idea-Generation in Naturally Occurring Contexts: Complex Appropriation of Simple Group Procedure," *Human Communication Research*, 29 (2003), pp. 560–591.

[10]Joann Keyton, *Communicating in Groups: Building Relationship for Effective Decision Making,* 2nd ed. (New York: McGraw-Hill, 2003), pp. 173–175.

[11]For further reading on research in small-group communication, see Marshall Scott Poole and Andrea B. Hollingshead (eds.), *Theories of Small Groups: Interdisciplinary Perspectives* (Thousand Oaks, CA: Sage, 2005).

APPENDIX

Speeches for Analysis and Discussion

Questions of Culture

Sajjid Zahir Chinoy

Seldom does a student commencement address upstage the featured speaker—especially when that speaker is a Pulitzer prize winner from Harvard University. Yet that is exactly what happened when Sajjid Zahir Chinoy spoke to his fellow graduates at the University of Richmond on May 12, 1996.

Born and raised near Bombay, India, Chinoy was selected to speak as the result of a campuswide competition. After describing the jumble of emotions that filled his mind as he came to the United States to attend school, he spoke movingly of the warm reception he received in Richmond and of how cultural differences can be overcome by attempting to understand other people.

Addressing his audience of 3,000 people extemporaneously and without notes, Chinoy received thunderous applause, and his remarks were widely reported in the press. His speech was so inspiring that the main speaker, Harvard psychiatrist Robert Coles, began his address by paying tribute to Chinoy. "I've been to a number of commencements," said Coles, "but I've never heard a speech quite like that."

The text of this speech has been transcribed from a video recording and is reprinted with permission from Sajjid Zahir Chinoy and the University of Richmond. It is also available on the CD-ROM and video supplements to *The Art of Public Speaking*.

1 Distinguished guests, faculty, staff, students, ladies and gentlemen, and, most of all, the Class of 1996:

2 I can visualize the scene again and again: 11:30 P.M., Saturday night, the fifteenth of August, 1992, Bombay International Airport, India. I was leaving home for the University of Richmond. And as I said that final goodbye to my parents, my family, and my friends; and as I saw hope, expectation, even a tinge of sadness, in their eyes; and as I stepped aboard the Boeing 747 in front, I knew my life had changed forever.

3 The next 36 hours on board the aircraft were a time of questions, of concerns, of tremendous uncertainty.

4 Had I made the right choice in leaving home? Had I made the right choice in leaving my parents, my family, my home? Had I made the right choice in leaving my country, my culture, my background? Had I made the right choice in choosing the University of Richmond?

5 And then, of course, there was that one nagging question, that one overriding concern: As one of only three Indian students on a Richmond campus of 3,000, would I ever fit in?

6 My country was different. My culture was different. My experiences were different. My background was different. My language was different. My accent was different. Would I ever fit in?

7 And so here I was, high above the clouds, grappling with questions of culture, of interaction, of ethnicity. What I didn't know was that 30,000 feet below, on the ground, the world was faced with these very same questions—the question of culture, the question of interaction, the question of ethnicity.

8 And so whether my aircraft took off from Bombay, where the Hindus and the Muslims lived together in a most fragile peace; or whether my aircraft was over Africa, where the Hutus and Tutsis of Rwanda and Burundi had long-standing animosity; or whether my aircraft was over Bosnia, where

the Serbs, the Croats, the Muslims, and the Bosnians had broken yet another truce, the question was the same—could different cultures ever come together to reinforce one another?

9 Ladies and gentlemen, after that bumpy aircraft ride, this young Indian student had found his answer. He had been witness to the four most spectacular years of his life at the University of Richmond. The academics were great; the extracurriculars were great; his graduate plans were great.

10 But what left an indelible impact on his mind was none of this. No, instead it was those special moments, those moments of human interaction, those human relationships that can never quite be translated into words:

11 The time this young Indian student spent his first Thanksgiving dinner with his debate team coach. That Thanksgiving evening when I ate my first American turkey and saw my first American football game, not knowing the difference between a tackle and a touchdown. And yet, all of a sudden, just like that, this very different Indian student had become an inherent part of the great American tradition of giving thanks.

12 The time I spent my first Christmas Eve with my journalism professor. That Christmas evening when the relationship wasn't of a faculty member and a student anymore, but of two buddies who fought fiercely over every point in Ping-Pong.

13 The time I had a long and honest talk with an American friend on the eve of a calculus exam. I didn't learn much calculus that night, but what I did learn was that as different as we are—different countries, different cultures, different continents—inherently we are still the same.

14 The time in December 1992 when India was hit by communal riots, when violence and bloodshed were but a few hundred yards from my family and my home, and when my fantastic roommate from my freshman year sat up the entire night, giving me hope, strength, and courage at every step.

15 Yes, four years after that bumpy aircraft ride, I have found the answer to the question of culture.

16 I have found that it has taken just a little understanding, just a little sensitivity, just a little open-mindedness, just a little empathy on the part of this community—this University of Richmond community—to change my life like never before.

17 I have found that it makes no difference what culture you follow, what your background is, what your experiences are, what language you speak, what accent you have. The commonality of the human bond far transcends these superficial differences.

18 And yet look around at the world today. Look around at the very regions that were faced with the same question of culture that I was faced with four years ago.

19 Look at Bosnia, where, between 1992 and 1996, 300,000 people had been slaughtered—Bosnians, Serbs, Croats, Muslims—all because they came from a slightly different heritage or culture or history.

20 Look at Bombay, India. In one maddening week in 1992, 2,000 Indians—Hindus and Muslims—lost their lives fighting with one another. They fought over a mosque; they fought over a structure made of brick and mortar. Two thousand human beings lost their lives.

21 Look at Africa, where, between 1992 and 1996, 1 million Hutus and Tutsis lost their lives. Just comprehend that for a moment. Between the time

you were a freshman and a senior, 1 million lost their lives fighting over culture, over history, over background.

22 Yes, just look at the madness. The world has fought hard to highlight its differences. We have forgotten our inherent similarities. All because what was missing was a little understanding. Just a little sensitivity. Just a little open-mindedness. Just a little empathy.

23 Two similar questions of culture in 1992. Two diametrically opposite results in 1996.

24 And so, to the Class of 1996, I say go and distinguish yourselves like never before. Go get the best of jobs, the most rewarding of careers. Go to the best of graduate programs. And make a real difference in your communities.

25 But not for one moment, not for one moment, ever forget the memory of these four years—the memory that just a little understanding, just a little sensitivity, just a little open-mindedness, just a little empathy on your part can mean the difference between complete despair for one young boy in Bosnia and remarkable hope for another young boy at Richmond.

26 Thank you.

Choices and Change

Barbara Bush

Barbara Bush's commencement address at Wellesley College on June 1, 1990, is one of the best known speeches of recent years. Bush was invited to speak by the senior class when their first choice, Alice Walker, author of *The Color Purple,* could not attend. In protest, 150 Wellesley seniors—about one-fourth of the graduating class—signed a petition charging that Bush was not a good role model for career-oriented students at a women's college and had been chosen because of the man she married rather than for her own achievements.

The petition touched off a storm of controversy. Throughout the month before Bush's speech, educators, newspaper columnists, and others debated the petition and the larger issue of women's role in American society. The media spotlight became so intense that Bush's speech was broadcast live by all the major television networks.

In her speech, Bush dealt with one of the most important issues facing modern women—how to balance their careers with their commitments to friends and family. She urged her audience to respect difference, to get involved in social issues, and to cherish human relationships as "the most important investments you will ever make." She capped off the speech by suggesting that someone in the audience might follow in her footsteps as the President's spouse. "I wish *him* well," she added, to thunderous cheering and applause.

Bush's blend of humility and humor won many accolades. NBC News anchor Tom Brokaw called her address "one of the best commencement speeches I've ever heard," while *The New York Times* judged it "a triumph." Many Wellesley students who had been skeptical about Bush's appearance also said they were pleasantly surprised by the speech. "She was wonderful and funny," one of them stated. "I think she could have addressed more women's issues. But she was sincere and she touched our hearts."

The text of this speech is taken from a videotape supplied by Wellesley College, and it includes several impromptu comments and other changes from the version published in the press. The speech is also included in the video supplement to *The Art of Public Speaking.*

1 Thank you very, very much President Keohane, Mrs. Gorbachev, trustees, faculty, parents, and, I should say, Julia Porter, class president, and certainly my new best friend, Christine Bicknell—and of course the Class of 1990. I am really thrilled to be here today and very excited, as I know all of you must be, that Mrs. Gorbachev could join us. These are exciting times—they're exciting in Washington, and I had really looked forward to coming to Wellesley. I thought it was going to be fun; I never dreamt it would be this much fun. So thank you for that.

2 More than 10 years ago when I was invited here to talk about our experiences in the People's Republic of China, I was struck by both the natural beauty of your campus and the spirit of this place.

3 Wellesley, you see, is not just a place, but an idea, an experiment in excellence in which diversity is not just tolerated, but is embraced.

4 The essence of this spirit was captured in a moving speech about tolerance given last year by a student body president of one of your sister colleges. She related the story by Robert Fulghum about a young pastor who, finding himself in charge of some very energetic children, hits upon the game called "Giants, Wizards and Dwarfs." "You have to decide now," the pastor instructed the children, "which you are—a giant, a wizard or a dwarf." At that, a small girl tugging at his pants leg asks, "But where do the mermaids stand?"

5 And the pastor tells her there are *no* mermaids. And she says, "Oh yes there are—I am a mermaid."

6 This little girl knew what she was and she was not about to give up on either her identity or the game. She intended to take her place wherever mermaids fit into the scheme of things. Where *do* the mermaids stand—all those who are different, those who do not fit the boxes and the pigeonholes? "Answer that question," wrote Fulghum, "and you can build a school, a nation, or a whole world."

7 As that very wise young woman said, "Diversity, like anything worth having, requires effort." Effort to learn about and respect difference, to be compassionate with one another, to cherish our own identity, and to accept unconditionally the same in others. You should all be very proud that this is the Wellesley spirit.

8 Now I know your first choice today was Alice Walker—guess how I know!—known for *The Color Purple.* Instead you got me—known for the color of my hair! Alice Walker's book has a special resonance here. At Wellesley, each class is known by a special color. For four years the class of '90 has worn the color purple. Today you meet on Severance Green to say goodbye to all of that, to begin a new and a very personal journey to search for your own true colors.

9 In the world that awaits you beyond the shores of Lake Waban, no one can say what your true colors will be. But this I do know: You have a first-class education from a first-class school. And so you need not, probably cannot, live a "paint-by-numbers" life. Decisions are not irrevocable. Choices do come back. And as you set off from Wellesley, I hope that many of you will consider making three very special choices.

10 The first is to believe in something larger than yourself, to get involved in some of the big ideas of our time. I chose literacy because I honestly believe that if more people could read, write and comprehend, we

would be that much closer to solving so many of the problems that plague our nation and our society.

11 Early on I made another choice which I hope you'll make as well. Whether you're talking about education, career, or service, you're talking about life, and life really must have joy. It's supposed to be fun!

12 One of the reasons I made the most important decision of my life, to marry George Bush, is because he made me laugh. It's true, sometimes we've laughed through our tears, but that shared laughter has been one of our strongest bonds. Find the joy in life, because as Ferris Bueller said on his day off: "Life moves pretty fast. You don't stop and look around once in a while, you're gonna miss it!" (I'm not going to tell George you clapped more for Ferris than you clapped for George!)

13 The third choice that must not be missed is to cherish your human connections: your relationships with family and friends. For several years, you've had impressed upon you the importance to your career of dedication and hard work—and of course that's true. But as important as your obligations as a doctor, a lawyer, a business leader will be, you are a human being first, and those human connections—with spouses, with children, with friends—are the most important investments you will ever make.

14 At the end of your life, you will never regret not having passed one more test, not winning one more verdict, or not closing one more deal. You will regret time not spent with a husband, a child, a friend, or a parent.

15 We are in a transitional period right now, fascinating and exhilarating times, learning to adjust to changes and the choices we, men and women, are facing. As an example, I remember what a friend said, on hearing her husband complain to his buddies that he had to babysit. Quickly setting him straight, my friend told her husband that when it's your own kids, it's not called babysitting!

16 Now, maybe we should adjust faster; maybe we should adjust slower. But whatever the era, whatever the times, one thing will never change: fathers and mothers, if you have children, they must come first. You must read to your children, and you must hug your children, and you must love your children. Your success as a family, our success as a society, depends not on what happens in the White House, but on what happens inside your house.

17 For over 50 years, it was said that the winner of Wellesley's annual hoop race would be the first to get married. Now they say the winner will be the first to become a CEO. Both of those stereotypes show too little tolerance for those who want to know where the mermaids stand. So I want to offer a new legend: the winner of the hoop race will be the first to realize her dream—not society's dream, her own personal dream. And who knows? Somewhere out in this audience may even be someone who will one day follow in my footsteps and preside over the White House as the president's spouse. And I wish him well!

18 Well, the controversy ends here. But our conversation is only beginning. And a worthwhile conversation it has been. So as you leave Wellesley today, take with you deep thanks for the courtesy and the honor you have shared with Mrs. Gorbachev and with me. Thank you. God bless you. And may your future be worthy of your dreams.

I Have a Dream

Martin Luther King, Jr.

Martin Luther King's "I Have a Dream" is widely regarded as a masterpiece. It was delivered August 28, 1963, to some 200,000 people who had come to Washington, D.C., to participate in a peaceful demonstration to further the cause of equal rights for African Americans. King spoke from the steps of the Lincoln Memorial, in the "symbolic shadow" of Abraham Lincoln, and the crowd filled the vast area between the Memorial and the Washington Monument. In addition, millions of Americans watched the speech on television or listened to it on the radio.

Like most ceremonial addresses, "I Have a Dream" is relatively short. Although it took King only 16 minutes to deliver the speech, he prepared it more carefully than any other speech in his career to that time. His purpose was to set forth as succinctly and as eloquently as possible the guiding principles of the civil rights movement, and to reinforce the commitment of his listeners to those principles.

One of the most interesting features of this speech is King's use of language to make the abstract principles of liberty and equality clear and compelling. Throughout, King relies on familiar, concrete words that create sharp, vivid images. He uses many more metaphors than do most speakers, but they are appropriate to the occasion and help to dramatize King's ideas. Finally, King makes extensive use of repetition and parallelism to reinforce his message and to enhance the momentum of the speech.

If you have heard a recording of "I Have a Dream," you know its impact was heightened by King's delivery. In his rich baritone voice, marked by the fervor of the crusader and modulated by the cadences of the Southern Baptist preacher, King gained the total involvement of his audience. As William Robert Miller says, "The crowd more than listened, it participated, and before King had reached his last phrase, a torrent of applause was already welling up."

The text of this speech was taken from a tape recording and is reprinted with permission of Joan Daves. Copyright 1963 by Martin Luther King, Jr. The speech is also available on the video supplement to *The Art of Public Speaking.*

1 I am happy to join with you today in what will go down in history as the greatest demonstration for freedom in the history of our nation.

2 Five score years ago, a great American, in whose symbolic shadow we stand today, signed the Emancipation Proclamation. This momentous decree came as a great beacon light of hope to millions of Negro slaves, who had been seared in the flames of withering injustice. It came as a joyous daybreak to end the long night of their captivity.

3 But one hundred years later, the Negro still is not free. One hundred years later, the life of the Negro is still sadly crippled by the manacles of segregation and the chains of discrimination. One hundred years later, the Negro lives on a lonely island of poverty in the midst of a vast ocean of material prosperity. One hundred years later, the Negro is still languished in the corners of American society and finds himself an exile in his own land. And so we've come here today to dramatize a shameful condition.

4 In a sense we've come to our nation's Capitol to cash a check. When the architects of our republic wrote the magnificent words of the Constitution and the Declaration of Independence, they were signing a promissory note to which every American was to fall heir. This note was a promise that

all men—yes, black men as well as white men—would be guaranteed the unalienable rights of life, liberty, and the pursuit of happiness.

5 It is obvious today that America has defaulted on this promissory note insofar as her citizens of color are concerned. Instead of honoring this sacred obligation, America has given the Negro people a bad check—a check which has come back marked "insufficient funds."

6 But we refuse to believe that the bank of justice is bankrupt. We refuse to believe that there are insufficient funds in the great vaults of opportunity of this nation. And so we've come to cash this check—a check that will give us upon demand the riches of freedom and the security of justice.

7 We have also come to this hallowed spot to remind America of the fierce urgency of now. This is no time to engage in the luxury of cooling off or to take the tranquilizing drug of gradualism. Now is the time to make real the promises of democracy. Now is the time to rise from the dark and desolate valley of segregation to the sunlit path of racial justice. Now is the time to lift our nation from the quicksands of racial injustice to the solid rock of brotherhood. Now is the time to make justice a reality for all of God's children.

8 It would be fatal for the nation to overlook the urgency of the moment. This sweltering summer of the Negro's legitimate discontent will not pass until there is an invigorating autumn of freedom and equality. Nineteen sixty-three is not an end, but a beginning. Those who hope that the Negro needed to blow off steam and will now be content will have a rude awakening if the nation returns to business as usual. There will be neither rest nor tranquility in America until the Negro is granted his citizenship rights. The whirlwinds of revolt will continue to shake the foundations of our nation until the bright day of justice emerges.

9 But there is something that I must say to my people, who stand on the warm threshold which leads into the palace of justice. In the process of gaining our rightful place, we must not be guilty of wrongful deeds. Let us not seek to satisfy our thirst for freedom by drinking from the cup of bitterness and hatred.

10 We must forever conduct our struggle on the high plane of dignity and discipline. We must not allow our creative protest to degenerate into physical violence. Again and again we must rise to the majestic heights of meeting physical force with soul force.

11 The marvelous new militancy which has engulfed the Negro community must not lead us to a distrust of all white people. For many of our white brothers, as evidenced by their presence here today, have come to realize that their destiny is tied up with our destiny. They have come to realize that their freedom is inextricably bound to our freedom. We cannot walk alone.

12 As we walk, we must make the pledge that we shall always march ahead. We cannot turn back. There are those who are asking the devotees of civil rights, "When will you be satisfied?" We can never be satisfied as long as the Negro is the victim of the unspeakable horrors of police brutality. We can never be satisfied as long as our bodies, heavy with the fatigue of travel, cannot gain lodging in the motels of the highways and the hotels of the cities. We cannot be satisfied as long as the Negro's basic mobility is from a smaller ghetto to a larger one. We can never be satisfied as long as

our children are stripped of their selfhood and robbed of their dignity by signs stating "For Whites Only." We cannot be satisfied as long as a Negro in Mississippi cannot vote and a Negro in New York believes he has nothing for which to vote. No, no, we are not satisfied, and we will not be satisfied until justice rolls down like waters, and righteousness like a mighty stream.

13 I am not unmindful that some of you have come here out of great trials and tribulations. Some of you have come fresh from narrow jail cells. Some of you have come from areas where your quest for freedom left you battered by the storms of persecution and staggered by the winds of police brutality. You have been the veterans of creative suffering. Continue to work with the faith that unearned suffering is redemptive.

14 Go back to Mississippi, go back to Alabama, go back to South Carolina, go back to Georgia, go back to Louisiana, go back to the slums and ghettos of our Northern cities, knowing that somehow this situation can and will be changed. Let us not wallow in the valley of despair.

15 I say to you today, my friends, so even though we face the difficulties of today and tomorrow, I still have a dream. It is a dream deeply rooted in the American dream.

16 I have a dream that one day this nation will rise up and live out the true meaning of its creed, "We hold these truths to be self-evident, that all men are created equal."

17 I have a dream that one day on the red hills of Georgia the sons of former slaves and the sons of former slaveowners will be able to sit down together at the table of brotherhood.

18 I have a dream that one day even the state of Mississippi, a state sweltering with the heat of injustice, sweltering with the heat of oppression, will be transformed into an oasis of freedom and justice.

19 I have a dream that my four little children will one day live in a nation where they will not be judged by the color of their skin but by the content of their character. I have a dream today.

20 I have a dream that one day, down in Alabama, with its vicious racists, with its governor having his lips dripping with the words of interposition and nullification, one day right there in Alabama little black boys and black girls will be able to join hands with little white boys and white girls as sisters and brothers. I have a dream today.

21 I have a dream that one day every valley shall be exalted, every hill and mountain shall be made low, the rough places will be made plane and the crooked places will be made straight, and the glory of the Lord shall be revealed, and all flesh shall see it together.

22 This is our hope. This is the faith that I go back to the South with. With this faith we will be able to hew out of the mountain of despair a stone of hope. With this faith we will be able to transform the jangling discords of our nation into a beautiful symphony of brotherhood. With this faith we will be able to work together, to pray together, to struggle together, to go to jail together, to stand up for freedom together, knowing that we will be free one day.

23 This will be the day—this will be the day when all of God's children will be able to sing with new meaning, "My country 'tis of thee, sweet land of liberty, of thee I sing. Land where my fathers died, land of the pilgrim's pride, from every mountainside, let freedom ring." And if America is to be a great nation, this must become true.

24 So let freedom ring from the prodigious hilltops of New Hampshire. Let freedom ring from the mighty mountains of New York. Let freedom ring from the heightening Alleghenies of Pennsylvania!

25 Let freedom ring from the snowcapped Rockies of Colorado! Let freedom ring from the curvaceous slopes of California!

26 But not only that. Let freedom ring from Stone Mountain of Georgia!

27 Let freedom ring from Lookout Mountain of Tennessee!

28 Let freedom ring from every hill and molehill of Mississippi. From every mountainside, let freedom ring.

29 And when this happens, when we allow freedom ring—when we let it ring from every village and every hamlet, from every state and every city—we will be able to speed up that day when all of God's children, black men and white men, Jews and Gentiles, Protestants and Catholics, will be able to join hands and sing in the words of the old Negro spiritual, "Free at last! Free at last! Thank God almighty, we are free at last!"

The Hidden World of Chili Peppers

Do you know where chili peppers originated and how they eventually spread around the world? Why some peppers are so much hotter than others? How the heat of a chili pepper is measured? What to do if you eat a too-hot pepper? The many medicinal benefits of chili peppers?

These are just a few of the interesting facts presented in the following informative speech. As you read the speech, notice how the speaker blends historical and scientific materials to produce an entertaining, yet highly instructive, look at chili peppers. Notice, too, how the speaker applies the principles of effective informative speaking discussed in Chapter 13.

This speech is also available on the CD-ROM and video supplements to *The Art of Public Speaking*. If you watch the speech, you will see that the speaker uses a number of well-designed visual aids to enhance the communication of his ideas.

1 Imagine your mouth burning like wildfire, your eyes squirting out uncontrollable tears, and your face red and sweating profusely. Are you sick? No, you just took a bite of a screaming hot chili pepper. Congratulations. You're partaking in a worldwide tradition that has been spicing up lives and diets for thousands of years.

2 My own desire for spicy meals led me to investigate why I get red in the face and salivate over the mere thought of eating a spicy chili. In the process, I've discovered there's a lot more to chili peppers than I'd ever imagined. Today I'd like to share with you what I've learned about the history of chili peppers, why they can be so spicy, what to do if you eat a too-hot pepper, and some of the ways peppers are used other than in foods.

3 The chili pepper has a long and fascinating history. Its scientific name is *Capsicum*. This is different from the common black pepper you have on your dining room table, whose scientific name is *Piper nigrum*. Black pepper was first cultivated in Asia and was prized in the West as early as the Roman Empire. In contrast, the chili pepper originated more than 5,000 years ago in South America, near what is today Bolivia and Brazil. Over time, it spread to Mexico, Central America, and the Caribbean.

4 But it wasn't until Columbus came in the 1490s that the chili pepper became known to the rest of the world. As stated in *The Cambridge World History of Food,* within fifty years after Columbus returned to Spain with sample plants, chili peppers could be found growing in coastal areas from Africa to Asia. From there, they spread inland, until they took hold of the taste buds of people around the globe. Today they're most widely used in Mexico, Central and South America, Africa, Asia, the Balkans, and the United States. Carolyn Dille and Susan Belsinger, authors of *The Chili Pepper Book,* estimate that 25 percent of the world's adult population uses chili peppers as a part of their daily diet.

5 Now that we know a little bit about the history of chili peppers, let's see why they can put such a fire in our belly. The pleasure and pain involved in eating chili peppers comes from a chemical called capsaicin. Capsaicin is concentrated in the pepper's veins and seeds. To enjoy the flavor of a chili pepper without burning your stomach or mouth, avoid the veins and seeds when cooking or eating them.

6 P. W. Bosland tells us in the book *Spices, Herbs, and Edible Fungi* that chili pepper intensity is measured in two ways. The first was developed by Wilbur L. Scoville in 1912. This method uses trained testers to measure chili peppers in Scoville Heat Units. These range from zero to 300,000. According to Bosland, this test is subjective because it relies on the individual tester's sensitivity to capsaicin.

7 The second, more widely used test is called the High Performance Liquid Chromatography test, more commonly known as HPLC. This is also measured in Scoville Heat Units, but it's more objective. The chili pods are dried and ground, and then the chemicals responsible for the heat are analyzed and rated according to pungency.

8 The hottest pepper on record is the deceptively small and unimposing orange habanero pepper. It's been rated as high as 300,000 Scoville Heat Units, and it's so powerful that some people have an allergic reaction just by touching it, which is why I'm holding it by the stem. The mildest pepper is the standard green bell, which you see at the grocery store everyday. It's been rated at zero Scoville Heat Units.

9 If you eat an orange habanero pepper, it's important to know how to deal with the burning sensation. Whatever you do, do not rinse your mouth with water. Dave DeWitt in *The Chili Pepper Encyclopedia* tells us capsaicin is not soluble in water. And even if you drink a gallon of ice water, it's not going to help. According to the Chili Pepper Institute at New Mexico State University, the best solution is to consume a dairy product such as milk or yogurt, which contain a substance that strips away capsaicin from the interior cells of your mouth. This is why some hot foods, like Indian foods, are served with yogurt sauce.

10 If you burn your skin, the Institute recommends cleaning the area with rubbing alcohol and then soaking it with milk. Above all, remember two things: First, always wear gloves when you cut a hot pepper such as a habanero. Second, never rub your eyes when working with hot chili peppers.

11 Although chili peppers are prized above all for the flavor they add to food, they have other benefits as well. Pepper sprays have become a standard weapon for the personal protection of individuals and law-enforcement

agencies. *The New York Times* reports that sales of pepper sprays have risen steadily and show no sign of slowing.

12 Chili peppers are also valued for their medicinal properties. According to Jack Challem, author of *The Nutrition Reporter,* there have been more than 1,300 medical studies on capsaicin, the active ingredient in peppers. Moderate doses have been proved to aid digestion, reduce hypertension, improve circulation, and help dissolve blood clots. Preliminary research by Professor Kenji Okajima at Japan's Kumamato University School of Medicine suggests that a combination of chili peppers and soybeans can promote hair growth and might hold promise as a cure for baldness.

13 In closing, it's difficult to imagine our lives without the spice added by chili peppers. From their origins in South America to their current popularity around the world, peppers have been used not only to flavor our food but also to improve our health and personal safety. While it remains to be seen whether or not chili peppers can actually cure baldness, we can be sure this ancient plant will continue to find new uses in our modern age.

Bursting the Antibacterial Bubble

During the past few years, the use of household antibacterial products has grown dramatically in the United States. Today Americans spend millions of dollars on everything from antibacterial soaps and hand wipes to tissues, sponges, shampoos, and even children's toys that have been treated with antibacterial chemicals.

The following persuasive speech argues that these products do not provide the benefits they claim and may, in fact, be contributing to long-term health and environmental problems. As a solution, the speaker recommends that the U.S. Food and Drug Administration institute regulations governing the use of antibacterial products and that consumers avoid using these products.

While you read the speech, study how the speaker uses examples, statistics, and testimony to support her position. Does she convince you that the heavy use of antibacterial products is a serious problem? Does she present an effective solution to the problem? How could she have made the speech more convincing?

This speech is also available on the CD-ROM and video supplements to *The Art of Public Speaking.*

1 In the film *The Boy in the Plastic Bubble,* a boy born with a deficient immune system is forced to live in a germ-free environment to prevent him from contracting infections. His room is sealed against bacteria and viruses, his food is specially prepared, and his only human contact comes in the form of gloved hands.

2 Today millions of Americans are trying to build a bubble around themselves and their families to keep out germs. The bubble is not made of plastic, however, but of billions of dollars worth of antibacterial hand wipes, tissues, soaps, and sponges.

3 Before I studied antibacterial products in my public health class, I always used antibacterial hand soaps and antibacterial all-surface cleaner for my apartment. I also know from my class survey that 70 percent of you use antibacterial soaps, cleaners, and other products.

4 But after learning about the subject in class and reading research studies for this speech, I'm here to tell you that, try as we might, we cannot build a bubble between ourselves and germs with antibacterial products and that these products actually create more problems than they solve. After looking at the problems created by antibacterial products, we'll explore some solutions.

5 The place to begin is by noting that antibacterial products are popping up just about everywhere. The next time you go to the store, try to find a liquid soap that is not antibacterial. According to the Alliance for the Prudent Use of Antibiotics, 75 percent of all liquid soaps and 33 percent of all bar soaps are antibacterial.

6 In fact, there are more than 1,000 antibacterial household products on the market. In addition to all the soaps and cleaning products, there are also antibacterial cotton swabs, tons of antibacterial shampoos, and this antibacterial cutting board from Williams Sonoma. You can even get antibacterial socks, mouthwash, toothpaste, and, to protect you while away from home, this travel toothbrush with antibacterial bristles.

7 The *Boston Globe* reports that larger items such as mattresses, countertops, high chairs, and even children's toys have been coated with antibacterial chemicals. *The New York Times* calls the antibacterial craze "the biggest marketing coup since bottled water."

8 There's no doubt that antibacterial products are popular with consumers, but there is a great deal of doubt about whether they're effective in stopping the spread of germs. Elaine Larson, associate dean of the Columbia University School of Nursing, studied 238 families who used antibacterial products and found that they were just as likely to get fevers, sore throats, coughs, rashes, and stomach problems as families who used regular products. Larson's findings are echoed by Eric Kupferberg, associate director of the Harvard School for Public Health, who states: "Antimicrobial products don't significantly eliminate the number of germs you encounter on a daily basis."

9 Nor do antibacterial products prevent the transmission of diseases such as colds and flus. Why? Because these illnesses come from viruses, not from bacteria. Antibacterial products don't kill viruses. As Dr. Larson explains, "most of the infections healthy people get are colds, flu, and diarrhea caused by viruses"—none of which can be prevented by the use of antibacterial products.

10 Not only do antibacterial products fail to deliver what they promise, but they actually increase your chances of getting sick. According to Stuart Levy, a professor of microbiology and medicine at Tufts University, excessive use of antibacterial products in the home can make children more likely to develop allergies and asthma.

11 In addition, people who use antibacterial products may become more susceptible to infections. Dr. James Chin, a research scientist in New South Wales, Australia, says: "The way we stay healthy is by low-dose exposure to bacteria and viruses. You need to exercise your immune system in the same way you need to exercise your muscles to be fit. If you don't do that, your immune system doesn't have a chance to do battle when it engages with an infection."

12 The problems caused by antibacterial products are so serious that Dr. Myron Genel, chairman of the American Medical Association's council on

scientific affairs, fears one result may be the creation of antibiotic-resistant bacteria "that are largely untreatable because they are resistant to existing drugs."

13 And that's not all. Besides being ineffective at preventing diseases and being potentially dangerous to our health, antibacterial household products also appear to harm the environment. Rolf Halden of Johns Hopkins University School of Public Health reports that each year the United States releases into the water supply more than 2 million pounds of the active chemicals in antibacterial soaps.

14 The U.S. Geological Survey reports that chemicals from antibacterial products are winding up in streams and groundwater from the Denver area to remote locations in the Rocky Mountains. These chemicals are known to pollute the water supply, disrupt fish reproduction and growth, and, because they do not decompose quickly, remain active for years and years.

15 Now that we've seen the seriousness of the problem, let's look at some solutions.

16 First, we need federal legislation regulating the use of household antibacterial products. Just as the Food and Drug Administration has regulations controlling the use of antibiotics, so, too, should it institute regulations controlling the use of antibacterial products.

17 We don't let people purchase antibiotics without a doctor's prescription, and there's no reason we should allow makers of soap, tissues, hand wipes, toothbrushes, and other products to add powerful antibacterial agents without oversight from the Food and Drug Administration. Given the problems being caused by these products, it is time for the federal government to take action.

18 Second, we all need to take action as consumers. Most obviously, we need to stop buying these products. The best way to avoid germs, says the Centers for Disease Control, is to wash your hands for 10–15 seconds with plain soap and water.

19 In fact, a study at the University of North Carolina found that washing your hands with soap and water is more effective at getting rid of germs than using antibacterial hand wipes. Emily Sickbert-Bennett, a public epidemiologist and co-author of the study, explains that when you use soap and water, the germs go down the drain, but with waterless antibacterial hand wipes, "you never rinse your hands. You are just rubbing a chemical into your hand and letting it dry."

20 In conclusion, Americans spend millions of dollars every year on products that promise to "kill germs on contact." But as we have seen today, the antibacterial craze is a marketing coup rather than a proven way of stopping either the spread of germs or the incidence of colds, flus, and other virus-borne illnesses. Worse, these products appear to contribute to health problems, and they are creating environmental problems in the U.S. water supply. The federal government should start regulating these products and we, as consumers, should stop throwing our money away on them.

21 We need to resist the false notion that we can use these products to create a bubble around ourselves to keep out germs and disease. Instead, we can burst the bubble of marketers who are selling us a false bill of goods and then we can thoroughly wash our hands of the whole mess.

The Ultimate Gift

As the Red Cross states, "Blood is like a parachute. If it's not there when you need it, chances are you'll never need it again." Although Americans take it for granted that they will be able to get a transfusion whenever they need one, blood donations have dipped so low in recent years that a serious, nationwide shortage could result. "When you need surgery, when you need cancer treatment, when a woman gives birth—we all assume the blood will be there," says Dr. Arthur Caplan of the University of Pennsylvania. "You can't make that assumption any more."

The following speech, given by a student at the University of Wisconsin, urges the audience to become regular blood donors. Like many speeches that seek immediate action, this one follows Monroe's motivated sequence. As you read it, study how the speaker develops each step in the motivated sequence. How does she gain the attention of her listeners? Does she present a convincing case that there is a need for blood donors? Is her plan explained in sufficient detail? How does she visualize the benefits of her plan? Does her call for action have strong persuasive appeal?

This speech is also available on the CD-ROM and video supplements to *The Art of Public Speaking.*

1 Are you at least 17 years old? Do you weigh more than 110 pounds? Do you consider yourself fairly healthy?

2 If you answered yes to all of these questions, you should be donating blood every two months. In my survey of the class, I found that only 50 percent of you have ever donated blood and that only 1 out of 13 of you donate on a regular basis. The lack of participation of eligible donors is a serious problem that requires immediate action. Through extensive research and two years of faithfully donating blood, I have come to realize the magnitude of this problem and just how easy the solution can be.

3 Today I would like to show why blood donors are in such desperate need and encourage you to take action to combat this need. Let's first take a look at the overwhelming need for blood donors.

4 The lack of participation of eligible blood donors poses a threat to the lives of many Americans. According to the American Red Cross Web pages, where I obtained an enormous amount of information, in the United States alone someone undergoes a blood transfusion once every three seconds, which amounts to 3,000 gallons of blood every hour, day and night. People who benefit from donations range from cancer patients to organ transplant patients to surgical patients; even premature infants and trauma victims benefit from donations. The need for blood never takes a vacation and neither should donors.

5 Let me tell you about Brooke, a three-year-old girl with long, curly blond hair and bright blue eyes. Brooke is a victim of cancer and had major surgery to remove a large tumor in her abdomen. She has spent approximately half of her life in the hospital receiving chemotherapy and other treatments for infections that resulted from a decrease in her white blood cell count after each session.

6 According to Texas Children's Hospital, Brooke's treatment will require blood products with a replacement value of 508 units of blood, of which only 250 units have been replaced. She still needs more than 250 units of

blood to continue her treatment. If she doesn't receive this blood, she will not live to attend kindergarten, to go to the prom in high school, or to get married—luxuries we all too often take for granted.

7 Cases like Brooke's are becoming all too common these days, with only 1 in 20 eligible Americans donating blood and the donor rate dropping steadily at 2 percent annually. These facts are particularly distressing considering that nearly half of us here will receive blood sometime in our lives.

8 You can now see the magnitude of the problem with the lack of blood donations. Fortunately, it is a problem that can be easily solved. Each and every one of you can be part of the solution. All you have to do to save priceless lives is go to the nearest Red Cross and donate your blood.

9 For those of you who have never donated blood before, the process is so simple and easy. First, you fill out a donor information form that asks you questions about your sexual history and health. You will then receive a miniphysical. They will take a drop of blood from your finger to measure the percent of red cells in your blood. Then they will take your blood pressure, as well as your temperature and pulse. So not only are you saving lives by donating blood, you are also checking on your own.

10 After your physical, you will be asked from which arm you prefer to donate. Then you will be asked to lie on a donor chair. A staff member will clean your arm and insert a sterile, nonreusable needle, so there is no way to contract AIDS from donating blood. After a pint of your blood has been taken, which usually takes about 10 minutes, you will be asked to rest for 10 to 15 minutes while you enjoy juice and cookies. The process is over, and in eight weeks you can donate again.

11 Many of you may be scared at the thought of the anticipated pain and needles. I admit I was terrified the first time I gave blood, but then I realized I was scared over nothing. The extent of the pain as they insert the needle is equivalent to someone scratching your arm for a brief second, and while the needle is in your arm, you don't feel a thing. And as I stated before, it is impossible to contract AIDS from donating blood.

12 Now that you know how easy and safe the solution is to the lack of blood donations, let's take a look at just how much difference your donations can make. Every unit of blood you donate can help save up to three lives. You see, the blood you donate is divided three ways—into red blood cells, white blood cells, and platelets. Each of these are stored separately and used for different types of treatment. Red blood cells are used to treat anemia. White blood cells are used to fight infections, while platelets are important to control bleeding and are used in patients with leukemia and other forms of cancer.

13 The joy you get from helping three people can be increased many times over. You see, you can donate blood six times in a year. Those six donations could help as many as 18 people. Just think, if you donated for 10 years, you could help save the lives of nearly 180 people. Who knows—one of those lives could be that of a friend, a family member, or even your own, since you can now donate in advance of your own surgery.

14 Now that you know what a difference just one donation can make, I want to encourage you to take action. I urge you to take a stand and become a regular blood donor. Forty-five minutes out of your day is a small price

to pay for the lifetime of satisfaction you receive by knowing you may have saved a life. If you have never donated blood before, pull deep inside yourself to find some courage and become a proud wearer of the "I am a first time blood donor" sticker. If you have donated before, think back to the feeling of pride you received from making your donation.

15 Finally, I ask all of you to think of a loved one you hold so dear to your heart. Imagine they need a blood transfusion and there is a shortage of donations that day so they can't receive the treatment they so desperately need—just like Brooke, the three-year-old girl I talked about earlier. Go to the nearest Red Cross in Madison, which is on Sheboygan Avenue, or attend the next blood drive here on campus. These drives are held in various parts of campus, including the dorms. In fact, the next drive will be held in the Ogg Residence Hall in two weeks.

16 Please take this opportunity to save lives and make yourself feel like a million bucks. Give the ultimate gift—the gift of life. Donate blood!

My Crazy Aunt Sue

The aim of a commemorative speech is to pay tribute to a person, a group of people, an institution, or an idea. In the following student speech, the speaker commemorates her aunt Sue and her heroic battle against the debilitating disease of rheumatoid arthritis.

As you read the speech, notice that it is not a biography that simply recounts the details of aunt Sue's life. Instead, it focuses on her courage, her sense of humor, and her refusal to complain about her fate. The speaker provides enough details to make clear why her aunt is so commendable, but her ultimate purpose is to inspire the audience rather than to inform it. The speaker also uses vivid language, repetition, and parallel structure to give the speech the kind of formal tone appropriate for a commemorative speech.

This speech is also available on the CD-ROM and video supplements to *The Art of Public Speaking.*

1 The strongest person I know cannot peel a potato. The strongest person I know has trouble putting on her makeup. The strongest person I know needs a special key holder to turn the key in her car's ignition.

2 For the past fifteen years, my 47-year-old aunt Sue has been living with rheumatoid arthritis, a painfully debilitating disease in which the joints of the body become intensely inflamed due to the immune system's activity. Yet despite the daily torments of this disease, my aunt Sue is stronger than any woman or man I have ever met.

3 Not a moment passes that my aunt Sue is not confronted with this demon of a disease and reminded of her disability through the pills she must take and the pain she must endure. It hurts to stand, it hurts to walk, it hurts to sit. After an infinite number of failed medications, aunt Sue is now undergoing her most aggressive treatment, which includes weekly oral chemotherapy. After half a dozen surgeries, her frail body is in need of still more.

4 And yet despite all of this, I can't recall ever hearing her complain about her fate. After all the indignities and inconveniences her illness has

thrown at her, my aunt Sue still finds the energy to devote much of her time not to herself, but to those less fortunate than her. This past Thanksgiving, for example, she helped organize a dinner for more than 500 poor and homeless people. My aunt Sue, who has her medications put in non-childproof containers so she can open them, helped coordinate a dinner for those in need.

5 The picture I have painted of my aunt Sue thus far is of a kind woman, a determined woman, a warmhearted woman whose own suffering seems inconsequential when compared to that of others. This is all completely true, but there is something else about my aunt Sue that makes me admire her so. Actually, it's what makes me love her as much as I do.

6 At five feet two inches, and 105 pounds, with the spunk of a teenager, she introduces herself as "Crazy Sue"—and sometimes I'd have to agree with her. Somehow she is able to approach this demonic disease with a sense of humor. And not just any sense of humor. My aunt Sue is one of the funniest people I know.

7 Years ago, when the disease began to hit her really hard, one of the attorneys at her law firm asked why she was limping. She told him she fell off a trapeze performing her weekend hobby—and he believed her! Following an ankle sprain and further complications, her ankle became deformed and the arch of her foot completely collapsed. Whereas most people would wallow in their misery, aunt Sue calls it her "cartoon foot."

8 My aunt Sue has made a positive impression on countless people throughout her life, but I hope she knows how much of an impression she has made on me—and how much I admire her.

9 I complain about trudging through the snow to class, but I'm walking pain free. I complain about driving my friends around town, but I'm steering the wheel pain free. I complain about the final exams I'll have to write, but I have the mobility in my wrist to write pain free. I have learned from my aunt Sue that I need to do a better job about being happy for the things that I have, rather than worrying about the not-so-perfect things in my life.

10 Aunt Sue may call herself crazy, but I call her phenomenal—a joy to be around and a reminder that having a physical disability in no way diminishes a person's spirit or inner beauty.

Photo Credits

Chapter 1

2–3: Bob Daemmrich/PhotoEdit; 7: Comstock Images (RF)/Creatas; 14: Chris Livingston/Zuma Press; 19: Jeff Greenberg/PhotoEdit; 25: Marcelo Hernandez/AP/Wide World Photos

Chapter 2

32–33: Debie Yazbek/AP/Wide World Photos; 37: G. Napolitina/La Presse/Zuma Press; 39: David Young-Wolff/PhotoEdit; 45: Bonnie Kamin/PhotoEdit; 49: John Eisele/Corbis

Chapter 3

54–55: Davis Barber/PhotoEdit; 59: Joe Tabacca/The New York Times; 65: Bonnie Kamin/PhotoEdit; 69: Patrick Ward/Corbis; **Appendix:** 73: Frank Siteman/PhotoEdit

Chapter 4

84–85: Ryan Donnell/The New York Times; 87: M.L. Sinibaldi/Corbis; 97: Michael Newman/PhotoEdit; 105: Sepp Seitz/Woodfin Camp & Associates

Chapter 5

110–111: Kevork Djansezian/AP/Wide World Photos; 115: Jack Kurtz/Zuma Press; 123: Mark Richards/PhotoEdit; 128: David Young-Wolff/PhotoEdit

Chapter 6

138–139: Rafael Macia/Photo Researchers, Inc.; 147: Digital Vision (RF)/Creatas; 154: David Young-Wolff/PhotoEdit; 163: Bob Daemmrich/Stock, Boston; 169: Mark Lewis/ TSI/Getty Images

Chapter 7

174–175: Chuck Burton/AP/World Wide Photos; 181: Ryan Connell/The New York Times; 185: Akira Ono/AP/World Wide Photos; 193: Mannic Media/McGraw-Hill, Inc.

Chapter 8

204–205: Stockbyte (RF)/Creatas; 208: Jim West; 211: Novastock/PhotoEdit; 221: Gary Conner/PhotoEdit

Chapter 9

226–227: Comstock Images [RF]/Getty Images; 230: Marilyn Humphries/The Image Works; 233: LWA-Sharie Kennedy Williams/Corbis; 235: Mannic Media/McGraw-Hill, Inc.; 239: Achmad Ibrahim/AP/Wide World Photos; 244: Al Goldis/AP/Wide World Photos

Chapter 10

252–253: Sepp Seitz/Woodfin Camp & Associates; 257: Michael Newman/PhotoEdit; 264: Joel Gordon

Chapter 11

270–271: Lucy Pemoni/AP/Wide World Photos; 275: Lora L. Gordon/ Radford University; 279: Photo: John Carnett. Copyright 2001 Time 4 Media, Inc. Reprinted with permission from POPULAR SCIENCE magazine. All rights reserved.; 283: E.A. Kennedy III/The Image Works; 289: Ross Woodhall/Corbis

Chapter 12

298–299: Larry Downing/Corbis; 303: Greg Baker/AP/Wide World Photo; 307: John Bilderback/Getty Images; 311: Shelly Castellano/Zuma Press; 316: Greg Wahl-Stephens/AP/Wide World Photos; 320: Brendan Smialowski/Getty Images

Chapter 13

326–327: John Marshall Mantel/AP/Wide World Photos; 330: Jim Zuckerman/Corbis; 349: Taxi/Getty Images

Chapter 14

370–371: Bob Daemmrich/PhotoEdit; 377: Getty Images; 381: Mary Katz; 385: Lora L. Gordon/Radford University; 390: Photodisc Collection/Getty Images

Chapter 15

398–399: William Philpott/Reuters/Corbis; 404: Peter Thompson; 407: Lynne Fernandes/The Image Works; 413: Jim West; 417: Najlah Feanny/Corbis; 422: Johnny Crawford/The Image Works

Chapter 16

432–433: Chris Pizzello/AP/Wide World; 436: Doug Mills/AP/Wide World Photos; 442: Bonnie Kamin/PhotoEdit; 449: Al Golub/Getty Images; 453: Peter Kramer/Getty Images; 456: Jim West; 459: Bryan Smith/Zuma Press

Chapter 17

468–469: Brook Kraft/Corbis; 472: Ed Bailey/AP/Wide World Photos; 476: Stuart Ramson/AP/Wide World Photos

Chapter 18

484–485: Comstock [RF]/Getty Images; 489: Ryan McVay/Getty Images; 495: RNT Productions/Corbis; 500: Image Source/Getty Images

Index